AF477786

IMISCOE
International Migration, Integration and Social Cohesion in Europe

The IMISCOE Research Network unites researchers from, at present, 28 institutes specialising in studies of international migration, integration and social cohesion in Europe. What began in 2004 as a Network of Excellence sponsored by the Sixth Framework Programme of the European Commission has become, as of April 2009, an independent self-funding endeavour. From the start, IMISCOE has promoted integrated, multidisciplinary and globally comparative research led by scholars from various branches of the economic and social sciences, the humanities and law. The Network furthers existing studies and pioneers new scholarship on migration and migrant integration. Encouraging innovative lines of inquiry key to European policymaking and governance is also a priority.

The IMISCOE-Amsterdam University Press Series makes the Network's findings and results available to researchers, policymakers and practitioners, the media and other interested stakeholders. High-quality manuscripts authored by Network members and cooperating partners are evaluated by external peer reviews and the IMISCOE Editorial Committee. The Committee comprises the following members:

Tiziana Caponio, Department of Political Studies, University of Turin / Forum for International and European Research on Immigration (FIERI), Turin, Italy

Michael Collyer, Sussex Centre for Migration Research (SCMR), University of Sussex, United Kingdom

Rosita Fibbi, Swiss Forum for Migration and Population Studies (SFM), University of Neuchâtel / Institute of Social Sciences, University of Lausanne, Switzerland

Agata Górny, Centre of Migration Research (CMR) / Faculty of Economic Sciences, University of Warsaw, Poland

Albert Kraler, International Centre for Migration Policy Development (ICMPD), Vienna, Austria

Jorge Malheiros, Centre of Geographical Studies (CEG), University of Lisbon, Portugal

Marco Martiniello, National Fund for Scientific Research (FNRS), Brussels / Center for Ethnic and Migration Studies (CEDEM), University of Liège, Belgium

Marlou Schrover, Institute for History, Leiden University, The Netherlands

Patrick Simon, National Demographic Institute (INED), Paris, France

Miri Song, School of Social Policy and Sociology, University of Kent, United Kingdom

IMISCOE Policy Briefs and more information on the network can be found at www.imiscoe.org.

European Immigrations

Trends, Structures and Policy Implications

edited by Marek Okólski

IMISCOE Research

AMSTERDAM UNIVERSITY PRESS

Cover design: Studio Jan de Boer BNO, Amsterdam
Layout: The DocWorkers, Almere

ISBN   978 90 8964 457 2
e-ISBN   978 90 4851 727 5 (pdf)
e-ISBN   978 90 4851 728 2 (e-Pub)
NUR   741 / 763

Table of Contents

Introduction

Marek Okólski

Not long ago, Europe was symbolically reunited – at least, such might be the perception of the first eastward enlargement of the European Union on 1 May 2004. The accession of eight Central and Eastern European (CEE) countries to the EU gave rise to further dismantling of those barriers between East and West that had been erected in the Cold War era. What followed was a softening of divisions across European societies and an intensification of mutual contacts and flows of knowledge and ideas. Many varied social phenomena in the East were expected to converge with those in other parts of the continent. Migration patterns, regimes and policies ranked among those phenomena.

At the beginning of 1989, when the Poles – and slightly later, citizens of other CEE countries – were granted unlimited freedom of international travel, a considerable part of western public opinion and western states reacted with anxiety, if not phobia. It was feared that freedom of movement – a basic human right that for decades prior to 1989 the West had unstintingly supported – could result in excessive flows of people from CEE to the West.

The East-West exodus did not happen, however. This was because the former communist countries of Europe, still aptly perceived in the late 1980s as politically and economically similar, set different goals for themselves and chose various strategies for transition to democracy and market economy, thus undergoing massive change. An important outcome of that change was a growing capacity to contain within the region itself the vast migration potential that had accumulated over the period of communist repression. This is why in the early 1990s, tens of thousands of Bulgarians, Romanians, Ukrainians and other CEE nationals opted for migration to other former communist countries, notably to the Czech Republic, Hungary and Poland, instead of following in the footsteps of their fellow countrymen who (in much smaller numbers than expected) headed for the West.[1] In comparison with Western Europe, the Czech Republic and some other economically booming CEE countries were both geographically and culturally closer for the migrants and thus involved less risk for the pioneers of international mobility of people from Ukraine, Romania or other source countries.

Over the 1990s the inflow of foreigners to CEE countries continued. Its forms became more mature; the earlier dominant form – the movement of petty traders and irregular workers engaged in various odd jobs – gave way to the flow of predominantly regular contract workers or small-scale entrepreneurs. By attracting considerable numbers of migrants from faraway countries, such as China (in Hungary and the Czech Republic) or Vietnam (in the Czech Republic and Poland), the national and ethnic composition of incoming foreigners became more diverse. At this time, communities of settled migrants began to appear, especially in large cities.

It appeared that those CEE countries in the forefront of political and economic transition were undergoing changes similar to those experienced a few decades earlier by four Southern European countries – namely, Italy, Spain, Greece and Portugal. These southern countries, along with the process of economic integration with Western Europe, rather rapidly changed their migration statuses. Having been important source countries for guest worker migration to many western economies in the 1950s and 1960s, while suffering from excess labour supply, they shifted to become new major European destinations for immigrant workers.

Since almost all Western European countries had also undergone such a transition, albeit at least a quarter of a century earlier, it seemed rather natural to predict that once Eastern Europe became economically integrated with the rest of the continent, the migration patterns in that region would change accordingly. Or, at least, to profoundly consider such a hypothesis.

*

Indeed, large scope of geographical coverage, long duration, high volume of migratory movements and a shift in migration balance from negative to positive on the European soil seem to be an unprecedented social phenomenon of modernity.[2] The beginning of mass emigration from Europe is usually dated to the early nineteenth century. Jean-Claude Chesnais (1986) argues that over a whole century, in the period 1815-1914, more than 60 million inhabitants of Europe (one fifth of its 1850 population) abandoned the continent of origin and, according to Russell King (1996), approximately 50 million Europeans moved to other continents between 1850 and 1914.[3] In roughly the same period (1861-1920), the United Sates, alone, saw the arrival of 30 million immigrants, 27 or 28 million of whom were probably of European origin (Miller & Castles 1993 after Borjas 1990).[4] In addition, many millions of European people migrated to other countries within the continent. For instance, between 1876 and 1920, from a total of fifteen million Italian immigrants, nearly seven million went to other European countries, notably to France, Switzerland and Germany. Similarly, a considerable proportion of Irish migrants moved to England and Scotland, whereas Germany was a destination of a large number of

Poles (Castles & Miller 1993). In a sharp contrast, until the late 1940s intercontinental migration to Europe did not match the emigration figures. It predominantly included returning emigrants whose proportion relative to the out-migrants was usually well below 50 per cent (King 1996).

In relative terms, (overseas) emigration per 1,000 resident population was very high in almost all European countries. In certain decades of the 1850-1910 period, it exceeded five per 1,000 on a yearly basis. In countries such as England, Scotland, Ireland, Norway, Sweden, Finland, Austria-Hungary, Italy, Spain and Portugal, it accounted for a large part of their natural increase (Baines 1991; Hatton & Williamson 2008).

The recent picture is strikingly different. Europe has become a continent of net immigration. From 1960 to 2010, the overall positive migration balance was around 32.9 million, that is approximately one fourth of the total 128.3 million increase in the European resident population in that period (UN 2009). According to the United Nations estimate, between 1960 and 2005, the number of international migrants in three of four major parts of the continent (northern, southern and western) rose from 10.3 million to 39.3 million or, in relative terms, from 2.8 per cent to 9.0 per cent of the total population (UN 2006).[5]

A growing importance of immigration to Europe can be best illustrated by the following observation: the first decade of the twenty-first century saw the rate of net migration close to (plus) 3.5 per 1,000 population in the group of 27 member countries of the European Union, whereas the respective rate of natural increase was below one per 1,000 (Eurostat 2009).

Corrado Bonifazi (2008) attempted to establish the time when Europe attained its status of net immigration. In the 1950s, the migration balance was still strongly negative (-4.8 million over the decade). In the 1960s, the net loss continued, but at a substantially lower level (-600,000). In the next decade, the balance became positive (+3 million). Thus, the 1970s witnessed a breakthrough. Since that time the gap between immigration and emigration in favour of the former has been systematically growing. Bonifazi, however, also stressed distinctive differences in migration trends between major groups of countries and individual countries themselves.

Western Europe turned to a net immigration regime in the 1950s, whereas Northern and Southern Europe only did so in the 1970s.[6] In turn, if the Russian Federation was excluded, Eastern Europe remained a net emigration region until the end of the century, if not beyond that date.[7] On the other hand, Belgium, France, Switzerland and Germany became a net immigration area as soon as in the 1950s,[8] while Italy only did so in the 1990s. In 1950, many countries of Europe which nowadays are perceived as immigration areas, hardly hosted foreign residents; in Finland, Greece, Ireland, Italy, the Netherlands, Norway, Portugal, Spain and the United Kingdom, their share in the total population was below 1 per cent (in some of them – below 0.3 per cent). After a half-century or so, the proportion of foreign residents in those countries multiplied by a factor five to ten (Bonifazi 2008).

*

Those simple empirical facts, besides the authors' intuition, became the inspiration for a research project from which this volume emanated.[9]

The emergence of ever-new immigration countries in Europe in recent decades makes the question of a common European migration pattern pertinent and indeed topical. Cultural proximity and common cultural heritage, comprehensive political, economic and historical links between societies and regions, similar contemporary socio-economic and demographic challenges and convergence of institutions and policies (partly through accession to the EU) can offer a provisional justification.

On the other hand, the succession of European countries in assuming the status of immigration area resembles the phenomenon of gradual entrance by those countries of the mass migration era over several decades in the nineteenth century. From a cross-country and inter-regional perspective, mass emigration from Europe in the period from the 1820s until the outbreak of World War I (and in some cases until the early 1950s) was by no means a uniform process, either in terms of its overall volume or time distribution. Similarly, in the period of intensified immigration, after World War II, European countries and their regions significantly differed with respect to the size and persistence of inflows over time. What particularly mattered in the later period from the European viewpoint were also the differences in forms of flows, the conditions of migrants' stay and employment and thus immigrants' propensity or ability to settle and integrate in the host society. Those differences notwithstanding, a general tendency appears clear and indeed unquestionable: until the mid-twentieth century, a great majority of European regions and Europe as a whole were primarily a sending area, whereas, since the second half of that century, they have gradually become a net receiving area.[10]

*

This volume is dedicated to a broadly conceived European migration pattern, to a unique coincidence and interplay of mass migration and the formation of modern Europe. Taking such a long and general view, the analyses in the ensuing chapters, however, focus on relatively recent (or future) phenomena transpiring in the group of countries that belong to the EU.

An underlying assumption is that a typical feature for modernising European countries is the change of a migration balance from net emigration to net immigration. In addition, two basic hypotheses explicitly mark the conceptual framework.

– Patterns of immigration in 'new' destination countries (latecomers) recall historical patterns observed in 'old' destination countries (early starters).[11]
– Each individual country – in the process of transformation from net emigration to net immigration – displays a number of important distinctive characteristics that are dependent on geographic location, previous migration links and routes, as well as the historical time of the transformation and international migratory context at the time.

Through systematising and examining the available body of knowledge about mass migration in Europe, the analyses in this volume seek to reconstruct immigration patterns in individual countries and groups of countries and identify major similarities and differences across those patterns. They also aim to link specific migration patterns with their root causes, historical contexts and structural factors. In particular, an attempt is made to evaluate the impact of migration policies on the course of immigration. Last but not least, the volume includes an exercise on the projection of immigration trends in the 'foreseeable' future that exploits the knowledge about past migration and innovative analytical tools.

These aims are to be achieved by in-depth analyses of causes, characteristics and effects of past and current migration flows to EU countries, especially those located in the southern and eastern rims of the European Community. A special importance is to be given to comparing and assessing the political background of immigration in the countries of destination, including its institutional and administrative setup.

The countries included in the analysis represent three parts of Europe that obviously differ according to geographic location and the time when net positive immigration status was (or will be) reached. The countries where the change in migration balance was accomplished before or during the third quarter of the twentieth century are named 'old' immigration countries. Those where such change occurred in the fourth quarter of the twentieth century are named 'new' immigration countries; and the remainder (the change to be completed some time in the twenty-first century) are named 'future' immigration countries. The respective breakdown of those countries is presented in Table 1.

The main concept underlying the framework and the method of analysis is that of country migration status. Migration status, perceived in terms of migration balance and inflows/outflows volume, became a crucial category in the analysis of migration transition – the process of a former emigration country acquiring the attributes of a new immigration country. In turn, those concepts and categories were framed by a more general conception of the migration cycle.

'Migration cycle' is an analytically useful, but by no means innovatory idea. For instance, as early as 1954, Brinley Thomas examined long swings

Table 1 *Breakdown of countries with respect to their migration status*

Part of Europe	*Time*		
	Early	*4th quarter of the twentieth century*	*Late*
West	Austria, France		
South		Italy, Greece, Portugal, Spain	
East			Czech Republic, Hungary, Poland

Source: Own elaboration

in trans-Atlantic migration (and urban development) in the period 1870-1910 within the concept of 'migration cycle',[12] while Castles and Miller (1993) suggested a cycle-like four-stage 'model' of migration as a tool for systematising and identifying the time-dependent internal dynamics of immigration.[13] Similarly, and also in 1993, Anthony Fielding argued that mass migration to, from and within Europe changes 'in tune with the stages of the business cycle' (Fielding 1993: 10). He distinguished four stages of the cycle, each being distinctly different with respect to basic migration characteristics. As economic activity fluctuates in a regular pattern, from an expansion (up to a peak) to a recession (down to a trough), and from a recession to an expansion, mass migration behaves in the way that is presented in Table 2.

Table 2 *Stages of a migration cycle dependent on the business cycle*

Stage 1 (expansion)	Immigration starts low and rises rapidly; emigration starts high and falls rapidly; net immigration replaces net emigration.
Stage 2 (peak)	Immigration peaks high; emigration bottoms out low; high net immigration
Stage 3 (recession)	Immigration starts high and falls rapidly; emigration starts low and rises rapidly; net emigration replaces net immigration.
Stage 4 (trough)	Immigration bottoms out low; emigration peaks high; high net emigration

Source: Fielding (1993: 11)

Moreover, the 'migration cycle' underlies such concepts as 'mobility transition' (Zelinsky 1971), 'migratory transition' (Chesnais 1986) and 'transition from trickle to flood' (Hatton & Williamson 2008), and has been exploited in many empirical studies. Some of those applications are referred to in chapter 1 of this volume. It might be mentioned here, however, that no universal or unequivocal sense and meaning is attributed in the literature to the concept of migration cycle.

The authors of the present volume apply 'migration cycle' in a flexible manner, in its narrower or wider meaning, according to analytical needs, aspect of migration or time-horizon of analysis. For instance, one of those applications followed the pioneering effort of Felice Dassetto (1990), who himself understood the cycle as a combination of cross-generation processes making migrants from poor countries enter and settle in a rich country. In this volume, it is exploited in the analysis of European countries passing to ever-greater 'maturity' with respect to immigration (see chapter 2 by Joaquín Arango in this volume). Another example was the application of the 'migration cycle' to the systematisation of stages in the change in country migration status, where the fundamental and constitutive process of the cycle comes to be the migration transition (see chapter 1 by Marek Okólski and chapter 3 by Heinz Fassmann and Ursula Reeger in this volume). The principal difference between the approaches adopted by the authors is that some of them (mainly chapter 1 and, to a lesser degree, also chapter 3 plus some others) take a very long view and reach as far back as to the origins of mass emigration, while others (mainly chapter 2) focus on relatively recent developments in European migration history, namely, the stage when European countries were experiencing sizeable and sustained flows of immigrants. The reason of this distinction seems obvious and it is purely functional. The former enables us to capture and compare the change in migration patterns in virtually all countries of Europe; the latter serves as an in-depth analysis of similarities and diversity in the establishment and maturing of the area and pertains exclusively to the present ('old' and 'new') net immigration countries.

*

This volume is organised as follows. The first two chapters focus on the recent history of European migration and the conceptual underpinnings of the analyses presented later in the volume. The next part (chapters 3 through 8) consists of three syntheses that test the concept of a regional immigration pattern in each of the three groups of countries and inquire into similarities and differences in migrant flows, immigrant integration and migration policies in those groups. It becomes clear that a synthetic perspective is more appropriate and manageable for countries with relatively long histories and rich experiences of immigration, as opposed to countries where immigration is a rather new phenomenon.

In the synthesis depicting immigration in 'old' immigration countries (chapter 3), the authors take a rather long and general view and offer stylised facts about migration. A corresponding chapter 5, related to 'new' immigration countries, while also attempting to draw a general picture, pays more attention to details and specificities of time, country and context of immigration. In contrast to these two, chapter 8, devoted to 'future' immigration countries – adhering to the cross-country comparative approach – mainly describes trends and patterns in individual countries; the author here is rather cautious in pointing to common regional characteristics of the analysed processes. The first two of those syntheses are accompanied by chapters 4, 6 and 7 presenting either different perspectives on the virtue of a 'regional' model of immigration or discussion of some of the key findings of those syntheses. The inclusion in the volume of these three critical chapters seems to have enriched the body of arguments in the debate on a 'European pattern of immigration'.

The next part of the volume (chapters 9 and 10) deals with migration forecasts. First, past attempts at migration forecasting, focusing mainly on inadequate data and techniques, are critically assessed and, in turn, an innovative approach to improving those forecasts is developed. Such a view is challenged and, to some extent, balanced in a brief rejoinder that follows. The final part of the volume (chapters 11 and 12) concentrates on lessons that can be learned from a comparative analysis of migration policies carried out in the individual countries and the groups of countries, as well as from recent trends in the management of migration in the context of European integration. In its conclusion, this part identifies the major challenges faced by the EU in the area of migration and immigrant integration policy. The volume closes with a brief account of major conclusions and an appraisal of the degree to which the authors' objectives have been accomplished. Here the hypothesis of European migration pattern is critically reassessed.

Turning to a more detailed look at the chapters, the first, by Okólski, deals with the premises of migration status change in European countries. It is based on the hypothesis that, in the long run, migration results primarily from the degree of disequilibrium between population and other resources, which at times manifests itself in various degrees of overpopulation or underpopulation. He points to the circumstances under which countries of Northern and Western Europe transformed from sending masses of their population overseas to receiving large numbers of people from all around the world and, consequently, from net emigration to net immigration. He also suggests that a similar shift in the migration pattern and balance, albeit after a certain time lag, occurred in a number of Southern European countries. This leads him to elaborate some considerations about the present migration status of Central and East European countries and basic prerequisites for their change of migration status in the near future. Okólski concludes that such a change in any country requires, above all, the outflow of excess population and, secondly, embarking on the path of sustained modern economic growth. When this is coupled with the completion of the demographic transition (natural increase close to zero and advanced ageing of the population), emigration starts to decline. On the other hand, economic competition and the search for cheap labour by employers induce segmentation of the labour market and increase demand for foreign workers. In effect, in the course of time the inflow of people becomes larger than the outflow.

In the following chapter, Arango seeks an answer to the question: Do different migration realities and experiences among European countries stem from historical factors (e.g. the moment when the migration pattern or regime started to change) or from structural socio-economic differences? In order to do so, he develops an analytical framework that serves as a basis for identification of distinct groups of immigration countries and a tool for the analysis of intra-group similarities and inter-group differences. This framework refers to the notion of a migration cycle conceived as a multi-stage process through which immigrants become better adapted to and (ultimately) integrated in the receiving society, and the socio-demographic characteristics of immigrants increasingly resemble those of the native population. It also implies the following four criteria of grouping and analysis of the immigration countries: age (stage of the migration cycle), generation (historical context of initial and formative phases of the cycle), historical precedence and socio-economic regime. In the next step, Arango applies that framework to examine the distinctiveness of the immigration patterns and characteristics of immigrant populations in the three groups of European countries. He concludes that the set of analysed countries presents great complexity and variation with respect to migration. This notwithstanding, the three different migration regimes in Europe seem to be a reality, where four Southern countries represent the highest degree of internal homogeneity and three CEE countries represent the lowest.

In the volume's first chapter devoted to a specific group of European countries, Fassmann and Reeger describe in a detailed manner the migration patterns observed in 'old' immigration countries. In doing so, they extensively use the concept of a migration cycle composed of three distinct stages: initial (pre-transformation), intermediate (transition) and adaptation (post-transformation). They also consider four characteristics of each stage: historical time, quantities (flows, stocks, pace of growth, fluctuations), public perception and legal measures. In their analysis, they include Germany and the UK in addition to Austria and France, and contrast those countries with Spain (as an example of a 'new' immigration country). Accounting for the differences between the countries at any given time, Fassmann and Reeger come to a straightforward final conclusion: with regard to immigration, European countries are developing in the same direction and in a similar way.

Godfried Engbersen's chapter widens the scope of analysis that deals with 'old' immigration countries. The author argues that the long-run approach adopted by Fassmann and Reeger, which he calls 'path-dependent', fails to recognise the importance of contemporary (or current) migration flows to Western countries, whose nature seems significantly different from the bulk of flows observed in the past. The essence of that new mobility, exemplified by the case of flows of people from CEE to the Netherlands, is a fluid (liquid) form of labour migration. In an institutional context entirely different from that of the old guest worker system of the 1960s and 1970s, the migration pattern in 'old' countries now seems to be deviating from the path depicted by the concept of a migration cycle. New migrations are, among others, characterised by a regular status of migrants' employment, temporary stay, individualised life strategies, multiplicity and multidirectionality of movements and loosely defined aspirations and options of migrants. All of this makes rather pertinent the question put forward by Engbersen: Are we witnessing a shift from the adaptation stage (according to Fassmann and Reeger, the final in the migration cycle) to a new initial stage?

The three succeeding chapters deal with the specificity of the so-called Southern (or Mediterranean) model of immigration, pertaining to 'new' countries of immigration. In the opening chapter, João Peixoto and six co-authors skilfully synthesise the immense research and new findings pertaining to four countries – Italy, Greece, Spain and Portugal (Arango, Bonifazi, Finotelli, Peixoto, Sabino, Strozza & Triandafyllidou 2009). They refer to earlier comparative analyses of immigration experiences in Southern European countries with the intention of testing their validity and updating them. In their analysis, Peixoto et al. focus on the phenomenon of irregular migration, the mechanisms of migrant workers' insertion in the labour market and migration policy responses. Special attention is paid to regularisation policies, executed – typical for Southern countries – ex post, as well as to their effectiveness and social costs. Through cross-country analysis, the authors scrupulously examine various aspects of migration-related experiences, tracking signs of both regional homogeneity and diversity. Despite the differences with regard to timing, quantity and types of migrant flows or to policy tools, ultimately, they seem to be convinced that a 'Southern model' does exist. They stress, however, that the model is dynamic because with time it acquires ever-new dimensions and meanings and includes new social frameworks and new policy instruments.

In turn, Martin Baldwin-Edwards presents a sceptical view about the utility and validity of a 'Southern model', identified in earlier years by the author himself and several others, especially when it comes to analyses of ongoing migration processes in the respective countries. Further, he adds a number of factors that – according to him – could enrich the analysis by Peixoto et al.; these include the role of local governance in policy directed at integration of immigrants, the role of NGOs and civil society in providing social support and acceptance of immigrants and the dependence of migration policy on political ideology and the operation of political parties.

In conclusion, Baldwin-Edwards suggests that a 'Southern model' might be too simple and too broad to adequately grasp all complexities and experiences acquired to date by the Mediterranean countries.

The last in the series of three chapters devoted to Southern European countries limits itself to Portugal and Spain, to what is called the 'Iberian model of labour migration'. Author Jorge Malheiros takes an in-depth look at a major feature of that model: the low degree of regulation of migration flows 'in a society characterised by practices marked by familiarism, informality and patrimony-based traditions'. He finds a close match between economic interests and migration policies that bring about a specific pattern of foreign worker recruitment, insertion and, ultimately, integration in the labour market. He argues that in this respect, Portugal and Spain, which are similar, differ significantly from Italy and radically from Greece.

The next chapter is devoted to immigration trends and patterns in three CEE countries: the Czech Republic, Hungary and Poland. In this chapter, Dušan Drbohlav draws extensively from a comprehensive cross-country analysis pertaining to the three countries (Grabowska-Lusińska, Drbohlav & Hars 2011). He points out that the three 'future' immigration countries, although expected to be experiencing similar migration-related processes, are in fact strongly differentiated. Migration flows to the Czech Republic are rather strong, emigration is low and the migration balance is clearly positive; Hungary has little immigration and hardly any emigration, resulting in a tiny surplus of immigrants; and in Poland emigration by far exceeds immigration, leading to a negative migration balance. On the other hand, Poland has a strong inflow of circular or short-term migrants (a good proportion of those migrants fit the concept of liquid migration, introduced in chapter 4) whereas in the Czech Republic and Hungary, long-term immigration is the predominant type. Drbohlav concludes that all three countries are undergoing migration transition, an intermediary stage between being an emigration country and being an immigration country, but find themselves in different phases of the transition. Poland is in its incipient phase, whereas Hungary and the Czech Republic, especially, are considerably further on in that process. Those differences notwithstanding, all three are at the moment too 'young' as immigration countries to justify a meaningful search for a 'regional model' of immigration or to draw a parallel between those countries and the rest of Europe.

The following two chapters deal with the issue of immigration in the future, or, strictly speaking, with the limits to migration forecasting. Arkadiusz Wiśniowski and his three co-authors argue that the relevant forecasts yield inevitably uncertain results if only for three reasons: the inability to adequately define migration, difficulty in its precise measurement and imperfections in knowledge about the nature of the processes involved. A considerable part of these weaknesses is attributed by them to the deterministic character of population forecasts, in general, and migration, in particular. In order to alleviate at least some of the weakness of migration forecasting, they suggest using a stochastic approach and, in particular, Bayesian statistics. This leads them to apply the concept of migration forecasting in a flexible manner, complementing official immigration data with expert data derived from a series of Delphi surveys. In turn, with help of autoregressive models and vector autoregressive models, Wiśniowski et al. present numerical results from that approach for a number of immigration countries representing various parts of Europe. Summing up, they seem to be confident that migration is mostly an unpredictable phenomenon and claim that 'precise forecasting of the exact values of immigration flows is virtually impossible'. Although the application of stochastic models to the forecasting of migration flows enables researchers to quantify and account for a degree of uncertainty, the lesson for policymakers is clear: any migration forecast must be viewed with great caution and all the more caution for longer time horizons.

Leo van Wissen, in the second chapter in this section, applauds the approach adopted by Wiśniowski et al., which he describes as innovative and elegant. However, he disagrees with their main message, namely that migration is hardly predictable. To support his view, Van Wissen discusses in a rather technical way a handful of factors that – in favourable circumstances – might make the results less uncertain. Thus, room for improvement can be found in the following: a better translation of expert ideas into distributions of the parameters of the forecasting model; more careful assumptions about the interdependency of model parameters; a lengthening of the time series for explanatory variables included in the model; a more accurate ('optimal') mathematical formulation of the model; and more internally consistent data on migration extracted from official statistics.

The two chapters preceding the final conclusions might be viewed as being practically oriented. They present policy recommendations that stem from analyses of most recent migration phenomena observed in Europe and attempt to refer those recommendations to the mainstream debate about a common European migration policy. First, Magdalena Lesińska lists the premises required by 'ideal' or 'mature' migration policy. Through this lens, she examines the process of learning by countries in earlier phases of the migration transition from countries in more advanced phases. In this context, she identifies and analyses the lessons to be learned, first, from the current 'old' immigration countries and then from the 'new' immigration countries. Lesińska also attempts to address the main questions she considers 'the pillars of migration policy'. She answers the question 'how should labour migration be managed?' by promoting the search for more flexible and effective rules and recruitment schemes. 'How should irregular immigration be coped with?' is met with a proposal for controls, regularisation and addressing root causes. Finally, she asks about the modes of solving 'the eternal problem of integration' and offers a very elaborate discussion that accounts for the integrity and coherence of policy aims and measures; the scope and organisational structure of integration policy; a variety of inclusion activities and combating discrimination and marginalisation; integration-promoting education and information; protection of vulnerable groups; and participation of migrants in the formulation and execution of integration policy.

The problem of integration in the context of so-called Europeanisation, with which Lesińska's chapter concludes, is further investigated by Theodora Kostakopoulou. She considers that aspect of migration policy from the legal and institutional perspective and, in doing so, she pays special attention to the evolution of the area of freedom, security and justice in the European Communities. Her analysis draws on a critical review of the development of policy goals and instruments in that area and she calls for a readjustment of European migration law and policy. As Kostakopoulou argues:

> [...] there is an urgent need to rethink the existing political frames of migration and integration, and to devise a coherent framework of migration governance that de-securitises migration, reflects international and European legal commitments and takes sufficiently into account the specificity of migration patterns in the 'old', 'new' and 'future' migration countries.

Bearing in mind that 'mobility is an integral part of the European integration project', a shift in paradigm is required – 'from perceiving and framing migration as a threat or nuisance to viewing it as a resource'.

Notes

1   The CEE's economic and political polarisation (the emergence of migration attraction poles in the region) proved to be a precondition for that shift in the expected out-migration of CEE populations. Other important underlying factors included: a dramatic liberalisation of migration policies (especially the rules of entry) throughout CEE, concomitant with the introduction of more rigorous admission rules in Western countries; intra-regional differences in demography and imbalances in labour markets in CEE; and – last but not least – the opening of ways for (until 1989, largely repressed) movements of various ethnic groups that were territorially divided or scattered by the redrawing of state borders in CEE during the Yalta Conference in 1945 (Okólski 2004).

2   A vast literature exists on this subject. Among the most influential works one might mention are: Bade (2003), Baines (1991), Castles and Miller (1993), Cohen (1987), Eltis (1983, 2002), Hatton and Williamson (1994, 1998, 2008), King (1996), Lucassen (1987), Potts (1990), Thomas (1954, 1958, 1972), Willcox (1929, 1931).

3   Stephen Castles and Mark Miller (1993 after Decloîtres 1967) offer a slightly lower figure (for 1800-1930) – namely, 40 million – but confine that estimate to the

overseas migration, thus excluding a huge migration of Russian population to Siberia and Central Asia since the 1890s (around 13 million according to McKeown 2004). Klaus Baade (2003) offers a variety of reliable estimates of European overseas emigration in a period of around 100 years between the beginnings of the nineteenth and the early twentieth centuries that range between 37 million and 63 million.

4   According to another account (Eltis 1983), in the period 1820-1880 13.7 million immigrants in the US arrived from Europe (in the period 1760-1820 the number was only 800,000).

5   In Eastern Europe, the increase also seemed very steep – from 6.8 million to 24.8 million (2.2 per cent to 7.5 per cent of the total population). These figures, however, to a large degree constitute an artefact. The initially large number of immigrants stemmed from the definition of international migrant adopted by the United Nations and based on the country of birth criterion. In turn, the period 1960-2005's growth owed to the collapse of the Soviet Union and the ensuing reclassification of persons who over that period moved within the boundaries of that country (and, of course, until around 1990 were considered internal migrants). From the time of the Soviet Union's disintegration they became international migrants. Those reservations are much less meaningful in the case of other parts of Europe (see Bonifazi 2008).

6   Precisely for that reason, the entities that compose Western Europe merit the name of 'old immigration countries', while those of Southern Europe are often called 'new immigration countries'.

7   The picture for Russia (and the whole former USSR, in fact) is blurred and cannot be compared with other parts of Europe due to reasons explained in note 5.

8   France presents a clear exception here. It was a country of net immigration already in some decades of the late nineteenth century and in the 1920s (King 1993).

9   IDEA – an acronym for the project known as Mediterranean and Eastern European Countries as New Immigration Destinations in the European Union – was conceived in early 2006 and carried out from 2007 to 2009. It benefited from financial support granted by the European Commission within the 6th Framework Programme (Priority SSP-5A, Area 8.1 B.2.5, Project no. 44446). IDEA was coordinated by the Centre of Migration Research (CMR) at the University of Warsaw and conducted by a consortium of eleven research institutions including, alongside the coordinator (in alphabetical order): the Central European Forum for Migration and Population Research (IOM Warsaw); the Centre for International Migration and Refugee Studies (Institute of Ethnic and National Minority Studies of the Hungarian Academy of Sciences, Budapest); the Centre of Research in Economic Sociology and Organisation (Lisbon); the Department of Social Geography and Regional Development (Charles University, Prague); the Hellenic Foundation for European and Foreign Policy (Athens); the Institute for Urban and Regional Studies (Austrian Academy of Sciences, Vienna); the Institute for Research on Population and Social Policies (National Research Council, Rome); the Institute of Political Science (Paris University X, Nanterre); the Mediterranean Laboratory of Sociology (National Centre of Scientific Research, Aix-en-Provence); Ortega y Gasset University Institute for Research (Madrid). Full documentation and all research outcomes of the project are available at www.idea6fp.uw.edu.pl.

10   Distinct exceptions to this tendency, however, could be observed even at the time of this writing. In particular, Poland and Romania from among the EU members and Ukraine from among non-EU countries ranked among important migrant-sending areas.

11   Strikingly, Timothy Hatton and Jeffrey Williamson (2008) speak about 'old' and 'new' emigrants from Europe during the period of mass overseas migration in reference to emigrants from Western and Northern Europe in the first instance and from Eastern and Southern Europe in the second. King (1996) referring to Michael Piore (1979) distinguishes between 'old' and 'new' immigration to the US (originating from North-Western and South-Eastern Europe, respectively).

12   In reference to Thomas' concept, Hatton and Williamson (1994) explicitly spoke of the 'emigration cycle'.

13   To be sure, in subsequent editions of the book, the concept of a four-stage model has been somehow diluted and presented in a very vague form.

References

Arango, J., C. Bonifazi, C. Finotelli, J. Peixoto, C. Sabino, S. Strozza & A. Triandafyllidou (2009), 'The making of an immigration model: Inflows, impacts and policies in Southern Europe', IDEA Working Papers 9, www.idea6fp.uw.edu.pl/pliki/WP_9_Southern_countries_synthesis.pdf.

Baade K.J. (2003), *Migration in European history*. Oxford: John Wiley/Blackwell.

Baines, D. (1991), *Emigration from Europe 1815-1930*. London: Macmillan.

Bonifazi, C. (2008), 'Evolution of regional patterns of international migration in Europe', in C. Bonifazi, M. Okólski, J. Schoorl & P. Simon (eds.), *International migration in Europe. New trends and new methods of analysis*, 107-128. IMISCOE Research Series. Amsterdam: Amsterdam University Press.

Castles, S. & M.J. Miller (1993), *The age of migration: International population movements in the modern world*. Houndmills: Macmillan.

Chesnais, J.-C. (1986), *La transition démographique: Etapes, formes, implications économiques*. Paris: Presses Universitaires de France.

Cohen, R. (1987), *The New Helots: Migrants in the international division of labour*. Aldershot: Avebury.

Dassetto, F. (1990), 'Pour une théorie des cycles migratoires', in A. Bastenier & F. Dassetto (eds.), *Immigration et nouveaux pluralisms: Une confrontation de sociétés*, 11-40. Brussels: De Boeck-Wesmael.

Eltis, D. (ed.) (2002), *Coerced and free migration: Global perspectives*. Stanford: Stanford University Press.

Eltis, D. (1983), 'Free and coerced transatlantic migrations: Some comparisons', *American Historical Review* 88: 251-280.

Eurostat (2009), 'Population and social conditions'. *Data in focus* 31: 1-11.

Fielding, A. (1993), 'Mass migration and economic restructuring', in R. King (ed.), *Mass migrations in Europe: The legacy and the future*, 7-17. London: Belhaven Press.

Grabowska-Lusińska, I., D. Drbohlav & A. Harš (eds.), *Immigration puzzles: Comparative analysis of the Czech Republic, Hungary and Poland before and after joining the EU*. Saarbrücken: Lambert Academic Publishing.

Hatton, T.J. & J.G. Williamson (2008), *Global migration and the world economy: Two centuries of policy and performance*. Cambridge: MIT Press.

Hatton, T.J. & J.G. Williamson (1998), *The age of mass migration: Causes and economic impact*. New York: Oxford University Press.

Hatton, T.J. & J.G. Williamson (eds.) (1994), *Migration and the international labour market, 1850-1939*. London: Routledge.

King, R. (1996), 'Migration in a world historical perspective', in J. van den Broeck (ed.), *The economics of labour migration*, 7-75. Cheltenham: Edward Elgar.

King, R. (1993), 'European international migration 1945-90: A statistical and geographical overview', in R. King (ed.), *Mass migration in Europe: The legacy and the future*, 19-39. London: Belhaven Press.

Lucassen, J. (1987), *Migrant labour in Europe 1600-1900*. London: Croom Helm.

McKeown, A. (2004), 'Global migration 1846-1940', *Journal of World History* 15: 155-189.

Okólski, M. (2004), 'The effects of political and economic transition on international migration in Central and Eastern Europe', in D.S. Massey & J.E. Taylor (eds.), *International migration: Prospects and policies in a global market*, 35-58. New York: Oxford University Press.

Piore, M.J. (1979), *Birds of passage: Migrant labour in industrial societies*. Cambridge: Cambridge University Press.

Potts, L. (1990), *The world labour market: A history of migration*. London: Zed Books.

Thomas, B. (1972), *Migration and urban development: A reappraisal of British and American long cycles*. London: Methuen.

Thomas, B. (ed.) (1958), *The economics of international migration*. London: Macmillan.

Thomas, B. (1954), *Migration and economic growth: A study of Great Britain and the Atlantic economy*. Cambridge: Cambridge University Press.

UN (2009), *World population prospects: The 2008 revision*. New York: United Nations.

UN (2006), *Trends in total migrant stock: The 2005 revision*. New York: United Nations.

Willcox, W.F. (ed.) (1931), 'International migrations', Vol. II, NBER Occasional Paper 18. New York: National Bureau of Economic Research.

Willcox, W.F. (ed.) (1929), 'International migrations', Vol. I, NBER Occasional Paper 14. New York: National Bureau of Economic Research.

Zelinsky, W. (1971), 'The hypothesis of the mobility transition', *Geographical Review* 61: 219-249.

1 Transition from emigration to immigration

Is it the destiny of modern European countries?

Marek Okólski

1.1 Purpose of this chapter

This book makes extensive use of two basic concepts: migration transition and the migration cycle. Expounded within its framework, the central premise of those concepts is such that, over time and under specific circumstances, individual European countries transform their migration status from one of emigration to one of immigration. This change in migration status has been termed the 'migration transition'.

As explained in the Introduction of this volume, the 'migration cycle' in its more general sense involves three distinct, consecutive phases: the first occurs when a country is overwhelmed by the outflow of its inhabitants, while the proportion of foreign nationals in the total population continues to be marginal; the second begins when the migration transition takes place; and the third begins when immigration systematically predominates over emigration and foreigners constitute a considerable proportion of the population. The central part of the cycle, the migration transition, also involves distinct parts (i.e. stages), which can be distinguished according to a given country's degree of maturity in terms of its immigration pattern or regime (see chapter 2 in this volume). A sequence of the stages – from immature to mature immigration country – makes up the 'migration cycle' (or rather 'immigration cycle') in a narrower sense.[1]

The main hypothesis underlying the analyses included in the present volume was that each European country finds itself in a specific stage of the immigration cycle. Consequently, countries included in the project were divided into three groups: the most advanced ('old'), the moderately advanced ('new') and the least advanced ('future'). As will be shown in part 3 of this chapter, of all countries analysed in depth in the present volume, Austria belongs to the first group ('old'); Greece, Italy, Portugal and Spain to the second group ('new'); and the Czech Republic, Hungary and Poland to the third group ('future'). Similarly, Ruby Gropas and Anna Triandafyllidou (2007) describe five types of European countries made distinct by their migration patterns: old host countries, recent host countries, countries in transition, small island countries and non-immigrant countries. Leaving aside 'small islands' (which include, according to Gropas and Triandafyllidou, Cyprus and Malta – and I would add Iceland here), this typology, apart from the three groups distinguished by the authors of this book, accounts for non-immigration status, the status attributed to the Baltic States, Slovakia and Slovenia.

This chapter specifically addresses the process a country undergoes to attain 'immigration country' status. To begin with, we should be more specific when using the notion of an 'immigration country' (or 'receiving area'). Does any type of inflow count, e.g. one comprising foreigners and/or return migrants; settlers and/or circular migrants – irrespective of its volume, durability or form – or should there be some additional requirements? It seems that immigration, in order to be studied as such (especially in the context of an immigration country) needs to attain a certain (high) critical mass and to be a relatively sustained phenomenon. Moreover, it seems conceivable that high-volume and sustained immigration goes hand in hand with net emigration. Assuming, then, that no country becomes an immigration country out of the blue, but rather reaches that status after a process of transformation from net emigration to net immigration, it seems useful – at least insofar as the Czech Republic, Hungary and Poland are concerned – to extend the concept of the migration cycle further, by adding an early stage ('prenatal' or 'embryonic') of the migration transition, where emigration declines and the nuclei of immigrant settlements are being set up.

For Central and Eastern European countries (and likely for other countries, e.g. Finland, Iceland and Ireland, as well) the real analytical crux, around which respective hypotheses could be tested empirically, is whether these countries are changing their statuses from net emigration to net immigration and, if so, how?

This sort of approach, however, requires taking a far-reaching retrospective view.

1.2   Factors of European migration in historical perspective

Whereas the present volume is about relatively recent migratory phenomena, in this chapter, I take a long view. This is because I argue that the change in the migration status of any European country (population/society/state) should be conceived of as embedded in a broader demographic context and analysed as a structurally determined phenomenon. Such an approach evidently requires a long-time perspective.[2]

Precisely speaking, in pre-modern contemporary societies migration plays an ancillary role in population reproduction. It becomes an important component of reproduction once mortality begins its systematic and secular decline. With the fall in death rates and ensuing, albeit delayed, fertility decline, the rate of natural increase reaches much higher levels than ever before and gives rise to several-decades-long, uninterrupted and relatively fast population growth. Thus, potential for mass emigration accrues. When the decrease in fertility rate is complete and fertility becomes close to the generation-to-generation replacement level, there is no longer need nor potential for massive and systematic emigration. On the contrary, under low and stable mortality, the close-to-replacement fertility brings about a very long process of population ageing. This, in turn, creates room for immigrant population. If, under such a reproduction regime, population is to increase and at the same time 'resist' fast ageing, steady immigration has to be reality. By this, migration maintains or reinforces its vital role in population reproduction, the role acquired at a certain point of the secular mortality decline.

Therefore, the demographic transition, the process that encapsulates the above-depicted phenomena, can be considered a structural foundation of the said change in migration status of European countries.

On the other hand, one might perceive the demographic transition as an intermediate stage of the modernisation-related[3] population cycle, whose initial (pre-modern) and ultimate (modern) stages assume some form of enduring population stability and a more or less erratic but also enduring equilibrium between the population size and its man-made environment. A shift in the predominant form and reproductive function of external migration, viewed from the perspective of any population that undergoes such a cycle, is, according to Jean-Claude Chesnais (1986), an integral part of the demographic transition and is called by him the migration transition.

Pre-modern migration is dependent upon political or economic conjuncture and rarely assumes mass scale.[4] Typically, short-term mobility of circulatory character predominates in the movements of population. Underneath, births and deaths – their high levels and short-term but rarely coherent variations notwithstanding – remain in a long-term balance.

Colin Clark (1977) and Jean-Noël Biraben (1979) suggest that over one thousand years (the period between 14 AD and approximately 1000), Europe's population size did not change at all,[5] though in between it displayed numerous ups and downs. Around the year 1400, its level was still not much higher than fourteen centuries earlier (Poursin 1976).[6] Since the fifteenth century, European population seemed evidently on the rise, and in the period 1400-1800 it grew (according to Carr-Saunders 1936) by a little more than 300 per cent (United Nations 1973: 21) or (according to a more up-to-date estimate) by some 180 per cent (Biraben 2006: 13).[7] This, however, was only a prelude to a really explosive increase.

In the nineteenth and early twentieth centuries, within the period of less than 100 years, European populations recorded unprecedented growth, usually by more than factor two. According to Walter F. Willcox (after

Chesnais 1986: 299), between 1800 and 1930, the population whose mother tongue was Russian increased by a factor of six; while in the case of English, the growth was fivefold; Italian and Polish: three-and-a-half-fold; Spanish: threefold; German: two-and-a-half-fold; and French: a bit more than twofold. Chesnais (1992: 319) estimates that in the presently highly developed countries, the growth of population size between the initial and final years of the demographic transition (on average, one hundred years) reached 300 per cent. It was mainly due to a systematic decrease of mortality and a consistently elevated natural increase. As alluded to in this volume's Introduction, a large part of that surplus population left for other continents.[8] This was due in some part to greatly improved means of transportation and good opportunities elsewhere that lured immigrants (Hatton & Williamson 2008; King 1996), but mainly because of a different and very special reason. That reason is verbalised in Chesnais' words (1992: 306):

> [...] emigration helped, at a time when the competition of young adults on the job market was at its highest, to reduce the threat of over-population [...]. External migration [was] a manifestly strategic variable in the process of a population's adjustment to its milieu.

As a matter of fact, Chesnais develops and substantiates empirically a hypothesis which posits a close to twenty-year time lag between time series of births (or natural increase) and emigration (Chesnais 1992: 171-175) and, by the same token, a 'substitution of mortality by migration'.[9] Russell King (1996: 35), in reference to the safety valve theory, offers a similar explanation:

> As the death rate in Europe declined and the birth rate failed to respond to keep population growth in check, emigration functioned as a safety-valve to skim off a significant proportion of the surplus.

By many accounts, mass emigration from Europe, which started in the early nineteenth century, can be considered a breakthrough in European population history. In reference to that phenomenon, Timothy Hatton and Jeffrey Williamson (2008) speak of the transition from a trickle to mass migration.[10] As a matter of fact, it is just one of the manifestations of a broader concept – the mobility transition, in terms of Wilbur Zelinsky's (1971) well-known hypothesis. Its essence is that 'physical and social mobility' always substantially increases as society ('community' in his own words) experiences the process of modernisation. Moreover, 'the course of the mobility transition closely parallels that of the demographic transition' (Zelinsky 1979: 171). One of the characteristics of early modernisation ('the early transitional society' phase) is a 'major outflow of emigrants to available and attractive foreign destinations', concomitant with a 'rapid decline in mortality [and] a relatively rapid rate of natural increase, and thus a major growth in size of population' (Zelinsky 1979: 173).

By a striking contrast, after around 100 to 150 years from the onset of mass intercontinental outflow of people, many countries of Europe witnessed exacerbated inflow of immigrants, largely of non-European origin, and at about the same time (if not a few decades earlier) European overseas emigration began to fade. Conspicuously, this new tendency generally appeared first in those countries where the mass emigration (and the demographic transition) was initiated at the earliest. In fact, labour markets in some of those countries had attracted large numbers of foreigners several decades before that time. At that time, however, the migrants originated as a rule from other (less advanced in the process of industrialisation) countries of Europe and often they assumed the role of temporary workers in their host countries.

The beginning of the 1970s saw some 10 million migrant workers in Europe, many of them from Turkey, India, Pakistan, British, Dutch and French colonies of the Caribbean, various African countries and the East Indies. Between the early 1950s and the early 1970s, the foreign population in Germany increased by around 3.5 million; in France and Britain by more than 2.5 million; in Switzerland by nearly 800,000; in Belgium by 400,000; and in the Netherlands and Sweden by 300,000 (King 1986; Castles & Miller 2003). Not only did foreign citizens become a part of the resident populations in Europe in the decades to follow, but, moreover, the number and geographical diversity of their origin greatly increased, as did the number of European destination countries.

That profound change also finds a reflection in the hypothesis of the mobility transition.[11] In the late phase of the transition, as Zelinsky (1979: 173, 174) argues, 'emigration is on the decline or may have ceased altogether' and next, the phase of 'advanced society' witnesses a 'significant net immigration of unskilled and semi-skilled workers from relatively underdeveloped lands'. All that is due to 'a slight to moderate rate of natural increase or none at all', caused by the decline of fertility which finally 'oscillates rather unpredictably at low to moderate levels'.

Levels of fertility in North-Western Europe after the mid-1960s (and later in other parts of the continent) turned out very low, in fact substantially below the replacement level. This was hardly predicted by the demographic transition model. Such unexpected fall in fertility prompted Dirk van de Kaa (1999)[12] to extend and adjust the classical model of demographic transition by assuming that the natural increase of population can be both positive and negative, and explicitly adding net migration as a component of the population change that continuously interplays with natural increase. He incorporated in the model the idea developed by Hatton and Williamson (1994), who suggested that, as natural increase (assuming systematically positive values) first rises and later declines, emigration goes through four phases – initiation, growth, saturation and regression – and with further decline in natural increase (within its negative values), immigration comes to the fore. Referring to contemporary Europe, Van de Kaa (1999: 29, 34) assumed that it

> will face a lengthy period of below-replacement fertility and, equally, a lengthy period of immigration […]. The region will surely come to grips with reality and will start acting as an immigration area. This will lead to a carefully controlled influx, possibly during a couple of generations.

Therefore an important conclusion might be drawn here. During the time of mass population movements, rates of migration are strongly linked (at least in the statistical sense) to rates of natural increase.[13] This is even more so when it comes to long trends (Chesnais 1992).

Coming back to the nineteenth century, all European societies experienced massive territorial mobility, including massive waves of emigration. Compared to the types of migrations observed in earlier periods of European history, the type of mobility that arose during the nineteenth century displayed two important, distinct characteristics. First of all, it was by and large intentional and usually included the aim of settlement. In addition, it was principally individualistic and economically oriented, as it was undertaken by entrepreneurs (including farmers) and workers in search of gainful employment.

It began, naturally, with capitalism and modernisation, and as a sustained quasi-unidirectional process of complex social change. The Industrial Revolution in England, an early component and factor of modernisation, gave rise to an unprecedented and long-lasting decline in mortality and accelerated population growth.[14] Shortly, the population explosion became an all-European phenomenon.

Increasing populations nourished industrial growth, both by enhancing the demand for goods and by supplying the labour market with ever more labour. Modernisation and the demographic transition became interwoven and mutually interdependent (Dyson 2001).

Initially, surpluses of population and labour occurred mainly in backward areas, which were barely influenced or penetrated by modern social change and the related institutions or social relationships.

Thus, the flow of people moving to fulfil the unsatisfied labour demand in modernising areas took a clear direction – from the peripheries with (mostly) subsistence (pre-capitalist) economies to metropolitan centres with full-fledged markets and highly monetised (capitalist) economies. This phenomenon, inter alia, contributed to the expansion of demand for goods and stimulated production growth. It should be mentioned that those flows of labour assumed the two forms, internal and international migration, both complementary or substituting for each other, depending on contextual circumstances, e.g. the phase of economic (business) cycle (Thomas 1954).

Population growth in Europe in the nineteenth century turned out to be so dynamic that the flows of people from the peripheries to the core, i.e. typically from rural to urban areas – both within particular countries and in the trans-European space – did not substantially reduce the population surplus and the emerging demographic-economic imbalance. As a consequence, a large overseas emigration movement emerged and attained an unprecedented scale. While in the early 1800s the population of all continents besides Europe consisted of less than 5 million European settlers or their ancestors, today the respective number has skyrocketed to between 550 million and 650 million (Grabowska-Lusińska & Okólski 2009).

With the phenomenon of modernisation and of colonisation by Europeans of countries overseas, the world has gradually been divided into a group of core (or centre) countries, where modern changes were either complete or highly advanced, and a group of peripheral countries, where these changes were only just pending. A long-term process that characterises this division is the movement of individual countries from the former group towards the latter.

Depending on the course of both modernisation and demographic transition, the demand for labour in the metropolitan centres occasionally exceeded the supply of migrant labour (originating predominantly in the peripheries), but sometimes the opposite happened. The former scenario favoured immigration, whereas the latter case favoured emigration. A general tendency, however, was that of net emigration in the early stages of economic and demographic change, and net immigration in the later stages. France, for instance, where the pace of demographic transition was relatively 'low' and social change was rather deep, experienced very little emigration and rather quickly became a net immigration country (Morokvasic-Müller, Dinh, Potot & Salzbrunn 2008).

That net immigration status is typical of advanced modernity – which, in turn, coincides with the end of demographic transition periods – is a result of the very nature of the latter phenomenon. The end of demographic transition means, among other things, very low fertility, close to zero population growth and fast population ageing. Under the circumstances of rapid economic growth, this unavoidably leads to labour shortages and to labour's 'importation' from outside (third countries).

The shift from a relative abundance of labour to a deficit could be seriously affected (amplified or impeded) by several other factors. One of these catalysts is the date when modern changes begin, or, strictly speaking, the relative level of modernity of a given society vis-à-vis other societies at the moment of the process's initiation. The later a society enters modernisation, the more it can borrow or copy from pioneers or predecessors, and the less consistent social changes in that society seem to be. Modernisation processes in Mediterranean and CEE societies serve as an illustration here. It might also be the case, however, that the latecomers encounter more acute and prolonged imbalances between the unsatisfied demand for labour generated by the centre and the excessive supply of labour generated by the periphery.

Another crucial factor that contributes to the increased diversity among various societies in the course of the migration status change involves inherent cultural differences between those societies. The societies that are culturally similar to each other are more likely to undergo a comparable course of transition from a net emigration to net immigration status than those more dissimilar. Finally, there is virtually a plethora of factors of more universal or more local reach that are believed to have facilitated or accelerated or modified the course and essence of the transition, such as transportation costs, wage level and rates, conjuncture (phase of the business/investment cycle), the Irish Famine, ethnic cleansing (e.g. persecution of Jews in the Russian Empire), structure of the world economy ('Atlantic economy'), public policy (e.g. government subsidies), the strength of kinship and social networks, etc. (e.g. Baines 1991; Chesnais 1986; Gliwic 1934; Hatton &Williamson 2008; King 1996; Thomas 1954, 1972). In a short term, under the influence of those factors, many cases were noted to be of significant deviation from the main trend or even distinct exceptions from that trend. In the long run, however, the impact of demographic phenomena, especially the change in the regime of (vital) population reproduction, turns out to be essential.[15]

Neither modern social change nor demographic transition is a uniform and linear process, and each one heavily depends on, among other things, starting points and cultural particularities. For instance, latecomer countries usually experience very rapid declines in mortality and strong surges in natural increase (i.e. the increase in native-born population)[16] relative to pioneer countries, but the persistence of traditional lifestyles and subsistence economies among the latecomers at the beginning of their transitions is comparatively larger, and makes their drift to modernity more arduous and slow. Under such circumstances, even if emigration attains a large size, the population surplus is sustained – if not increased – which hampers or undermines social change.

In order to synchronise the two processes, i.e. demographic and social change, a bit of luck is necessary. In the case of the Mediterranean countries (Italy, Spain, Greece and Portugal), 'luck' meant a contemporaneous decline in fertility and increase in the outflow of surplus population, which responded to an unfulfilled demand for foreign labour in the pioneer countries of Western and Northern Europe. This happened in the 1950s and 1960s, when the Mediterranean countries were already fairly advanced not only in the modernisation of their institutions and socio-economic structures, but also in imitating 'Western' patterns of culture. The outflow of redundant population then brought about a crowding-out effect and made room for the completion of modern changes.[17]

1.3   Diversity of migration trends across Europe

Let me now take a more restricted view and focus on European migration in the post-World War II period. Looking at basic migration trends in that period, and especially at migration status transformation from net emigration to net immigration, it becomes apparent that, although major characteristics of that change were preserved, it was by and large influenced by a new post-war political reality. To clarify this point, I rely on a division of the post-war period into five stages presented in Table 1.1.

Table 1.1   *Stages of post-World War II migration processes*

Stage/sub-period	Key characteristics
1. 1945-1947	Post-war reconstruction; new partition of Europe; adjustment migration
2. 1948-1973	Political bipolarity; Cold War and the arms race; blooming western market economies vis-à-vis state-controlled and non-efficient economies of Southern Europe and CEE; western economic integration (European Economic Community); strong labour flow from the South to the West and suppressed labour mobility in the East
3. 1974-1988	Political détente; major cracks in the political system in CEE (1980, Poland); globalisation challenges; economic restructuring and deeper integration (inclusion of the South); search for available low-cost labour; inflow of irregular migrants from CEE (including many 'ethnic Germans' leaving their CEE countries of origin and entering Germany as tourists) and non-European countries; failure of 'socialist modernisation'
4. 1989-2004	Breakdown of the Communist bloc; end of bipolarity; sudden increase in population displacements; regional conflicts and wars; new political entities; a complete project of European integration (including common immigration policy and management); economic transition in CEE
5. after 2004/2007	Restoration of European unity; strong competition on the part of non-European economies; human capital deficits; continuous demand for immigrants vis-à-vis intensified difficulties in migrant integration

Source: Own elaboration

Having identified these stages and sub-periods, I will highlight basic differences in migration trends between three groups of countries: Western and Northern Europe (WNE), Southern Europe (Mediterranean) and Central and Eastern Europe (CEE). What is an essential component of this geographical breakdown is, among other things, the temporal distance between respective initiations of modern social change. For example, WNE countries preceded Mediterranean countries, and Mediterranean countries preceded CEE countries. To further elucidate this point, subsequent sub-periods can be distinguished by their predominant characteristics and be considered specific to a given sub-period flow of people. These can be termed, respectively: 'post-war adjustment migration', 'migration related to labour recruitment', 'migration related to a "new globalisation"', 'post-communist migration' and 'post-enlargement migration'. They are succinctly described in Table 1.2.

Directly after the period of post-war adjustment migration, WNE countries, facing serious labour deficits and the challenge of deep economic restructuring, were prepared for a massive intake of foreign workers. A

Table 1.2 *Sub-stages of post-World War II migration processes*

Stage/ sub-period	Region		
	Western and Northern (WNE)	*Southern (Mediterranean)*	*Central and Eastern (CEE)*
1. Post-war adjustment migration (1945-1947)	Post-war return migration; politically and ethnically motivated displacements		
	(Germany)	(Greece)	(All countries)
2. Migration related to labour recruitment/ bilateral agreements (1948-1973)	Labour shortages; foreign recruitment; towards net immigration; Finland, Ireland (major exceptions); fears of brain drain in some WNE countries	(Low-skilled) labour outflow; freeing labour markets of redundant workforce; high net emigration; networks and ethnic niches in WNE	Ban on international movements;under-urbanisation; GDR, Hungary, Czecho-slovakia (political exceptions), Yugoslavia (economic exception)
3. Migration of the onset of 'new globalisation' (1974-1988)	Cessation of recruitment; labour market segmentation; inflow for family reunion; inflow of asylum seekers; irregular employment of foreigners	Rapid decline in outflow; labour deficit leads to admission of foreigners (large scale of irregular work); towards net immigration	Movements con-tained within CEE region; resumption of ethnicity-motivated outflow; onset of in-complete migration

Table 1.2   *(continued)*

Stage/ sub-period	Region		
	Western and Northern (WNE)	*Southern (Mediterranean)*	*Central and Eastern (CEE)*
4. Post-communist migration – related to disruption of communism and orientation towards 'Fortress Europe' (1989-2004)	Advanced segmentation of labour market (secondary jobs for foreigners); massive inflow of undocumented migrants and asylum seekers; migrant smugglers and traffickers; selective admission for the highly skilled		Incomplete migration; post-communist adjustment migration; economic polarisation within CEE → intra-regional movements; towards net immigration (Czech Republic)
	Prospective trends in the 10-15-year time span		
5. Post-enlargement migration – integrated European migration space (after 2004/2007)	Inflows due to population stagnation and ageing (main underlying factors); further segmentation of labour markets; intra-EU competition for the highly skilled; low level of intra-EU mobility (some but shallow potential in Poland, Romania, Bulgaria and the Baltic states; towards completion of labour market draining of redundant labour in CEE)		

Source: Own elaboration

continuous flow of immigrants was soon triggered and, after some time, the WNE countries, one by one, turned into net immigration areas.

Many of the migrating workers originated from the Mediterranean countries. According to numerous accounts, between 1950 and 1970, anywhere from 7 million to 10 million persons emigrated from Italy, Spain, Greece and Portugal (circa 8 to 10 per cent of the mid-period population), of which a half went to WNE (Layard, Blanchard, Dornbush & Krugman 1992). Massimo Livi Bacci (1972: 17) estimates that in the period 1965-1970 'emigrant workers [from southern countries][18] make up about 50 per cent on the average, of the potential increase of the labour force', of which 89 per cent in the case of Italy, 85 per cent in the case of Portugal, 65 per cent in the case of Greece and 46 per cent in the case of Spain.[19] An outflow of this huge magnitude was possible due to considerable underemployment or 'disguised' unemployment in those countries.[20] In more underdeveloped areas of the Mediterranean countries, the outflow comprised up to 85 to 90 per cent of the potential increase of the labour force (Danieli 1972). Running parallel to this, from the late 1960s onwards, all four Mediterranean countries experienced a rapid and consistent decline in fertility – from a maximum total fertility rate (TFR) of 2.4-3.1 to 1.4-1.7 around 1985 (United Nations 2007). The labour potential at the time was therefore significantly reduced due to emigration, and a continuously diminishing labour potential was stabilised largely due to below-replacement fertility.

Those were the main demographic underpinnings for major social change and sustained modern economic development. Social change in Italy accelerated in the 1950s, in Spain in the 1960s, but in Greece and Portugal only in the 1980s. In each case, however, a breakthrough occurred when economies opened up and integration with more developed European countries became a structural process.

As a result, after 1973, in the sub-period of migration related to the process of 'new globalisation', the Mediterranean countries – first Italy and later the three others – were strongly affected by shortages of labour. The worker outflow was drastically reduced and, soon thereafter, the labour markets were opened to the inflow of foreigners. By the end of the 1980s, all four countries changed their migration statuses and came to be new net immigration areas.

Contrary to WNE and Mediterranean Europe, the population movements in CEE over the period leading up to the late 1980s were strongly subordinated to political factors. In fact, after the abrupt interruption of massive post-war resettlements in 1948, both the outflows and the inflows were almost completely reduced to exceptional cases. Not only did international migration come to a halt, but also any cross-border mobility was effectively stopped. Under the circumstances of high natural increase and sluggish economic development, a large backlog of unrealised migration arose in many CEE countries, notably in Poland and Romania.[21]

Over time, however, and alongside a softening grip on human freedoms, a variety of forms of out-movement began emerging that became alternatives to 'regular' emigration. These movements, heavily controlled by the authorities, reflected a specific pattern that ran concomitantly with an internal political cycle. In particular, compared to periods characterised by a 'hard grip' on international mobility, many more people were allowed to leave the country in times of political turmoil and during shifts in political leadership. Gradually, more and more CEE residents who managed to travel abroad became residents of foreign countries – as immigrants or temporary workers, refugees, co-ethnics or undocumented migrants (e.g. 'overstaying tourists').

What greatly differentiated CEE countries from other important migration source countries were, until at least 1989, their migrants' concealed motives and forms of movement. While a great majority of migrants from CEE countries sought employment in foreign countries – which undoubtedly constituted the main motive of their migration – they were compelled to declare other purposes both to the government of their country of origin and that of the host countries in order to be allowed to leave or enter and stay. This forced them into an unstable and disadvantageous, if not precarious, situation in the labour market and in social life in general. Even after

1989, when departures from CEE countries were newly permitted and residents could easily enter many traditional destination countries, they could do so legally only as tourists – which was seldom an actual motive for journeying abroad.

Because of their somewhat irregular status, most migrants originating from CEE countries endured discriminatory practices of employers and were usually grossly underpaid. In order to cope with that reality, CEE migrants developed a peculiar pattern of mobility that enabled them to boost the real value of their foreign earnings. It was incomplete migration, a sort of circulation of individual household members, often repeated, and characterised by short-term employment abroad and a very high proportion of earnings being remitted or repatriated to the migrant's home country, where the cost of living was substantially lower. By spending most of the 'foreign money' they earned abroad in their countries of origin, the migrants' real wages became relatively high and enabled migrant households to survive, if not enjoy a decent lifestyle. At the same time, however, migrant households remained anchored and indeed enmeshed in the peripheries of CEE countries, despite the significant mobility of some of their members.

As a result, throughout the entire sub-period of post-communist migration, the outflows of people from CEE countries barely contributed to unburdening them of redundant people. Despite growing out-migration, labour surpluses were sustained. At the same time, however, at least one radical change occurred that was in line with what happened earlier in WNE countries and Mediterranean Europe: fertility decreased to levels far below replacement. While in 1985 the TFR was still as high as 2.3 in Poland, Romania and Slovakia (then a part of Czechoslovakia) and 2.1 in the Baltic States, in 2000 it reached a level of around 1.3 throughout the entire region (United Nations 2007). This marked the beginning of a rapidly shrinking demographic labour potential.

Now it would seem opportune to question whether the accession of CEE countries to the European Union resulted in any significant changes in the migration trends of their populations.

It will not be possible to attain reliable estimates of the post-enlargement outflow until the results of the forthcoming population censuses are released. For now, we can venture only guesstimates at best. This is because no existing record adequately measures various types of flows and stocks of migrants. Typically, the size and composition of migrant stocks differ from country to country because the definition of an immigrant resident differs. Some countries do not distinguish, for example, between migrants who moved before their home country's accession date and those who moved later. This is especially pertinent when the act of accession provided migrants with an opportunity to change their statuses from clandestine and undocumented to regular and documented. Migrant flows are thus not broken down according to the length of migrants' sojourns in the destination countries, which could result in multiple counts and other deficiencies.

These caveats aside, it can be said that the date of the first eastward EU enlargement, 1 May 2004, marked the beginning of a new quality in the outflow of people from CEE countries. It has become quite clear, after two and a half years, that the change in differentia specifica of migration affected many of its aspects: the volume of flows, which increased substantially, and their composition – regional, social, economic and demographic. Forms of flows and the motives of migrants also became more diversified.

A cautious World Bank (2006) estimate of the outflow from the EU-8 accession countries to the three EU-15 countries, which, on 1 May 2004, did not introduce transitory precautions to protect their labour markets, suggested a very large scale of mobility. It found that, over the first twenty months, until 31 December 2004, Lithuania lost 3.3 per cent of its working-age population, Latvia 2.4 per cent, Slovakia 1.3 per cent, Poland 1.2 per cent and Estonia 1.1 per cent. That came as a surprise to many analysts, seeing as during the pre-accession period little was known about the migration potential of such countries as Latvia or Slovakia and the populations of those countries were not regarded as highly prone to emigration.

It could be safely assumed that, between 1 May 2004 and 1 January 2007, at least 1 million persons, 80 to 90 per cent of whom were job-seekers, emigrated from Poland. This corresponds to slightly more than 4 per cent of the total working-age mid-period population (2.6 per cent of the entire population). Keeping in mind the estimates of the outflow during the 1980s (more than 1 million long-term emigrants), and between 1991 and 2003 (approximately 750,000), it can be argued that, over the last quarter of a century, around 2.5 million Poles emigrated – which amounts to over 67 per cent of the natural population increase in that period and over 6.5 per cent of the total population (Grabowska-Lusińska & Okólski 2009). Comparing the rate and volume of that outflow to the outflow recorded in Mediterranean Europe during labour recruitment-related migration, we can conclude that Poland might not be far from completing the crowding-out process.

Polish Labour Force Survey (LFS) data leave no doubt that the accession date constituted a breakthrough in outflow trends. Until the beginning of 2004, the stock of temporary migrants, who traditionally predominate in the outflow from Poland, was fairly stable at a level of around 200,000.[22] This was especially true for the number of long-term migrants; the stock of short-term migrants slowly decreased over the 1990s and slowly increased from 2000 to 2003.[23] In the middle of 2005, the migrant stock surpassed 300,000; by mid-2006 it reached 450,000; and, at the end of that year, 500,000 Poles were recorded (by account of LFS) as temporary migrants.

A similar conclusion can be drawn on the basis of host countries' sources. For instance, an accelerated inflow to Britain is documented by the National Insurance Number statistics, where Poles, along with Slovaks and Lithuanians, became leading nationalities among those issued a new number. One year before the accession date, they were barely featured at all in those statistics, with an overall share of around 4 per cent of all foreigners. Just one year later, Poland became a clear leader in the statistics, and in the year 2006/2007, of the top six nationalities, three were CEE countries, which accounted for an overall share of 39 per cent. The British International Passenger Survey data also confirm that the movements of the citizens of accession countries into the United Kingdom, Poles in particular, increased rapidly after 1 May 2004. The same trend was observed in Sweden, where not only did the inflow from CEE accelerate, but, in addition to migrant workers, it comprised proportionally more family members. The case of the inflow into Ireland presents another striking illustration of this phenomenon. Until the middle of 2004, Ireland hosted few immigrants from CEE countries, but in 2006 CEE, citizens became a clearly predominant group among the newly arrived (Grabowska-Lusińska & Okólski 2009).

The three countries that did not limit access to their labour markets were not the only ones to have experienced elevated inflows from CEE countries. With the one distinct exception of Germany, a significant increase was also observed in other WNE countries.

Taken together, a considerable outflow of people from the CEE countries during the post-enlargement sub-period, which coincided with a rapid decline in fertility and a soon-to-be reduced demographic labour potential, provided for a historic opportunity to unburden CEE countries' labour markets of superfluous people and, as a consequence, improve their efficiency. Since this went hand in hand with modern economic change – which was a requisite for economic integration with the EU – the CEE accession countries could soon experience a breakthrough in the transformation of their migration status from net emigration to net immigration. As was historically the case for the four Mediterranean countries, a bit of luck in bringing about that major change proved helpful, if not indispensable. This time, for the CEE countries, the bit of luck came from Britain: it materialised in the visionary and strong-willed British polity and in the huge capacity of the booming British economy to absorb incoming labour.

The significance of the outflow of people from CEE countries in the post-accession period cannot be overestimated. The crowding-out of those countries' labour markets was a major, structurally determined social phenomenon, a foundation for further modern social change and, ultimately, an impetus for convergence with the core objectives of the EU.

1.4   Transformation of migration status: An outline of the model

Taking the long view, migration can be perceived as a response to a disequilibrium that arises between population size and growth and the stock and composition of resources that a given population uses or needs to support itself (Coleman 2006). As pointed out in section 1.2 of this chapter, modernisation stimulates two processes that are of vital importance for migration, namely:
- The shrinking of the subsistence sector of the economy, which has historically symbolised backwardness and, by diminishing, makes way for an expanding and highly monetised market sector.
- A specific change in population (called the demographic transition) whose major traits include a systematic and accelerated increase in the number of people that goes parallel with, on the one hand, a clustering of those people in the enclaves of backwardness or the peripheries of modernity, and, on the other hand, a growing shortage of people in emerging economic growth poles (centres).

This sort of social change entails a mass migration from the periphery to the centre, whose direct cause is the relatively uneven distribution of the population. This is a multistage phenomenon, ranging from the strictly local through the global stage.

It could be argued that population surpluses hamper or occasionally preclude the modernisation of peripheries. The outflow of redundant people constitutes one major impetus for the completion of the modernisation project – though it is not capable of either initiating or substituting modern reforms.

A rapidly onsetting period of modernity, due to an increasing (and usually relatively high) natural population increase, is conducive to emigration. Outflows generally originate in overpopulated rural areas (including tiny towns located in the middle of those areas), then expand to include developing urban areas or colonised lands. A mature level of modernisation coincides with a declining (and usually relatively low, sometimes negative) natural population increase. Population ageing is also usually set in motion. What ensues is a structural deficit in a given population, manifested above all in a steady labour shortage. Needless to say, this is conducive to immigration.[24]

An additional factor determining the flow of people from country peripheries to centres that is related to modernisation and relevant from an international perspective is the timing of the initiation of modern changes in particular countries (a 'generation effect').[25] As a rule, pioneer countries in early stages of modernisation, apart from sending population surpluses generated by their peripheries to modernity poles (centres), export some of these surpluses to other countries – typically to colonies overseas.

Latecomer countries, however, usually lack such opportunities. What eventually facilitates migration for the latecomer countries is, quite paradoxically, a difference in the timing of the transformation process' initiation between them and the pioneer countries: the latter are converted sooner from countries of net emigration to net immigration. The erosion of traditional socio-economic structures and institutions within the latecomer countries goes hand in hand with an advanced level of modernity and often with labour shortages within the pioneer countries (Massey 1999).

The subsistence (natural) sector in a modernising society can be thought of as something of a vestigial organ or other archaic remnant in the body of an advancing economy. No convergence mechanism exists to make it compatible with the market (capitalist) sector. In the long run, it can only perish or become parasitic for the latter. People functioning in subsistence sectors have little chance of changing their social and economic roles and positions unless they abandon their outdated lifestyles or occupations. In the vast majority of cases, however, abandonment means out-migration.

There is something of a structural incompatibility between the subsistence and market economy. The virtues of the former include a 'closedness' or semi-isolation, a struggle for survival and continuity. The virtues of the latter include an openness and a tendency towards expansion. The mentality, work culture and skills of the people in one sector are useless in the other. The characteristics of cultural and human capital – indefinitely reproduced and propagated in the subsistence sector – do not fit the market sector. There is thus a kind of superfluity of population resources in the subsistence sector.

In modern society, with welfare states as its prominent institution, the natural or subsistence sector gives rise to extra social costs. These costs are particularly acute under conditions of low mobility or when mobility (outflow) is impeded by existing institutions. This is because the natural increase of people living in the subsistence sector is relatively high, which puts pressure on social benefits and leads to increasing related costs. The preservation of the subsistence sector under otherwise modern conditions thus impairs or impedes development. The scale of modernising reforms (e.g. investment in modern infrastructure and R&D) is severely limited by competition stemming from the necessary financing of extra social costs that result from the very existence of a subsistence sector.

Modern and self-sustained development within a country is possible and particularly beneficial if three conditions are met at about the same time:
– Deep reforms leading to the expansion of the competitive market sector.
– A reduction in fertility, bringing about a low natural increase.
– High mobility (especially spatial mobility) of the population, which facilitates internal transfers of demographic surpluses within the

subsistence sector and outflows of the remaining redundant population to third countries.

The subsistence sector then rapidly diminishes and sources of superfluous population begin to dry out. A modern, liberalised economy is strengthened and consolidated when, among other things, strong international competition exists and no population pressure is exerted (close to zero natural increase) on it. The attempts of economic actors (firms) to lower labour costs (or at least to prevent their increase) are accompanied by and, in a way, confronted with a diminishing local workforce and a weakening propensity of local workers to accept low-paying jobs. This tendency results from, and is reinforced by, the very nature of the institutions of the welfare state. The ensuing evolution of the labour market gives way to a specific structural form called a 'dual labour market', which displays a characteristic segmentation pattern. The expansion of a labour market segment with lax regulatory standards and wage rigidities becomes a source of comparative advantage to certain firms linked to that segment. However, with an insufficient supply of local labour, the inflow of migrant workers from peripheral economies is a fundamental prerequisite of such a sector's expansion.

Specific institutions and mechanisms exist to facilitate the inflow of workers responding to the volume and structure of modern economies' demand for labour. Systematic immigration contributes to the emergence and growth of a 'foreigners' sector' within the labour market. Migrant workers in foreigners' sectors become over-represented relative to their share in the total labour force and, in some cases, even outnumber the local workers.

In sum, the indispensable requisites for any country to transform its migration status are, first, the outflow of redundant population (the crowding-out) and, secondly, embarking on the path of sustained modern development. Under these circumstances, emigration declines rapidly. In turn, the completion of the demographic transition (natural increase at close to zero and rapid ageing of the population, including the workforce) and the economic competition-led segmentation of the labour market bring about an inflow of foreign workers whose number, over time, becomes larger than that of outgoing local workers. A former emigration country thus becomes an immigration country.

Notes

1   In this very meaning, 'migration cycle' is narrower from a historical time perspective, but it goes more deeply as far as contextual matters are concerned.
2   I adhere here to an approach of studying historical structures evolving over a long time by means of problem-oriented and comprehensive analyses (*lire l'histoire à rebours*, according to Marc Bloch), as developed by French historians and known as *longue durée* (Braudel 1999). Akin to that approach in the area of migration study

    are such seminal works as Zelinsky (1971), Piore (1979), Chesnais (1986) and Massey (1999).

3   One of the key notions used in this chapter and to some extent throughout the entire volume is 'modernisation'. I realise how ambiguous, if controversial, this term might sound nowadays. My preferred meaning of modernisation is rather simple and refers to a dichotomous typology of European societies, often applied to the history of the recent few hundred years, which distinguishes between 'pre-modern' (traditional) type and 'modern' type. In accordance with this, each European society evolves from the former to the latter; between the pre-modern and modern type there is a specific transition, an all-embracing structural social change, called modernisation. While the outcome of modernisation seems clear – it is a structurally and strikingly *different* society – the criteria of that difference are numerous and by no means mutually exclusive. They depend on the cognitive perspective represented by those who are or were involved in the study of that process. The perspectives adopted by such scholars as Herbert Spencer, Ferdinand Tönnies, Max Weber, Emile Durkheim, Talcott Parsons, Henry Maine, Robert Redfield and Krishan Kumar evidently differed, but probably none of them would have found it difficult to point out fundamental differences of structural character between a pre-modern and a modern society, and even less to indicate the time and place on Earth where the change called 'modernisation' came about. Needless to add, in this volume we distance ourselves from 'modernisation' in Walt Rostow's sense.

4   Apart from periods of war or conquests and colonisations, international migrants include mostly relatively small numbers of merchants, mercenaries or missionaries. David Coleman (2006: 37) argues that 'labour movement does not become generally international until a much later date, particularly during the Industrial Revolution [...]'.

5   It was estimated at some 39.5 million in AD 14 and at 39.2 million circa the year 1000 (Clark 1977: 64).

6   Jean-Marie Poursin's (1976: 21) estimate for circa 1400 is 45 million. Biraben (2006: 13), however, puts the number of Europeans around that year much higher, at some 52 million.

7   All estimates exclude the population living on the territory of the former USSR. Here, similarly, its size did not change between Anno Domini and 1400, while in the period 1400-1800 it grew by a little less than 300 per cent (Biraben 2006).

8   According to Poursin (1976: 23), between 1650 and 1950, the population of European origin became larger by over 800 million and reached 940 million, 300 million of whom lived outside of Europe.

9   According to Chesnais (1992: 165): 'Migration is at its highest during the period when, following the decline in mortality, the curve of natural increase approaches its apex; and the size of the wave of departures is closely connected with the level of natural increase and hence with patterns of demographic transition. The traits of migration are inseparable from the profiles of transition, and vice versa.'

10   In an earlier work (Hatton & Williamson 1994), the authors spoke of the 'emigration cycle', which extends from a growing emigration rate to receding emigration.

11   A very similar perspective is represented by the concept of the 'migration curve', i.e. a historical process in which populations make the transition from net emigration to net immigration (Ackerman 1976 quoted after Massey 1999).

12   Earlier Van de Kaa (together with Ron Lesthaeghe) developed a concept of the second demographic transition, a phenomenon typical of North-Western Europe, where it developed since the mid-1960s. He distinguished the two transitions in the following way: 'While mortality decline provided the "engine" for the first transition, fertility decline is the "engine" of the second. In both instances international migration

plays a significant role in the balancing equation, but while it provided a safety valve of sorts in the first, it is a carefully guarded inlet in the second' (van de Kaa 2004: 8).

13   Brinley Thomas (1954) suggested that it is much more than a statistical relationship. He argued that, contrary to widespread opinion, the volume and fluctuations of European immigration to the United States depended not only on the demand for labour in this country, but above all on demographic changes in the countries of origin. Thomas found that all four main upsurges of emigration from Europe until the outbreak of World War I followed, with a 25-year time lag, a peak in natural increase.

14   King (1996: 45) cites interesting observations made by Friedrich Engels, who was one of the first to recognise the important role of population growth in the development of English industry.

15   The opposite view is represented by Anthony Fielding (1993). According to him, until recently mass migration in Europe was determined by the medium-term economic fluctuations (the business cycle). After the mid-1970s, however, Western Europe underwent fundamental change in the production system – from Fordist to post-Fordist, which substantially affected migration: 'the most important feature of mass migration under post-Fordist forms of production organization is its absence!' (Fielding 1993: 14). Mass migration gives way to 'small-scale and more individualistic forms' of inter-regional and international mobility.

16   It is not rare that in the initial stage of changes fertility rises, which is due to, among other things, the deep mortality decline itself (better chances of potential mothers' survival).

17   For the discussion of the 'crowding-out effect', see Kaczmarczyk and Okólski (2008).

18   Including also the former Yugoslavia and Turkey.

19   Taking into account migration of seasonal and temporary workers, however, would significantly increase that estimate. Thus, according to Livi Bacci (1972: 18), 'we can by all means say that [...] the number of emigrant workers has been greater than the natural increase of the labour force'.

20   Excess supply of manpower in the agricultural sector, especially the unemployed or underemployed peasants searching for a job in foreign countries, was believed to be the main source of emigration potential in the Mediterranean countries (Livi Bacci 1972).

21   Interestingly, a study carried out in the 1960s by the UN Economic Commission for Europe (UN ECE 1968), devoted to the determinants of labour supply in Europe until 1980 – which inter alia evaluated labour market situation in CEE – found strong but latent migration pressures in the then socialist countries, which at that time were contained by the existing legislation and administrative order. Referring to that study, Luisa Danieli (1972) pointed to Poland and Romania as CEE countries having a vast surplus of manpower (from one fifth to one half of the active population) and to Czechoslovakia and Hungary as countries with probably insufficient labour supply.

22   Polish LFS provides quarterly estimates of the stock of temporary migrants (i.e. those who at the time of survey are registered as 'permanent' residents of Poland). In general, the survey is limited to households where at least one member is present in his or her domicile at the time of survey and, if that condition is met, to the household members fifteen years old or more. Thus, the migrant count based on LFS might be seriously underestimated.

23   Short-term migrants are defined as those whose uninterrupted stay outside of Poland does not exceed twelve months at the time of survey; otherwise, the migrants are considered to be long-term.

24   Massey (1999: 40), referring to Michael Piore's theory of immigration driven by the mechanisms of segmented labour market, notes that the main factor of immigration, 'the imbalance between the structural demand for entry-level workers and the limited domestic supply of such workers [...] in developed countries', stems from two major root causes. One of them is a combination of 'fundamental socio-demographic trends', such as very low natural increase of the working-age population, the depletion of labour reserves in rural communities and the rise of female labour-force participation together with the transformation of women's jobs into a source of primary income support. Another main root cause is 'the built-in demand for inexpensive and flexible labour' in modern industrial societies, which results from 'fundamental characteristics of advanced industrial societies and their economies', such as: 'structural inflation', 'social constraints on motivation embedded within occupational hierarchies' and 'the inherent duality of labour and capital', producing a segmented labour market structure (Massey 1999: 37-39).

25   See chapter 2 in this volume.

References

Baines, D. (1991), *Emigration from Europe 1815-1930*. London: Macmillan.

Biraben, J.-N. (2006), 'The history of the human population from the first beginnings to the recent day', in G. Caselli, J. Vallin & G. Wunsch (eds.), *Demography: Analysis and Synthesis. A Treatise in Population Studies*, 5-17. Burlington: Academic Press.

Biraben, J.-N. (1979), 'Essai sur l'évolution du nombre des hommes', *Population* 34 (1): 13-26.

Braudel, F. (1999), *Historia i trwanie*. Warsaw: Czytelnik.

Castles, S. & M.J. Miller (1993), *The age of migration: International population movements in the modern world*. Houndmills: Macmillan.

Chesnais, J.-C. (1992), *The demographic transition: Stages, patterns and economic implications*. Oxford: Clarendon Press.

Chesnais, J.-C. (1986), *La transition démographique: Etapes, formes, implications économiques*. Paris: Presses Universitaires de France.

Coleman, D. (2006), 'Migration as a primary force in human population processes', in G. Caselli, J. Vallin & G. Wunsch (eds.), *Demography: Analysis and Synthesis. A Treatise in Population Studies*, 19-40. Burlington: Academic Press.

Clark, C. (1977), *Population growth and land use*. London: The Macmillan Press.

Danieli, L. (1972), 'The demographic and social pattern of emigration in Europe', in M. Livi Bacci (ed.), *The demographic and social pattern of emigration from Southern European countries*, 377-394. Florence: Universita di Firenze.

Dyson, T. (2001), 'A partial theory of world development: The neglected role of the demographic transition in the shaping of modern society', *International Journal of Population Geography* 2 (7): 67-90.

Fielding, A. (1993), 'Mass migration and economic restructuring', in R. King (ed.), *Mass migrations in Europe: The legacy and the future*, 7-17. London: Belhaven Press.

Gliwic, H. (1934), *Materjał ludzki w gospodarce światowej*. Warsaw: Trzaska, Evert i Michalski.

Grabowska-Lusińska, I. & M. Okólski (2009), *Emigracja ostatnia?* Warsaw: Wydawnictwo Naukowe Scholar.

Gropas, R. & A. Triandafyllidou (eds.) (2007), *European immigration: A sourcebook.* Aldershot: Ashgate.

Hatton, T.J. & J.G. Williamson (2008), *Global migration and the world economy: Two centuries of policy and performance.* Cambridge: MIT Press.

Hatton, T.J. & J.G. Williamson (1994), 'International migration 1850-1939: An economic survey', in T.J. Hatton & J.G. Williamson (eds.), *Migration and international labour market: 1850-1939*, 3-32. London: Routledge. Dordrecht: Kluwer Academic Publishers.

Kaczmarczyk, P. & M. Okólski (2008), 'Demographic and labour-market impacts of migration on Poland', *Oxford Review of Economic Policy* 3 (24): 599-624.

King, R. (1996), 'Migration in a world historical perspective', in J. van den Broeck (ed.), *The economics of labour migration*, 7-75. Cheltenham: Edward Elgar.

Layard, R., O. Blanchard, R. Dornbush & P. Krugman (1992), *East-West migration: The alternatives.* Cambridge: MIT Press.

Livi Bacci, M. (ed.) (1972), *The demographic and social pattern of emigration from Southern European countries.* Florence: Universita di Firenze.

Massey, D.S. (1999), 'Why does immigration occur? A theoretical synthesis', in C. Hirschman, P. Kasinitz & J. DeWind (eds.), *The handbook of international migration: The American experience*, 34-52. New York: Russell Sage Foundation.

Morokvasic-Muller, M., B. Dinh, S. Potot & M. Salzbrunn (2008), 'Immigrant France: Colonial heritage, labour (im)migration and settlement', IDEA Working Papers 2, www.idea6fp.uw.edu.pl/pliki/WP2_France.pdf.

Okólski, M. (2008), 'Europa en moviemento: La migracion desde y hacia Europa Central y del Este', *Revista CIDOB d'Afers Internacionals* 84: 11-32.

Okólski, M. (2007), 'Europe in movement: Migration from/to Central and Eastern Europe', CMR Working Papers 22 (80).

Piore, M.J. (1979), *Birds of passage: Migrant labour in industrial societies.* Cambridge: Cambridge University Press.

Poursin, J.-M. (1976), *Ludność świata.* Warsaw: Państwowe Wydawnictwo Naukowe [originally published in 1971 as *La population mondiale*, Paris: Éditions du Seuil].

Thomas, B. (1954), *Migration and economic growth: A study of Great Britain and the Atlantic economy.* Cambridge: Cambridge University Press.

United Nations (2007), *World population prospects: The 2006 revision.* New York: United Nations.

Van de Kaa, D. (2004), 'Is the second demographic transition a useful research concept. Questions and answers', *Vienna Yearbook of Population Research* 2: 4-10.

Van de Kaa, D. (1999), 'Europe and its population: The long view', in D. van de Kaa, H. Leridon, G. Gesano & M. Okólski (eds.), *European populations: Unity in diversity*, 1-50. Word Bank (2006), 'Labour migration from the new EU member states', *World Bank EU-8 Quarterly Report* September.

Zelinsky, W. (1979), 'The demographic transition: Changing patterns of migration', in *Population science in the service of mankind*, 165-190. Vienna: Institute of Life/ International Union for Scientific Study of Population.

Zelinsky, W. (1971), 'The hypothesis of the mobility transition', *Geographical Review* 61: 219-249.

2 Early starters and latecomers

Comparing countries of immigration and immigration regimes in Europe

Joaquín Arango

'Seek simplicity and distrust it' (J. Davis)

2.1 Introduction

In recent decades, Europe has become one of the major immigration-receiving regions in the world. No other region receives more immigrants in absolute terms, although not in relation to population size. Put in historical perspective, this represents an epochal change, since Europeans tended to predominate in international migration flows until the 1960s. Taken as a whole, it can be said that Europe's migration transition – i.e. its transformation from a primarily sending region to a primarily receiving one – took place in the two decades that followed the end of World War II, albeit a handful of countries had experienced it well before. This fact notwithstanding, the present configuration of Europe as an immigration-receiving region is better understood as the outcome of a gradual accumulation of national migration transitions, some of which are still in process. Further national transitions can be expected in the coming years.

In the specialised literature, Europe is often referred to as an international migration system. Since the 1990s, the notion of migration systems has gained momentum. The idea of applying system analysis to the study of migration is no doubt an appealing concept, one that emphasises the bi-directionality that exists between groups of countries that exchange migration flows alongside other exchanges. It was effectively applied by the geographer Akin Mabogunje in a seminal study of international migration flows in Western Africa (Mabogunje 1970) and later promoted by Mary Kritz, Lin Lean Lim and Hania Zlotnik at the beginning of the 1990s (Kritz, Lim & Zlotnik 1992). At present, however, it is still richer in undelivered promises than in tangible results. It suffers from considerable ambiguity, as its central premise is used with a diversity of meanings that are seldom made clear. In its most common application, it pertains to groups of more or less contiguous or proximate receiving countries that have important elements in common – thereby excluding the countries where the bulk of immigrants originate, as the initial and more orthodox version of the notion would have it (Zlotnik 1992). In so doing, it does not go far beyond what geographers used to term 'migration regions'.

Defined in this limited way, Europe is one of the four major systems in the contemporary world, together with North America, the Persian Gulf and the Asia Pacific region (Massey, Arango, Hugo, Kouaouci, Pellegrino & Taylor 1998). Put in a global perspective and compared with the remaining three, Europe appears to be a relatively homogeneous entity. Yet, taken in itself, and looking inwards rather than outwards, there can be little doubt that, if anything characterises Europe, it is a high degree of diversity – an unsurprising fact given the large number of countries that it comprises. Europe is synonymous with heterogeneity, and this applies to migration realities as well as to many other factors.

A minor semantic clarification might be advisable before proceeding further. In recent years the age-old distinction between sending and receiving countries has been increasingly questioned. No doubt, strictly speaking, it can be said that all countries are sending, receiving and transit countries at the same time. The distinction justifiably often rests, however, on solid foundations and is analytically useful, as out-migration and immigration are phenomena that yield very different outcomes and impacts, and they result in different realities, needs and policies. Doing away with these well-established concepts implies renouncing useful labels and putting countries that are markedly different in terms of migration in a single bag, which could serve to blur the analysis rather than to clarify it. Some countries are primarily immigration-receiving ones and others are, above all, sending ones, while some may be significantly sending and receiving at the same time. The decisive criterion for defining a country as immigration-receiving is not so much net migration in a given year – in a receiving country it can be occasionally negative – but rather the societal impact of receiving or hosting significant numbers of immigrants. And, mutatis mutandis, the same goes for defining sending or transit countries. In other words, in this chapter a receiving country is one in which the most socially significant phenomenon in terms of international mobility is immigration.

Understood in this way, the condition of immigration-receiving can be applied to a large number of countries in Europe. It is clearly the case of the fifteen that were members of the EU before the 2004 enlargement, as well as of Switzerland and Norway. It is also the case of some of the countries that joined the EU in 2004, including some that are significantly sending and receiving at the same time.[1]

Comparing the countries that form the European migration system, conservatively defined as comprising only its receiving end, can help improve the knowledge of national immigration experiences and their determinants and provide a better understanding of the latter's implications for policy. The heuristic potential of the comparative perspective has been sufficiently substantiated in the social sciences, and does not require further examination here. Yet, the large number of countries involved in this case makes the comparison difficult, though not impossible. Comparing countries that have long hosted populations of immigrant background with others that started to receive significant numbers of immigrants a few years ago further compounds the analytical difficulties. No doubt, every country is particular and different from all the others, also in matters of migration. Nevertheless, significant similarities among countries can be found as well.

Indeed, identifying meaningful groups of receiving countries might be an effective way of reducing the high degree of complexity resulting from heterogeneity. If the aim is to seek significant patterns, it can be posited that the comparative exercise will be analytically richer if it is carried not only among a large number of individual countries, but also among a much smaller number of meaningful groups of countries. In turn, it can be surmised that these groups could be seen as representative of different types of immigration-receiving countries, as ideal types that may have analytical value and prove useful in the explanation of different migration realities. Identifying their core characteristics may have analytical value in itself, and could help explain policy outcomes.

This chapter aims to identify and analyse factors that may help to significantly group sets of immigration-receiving countries in Europe, factors that, in other words, bundle together a set of countries by relevant similarities and distinguish them from other sets of countries. Admittedly, doing so constantly incurs the risk of overgeneralisation – difficult to avoid given the nature of the subject matter. Existing theories are of little or no use in this exercise. The analytical framework has to be developed inductively, going back and forth between models and reality and taking relevant notions from both.

The identification of different types of immigration countries and their implications commands increasing attention in these times (King 2000; Gropas & Triandafyllidou 2007). This exercise can be particularly relevant in the case of an EU that has now formally embarked on the construction of a common immigration and asylum policy. The existence of significant differences, in terms of migration realities and orientations among member states, can add to the staggering difficulties that this ambitious enterprise entails, as experience so far suggests. Ascertaining which differences are more relevant and how they affect national stances towards common policy could be one of the outcomes of this comparative exercise. Determining what recent destination countries can learn from the experiences of those that preceded them as receiving countries could be an additional outcome.[2] This exercise should help to improve understanding of the core characteristics of each group or of each type of receiving country. In turn, these characteristics could help to understand different policy approaches and to identify priorities. They could also clarify their underlying determinants, including prevailing attitudes towards immigration that, in turn, may be affected by the impacts of immigration as they are perceived by different societies.

2.2   Analytical considerations and hypotheses

This chapter departs from the basic proposition that, on the basis of both similarities and differences, meaningful groupings of immigration-receiving countries in Europe can be identified. To be significant, each group will comprise those countries that show greater similarities among them and greater differences with the remaining countries. The groups selected will be meaningful and relevant if similarities prevail over differences, and if differences with countries in other groups are generally larger than those among them. A set of hypotheses relative to the variables that are relevant to the grouping of countries will be put forth. Historical and socio-economic factors will be the foremost candidates for the explanation of similarities and differences. In theory, the hypotheses ought to be tested against the existing wealth of empirical data. Yet, testing them against the empirical evidence available for a large number of countries is a Herculean task, one that goes well beyond the possibilities of this chapter. Instead, some general, impressionistic remarks about their possible validity will be offered.

The comparative exercise requires identification of the criteria upon which the grouping of countries rests. Are they chiefly structural factors, i.e. having to do with significant differences in socio-economic regimes and other societal characteristics? Are they mainly historical in nature, i.e. related to the length of the immigration-receiving experience and the implications that derive from chronology or timing? In other words, are migration experiences and realities among European regional groups of receiving countries significantly different because they are structurally different – and because structural socio-economic differences are the result of different migration patterns – or because some countries developed earlier as immigration-receiving countries, or both? Finally, are these groupings regional in character, i.e. do they roughly coincide with well-defined geographic regions?

2.2.1   Hypothesis 1: The 'age effect'

Immigration-receiving countries are bound to differ significantly depending on the stage of the migration cycle in which they find themselves, as migration stages decisively affect the composition of the immigrant population and its changing relationship with the general population. In the course of their immigration experience, receiving countries go through a migration cycle – a notion inspired by the life cycle concept, borrowed by the social sciences from biology (Clausen 1986; Glick 1947). Certain socio-demographic structures and aggregate characteristics of the immigrant population correspond to each stage of the cycle, which, in turn, makes for different socio-economic impacts and contributes to different perceptions from among the general population. Borrowing from the demographic parlance, this can be referred to as an 'age effect'. Immigration realities are very much affected by the stage of the migration cycle in which countries find themselves and they tend to evolve as countries advance into later stages.

The notion of a migration cycle was proposed by the Belgian sociologist Felice Dassetto as the set of processes through which immigrants from less developed countries enter and settle in more developed ones, in a time sequence that affects – and requires adaptation by – the immigrants themselves, the native population and the institutions of the receiving societies. Within the migration cycle, certain stages can be identified. Dassetto points out three: in the first stage, immigrants are, above all, socially marginalised foreign workers; the second stage is dominated by family reunion – and therefore by the appearance of new actors – as well as settlement and acculturation, and is often further accompanied by social tensions between the immigrant population and segments of the receiving society, connected with the schooling of immigrant children, the use of public services, particularly health, and the establishment of immigrant families in the neighbourhood; the third stage has to do with the long-term inclusion and integration processes of long-term residents (Dassetto 1990).

Typically, young adults – often single or unaccompanied by their families – tend to prevail in the initial stages. Family reunion flows follow after a certain, often variable time. A second generation develops over time, and the number of elderly members increases. Gradually, the demographic composition of the immigrant population tends to resemble that of the general population. After several decades, it becomes multigenerational. Of course, different immigration societies go through the immigration cycle in different forms and at different speeds. The persistence or intensity of flows at later stages obviously makes an impact on the composition of the immigrant population.

Yet, the realities of countries that have, historically, long experienced significant immigration, and which have a multigenerational immigrant population, tend to be very different from those of countries of recent immigration, in which the first generation is still prevalent or of those in which the second generation is still in the making. Immigrant populations made up primarily of individuals greatly differ from those organised around families containing more than one generation and around communities. Different socio-demographic profiles determine very different effects, in terms of labour force participation rates, consumption of public services and social benefits, patterns of housing and settlement, social visibility and the like. In turn, different impacts, real or perceived, may affect societal attitudes towards immigration. The 'age effect' also affects policies, usually entailing a greater concern for integration as time goes by.

Taking the long view, it can be argued that the effect of age as a differentiating factor is transitory, and it will fade away after a few decades, once a receiving country reaches the mature stage. This consideration somewhat lessens its appeal. There is, however, another implication of the timing variable, more precisely of the birth date of a country as an immigration-receiving one, which is relevant in a different sense and for reasons that go beyond the different composition of the immigrant population. It can be referred to as the 'generation effect', to use demographic jargon once again, and paves the way for another hypothesis.

2.2.2   Hypothesis 2: The 'generation effect'

The timing factor has another implication that can be understood as a 'generation effect'. It stems from the influence exerted on the course and characteristics of the immigration experience by the historical context in which its initial and formative phases took place. Especially influential elements of this context are the types of immigration flows prevailing in that period and the socio-economic conditions that determine them, the dominant conceptions of migration, and the main characteristics of the international economic order and of socio-economic regimes. These influences may leave a long-lasting imprint on later stages of the immigration experience. These formative years may shape dominant social orientations towards immigration that would have a long-lasting effect or produce facts or policies that further impact future developments.

As a matter of fact, this last observation opens the door to a third hypothesis, also related to timing, and borrowed this time from economic history. It could be termed the hypothesis of the 'influence of historical precedence'.

2.2.3   Hypothesis 3: The influence of historical precedence

Nearly half a century ago, the economic historian Alexander Gerschenkron, in his seminal analysis of historical patterns of industrialisation, pointed out that the experience of latecomers is bound to be markedly different from that of early starters, if only because of the influence that the experience of the forerunners exerts on those that follow. Not only is the pace usually quicker – there is often an advantage in catching up – but the structures of production and industrial organisation are different, as is the intellectual climate which harbours the process (Gerschenkron 1962). Industrialisation and immigration are admittedly very different in nature, but mutatis mutandis the distinction between early starters and latecomers may provide a useful perspective for understanding the immigration experience of the latter in Europe, especially as far as the adoption of policies is concerned. Of course, historical precedence is by no means the only source of differences. In the case of Europe, the influence of the early starters' experience over that of the latecomers is very much reinforced by the common membership in a supranational structure such as the EU.

According to all the foregoing, the 'timing' factor is likely to be a very relevant criterion for any meaningful grouping of countries in Europe, for reasons that have to do with the 'age effect', the 'generation effect' and the 'precedence effect'. Yet it is certainly not the only one, and maybe not even the most relevant one. Socio-economic regimes, or a number of socio-economic structural characteristics, constitute another obvious candidate. To begin with, different chronologies of the immigration experience relate to such structural differences and, more precisely, to diverse degrees of development. It is there that reasons explaining why some countries experienced the migratory transition before others have to be sought.

2.2.4 Hypothesis 4: The influence of structural characteristics

It can be posited that immigration-receiving countries in Europe are also bound to differ on account of their defining structural characteristics, i.e. types of economy and social systems, which result in different intensities and types of labour demand, in different orientations towards the inclusion or exclusion of foreigners, and in different degrees of openness or closedness towards the admission and incorporation of immigrants. Different socio-economic regimes – i.e. more liberal or more corporatist; more adapted to the European social model or closer to the Anglo-Saxon model (Jordan 2007); with strong or weak labour union bargaining; with higher or lower degrees of social protection; with higher or lower rates of female labour force participation; with larger or smaller informal sectors – significantly influence labour demand, admission policies, types of flows, public perceptions of immigration and more accepting or more restrictive stances.

Different types of socio-economic structures or regimes result in a different demand for immigrant labour. Some socio-economic regimes are more prone than others to admit foreign workers and to facilitate their insertion into the labour market. The strength of labour demand and the degree to which it is filled by immigrant workers may, in turn, affect public perception, which can then influence admission policies.

2.2.5 Three major groups

Three major groups of countries can be identified in Europe, and they roughly correspond to well-defined regions. Each of them is relatively homogeneous and different from the other groups, chiefly on account of historical and structural factors. The first group encompasses a number of countries located in the north-western quadrant of Europe, which became countries of immigration in the third quarter of the twentieth century or earlier and which today can be termed 'mature' or 'old'. The second is made up of four countries in Southern Europe, which experienced their migratory transition in the final quarter of the twentieth century and which can be considered as the second generation of immigration-receiving countries in Europe. The third includes a number of countries in Central and Eastern Europe (CEE), which started their migratory transitions in the years around the turn of the century, and can be seen as 'recent' or 'future' countries of immigration.[3] At least the first two groups are representative of different types or patterns of immigration-receiving countries. It is too soon to determine whether the third group will yield a third, distinct type.

No doubt, the three aforementioned categories clearly coincide with three regions often identified in Europe. North-Western Europe, Southern Europe and Central-Eastern Europe are usual regional labels. A wide range of different variables underlie and justify this regionalisation. Among them, and without disregarding the influence of geographic factors – which are especially clear in the case of the South – are those that have to do with the economy, e.g. the degree of development or type of socio-economic regime and welfare system and recent political history seem the most relevant. In the case of immigration, historical factors that have to do with the chronology of the migration experience should also be considered. It can be posited that the timing of the immigration experience – that is, the temporal distance that separates the present from the date in which they became an immigration-receiving country – is relevant in more than one instance.

2.2.6 'Age effect'

The stage of the migration cycle in which different countries find themselves is likely to bring about decisive differences as far as immigration realities are concerned. As far as this 'age effect' goes, there is little doubt that the members of each regional group basically share a common chronology. The mature countries of the north-western quadrant – namely France, Germany, Great Britain, Belgium, the Netherlands, Luxembourg, Switzerland, Sweden and Austria – became immigration-receiving countries in the third quarter of the twentieth century or earlier. Indeed, France did so much earlier. Yet, regardless of the particular chronology of the migration transition in each case, all of the countries received large numbers of immigrants in the 1950s and 1960s. Although quite a few of them returned home, a large part of them remained after the crisis of the mid-1970s that followed the first oil shock after the Yom Kippur War. Family reunion had started to take place before that date and greatly intensified afterwards. As a result, all these countries today host populations of immigrant background that span several generations.

Many implications derive from this fact. The socio-demographic profile of the populations of immigrant background, initially biased towards a marked preponderance of young adults, tended gradually to resemble that of the general population. Their activity rate tended to decline, and the level of unemployment to go up. Consumption of public services increased, as did the degree of dependency on the welfare system. Immigrants became more visible as families settled in neighbourhoods and residential segregation processes set in (Tapinos 1993). All this is likely to have had a considerable impact on perceptions and attitudes towards immigration.

Admittedly, the immigration cycle can be travelled in different ways, and not necessarily in a linear one. In particular, it will depend on whether the volume of initial and intermediate flows is sustained or reduced after these stages. The structure of the immigrant population and some of its attendant characteristics, such as the activity rate, can be reinvigorated by intense flows in mature stages, as recently happened in some countries – namely the United Kingdom in the early years of this century. In the case of north-western countries, massive flows tended generally to decline from the mid-1970s onward, except for family reunion and asylum flows, at least until the mid-1990s. The massive arrival of ethnic Germans (the *Aussiedler*) to Germany in the early 1990s may have been the major exception to this pattern.

The countries of Southern Europe find themselves at a much earlier stage of the immigration cycle. Out-migration prevailed until the mid-1970s, then return migration was prominent, and only since the 1980s could they be perceived as primarily receiving countries. This pattern is less clear in the case of Portugal, where out-migration continued to be significant after these dates and has intensified in recent years. Italy and Greece received large flows during the 1990s, and Spain underwent a vigorous immigration boom between the late 1990s and 2008. As a result, young adults in the prime of working age are preponderant in their immigrant populations. Paramount implications of such a demographic profile include an aggregate labour force participation that is higher than that of the rest of the population; more geographic mobility; a relatively limited consumption of public services – especially in the areas of healthcare and pensions – and welfare benefits; a favourable fiscal balance; and a significant contribution to the growth of GDP. A second generation is in the making, though it is not yet as prominent as it is in more mature receiving countries.

As for the countries that make up the third group, in CEE – they are still at an earlier stage of the immigration cycle, in which first-generation immigrants, often single or unaccompanied by relatives, overwhelmingly prevail.

2.2.7   'Generation effect'

The experience of Southern European countries is likely to diverge from that of their North-Western counterparts not only because of 'age', but also because their formative years as immigration countries occurred at a time when both international migration flows and the historical context in which they took place were structurally different from what they had been a quarter of a century before. The same can be said of CEE countries with respect to the other two groups of countries.

It can be surmised that the 'mature' countries of North-Western Europe underwent their socialisation processes as immigration recipients in the course of the third quarter of the twentieth century. This statement can easily be challenged by arguing that France, by far the oldest country of immigration in Europe, had done so much earlier. Notwithstanding this truth, it can be posited that France underwent something akin to what psychologists call a second adult re-socialisation process during the 1950s, 1960s and early 1970s, and that it probably was no less influential for later developments than any preceding experience.

Unlike nowadays, the third quarter of the twentieth century was a time when international migration flows were not yet global. The number of sending countries significantly participating in out-migration was much smaller than today. The fact that several European countries had to resort to recruitment to meet their labour needs suggests a much more limited scope. An unlimited, spontaneous supply of migrant labour as it exists today could not be taken for granted then. The fact that international migration flows were not global, and that only a relatively limited array of sending countries took part in them, has left its imprint on the ethnic composition of the populations of immigrant background in several receiving countries – France, the UK, Germany, the Netherlands, Belgium, Austria and Switzerland – by the strong preponderance of a few national groups, mostly from the Mediterranean basin or the Indian subcontinent and the English-speaking Caribbean in the case of the UK. Although recent flows have added a considerable degree of diversity, the birthmark of that period is still perceptible.

It was also a time in which the demand for labour – and for immigrant labour, for that matter – arose to a large extent from the central sectors of the economy, including manufacturing and mining. These were sectors that were still relatively labour-intensive and that very often consisted of firms organised along Fordist lines. It was also a time when informal employment was much less expansive than it is currently, when industrial relations were more regulated and when the welfare states were growing rather than being questioned or reduced, as they are today.

Additionally, the third quarter of the twentieth century was a time when much less was known about the dynamics of international migration than what would later be known. For instance, lacking the benefit of hindsight that is available today, the immigration authorities of the time thought that temporary schemes such as the guest worker system could be the solution to labour needs that were often perceived as transitory. Today, few would think the same, as it was precisely the experience of those countries that made clear that democratic states are at pains when trying to enforce temporariness.

The relative failure of that option – not so much in solving the acute labour shortages that constituted a bottleneck for economies undergoing super-growth, as someone called it (Kindleberger 1968), but in enforcing temporariness and preventing the settlement of the guest workers when they were invited to return – would decisively mark the immigration history of several countries. The unforeseen consequences of such an option may have contributed to the growth of a negative perception of immigration that seemed to be shared by large segments of the population; that is, the perception of immigration as unwanted, as the outcome of an error in calculation. The closure of borders to further immigration in the early or mid-1970s, which was initially temporary, soon became permanent and, in the context of a protracted economic slump, gave way to a new paradigm that would be known as 'zero migration'. In turn, the impossibility of closing the doors to immigration flows stemming from entitlement – family reunion and asylum – meant that the flows that were drastically curtailed were those of labour migration. This would reinforce the perception of a large part of immigration as unwanted or, as it has been recently termed in France, as *immigration subie* instead of *immigration choisie*.

In the case of north-western countries, the combination of a peculiar immigration history with a lesser demand for immigrant labour more recently, as will later be argued, has resulted in a greater proportion of family migration and asylum seekers and refugees, and a lesser one of workers. This constitutes an important difference with respect to the countries of Southern Europe and has pervasive implications. In fact, the relative weight of the different types of immigration flows – chiefly labour migration, family reunion, asylum and irregular streams – among countries and possibly groups of countries is likely to be a powerful differentiating variable, as they have different socio-economic impacts and contribute to different perceptions of immigration from the general population. The relative weight of the types of flows in each country may have an impact on the economic and social consequences of immigration and on the perception the public has of it (wanted or unwanted). In turn, both consequences and perceptions may affect policies, flows and integration outcomes. The

relative weight of types of flows in each country depends, inter alia, on admission policies, but these may be affected by the demand of labour that
different socio-economic regimes make, past immigration impacts and their
evaluation and the ability to control flows. All of these affect the consistency of policies and outcomes.

The influence of that period is so pervasive that the north-western countries are sometimes referred to in the literature as 'post-migration societies',
in the sense that they are primarily concerned with managing the consequences of past migration.

Being 'socialised' as countries of immigration in the 1950s and 1960s,
with Fordist economic structures and with a guest worker approach, is
bound to give way to an immigration experience very different from that
of the latecomers, who became countries of immigration in the 1980s and
1990s or later, when globalisation was in full swing and informalisation
and deregulation were (and are) rapidly increasing. Indeed, the Southern
European countries are now experiencing a 'generation effect' very different from the one that marked the experience of north-western countries.
First of all, having surfaced as countries of immigration in an era of global
flows can, by itself, give way to greater diversity from the very beginning
of the immigration experience. This is especially true of Italy and Spain –
though not so much of Portugal, where the influence of the colonial past is
paramount – and of Greece, where geographic proximity is decisive. This
is not the proper place to discuss the implications of a larger degree of diversity, but its relevance as a variable leaves little doubt.

The Southern European countries have become countries of immigration
in a time agitated by intense winds of deregulation, informalisation and labour precariousness, something that by itself generates very different conditions for the insertion of immigrants into labour markets and entails different social consequences. It is also a time when the nexus between the
underground economy and irregular migration has grown in importance
(Berggren, Likic-Brboric, Toksöz & Trimikliniotis 2007). Although it is
certainly not the only driver, it contributes to a higher incidence of irregular migration in the South. It would be unsurprising if something similar
were said of CEE countries when sufficient time has elapsed to be able to
characterise their immigration experience.

Both the southern and the eastern groups of countries have become
countries of immigration at a time when the guest worker model is seldom
seen as a realistic option on account of the north-western experience – the
recent popularity of the notion of 'circular migration' notwithstanding.

2.2.8   The influence of historical precedence

It can be posited that the influence of historical precedence has significantly conditioned the immigration policies of Southern and Eastern

European countries, and therefore their experiences and realities. This is because they have grown, or are starting to grow, as countries of immigration at a time when other, more developed immigration countries existed nearby. The more developed were capable of influencing the policies of the less developed basically, but not only, through their common membership in the EU. Very likely, this has de facto limited the policy options of the latecomers. The influence of the 'zero migration' paradigm is perceptible in the experience of the southern countries not because they have accepted few immigrant workers – which is certainly not the case – but because they have done so through restrictive admission policies based on the premise that hiring an immigrant worker usually requires passing the labour market test; that is, proving that there are no national or communitarian workers available for that job. Combined with factors that will be discussed later, these policies have contributed to high rates of irregular migration, as they conflict with an often vigorous demand for immigrant labour. Another example of this sort of influence has been the requirement imposed on the accession countries of 2004 and 2007 to accept the entire Schengen *acquis* as a *conditio sine qua non* of their entry into the EU. In itself, the influence arising from historical precedence would determine that the path leading to the mature stage would be differently walked by the latecomers.

2.2.9   *The influence of structural differences*

The foregoing suggests that migration realities and experiences are likely to differ among the three groups of countries because the economies and societies of North-Western Europe are structurally different from those of the South and those of CEE.

Risking, perhaps, excessive generalisation, it can be said that the economies of the southern countries today demand more immigrant labour as a rule than their north-western counterparts. This is due both to the fact that they are more labour-intensive than the north-western countries and to the greater weight in their economies of sectors more likely to rely on immigrant labour. These include personal services, such as domestic work and the care of dependent or elderly persons, the tourist and hospitality industry, construction and the building trades, and intensive agriculture and fruit-picking. All these sectors are relatively larger in southern economies. Sectors that are larger in north-western economies, such as manufacturing, have become capital-intensive and make a scant demand for labour, especially of the less-skilled sort.

In today's migration setting, which is characterised by a marked segmentation of labour markets, the secondary labour market is the one that contains the least appealing jobs – which are very often filled by immigrant workers. There are good reasons to believe that this segment is relatively larger in southern and eastern countries, which have a higher proportion of low-skilled occupations in their economic structures. In mature countries, a significant proportion of such jobs seems to be performed by the offspring of previous immigrants.

Not surprisingly, on account of the foregoing, immigration rates in the last two decades have tended to be higher in southern countries than in north-western ones. Spain and Italy have been, by far, the countries that have received the largest numbers of immigrants in the EU in recent years, and Greece and Portugal have also registered considerable intakes at certain points.

Higher immigration rates in southern countries can be explained not only by higher demand for immigrant labour, but also by less restrictive labour migration policies, either de jure or de facto, than those prevailing in north-western countries, with the exception of the UK and Ireland – another latecomer – in the first decade of the twenty-first century. In general terms, southern countries have made more efforts to widen the avenues for the legal access to the labour market, whether through quotas, mechanisms of nominal invitation, shortage lists and other schemes.

The economies of north-western countries are, as a rule, more regulated and controlled – especially in countries with corporatist regimes – with a larger intervention of stakeholders in the functioning of the labour market. This reduces some of the advantages of immigrant labour, including its typically lower cost.

In Southern European countries, a considerable part of the immigrants required by the economy either entered illegally or became irregular later by overstaying – probably in a higher proportion than in north-western countries. This would constitute an important difference in itself. But, in addition, it paves the way for other relevant differences, such as larger underground economies, more staggering difficulties for the control of entries and stays, more permissive legal cultures and, maybe, more tolerant stands towards irregular migration. A number of studies have suggested that the relative ease of accessing the labour market without work or residence permits in informal sectors of southern countries may constitute an alternative option to asylum demand (Finotelli 2007).

Another structural difference has to do with the size and type of welfare systems. It can be argued that the larger welfare systems of north-western countries provide an institutional context less favourable for the incorporation of cheap labour. In addition, they may generate a higher degree of reluctance to share public goods (Brochmann & Dölvik 2006). On the southern side, smaller, more conservative and family-oriented welfare systems contribute to a larger demand for care workers, which is often satisfied by immigrants.

2.3 Concluding remarks

Comparing and contrasting immigration-receiving countries may help to better understand each country, what it has in common with others as far as its immigration experience is concerned and how it differs and why. This chapter has presented a series of reasons, expressed as hypotheses, as to the basic similarities and differences that exist among different countries and groups of countries in Europe. On the basis of these hypotheses, a considerable degree of internal homogeneity within each of the three regional groups identified in the volume could be expected, as could be significant differences among the groups. All three groups seem to be meaningful, but the second, made up of the four southern countries of Portugal, Italy, Greece and Spain, seems to be the most homogeneous. The 'old' group of the north-western quadrant appears to be more heterogeneous. Indeed, it could be easily and usefully disaggregated into subgroups, especially since different socio-economic regimes can be identified within it (Massey et al. 1998; Jordan 2006). It is too soon to say much about the third group, constituted by the recent or 'future' countries of immigration in CEE – especially if other countries are included in the picture in addition to Poland, the Czech Republic and Hungary. Because the experience of this group is still incipient and because it is too soon to try to characterise it, this chapter has dealt primarily with the first two groups – although parts of what has been said about the southern countries could be extrapolated to their eastern counterparts. This would obviously be the case, even a fortiori, as far as the implications of the 'age effect' and of the 'precedence effect' are concerned, given that immigration-receiving countries in CEE are even younger than those in Southern Europe and that the EU's influence on the design of immigration policies has become stronger, as attested to by the conditions set for the 2004 enlargement. It would also apply to the influences stemming from the 'generation effect', as the defining traits of informalisation and deregulation are no less prevalent in the first decade of the twenty-first century than they were a quarter of a century ago.

As for the reasons underlying the basic differences among the three groups, the first one has to do with their degree of newness or seniority as immigration-receiving countries, something that has been referred to here as the 'age effect'. It is obvious that this factor clearly differentiates the three groups. But by its very nature, this is a transient factor that will fade away with the passage of time and is therefore of limited interest. Should this be the only or foremost differentiating factor, there would be no reason not to think that latecomers could replicate the experience of the early starters.

Of course, it is not the only factor. A second hypothesis posits that the birth date of countries as immigration-receiving ones may also be relevant because of the long-lasting influences that they may be subject to during their formative years, in a sort of 'generation effect'. In the case of Europe, there is little doubt that the historical context in which the 'mature' north-western countries grew as immigration receivers and some of the strategic orientations adopted in that context decisively conditioned their further experience with immigration, especially the option for the guest worker model and its relative failure. It is too soon to know what the legacy will be in the case of the southern countries, but it is likely to be as different from that of the early starters as the global context in which they have become socialised as countries of immigration. The same, mutatis mutandis, can be expected for CEE countries.

In addition, it could be expected that the three groups of countries would differ on account of structural differences in their economies and societies because different socio-economic regimes determine different migration regimes. The migration regimes of North-Western and Southern Europe are indeed different. In southern countries immigration rates have tended to be higher in the last two decades; their economies have a larger demand for immigrant labour, and immigration in them is, above all, labour migration; asylum demand is much less prominent, and rates of favourable resolutions are lower; the demand for immigrant labour is more geared to fill unskilled jobs; the demand for highly skilled immigrants is smaller; labour migration policies have tended to be more open, proactive and relatively innovative; immigration seems to have been more accepted, in general terms; the proportion of immigrants in an irregular condition is higher; extraordinary regularisations have been more frequent; and the control of flows is more difficult. The CEE countries of Poland, Hungary and the Czech Republic show significant differences with respect to the preceding groups, but their migration regime is still in the making. This notwithstanding, there are good reasons to believe that it will be as different from the two other groups as are their respective socio-economic regimes.

Both structural characteristics and historical factors therefore differentiate the migration regimes of the three groups. Given that the chronology of the immigration experience may be highly correlated with the chronology and degree of economic development, and that the latter may be associated with different types of socio-economic structures or regimes, it can be surmised that both criteria for the grouping of countries – timing and structural characteristics – may coincide to a large extent and in most, though not all, cases. In other words, there is a certain degree of covariance between the two orders of factors. Yet, identifying nuances and exceptions in this coincidence can do justice to complexity. Countries such as Ireland and Finland, which have much in common structurally with the north-western group, but are relative latecomers, may complicate a framework that rests on a degree of symmetry between the chronology of the immigration experience and certain socio-economic characteristics. Their inclusion in the analysis could clarify which of the two bundles of factors, structural or historical, is the most relevant. Comparing Malta and Cyprus, which are structurally similar but more recent as immigration countries, or even Slovenia, with the four southern countries that have been considered here might also be enlightening (King & Thomson 2008).

Admittedly, cultural differences could also contribute to explaining variation in migration regimes. Cultural variables have been left aside in this chapter because they are elusive and hard to operationalise, not because they are irrelevant. On the contrary, societal attitudes – which could amount to a sort of national ethos – towards immigration may result in different degrees of acceptance or reluctance and explain, for instance, the decision to implement a guest worker model or persistent reservations by some countries to accept the conditions of a country of immigration (Tränhardt 1995).

In any case, all the factors as addressed by the hypotheses put forth here suggest that the migration experiences of the three groups of countries are bound to be significantly different, and that they may correspond to three different types of migration regimes. This seems to be clear already in the case of the two less recent groups. It is therefore quite unlikely that latecomers will replicate the experience of the early starters. Additionally, they will not do so on account of the precedence effect. All this limits the potential for more recent countries to learn from the experience of those that preceded them, although it does not rule out the possibility of learning from specific decisions or courses of action.

Finally, the existence of substantial differences in migration regimes and experiences among European countries cannot but deeply condition the construction of the common immigration and asylum policy in the EU. If such a policy is to benefit all, these differences should not be disregarded.

Notes

1   Countries outside the EU whose population numbers less than one million are not considered here.
2   The very title of the IDEA project from which this chapter arose – Mediterranean and Eastern European Countries as New Immigration Destinations in the European Union (see note 9 in the Introduction of this volume) – implicitly alluded to three groups of countries: on the one hand, the Mediterranean or Southern and the Eastern European Countries that represent the 'new' immigration destinations in the EU; and on the other, the 'old' ones in respect to which the former are new. Additionally, it could be easily reckoned that the degree of *newness* is rather different among the two 'new' groups of destination countries.
3   The IDEA project started with these three predefined groups of countries, but the criteria underlying the grouping were not made explicit. It can be surmised that it was done intuitively or on the basis of common sense – a widely shared common sense at that.

References

Allum, P. (1995), *State and society in Western Europe*. Cambridge: Polity Press.

Arango, J. (2003), 'Is there a Southern European model of immigration?', paper presented at the European Population Conference EPC 2003, Warsaw, August 2003.

Arango, J. (1999), 'Immigrants in Europe: Between integration and exclusion', in *Metropolis international workshop: Proceedings*, 231-256. Lisbon: Luso-American Foundation.

Arango, J. (1999), 'Becoming a country of immigration at the end of the 20th century: The case of Spain', in R. King, G. Lazaridis & C. Tsardanidis (eds.), *Eldorado or fortress? Migration in Southern Europe*, 253-276. London: Macmillan Press.

Baganha, M.I. (ed.) (1997), *Immigration in Southern Europe*. Oeiras: Celta.

Baldwin-Edwards, M. & J. Arango (eds.) (1999), *Immigration and the informal economy in Southern Europe*. London: Frank Cass.

Berggren, E., B. Likic-Brboric, G. Toksöz & N. Trimikliniotis (eds.) (2007), *Irregular migration, informal labour and community: A challenge for Europe*, 40-50. Maastricht: Shaker Publishing.

Bonifazi, C. (2008), 'Evolution of regional patterns of international migration in Europe', in C. Bonifazi, M. Okólski, J. Schoorl & P. Simon (eds.), *International migration in Europe: New trends and new methods of analysis*, 107-128. IMISCOE Research Series. Amsterdam: Amsterdam University Press.

Brochmann, G. & J.E. Dölvik (2006), 'Is Immigration an enemy of the welfare state?', in D. Papademetriou (ed.), *Europe and its immigrants in the 21st century: A new deal or a continuing dialogue of the deaf?*, 155-178. Washington, D.C.: Migration Policy Institute; Lisbon: Luso-American Foundation.

Castles, S. (1986), 'The guest-worker in Western Europe: An obituary', *International Migration Review* 20.

Clausen, J.A. (1986), *The life course: A sociological perspective*. Englewood Cliffs: Prentice-Hall.

Dassetto, F. (1990), 'Pour une théorie des cycles migratoires', in A. Bastenier & F. Dassetto (eds.), *Immigration et nouveaux pluralisms: Une confrontation de sociétés*, 11:40. Brussels: De Boeck-Wesmael.

Edye, D. & V. Lintner (1996), *Contemporary Europe: Economics, politics and society*. London: Prentice Hall.

Esping Andersen, G. (1990), *The three worlds of welfare capitalism*. Cambridge: Cambridge University Press.

Finotelli, C. (2007), *Illegale Einwanderung, Flüchtlingsmigration und das Ende des Nord-Süd-Mythos*. Münster: LIT.

Gerschenkron, A. (1962), *Economic backwardness in historical perspective*. Cambridge: Harvard University Press.

Glick, P. (1947), 'The family life cycle', *American Sociological Review* 12: 164-174.

Heckmann, F. & D. Schanapper (eds.) (2003), *The integration of immigrants in European societies: National differences and trends of convergence*. Stuttgart: Lucius & Lucius.

Jordan, B. (2007), 'Migration regimes and irregular migration', in E. Berggren, B. Likic-Brboric, G. Toksöz & N. Trimikliniotis (eds.), *Irregular migration, informal labour and community: A challenge for Europe*, 40-50. Maastricht: Shaker Publishing.

Kindleberger, Ch.P. (1967), *Europe's post-war growth: The role of labor supply*. Oxford: Oxford University Press.

King, R. (2000), 'Southern Europe in the changing global map of migration', in R. King, G. Lazaridis & C. Tsardanidis (eds.), *Eldorado or fortress? Migration in Southern Europe*, 1-26. London: Macmillan.

King, R. & M. Thomson (2008), 'The Southern European model of immigration: Do the cases of Malta, Cyprus and Slovenia fit?', *Journal of Balkan and Near Eastern Studies* 10 (3): 265-291.

Kritz, M.M., L.L. Lim & H. Zlotnik (eds.) (1992), *International migration systems*. Oxford: Clarendon Press Oxford.

Kuijsten, A. (1994), 'International migration in Europe: Patterns and implications for receiving countries in Europe', in United Nations Economic Commission for Europe, *International migration: Regional processes and responses*. New York and Geneva: United Nations.

Mabogunje, A.L. (1970), 'Systems approach to a theory of rural-urban migration', *Geographical Review* 2(1): 1-18.

Massey, D.S., J. Arango, G. Hugo, A. Kouaouci, A. Pellegrino & J.E. Taylor (1998), *Worlds in motion: Understanding international migration at the end of the millennium*. Oxford: Clarendon Press Oxford.

Organization for Economic Co-operation and Development (several years), *Trends in international migration Sopemi*. Paris: OECD.

Reyneri, E. & M. Baganha (2001), 'Migration and the labour market in Southern Europe', *IMIS-Beiträge* 17: 33-53.

Schierup, C.-U. (2007), ' "Bloody subcontracting" in the network society: Migration and post-Fordist restructuring across the European Union', in E. Berggren, Br. Likic-Brboric, G. Toksöz & N. Trimikliniotis (eds.), *Irregular migration, informal labour and community: A challenge for Europe*, 40-50. Maastricht: Shaker Publishing.

Tapinos, G. (ed.) (1993), *Inmigración e Integración en Europa*. Barcelona: Fundación Paulino Torres Domènech.

Tränhardt, D. (1995), 'Germany: An undeclared immigration country', *New Community* 21 (1): 14-36.

Triandafyllidou, A. & R. Gropas (eds.) (2007), *European immigration: A sourcebook*. Farhan: Ashgate.

Werner, H. (1986), 'Post-war labour migration in Western Europe: An overview', *International Migration* 24 (3): 543-557.

Zlotnik, H. (1992), 'Empirical identification of international migration systems', in M.M. Kritz, L.L. Lim & H. Zlotnik (eds.), *International migration systems*, 19-40. Oxford: Clarendon Press Oxford.

3 'Old' immigration countries in Europe

The concept and empirical examples

Heinz Fassmann and Ursula Reeger

3.1 Introduction

In the course of their immigration experience, transitioning receiving countries go through a specific demographic development and policy learning process that is called a migration cycle. It appears that this migration cycle is to some extent similar to that which old immigration countries experienced in the past. Migration processes of the past will never be repeated in exactly the same way, but if the stages of the migration cycle are generalised, the similarities become apparent. This chapter applies this conceptual model to the past and recent migration history of the 'old' immigration countries in Europe. The authors critically evaluate the grouping of the old immigration countries, prod for specific as well as general driving forces and look for a general model to be applied to the shift that countries undergo from emigration to immigration. For this purpose, the most important 'old' immigration countries are included in the considerations – namely Germany, France, Great Britain and Austria. Also elaborated is the case of Spain as an illustration of a 'new' immigration country in order to show how the concept can also be applied (for more detailed information on Spain, see chapters 5 and 7 in this volume).

3.2 Notions and concepts

3.2.1 *The notion of 'old immigration countries'*

The notion of an 'immigration country' plays an important role in public debate and signals a change in perception, but there is no commonly accepted definition. There are at least two approaches to operationalise this concept. The first one defines an immigration country as a declared self-perception. The political elite and the general public agree that immigration is part of the nation-building process. Society is built upon migration – that is the general idea. Whether the real number of immigrants is high or low does not play a significant role; what is important is general self-perception. The so-called classical immigration countries (the United States, Canada, Australia) adhere to this definition. The other approach is more statistically based. Immigration countries are defined by a considerable and systematic surplus of immigration over emigration over time, and thus by positive net migration. It is assumed that positive net migration is not a singular event and is more or less a steady, stable situation. There are no defined thresholds for how many years net migration must be positive in order to label a country an immigration country, but clearly the majority of years in a given period should show a positive balance.

There can be a discrepancy between the statistical definition of an immigration country and self-perception. For example, Germany should be categorised as an immigration country as of the end of the 1950s or 1960s, but its acceptance as such by the law, its population and politicians came about only just recently, at the beginning of the twenty-first century. Austria experienced the same situation, with an excess of immigration over emigration since the 1960s, though this statistical fact has not been accepted by the public without reservation. In this chapter (and throughout the present volume), the statistical definition is used to designate an immigration country.

The second point to be clarified is the attribute 'old'. What is an old immigration country? In the context of this volume, 'old' is a relative term which has little to do with an absolute number of years. The surplus of immigration over emigration occurred sometime in the past, without an exactly pinpointed moment in time. But the attribute 'old' also implies that 'young' immigration countries exist, where the excess of immigration over emigration is a more recent phenomenon. The terminology of 'old immigration countries' is linked inevitably and necessarily to a time-dependent process. The basic assumption is that European countries are shifting from emigration to immigration statuses, and from young to old.

3.3   The concept of a migration cycle

The transition from a young to an old immigration country is not a linear process (as was described by Zelinsky 1971), or one without any friction. International migration changes societal compositions, highlights the question of national or regional identity and sharpens distributional conflicts over workplaces, on the housing market and in the public space. Especially in times of an economic downswing, conflicts between the native and the newly arriving population may emerge.

To better explain these processes of change, to underline the importance of the transition of an emigration country or a country without any significant immigration to one where immigration becomes the dominant demographic event, the IDEA project (see note 9 in the Introduction of this volume) developed the concept of a migration cycle. It is based on the general idea that the society and the legal system of a country adapts to a new situation and develops a mechanism to handle new or evolving migratory circumstances. Countries and societies are 'learning', absorbing past experiences and developing new adaptation strategies. Learning processes are time-dependent and embedded in a certain temporal and spatial context. As for the sources of this learning process, they include not only the country's own past, which certainly merits mention, but also countries' ability to learn from the experiences, successes and failures of other countries that became immigration countries earlier. By no means does this imply, however, that all European countries pass through exactly the same cycle. Furthermore, it is not postulated that the individual stages of the cycle last for the same amount of time or exhibit identical characteristics. Countries that are entering the transition process later could potentially require a shorter period of time to adapt than the states that transitioned earlier. The concept can nevertheless be used as a blueprint, or as a mirror for the development of widespread immigration and emigration trends.

To newly emphasise the idea of a cycle, and in an attempt to further clarify the concept, 'migration transition' connotes a time period of indeterminate duration when a country or region adapts to a new immigration situation. Former emigration countries, for example, become immigration countries – or vice versa – and, during this process, go through at least three different stages: an initial, pre-transition or preliminary stage; an intermediate or transition stage; and a net immigration stage. These stages are the main components of the migration cycle and correspond to a very general process involving system stability, disturbances and, finally, the emergence of a new stability.

During the initial, pre-transformation or preliminary stage, emigration is more important than immigration, or else net migration is zero. Stability is a key factor in the initial stage. A certain and specific demographic situation is constant for a long period of time and, usually, both political and social dynamics are attuned to it.

The second stage is of particular importance because the system begins to undergo fundamental changes. During the intermediate or transition stage, a former emigration country becomes, step by step, a new immigration country. The steps are of different lengths and of varying substance, e.g. a given country's transition could begin with a significant migration surplus and could then be followed by a period of stagnation or a short-term negative balance. But the general trends appear to be changing and, from the transition's inception, immigration typically outweighs emigration. Changes in the general trend do not happen invisibly, or without any trace. The first economic crisis and the relative 'overshooting' of immigration usually cause the issue to become more and more prominent in public discussions and debates. Immigration and migration control come to be hot-button political topics and electoral votes are won or lost depending on the way politicians address the migration issue. New mechanisms to control migration are imposed, step-by-step and over time.

The intermediate or transition stage then fades out into a third stage, which is called the adaptation stage or post-transformation stage. This stage's main characteristic is newfound stability. Immigration is more or less acknowledged as a necessary supplement to a demographically diminishing working population, on the one hand, and a growing economy, on the other hand. Extreme expressions of opinion in support of one solution or another lose popularity, and a new political rationality emerges by integrating into a differentiated legal system a means of controlling international migration. Whereas during the pre-transition and transition stages the legal system provided, at best, one means of entering the state, by the end of the transition period, a whole panoply of strategies to obtain residence and settlement titles would have likely developed. Conceptual differentiations of the inflows and legal or judicial differentiations of the individuals who are legally allowed to immigrate are important features of this phase.

The various stages of the immigration cycle are thus found in the transitions from new or young immigration countries to old immigration countries, or else from emigration countries to immigration countries. Many European countries are on their way to becoming full-fledged immigration countries, and can be classified according to the stage they find themselves in. Most of the new member states are in the initial or pre-transition stages, though it appears some of them will be entering the transition stage sooner (e.g. the Czech Republic, see chapter 8 in this volume), others, some time later (e.g. Poland). Most of the Western European countries are in the intermediate or post-transition stages, and some of them are entering the adaptation phase or post-transition stage. Most of the Southern European countries currently find themselves in the transition stages, albeit with high fluctuations, wherein very contentious debates on migration and searches for viable legal solutions are pervasive.

3.4   The main drivers

If a migration cycle is loosely defined as an adaptation and learning process that becomes necessary when new demographic and economic conditions arise, it begs the question of which factors are primarily responsible for the new circumstances. This question leads us to the concept of main drivers, which are defined as the most important independent variables that explain the change. Why do most European countries enter the second transition stage and leave the stable situation in which emigration outnumbers immigration, or where net migration was zero? Which factors are the most relevant for a country's entering the migration cycle?

The question of which drivers matter most can be at least partly addressed by the usual migration theories for labour migration, such as the push-and-pull model or the migration system theory, and depends on which kind of migration is put into primary focus. The main drivers for asylum seekers are different than those of labour migrants. For asylum seekers, political crises, wars and persecutions in neighbouring countries and regions, the geographical distance between their region of origin and the first receiving country and the attractiveness of the receiving country's asylum procedure are all important drivers.

Regarding labour migration, the main drivers are to be found in demographic realities, in economic and sectoral development and in the structure of the labour market. The effects of demographic development and the structure of the labour market are rather long-term considerations, while economic development is often a short-term factor.

First, it is a demographic reality that decreasing numbers of births lead – after a time delay – to diminishing numbers of entries into the labour market and to an ageing of the workforce. In this situation, the demand for new labour increases, especially when economic growth is high and productivity gains are less than or equal to a reduction in working time. A shrinking and ageing labour force will have a direct effect on pull factors and will stimulate immigration, especially when economic development leads to an increase in labour demand. Furthermore, an ageing society will manifest some effects not only on the quantity of immigration, but also on the public's selectivity. An ageing society will increase the demand[1] for health and care services, which are performed mainly by the female labour force.

Second, increasing economic growth leads to an increasing demand for new labour migration, especially when the demographic transition is in full swing. Growth in GDP is usually highly correlated with a positive net migration balance. Short-term external events sometimes cause an above-average increase in the demand for labour. Such events may be large investments in short periods of time, such as world championships or Olympic Games. Besides this short-term and cyclical effect, the long-term structural change resulting from industrial economies' shifts to service-based economies during the past several decades should be taken into consideration. Productivity gains in the service sector are limited, and the qualities of the services are connected to human beings, not to machines. Especially in domains such as tourism and health and personal services, economic growth automatically leads to an increase in the work force.

The third independent process is the segmentation of the labour market and rising tendency for natives – and, albeit more slowly and to a lesser degree, the immigration population – to be more highly qualified. As industrial development comes into full swing, labour market segmentation becomes more and more important, and actually acts as a source for further immigration. A well-developed labour market is characterised by the division of the entire market into at least a primary and a secondary segment. The primary segment employs well-educated labourers, who are the source of high-ranking firms' specific knowledge bases. These well-educated labourers receive high wages and enjoy stable careers. In the secondary labour market segment, the less-qualified labourers are concentrated, the wages are lower and the careers are unstable. With the increasing qualifications of the native and some immigrant population, more and more graduates attempt to enter the primary segment, leaving the jobs in the secondary segment vacant and increasing the demand for new labour migration (Hudson 2007).

Finally, the state and related means of regulation of international migration must be included as main drivers. With its laws, regulations and related practices, the public authorities shape immigration in a direct and sustained way. Of course, the state does not act independently of the previously mentioned factors, and indeed state action is normally closely tied to demographic and economic developments. Especially during times of a diminishing labour supply and the economy needing more labourers, public authorities become active in and reactive to that situation. Thus, the state is not only a key driver, but is, at the same time, influenced by other drivers.

It is important to note that these drivers interact or are mutually dependent on one another. They also display different temporal characteristics. Drivers like demographic development have a long-term effect, while economic influences show short-term effects. These should be seen from a double perspective: the way in which they manifest themselves both in target countries of migration and in potential countries of origin.[2]

3.5   Europe: Convergence and diversity of international migration

During the nineteenth and early twentieth centuries, Europe was a continent of emigration. Imre Ferenczi and Walter F. Willcox claim that roughly 50 million to 55 million people emigrated from Europe to the United States, and approximately another ten million Europeans left for Argentina, Canada and Brazil between 1846 and 1924 (Ferenczi & Willcox 1929: 185). But after 1945, a new era began – one that also affected European migration. Nothing better illustrates the new economic and political rise of Europe than the change in migration trends after World War II. Gradually, most European countries were transformed into de facto immigration countries. But this was not the result of any comprehensive or concerted strategy, but of specific economic, demographic and political developments. During the second half of the twentieth century, Europe became an immigration continent 'against its will', and the main countries involved in this development were those termed, 'old immigration countries' in this volume.

3.5.1 *The general pattern*

There are good arguments in support of the use of both flow data and net migration data to identify immigration countries. However, for both cases, the availability and accuracy of migration statistics in European countries is an unsolved problem. The individual nation-states use long-established but very different instruments to determine population and migration statistics, which are not generally easy to harmonise with each other. One possibility for using long-term net migration data is offered by the Population Division of the United Nations. They provide calculated net migration as the result of comparing population figures from two different years. Calculated net migration is arrived at using the main demographic equation: the population of $t + 1$ is the population of t plus birth and minus death between t and $t + 1$. Net migration is therefore not only the result of 'real' migration flows; it also reflects any statistical changes and uncertainties. However, these data provide net migration figures for every country of the world since 1950, and therefore allow for a recalculation of the net migration of the EU-27 countries for more than five decades.

It becomes apparent from these data that, until the beginning of the 1960s, more people left the EU-27 than came in. Back then, Europe was still an emigration continent. Negative migration balances of more than 200,000 persons per year changed, for the first time, during the quinquennium 1960-1965. The recruitment of foreign labour prevailed as a labour market-related measure, and many European countries satisfied their additional demand for labour – which was usually accompanied by positive economic developments due to immigration.

The positive balance only went down, or failed to grow with the intensity most expected, during times of economic crisis (1968, 1973, 1980). From the middle of the 1980s onwards, the international migration balance of the EU-27 vis-à-vis the 'rest of the world' has always been positive, and in fact grew from quinquennium to quinquennium. Between 2005 and 2010, it grew to 1,311,000 people, meaning that, year by year, the difference between the number of people coming to the EU-27 and those leaving was 1,300,000 people. Taken as a long-term average (1950-2010), the annual net gain from migration amounts to 420,000 people.

A further fact that can be illustrated using the net migration data of the United Nations is the convergence of European migration. In the EU-27, the variation in different nations' net migrations decreased, but the process was not linear. It was low during the 1950s, because almost all nation-states were characterised by a prevalence of emigration. During the 1960s, the variance grew remarkably fast because some countries had already turned into immigration countries and others still were dominated by emigration. The variation diminishes again during the 1980s, as the postulated pattern – Europe turning into an immigration continent – generally wins through. For the time being, there are only a few remaining countries in Eastern Europe that still display a negative migration balance. But even in that region, it is only a matter of time until immigration exceeds emigration. A main reason for this is a likely strong drop in fertility, which translates into a decreasing domestic labour supply. This process is typically delayed for a time as a relatively fast-growing economy suddenly experiences a need for a larger workforce. In the Czech Republic, Hungary, Slovenia and Slovakia, immigration has been outweighing emigration since the beginning of the 1990s – the international migration balance has been positive since then.

3.5.2   Country-specific differentiations

As just pointed out, this development was not the same or even parallel in all European countries. Some of them showed a positive migration balance during the whole time period in question; other European countries only did so in recent years. Table 3.1 displays these differences in temporal dynamics. The following section discusses the differences further.

During this entire time period, France displayed positive net migration. On the one hand, this resulted from an active recruitment policy that was specifically organised by the public authorities in order to attract a foreign workforce. On the other hand, France received returning settlers, soldiers and civil servants, as well as citizens of the former colonies, in the course of the decolonisation process. This immigration was not only economic and related to the labour market, but also dependent on external events. For the entire period between the 1950s and 2007, net migration was positive (2007: +73,000). France can therefore indubitably be dubbed an 'old immigration country'. Its turning point from emigration to immigration, however, dates back to the second half of the nineteenth century, and the shape of its graph is different than the one for Germany. The average positive net migration for the whole time period (1950-2010) is 112,000 persons. In 2008, there were about 3,650,000 foreigners living in France and 6,500,000 people who had been born abroad, a fact that underlines the importance of colonial immigration and the quick granting of citizenship, mostly for the second-generation children born in France. With a share of foreigners at 5.7 per cent, France finds itself in the middle of the European playing field.

Figure 3.1 *Net migration in France, 1950-2010*

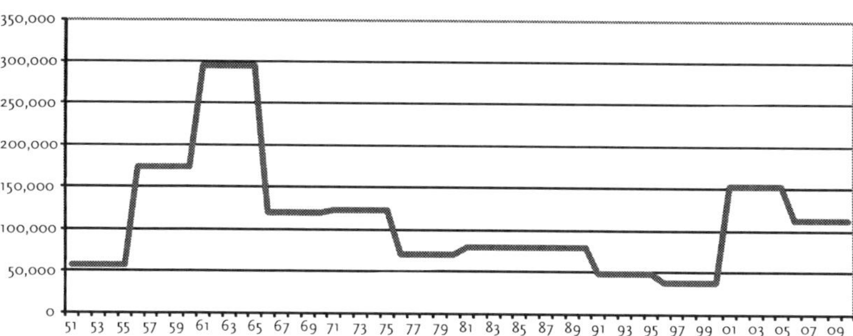

Source: United Nations Population Division; own design

Germany has experienced a near-constant positive net migration since the 1950s, though it was more strongly reflective of economic trends. The economic crises following the first and second oil price shocks led to considerably shrinking net migration. Fewer foreign labourers were recruited, or else return migration was actively promoted. During the entire period between the beginning of the 1950s and the end of 2010, net migration was positive. Only during a few years around 1975 and 1980 did the migration balance become negative. Apart from labour market-oriented inflows of immigrants into Germany, there was also a massive inflow of people of German descent from Eastern Europe (including from the German Democratic Republic to the Federal Republic of Germany before 1961). The official figures for the inflow of labour into Germany (West Germany) until 1989 are significantly biased due to the influx of 'ethnic Germans' from other countries. The peak period of net migration between the mid-1980s and mid-1990s was mainly caused by the influxes of asylum seekers and the ethnic Germans from the eastern parts of Europe.

Figure 3.2 *Net migration in Germany, 1950-2010*

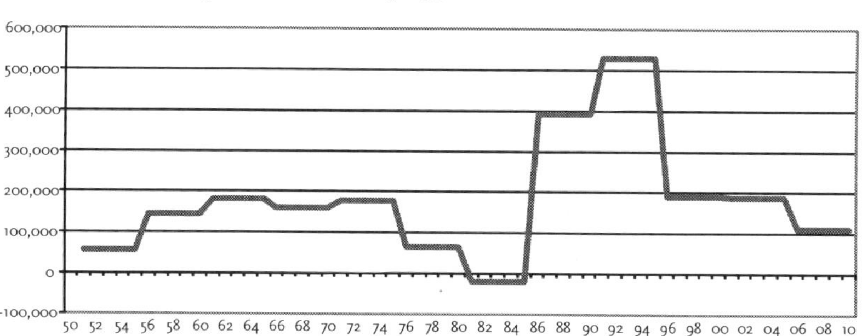

Source: United Nations Population Division; own design

Germany is indisputably an old immigration country, but still saw more than one turning point during its transition from a country of emigration to one of immigration. Its average annual net migration is currently +181,000 persons, the highest of all the EU-27 countries. The stock of immigrants totals about 10,500,000 people born abroad and 7,300,000 foreign citizens, which makes for an 8.8 per cent share of foreigners.

The Austrian case is strongly reminiscent of the German example, as it is also characterised by a strong link to economic trends. But there are two main differences between the two countries. For one, Austria never implemented a system tailored specifically to ethnic migration, whereby descendants of Austrians living in the countries of Eastern Europe were granted privileged statuses when they 'returned'. Secondly, Austria experienced an economic upswing later than Germany and, consequently, initiated active recruitment policies later than Germany. Germany began signing recruitment contracts in the middle of the 1950s, whereas the Austrian government did so only at the beginning of the 1960s. The long-term average of net migration in Austria during the past six decades amounts to +14,000, but the total is +34,000 during the past two decades. Austria is undoubtedly an immigration country, but only in the statistical sense, because its popular 'self-perception' is rather different – especially that of the political elite. The stock of immigrants in Austria amounts to about 1,400,000 foreign-born and 800,000 foreign citizens, which together results in a 10 per cent share of foreigners. This significant share places Austria in the leading European group.

Table 3.1   *Calculated net migration, 1950-2010 (in 1,000)*

Years	Spain	France	UK	Germany	Austria	EU-27
1950-1955	-51	57	-101	55	-15	-267
1955-1960	-104	174	-15	144	-10	-201
1960-1965	-78	295	44	180	3	257
1965-1970	-43	120	-50	161	10	-71
1970-1975	3	123	-38	178	17	314
1975-1980	23	71	-11	66	1	309
1980-1985	-26	80	-50	-22	4	28
1985-1990	-15	80	6	391	22	436
1990-1995	65	48	33	530	47	760
1995-2000	159	38	99	190	13	578
2000-2005	501	152	190	186	44	1,605
2005-2010	350	100	190	110	32	1,311
Average per annum	65	112	25	181	14	422

Source: World Population Prospects: 2008 revision (http://esa.un.org/unpp); own calculation

Figure 3.3   *Net migration in Austria, 1950-2010*

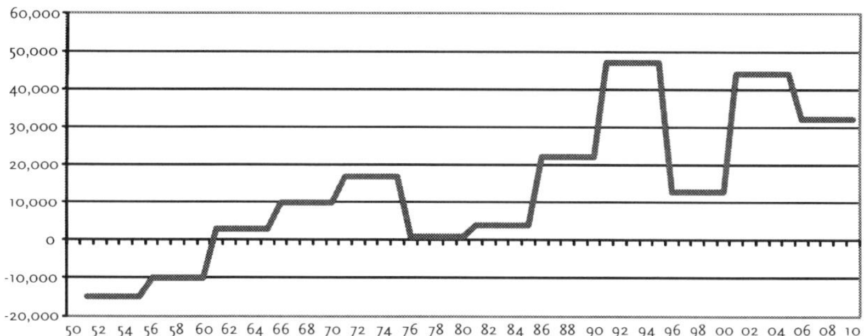

Source: United Nations Population Division; own design

The United Kingdom clearly represents a different type: only since the mid-1980s has the UK shown a continuously positive migration balance. Before that time, the UK was characterised more by emigration than immigration. For many decades, UK citizens leaving for the US, Canada and Australia outnumbered the return migrants from present or former colonies. In addition, the immigration of citizens from the former colonies was more and more restricted in both political and legal terms. The image of 'Britain under siege' disseminated by the media also had political implications. However, applying the strictly statistical definition already used here, the UK did become an immigration country – a very young one, compared to France. The turning point from emigration to immigration lies only two decades back. But public self-perception did not change. The British public has been surprised by the increase in immigration in recent years. Overall, positive net migration amounted to 25,000 since the beginning of the 1950s, but reached 128,000 since the beginning of the 1990s. As of 2008, about 3,700,000 foreign citizens are residing in the UK, and 6 million people have been born abroad. As is well known, the UK has – just like Ireland and Sweden – forgone temporary arrangements for controlling labour immigration from the new member states and has thus turned into an important target for Polish and Lithuanian workers. The share of foreigners was 4.2 per cent in the year 2000, increasing to 6.5 per cent in 2008.

Only the Southern European countries are younger immigration countries than the UK. The case of Spain will be briefly described here. At the beginning of the 1990s, Spain experienced the same transformation process as Germany and Austria several decades prior – namely, the conversion of the migration balance to positive values. Following its accession to the European Union and positive economic developments, not only did emigration stop, but a notable surge began of labour immigration targeting agriculture, tourism and private households. The immigration of elderly people from the UK, Germany and the Scandinavian countries – who

Figure 3.4   *Net migration in the UK, 1950-2010*

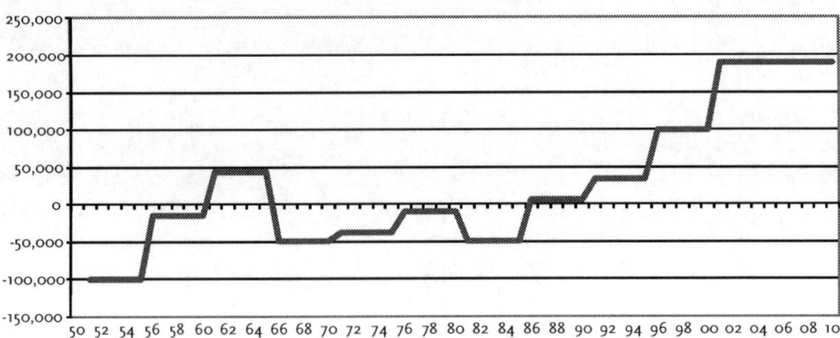

Source: United Nations Population Division; own design

wanted to spend their sunset years in the European sunbelt – is also a considerable immigration factor. The long-time average of net migration since the 1950s was more than +65,000 persons, but since the beginning of the 1990s, it has been as high as +296,000. It thus exceeds the international net migration of Germany, a fact impressively documenting its evolution towards an immigration country, and the growing convergence in this respect. In 2008 about 4,600,000 foreign citizens were registered in Spain, which results in a share of immigrants of 11.5 per cent. Spain thus finds itself among the European countries with the highest shares of immigrants: it is surpassed only by mini-states, which display even higher shares.

Figure 3.5   *Net migration in Spain, 1950-2010*

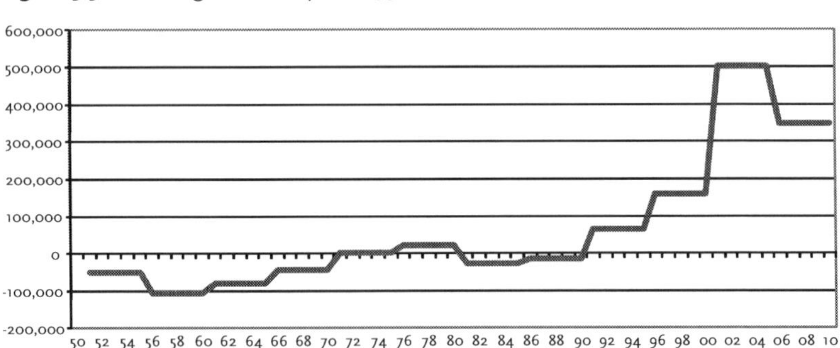

Source: United Nations Population Division; own design

3.6 The migration cycle: The Austrian example

In the following sections, the perspective taken is that of a single member state, rather than from the European level. Austria is an apt example for demonstrating, in detail, the transition from an emigration into an immigration country. It also exhibits the nuanced applicability of the concept of the migration cycle. Upon closer inspection, it becomes apparent that the differentiation of the cycle and its stages are always relative. There are persuasive arguments showing that Austrian migration history since 1945 can be accurately described as a single cycle: one with a stable stage until the beginning of the 1960s, an intermediate stage until the end of the 1990s, and, finally, a stage of renewed stability. But the intermediate stage in Austria could just as well be described using as two separate sub-stages: the first one lasting until the mid-1980s, when the classic 'guest worker regime' came to an end and stability returned; and a second one associated with the fall of the Iron Curtain and in which stability and a new balance only recently made an appearance.

3.6.1 Migration history in retrospect

Until the end of the 1950s, Austria was decidedly an emigration country. The country was poor, unemployment was high and any hope for an economic upswing came later than it did in Germany. The out-migration of Austrian nationals exceeded immigration levels, with the most important target regions being the US, Canada and Australia, as well as the neighbouring countries of Germany and Switzerland. From the Austrians' perspective, there were many advantages related to employment in these two neighbouring countries: small distances, no language barriers and higher levels of income than those available at home made emigration for labour purposes an attractive option (Münz, Zuser & Kytir 2003: 20).

This emigration continued into the 1960s, with about 92,000 Austrians leaving between 1962 and 1973. This number does not include commuters (most of whom were located in Western Austria) or seasonal workers, who kept their main residences in Austria. This means that the total number of Austrian employees in Germany and Switzerland was even higher. In 1973, the total number of Austrians residing in Germany was 177,000, with 101,000 gainfully employed; in Switzerland, the number of Austrians amounted to 40,000 until just before the oil crisis (Münz et al. 2003: 20).

International immigration was a rarity, and only happened in the form of political refugees. In 1956-1957, 180,000 Hungarians sought asylum in Austria; in 1968-1969, 160,000 Czechs and Slovaks left via Austria, but only 12,000 attempted to obtain asylum in Austria. Austria was not really a target destination for many of these migrants – rather, it only happened to be nearby and a direct neighbour, thus serving as a transit country for

Table 3.2 *Stock of the population by nationality in Austria, 1961*

Country of origin	Foreign nationals		
	Absolute number	*In % of total population*	*In % of foreign population*
Total population	**7,073,814**	**100**	
Austrian nationals	6,971,648	98.6	
Foreign nationals	**102,166**	**1.4**	**100**
EU-14	59,215	0.8	58.0
Yugoslavia	4,565	0.1	4.5
Turkey	217	0.0	0.2
Visegrad*	6,498	0.1	6.4
Other	31,671	0.4	31.0

* Poland, Romania, Czech Republic, Slovakia, Hungary
Source: Census 1961, Statistics of Austria; own calculation

refugees. Many of them preferred to travel on to other Western European or overseas destinations, which were more attractive to them than a country so close to the Iron Curtain and the countries they had just fled; some also simply returned home. The Austrian public expressed sympathy for refugees from behind the Iron Curtain, whom they saw as victims of communism.

The 1961 census counted a foreign population of only 1.4 per cent, or a little more than 100,000 people in absolute terms. The majority came from Western Europe, with all other origins playing an insignificant role. The immigration of the foreign population was neither a subject of public concern nor an issue addressed by labour market policy. The situation changed with the Austrian *Wirtschaftswunder* – a period of economic growth beginning in the 1950s – and with the return of high fertility rates.

In the early 1960s, Austria faced a growing demand for labour as the economy was still booming: the industrial sector was expanding, the currency had stabilised, inflation was below 5 per cent and the unemployment rate was below 3 per cent. Taken together, this meant the goal of full employment had been achieved. The rates of labour force participation among females decreased because many women had to leave their jobs in order to take care of their newborns. The subsequent shortages within the labour force – which primarily affected the industrial sector – had several underlying sources. First, it could be perceived as a long-term consequence of the human losses during World War II. Second, the high number of births and the lack of childcare kept women away from the labour market. Third, the temporal extension of education released fewer people directly into employment.

Facing the need for additional labour, social partnerships agreed upon contingents (quotas) for the employment of guest workers in 1961, with the goal of letting them in only on a temporary basis and sending them back should there be any unfavourable economic developments. They were to just serve as additional temporary workers. Generally speaking, Austrian migration policy was a reflection of the needs of the labour market in this first phase of guest worker immigration. Migration policy as such was not an issue. The interests of entrepreneurs were dominant. Guest workers were welcomed and seen as an additional source for wealth – but not as a part of the Austrian society. Integration was not on the agenda, and long-term residence of the imported labour force was not intended.

The Austrian recruitment of labour migrants happened later than in Germany, Switzerland or Scandinavia. The first intergovernmental recruitment agreements were established with Spain in 1962 (though in reality these remained irrelevant), with Turkey in 1964 and with Yugoslavia in 1966. The so-called 'rotation principle' formed the basic idea at the beginning of the immigration of guest workers. They were to stay only on a temporary basis, with no opportunities for permanent settlement, family migration or societal integration. But this idea failed, due to resistance from both the employers' and the foreign employees' sides. Businesses were reluctant to relinquish the workforce they had taken care to train, and the migrants stayed because they were employed and earned more money than they could at home (see Fassmann 1992: 101).

In practical terms, the Austrian Federal Economic Chamber established recruitment centres in the sending countries and, in 1967, a provisional employment centre was installed directly at Ostbahnhof, one of Vienna's main train stations. But this concept of direct recruitment became less effective over time, with ongoing immigration and the formation of networks between businesses and guest workers already present in Austria; workers actively recruited friends and relatives in the sending countries (Bauböck 1996: 13). These new labourers entered Austria as tourists, but under the economic boom conditions of the early 1970s, it was quite easy for them to get an employment permit.

Beginning in the larger cities in the northern republics of Yugoslavia, and with high proportions of Slovenians and Croats, guest worker migration in its initial phases brought individual young people to Austria. These individuals were not able to find employment in their home countries after having finished school, or else were interested in earning more money abroad. The quantitative increase from 1969 onwards went hand in hand with social and geographical expansion. More and more older people with lower qualifications from rural areas in the south-eastern parts of Yugoslavia (Serbia, Bosnia and Herzegovina, Macedonia) were also involved in the process. The motives of these guest workers were all the same: maximising income and, at the same time, minimising the costs of the stay abroad in order to be able to send as much money as possible back home (Fassmann 1992: 102).

As it was increasingly successful in recruiting foreign labour, Austria was facing a first wave of immigration of guest workers in the mid-1960s, with an annual growth of more than 10,000 foreign workers from 1965 (11,200) until 1967 (14,700). This number rose to around 40,000 in the period 1971-1973, ultimately representing the heyday of guest worker immigration. The economic boom went on and the employment of foreign labour reached its peak in 1973 with around 227,000 persons, 78.5 per cent from Yugoslavia. Guest workers made up about 10 per cent of the total Austrian labour force.

The national census only provides limited information about the stock of the foreign population in the early phases of guest worker recruitment. Guest workers whose families still resided in their countries of origin were not counted as parts of the resident population, which was also characteristic of the way politicians and decision-makers dealt with guest worker migration. But questions also arose regarding those workers whose families were still back home: a publication was issued containing information on 'guest workers living in Austria but not belonging to the resident population' (Österreichisches Statistisches Zentralamt 1974: 3). Table 3.3 comprises both groups. While the share of foreigners was only 1.4 per cent before Austria's transformation from a country of emigration to immigration (1961), it had doubled to 2.8 per cent in 1971, with the census already reflecting the dominance of immigration from the Balkans.

A comparison of the composition of the population in 1961 and 1971 clearly shows that the total increase in the foreign population (more than 100,000 persons) to a great extent resulted from immigration inflows from Yugoslavia and Turkey. Yugoslavia was the main sending country, with 44 per cent of the 211,896 foreign nationals residing in Austria in 1971. All in all, the guest workers made up 52 per cent of the total foreign

Table 3.3 *Stock of the population by nationality in Austria, 1971*

Country of origin	Foreign nationals			Females in %
	Absolute number	*In % of total population*	*In % of foreign population*	
Total population	**7,491,526**	**100**		
Austrian nationals	7,279,630	97.2		53.2
Foreign nationals	**211,896**	**2.8**	**100**	**39.4**
EU-14	64,594	0.9	30.5	48.5
Yugoslavia	93,337	1.2	44.0	36.9
Turkey	16,423	0.2	7.8	12.7
Visegrad*	6,853	0.1	3.2	42.1
Other	30,689	0.4	14.5	41.9

* Poland, Romania, Czech Republic, Slovakia, Hungary
Source: Census 1961, Statistics of Austria; own calculation

population. Western Europe accounted for one third of the foreign resident population in 1971.

The number of Turks immigrating to Austria was still comparatively low at the beginning of the 1970s, with only 16,423 entering, with a clear dominance of men: only 12.7 per cent of the Turks in Austria in 1971 were women, while 37 per cent of the residing Yugoslavs were women. This was a clear indicator that family migration or the independent immigration of women, in their case, must already have started – to at least some extent before 1971. But Yugoslav women had also entered Austria as guest workers.

In the first half of the 1970s, the economic situation in Austria changed enormously due to two parallel developments. The first was pronounced economic stagnation after the first oil price shock in 1973, which marked the end of the boom era that had lasted for a long period of time. Stagnation led to growing unemployment, reduced working hours, increased inflation and public debt as well as failing enterprises. Secondly, the arrival of the baby boom cohorts on the labour market marked the end of the internal labour shortage.

Public opinion about immigration and guest workers as such changed rather dramatically. While people from the former Yugoslavia and Turkey were tolerated in times of good economic performance, the public increasingly perceived them as a threat and as those who short-changed the welfare system. In an effort to fight the rising xenophobia, the 'Kolaric' poster was hung in the streets of Vienna in 1973, and it is still famous today. Featured in the poster is a man who was working in a Vienna slaughterhouse and whose real name was Kolaric. He is asked by a small, obviously Austrian boy, why they call him 'Tschusch' (a swear word for people from the Balkans), even though they (man and boy) have the same family name. The dialogue between the Austrian boy and the man was supposed to bring migration history back into the public sphere. The boy and the man are migrants (or descendents of migrants), but one is treated in a xenophobic way by the other, which is neither fair nor logical. Launched by the Aktion Mitmensch of the Austrian advertising industry, the placard is an early example of the promotion of tolerance towards migrants and their integration.

From 1974 to 1976, there were massive attempts to reduce the foreign labour force in Austria and the official recruitment was thus stopped completely. The failure of the rotation principle and the trend towards permanent settlement quickly became apparent. Contrary to official political plans and expectations, the recruitment ban provoked a consolidation of permanent residences for a part of the foreign workers, who earlier had travelled back and forth, depending on the labour market situation, but now – in fear of losing the right to live and work in Austria – decided to stay permanently (Münz et al. 2003: 23).

In 1974, the Ministry for Social Affairs decreed a stepwise restriction of labour immigration after negotiations with the social partners. At the level of the federal states, a so-called Landesverhältniszahl was implemented; it aimed at regulating the size of the average foreign labour force within the total labour force. In 1976, the Aliens' Employment Act (*Ausländer-beschäftigungsgesetz*), aimed at regulating the admission of foreigners to the Austrian labour market, came into force. The Aliens' Employment Act was based on the premise that foreigners could only be employed if the situation on the Austrian labour market – as well as public and overall societal interests – allowed for further immigration. The Aliens' Employment Act introduced a system of graduated access to different types of permits with differing durations: first, there were employment permits (*Beschäftigungsbewilligung*), after one year, a work permit (*Arbeitserlaubnis*) and, finally, a certificate of exemption (*Befreiungs-schein*) after five years of employment.

All these measures led to significant reductions in the guest worker quotas and to an 'exportation of unemployment'. More than 31,000 guest workers left in 1975 and another 19,000 in 1976. This reduction continued – with only two years of an increase in foreign labour (1977, 1980) – until 1984, when the foreign labour force comprised only 139,000 persons, 40 per cent less than ten years before. Yugoslavians were more strongly affected than Turks: the number of employed Turks only dropped from 30,000 (1974) to 27,700 in 1984, whereas more than 50 per cent of the Yugoslav labour force left Austria and its labour market (1974: 169,400; 1984: 84,144). As naturalisations did not yet play an important role in quantitative terms, one can assume that these guest workers actually did go back home or else tried to seek employment elsewhere.

Table 3.4   *Stock of the population by nationality in Austria, 1981*

Country of origin	Foreign nationals			Females in %
	Absolute number	In % of total population	In % of foreign population	
Total population	**7,555,338**	**100**		
Austrian nationals	7,263,890	96.1		53.0
Foreign nationals	**291,448**	**3.9**	**100**	
EU-14	57,823	0.7	19.8	49.9
Yugoslavia	125,890	1.7	43.2	44.8
Turkey	59,900	0.8	20.6	40.0
Visegrad*	11,722	0.2	4.0	37.6
Other	36,113	0.5	12.4	44.1

* Poland, Romania, Czech Republic, Slovakia, Hungary
Source: Census 1981, Statistics of Austria; own calculation

The 1981 census results show that the process of family reunification had increased the number of women from Yugoslavia and Turkey in Austria, to almost 45 per cent women for Yugoslavia and 40 per cent for Turkey. Those who had not left after the oil crisis decided to stay in Austria for a longer period of time and therefore managed to realise the plan to bring their families to Austria. Thus – and despite the government's successful attempts to reduce the foreign labour force – the size of the foreign resident population grew from 212,000 in 1971 to 291,000 in 1981 (or by 37 per cent). At 63.8 per cent of the total foreign population, the dominance of guest worker migration was substantial.

The time period between 1985 and 1994 saw two huge political changes that had massive effects on the development of international migration, not only for Austria, but for Europe as a whole. First of all, the fall of the Iron Curtain in the late 1980s brought the newfound freedom of travel to people of the former Eastern bloc, meaning i.e. the old paths of East-West migration were reopened. Furthermore, at the beginning of the 1990s, the wars in Croatia (1991-1995) and Bosnia-Herzegovina (1992-1995) forced millions of refugees to flee from their countries. The annual net migration of foreigners grew from +12,000 in 1985 to up to +85,000 in 1991, and remained rather high until 1994 (+13,200).

Table 3.5 *Stock of the population by nationality in Austria, 1991*

Country of origin	Foreign nationals			Females in %
	Absolute number	In % of total population	In % of foreign population	
Total population	**7,795,786**	**100**		
Austrian nationals	7,278,096	93.4		52.4
Foreign nationals	**517,690**	**6.6**	**100**	
EU-14	79,437	1.0	15.3	51.8
Yugoslavia	197,886	2.5	38.2	43.1
Turkey	118,579	1.5	22.9	40.3
Visegrad*	58,731	0.8	11.3	39.6
Other	63,057	0.8	12.2	42.9

* Poland, Romania, Czech Republic, Slovakia, Hungary
Source: Census 1991, Statistics of Austria; own calculation

As the census data show, the size of the foreign resident population grew enormously between 1981 and 1991, namely from 291,000 to 518,000 (+227,000 persons). With a share of more than 60 per cent of the total foreign population, it was once again Yugoslavia and Turkey playing the dominant role in the composition of the stock of foreigners in Austria in 1991. At this point, the massive wave of immigration due to the Balkan Wars had not yet started. As for other regions of origin, the number of people residing in Austria who were nationals of its eastern neighbouring countries – including Romania and Poland – was four times higher in 1991 as compared to 1981, but was, in absolute numbers, still very low. The share of females still varied substantially by sending region: the lowest share (39.6 per cent) came from the then rather new immigration countries from Eastern Europe.

These severe changes in Austria's migration landscape led directly to changes in public opinion about immigration, driven by fears of Austria being 'flooded by foreigners' and, later on, in marked reforms of migration policy. The right-wing party, FPÖ, increased its share of voters from 5 per cent to 26.9 per cent by the end of the 1990s. In 1992, they launched a referendum called 'Austria first', which was signed by 416,500 Austrians (7.3 per cent of all eligible voters). During the referendum, the following demands, among others, were made: an expulsion of delinquent foreigners, a stricter naturalisation act and a complete stop to immigration. The immediate reaction of those opposing the referendum was the 'sea of lights' on the Heldenplatz in Vienna in January 1993, in which about 300,000 persons took part. Organised by the NGO SOS Mitmensch, people demonstrated against xenophobia and racism in the biggest protest the Second Republic had ever seen.

Thus, in the first half of the 1990s, the Austrian political system was reactive. In 1993, the 'Aliens Act' became effective. Half a year later, Austria passed a new, so-called Residence Law, which was in fact an immigration law. Against the backdrop of the migration movements that took place after the political changes in Europe, it aimed at regulating and restricting new immigration (König & Stadler 2003: 226). Policy started to evolve towards a system of controlling migration. Austria was one of the first Western European countries that established an immigration law.

An annual quota for new immigration was established and potential immigrants were divided into different groups: most fundamentally, either EU citizens or third-country nationals. Persons wanting to immigrate to Austria needed a residence permit and had to provide evidence of their lodging and means of subsistence. This meant that potential immigrants from outside the EU already had to have secured employment before arriving. The residence permits were subject to the above-mentioned quota, and the first application had to be filed from their country of origin. EU and European Economic Community (EEC) citizens were exempted from these restrictions: they needed neither special authorisation for immigration nor a residence permit.

The residence law of 1993 was successful in curbing high rates of immigration from third countries in the early 1990s. The size of the foreign labour force, as well as that of the foreign population, remained relatively stable between 1995 and 1999, and only grew slightly until 2002. But comparison with the 1991 stock data shows that the foreign population had grown enormously, by around 190,000 persons. They made up 9 per cent of the total population in 2001, even though the number of naturalisations was very high in the 1990s, and many foreign nationals in 1991 became Austrians by 2001. With regard to the composition of the foreign population residing in Austria, the situation did not change much between 1991 and 2001: 63 per cent of all foreign nationals still had their roots in one of the classic sending countries, either Yugoslavia or Turkey.

Table 3.6 *Stock of the population by nationality in Austria, 2001*

Country of origin	Foreign nationals			Females in %
	Absolute number	In % of total population	In % of foreign population	
Total population	**8,032,926**	**100**		
Austrian nationals	7,322,000	91.1		52.0
Foreign nationals	**710,926**	**8.9**	**100**	
EU-14	106,173	1.3	14.9	50.5
Yugoslavia	322,261	4.0	45.3	47.0
Turkey	127,226	1.6	17.9	44.0
Visegrad*	67,092	0.8	9.4	49.4
Other	88,174	1.1	12.4	47.8

* Poland, Romania, Czech Republic, Slovakia, Hungary
Source: Census 2001, Statistics of Austria; own calculation

After 2001, many laws were reformulated more restrictively in an effort to limit new arrivals. The so-called Aliens' Law Package (*Ausländerpaket*) of 2002 is of special relevance. The Aliens' Law Package comprised the Asylum Act, the Aliens' Police Act and the Settlement and Residence Act, and was influenced by five EU directives (long-term residence, family re-union, free movement of EU citizens, students, et al.), which had to be ful-filled as soon as possible. On the whole, Austria became more restrictive for third-country nationals in terms of both immigration and integration. But it also facilitated the employment of seasonal workers as well as the immigration of key personnel. It established mandatory integration courses, which included language classes and beginners' lessons on various legal and historical aspects of the country.

Austria developed a complex system to distinguish different immigrant groups in order to fulfil the needs of the economy and, more generally, to keep the influxes low. The public debate on the issues of migration, of foreigners and other societal development was once again highly politicised, but the intellectual quality of the argument changed. Only a minority asked for 'Ausländer raus' ('go away, foreigner'), which was neither legal nor rational, while another minority demanded open borders and unlimited immigration. Political discourse was more based on the acceptance of reality than it was in the beginning of the 1990s. And the issue of integration became more and more important, as it became clear that the idea of guest workers as temporary migrants was, at least to some extent, an illusion. In a shrinking demographic and ageing society with a simultaneously growing economy, immigration became a structural phenomenon of both the present and the future.

3.6.2   Generalising migration history

The Austrian case demonstrates how a former emigration country became an immigration country. The example shows the changes in migration as well as the adaptation of the society and the legal system to a changing migration pattern. Austria 'learned' to manage the new situation and to accept its various consequences. This learning process was neither free from friction nor linear. In accordance with the concept of a migration cycle, significant stages of this learning and adaption process can be identified, including the initial stage, the intermediate stage and the adaptation stage.

Generally, the initial stage is characterised by low rates of immigration and a public sphere that is not oblivious to international migration – unless emigration is of comparatively more significance, which was the case for many European countries. There are no specific political measures to regulate immigration; only emigration is controlled, mostly in the sense of impeding or restraining citizens from departure. For a long time, Austrian legislation envisaged emigrants asking for permission before leaving the country.

This situation changes in the intermediate stage. Immigration begins when a growing national economy displays increased demand for additional labour, on the one hand, and a demographic development occurs that leads to a diminishing internal labour supply, on the other. Immigration is coupled with economic cycles and thus tends to fluctuate strongly. The public and politicians willingly accept this additional labour force as immigrants take on jobs that are poorly paid – thus helping domestic businesses. The increase in demand-driven labour migration appears almost formally regulated (*Anwerbeabkommen*) and is accompanied by the unregulated immigration of irregular workers. The migration regime is still poorly developed, as in the case of guest worker countries, and this occurs often through a revival of the *Fremdarbeiter* regime.

This kind of immigration is not perceived as a regular inflow, but rather as an exceptional phenomenon in a booming economy. The terms 'guest work' and 'guest worker' imply temporal limitation. Similarly, the legalisation of labourers entering or being employed on an irregular basis is carried out on the basis of the erroneous expectation that these are only exceptional cases, and ones that can be 'repaired'. In the early intermediate phase, the public almost completely ignores immigration, as the immigrants are predominately single males and thus not visible in the public

Table 3.7 *Stages of the cycle: A non-immigration country becomes an immigration country*

Stages	Temporal (example Austria)	Quantitative dimension	Public perception	Legal measures
Initial	Until the late 1950s	International immigration remains the exception, emigration is dominating	The public does not perceive immigration, at best only emigration	No specific immigration policies at hand, if at all, emigration is regulated
Intermediate	1960 up to approximately 1994	Emerging immigration becomes more important than emigration, but is still related to cyclic phenomena, high fluctuation of balances	Immigration becomes part of the public discourse when economy is declining and the labour market is closing	Oscillating between liberalisation and tightening of political measures
Adaptation	After 1994	Immigration is a constant phenomenon, high fluctuations are over	Slowly growing acceptance	Differentiated legislation with a multitude of 'channels of immigration'

Source: Own design

space or in schools. Furthermore, they usually reside in the outskirts of city centres, on construction sites and in barracks.

As the intermediate stage proceeds, immigration becomes a constant phenomenon, and more and more comes to the awareness and attention of the public. The structure and composition of immigration changes from single males to family migration, and these move from the outskirts to inner city areas. The reactions of the public range from surprise to indignation. Arguments like 'we are being flooded', 'we will lose our culture' and 'foreigners are a threat to social peace' are often pervasive and are nothing more than expressions of surprise at a new immigration situation. Another part of the public is pleased by the cultural enrichment that accompanies immigration, or feels sympathy for the comparatively worse-off immigrants and their socially problematic situation in the host country. All of this results in political polarisation and legal measures that oscillate between liberalisation and increased stringency.

Finally, the intermediate stage passes into a stage of adaptation. Immigration is recognised as a necessary supplement to a demographically decreasing working population. The public is not surprised anymore and comes to terms with a culturally heterogeneous society. Extreme expressions of opinion in support of one way or another lose popularity and a new political rationality surfaces. This can also be seen as regulating immigration. While there was a certain type of 'labour migrant' during the intermediate stage, a whole panoply of residence and settlement titles was developed over time.

3.7   Conclusion

This chapter has shown that Europe became an immigration continent with a significant surplus of immigration, and that most European countries are developing in a similar way. There is strong evidence to suggest that the Southern European countries are becoming immigration countries, and that the Eastern European ones are or will soon be heading in the same direction. But this discussion has also demonstrated that the timing and pattern of the shift from a predominantly emigration country to one of immigration differs from case to case. Economic and demographic developments, as well as historical framing and context, are all extremely important for explaining different migration realities.

This chapter also discussed the content and the applicability of the migration cycle concept. The migration cycle concept assumes a general shift from an emigration to an immigration situation and identifies significant phases within this shift. It is illustrated by the Austrian example and proves itself a useful conceptual tool for analysing migration history. It sets forth a general guideline and reporting grid in order to make country reports more analogous and easily compared. But it is essential to note that such a heuristic phase model is a very rough simplification. It does not aim to suggest that all European countries go through these exact phases, and it should not be understood as an automatic phenomenon. It does, however, reflect an ordered, observable sequence of actual migration, public perception and political measures, and serialises them in order to make them more easily comprehended. This is extremely helpful because simple and descriptive country reports were produced in large numbers: in this respect, the IDEA project brought about significant scientific progress.

Notes

1   The bivariate correlation between the birth rate and net migration is indeed negative and highly significant. Based on a long time series for Austria, it can be shown that the correlation between the birth rate and net migration was -0.6 between 1950 and 2008: the higher the birth rate, the lower net immigration, and vice versa.

2   To test the postulated links empirically at least to some extent, a dataset has been compiled from the Eurostat database (New Cronos) containing all EU-27 countries. For the decade 1998-2008, the annual migration balances of each member state have been extracted as dependent variables and the GDP per capita, the total fertility rate and the unemployment rate have been added as independent factors. The explanatory value of the regression model is 28 per cent and the GDP per capita turned out to be the most relevant variable: the higher the GDP per capita, the higher the positive migration balance. The second variable, 'unemployment', is also significant, but with a negative sign: the higher the unemployment in the EU-27 countries, the lower the migration balance. Finally, the total fertility rate also displays a significant effect: the lower it is, the higher the international migration balance.

References

Bauböck, R. (1997), 'Migrationspolitik', in H. Dachs (ed.), *Handbuch des politischen Systems Österreichs: Die Zweite Republik*, 678-689. Vienna: Manz.

Bauböck, R. (1996), *'Nach Rasse und Sprache verschieden': Migrationspolitik in Österreich von der Monarchie bis heute*. Vienna: IHS.

Biffl, G. (2006), *SOPEMI report on labour migration*. Vienna: WIFO.

Fassmann, H. (1992), 'Funktion und Bedeutung der Arbeitsmigration nach Österreich seit 1963', in A. Hohenwarter & K. Althaler (eds.), *Torschluß. Wanderungsbewegungen und Politik in Europa*, 100-110. Vienna: Verlag für Gesellschaftspolitik.

Fassmann, H. (2009), 'European migration: Historical overview and statistical problems', in H. Fassmann, U. Reeger & W. Sievers (eds.), *Statistics and reality: Concepts and measurements of migration in Europe*, 10-27. IMISCOE Reports Series. Amsterdam: Amsterdam University Press.

Fassmann, H. & R. Münz (1996), 'Österreich: Einwanderungsland wider Willen', in H. Fassmann & R. Münz (eds.), *Migration in Europa: Historische Entwicklung, aktuelle Trends, politische Reaktionen*, 209-230. Vienna/New York: Campus.

Ferenczi, I. & W.F. Willcox (1929), *International migrations, Volume I: Statistics*. New York: National Bureau of Economic Research.

Hudson, K. (2007), 'The new labor market segmentation: Labor market dualism in the new economy', *Social Science Research* 36 (1): 286-312.

König, K. & B. Stadler (2003), 'Entwicklungstendenzen im öffentlich-rechtlichen und demokratiepolitischen Bereich', in H. Fassmann & I. Stacher (eds.), *Österreichischer Migrations- und Integrationsbericht: Demographische Entwicklungen – sozioökonomische Strukturen – rechtliche Rahmenbedingungen*, 226-260. Klagenfurt: Drava.

König, K. & B. Perchinig (2005), 'Austria', in J. Niessen, Y. Schibel & C. Thompson (eds.), *Current immigration debates in Europe: A publication of the European migration dialogue*. Brussels: MPG.

Kraler, A. (2007), 'The case of Austria', in G. Zincone, R. Penninx & M. Borkert (eds.), *Migratory policymaking in Europe: The dynamics of actors and contexts in past and present*, IMISCOE Research Series. Amsterdam: Amsterdam University Press. www.demokratiezentrum.org/de/startseite/wissen/timelines/arbeitsmigration_nach_oesterreich_in_der_zweiten_republik.html.

Münz, R., P. Zuser, P. & J. Kytir (2003), 'Grenzüberschreitende Wanderungen und ausländische Wohnbevölkerung: Struktur und Entwicklung', in H. Fassmann & I. Stacher (eds.), *Österreichischer Migrations- und Integrationsbericht. Demographische Entwicklungen – sozioökonomische Strukturen – rechtliche Rahmenbedingungen*, 20-61. Klagenfurt: Drava.

National Contact Point Austria (ed.), (2006), *Policy report: Immigration and integration in Austria*. Vienna.

Österreichisches Statistisches Zentralamt (ed.) (1974), *Ausländer. Ergebnisse der Volkszählung vom 12 Mai 1971*. Vienna.

Reeger, U. (2009), 'Austria', in H. Fassmann, U. Reeger & W. Sievers (eds.), *Statistics and reality: Concepts and measurements of migration in Europe*, 111-130. IMISCOE Reports Series. Amsterdam: Amsterdam University Press.

Tazi-Prevem I., J. Kytir, G. Lebhart & R. Münz (1999), *Bevölkerung in Österreich: Demographische Trends, politische Rahmenbedingungen, entwicklungspolitische Aspekte*. Vienna: Institut für Demographie der ÖAW.

Zelinsky, W. (1971), 'The hypothesis of the mobility transition'. *Geographical Review* 61 (2): 219-249.

4 Migration transitions in an era of liquid migration

Reflections on Fassmann and Reeger

Godfried Engbersen

4.1 Introduction

It is a pleasure to have the opportunity to respond to the compelling contribution of Heinz Fassmann and Ursula Reeger. Their work demonstrates their ability to reduce the complexity of international systems in a very elegant way. Their conceptual model of a migration cycle offers an important heuristic device for analysing migration history. To further illustrate its applicability, I will apply it to my country, the Netherlands. However, this sort of application and a closer look at current migration flows to 'old' immigration countries will necessarily provoke one major question. This question is related to the emphasis given in their chapter to historical context and its effects on emigration and immigration. This includes, for example, a colonial past or certain labour recruitment policies in the 1950s and 1960s. The question is whether such a historical, 'path-dependent' approach offers an adequate explanation for contemporary, rather unexpected labour migration flows from Central European Countries (CEE) to Western Europe. The European Union enlargements of 2004 and 2007 have generated substantial labour migration from CEE through the successive lifting of restrictions to the majority of labour markets from the old EU member states. Hundreds of thousands of migrants from Poland, Romania and Bulgaria went to Western European countries as a consequence (Black, Engbersen, Okólski & Panțîru 2010). This issue, which is related to labour migration, does not do justice to the full complexity of the analysis by Fassman and Reeger. However, I think it is relevant to analyse whether the nature of contemporary labour migration differs from labour migration flows in the past.

4.2   Path dependency versus new pathways of migration

For decades, the Netherlands was – like Germany and Austria – a 'reluctant country of immigration' (Cornelius, Tsuda, Martin & Hollifield 2004; Muus 2004). Although the Netherlands has had a positive immigration surplus since the early 1960s, successive governments have continued to officially deny that the Netherlands was a country of immigration. It was not until 1998 that the Dutch government officially acknowledged the fact that the Netherlands had become an immigration country. The different stages in a 'migration cycle', as proposed by Fassmann and Reeger, can be applied to the Netherlands (Engbersen, Van der Leun & De Boom 2007).

Preliminary phase

After World War II, the Netherlands was a country of emigration. Many Dutch citizens emigrated to immigration countries such as Australia, Canada and New Zealand and, to a lesser extent, Brazil and South Africa. Between 1946 and 1969, nearly 500,000 Dutch citizens left the Netherlands. In the same period, the Netherlands was experiencing a massive inflow of migrants (repatriates and Eurasians) from the former Dutch East Indies (now Indonesia) after Indonesia's independence in 1949 (see Figure 4.1). More than 50 years later (in 2003), there were 400,000 people in the Netherlands who had either been born in Indonesia or had at least one parent who had been born there.

Figure 4.1   *Net migration in the Netherlands, 1950-2009*

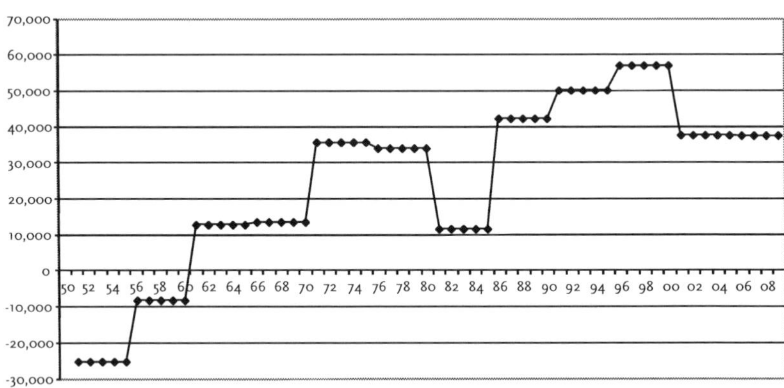

Source: Statistics of the Netherlands; own design

Transformative phase

A new pattern arose in the early 1960s with the arrival of guest workers from the Mediterranean (especially from Turkey and Morocco). When guest workers started bringing their families over to the Netherlands, it finally began to dawn on the Dutch that many of them were going to stay. After Surinam's independence in 1975, major flows of post-colonial immigrants from Surinam began to arrive in the Netherlands as well. In the 1970s, almost half of the non-Dutch immigrants to the Netherlands came from just five countries: Turkey, Morocco, Surinam, Netherlands Antilles and Indonesia. These migration patterns are perfectly aligned with the argument made by Fassmann and Reeger.

From the adaptation phase to a new initial phase?

After the transformative phase, there was indeed in the Netherlands a stage of adaptation. However, in the 1990s, the percentage of the five major immigrant groups steadily declined to less than 25 per cent of the foreign-born immigrants. Large groups of asylum seekers came to the Netherlands, especially in the period 1990-2000. Today, there are nearly 60 immigrant groups of at least 4,000 to 5,000 persons in the Netherlands. The total number of different nationalities in the Netherlands is around 180. The new immigrant groups come from countries to which the Netherlands has had rather limited political or economic ties, such as Iraq, Afghanistan, Iran, Poland, the former Soviet Union and the former Yugoslavia. Migrants from the former Yugoslavia, for example, are now the fifth main migrant group in the Netherlands. There are also a number of smaller migrant groups from Somalia, Ghana, Egypt, Vietnam, Pakistan and Hong Kong. Steven Vertovec makes similar observations about Britain in his recent work on 'super-diversity'. In the 1950s and 1960s, almost all migrants in Britain came from colonies or former colonies or Commonwealth countries. Today, migrants come from practically every country in the world. The city of London harbours people from some 180 countries (Vertovec 2007: 1029). The same is true for Dutch cities such as Amsterdam, Rotterdam and The Hague. Amsterdam and The Hague are among the 25 cities with the largest number of foreign-born residents in the world (Samers 2010: 31).

Another fundamental development is the rise in labour migration from CEE. According to the official migration and population figures of Statistics Netherlands, around 4,500 CEE workers moved to the Netherlands in 2003. In 2008, 26,000 immigrants from CEE countries came to the Netherlands, primarily from Poland, Bulgaria and Romania. As a result of this immigration, the number of CEE nationals officially residing in the Netherlands increased more than sixfold since 1996, from just over 10,000 in 1996 to nearly 65,000 in 2009.[1] Within this category, the Poles make up a clear majority (De Boom, Weltevrede & Engbersen 2009).

Apart from the migrants who settle officially in the Netherlands, there is a large category of labour migrants who do *not* appear in the official population statistics, because they do not or cannot register in the Municipal Personal Records Database (*Gemeentelijke Basisadministratie Persoonsgegevens*, GBA). Figures from the Employee Insurance Agency (UWV) show that, in December 2008, there were 87,000 employees from CEE countries working in the Netherlands who were *not listed* in the GBA.[2] In addition, there were around 7,000 employees of Polish-German nationality and approximately 7,700 entrepreneurs from one of the CEE countries in the Netherlands who were not registered in the GBA. Accordingly, the number of CEE workers in the Netherlands at the end of 2008 who were not listed in the GBA – and therefore not included in the official population figures of Statistics Netherlands – was estimated at more than 100,000. If we add these 100,000+ labour migrants not registered in the GBA to the nearly 65,000 migrants listed in the GBA, the number of CEE nationals residing in the Netherlands on 1 January 2009 was approximately 165,000[3] (De Boom et al. 2009). Nobody foresaw that so many migrants from Poland would migrate to the Netherlands, or even earlier to rather new destination countries like the UK or Ireland (Black et al. 2010). In other words, migration theory, with its strong emphasis on historical embeddedness and path dependency, faces difficulties explaining these new pathways of migration and settlement.

4.3   The invisibility of current flows of labour migration

How should we evaluate the current temporary, circular forms of labour migration from CEE? As the case of the Netherlands shows, contemporary labour migrants are often *not registered* in official migration statistics as compiled by national statistical bureaus, the United Nations or Eurostat. The missing aspects of these 'liquid' forms of migration can be illustrated with official Eurostat data on the inflow of nationals from CEE countries into four 'old' EU member states (Austria, Germany, the Netherlands and the UK). These data show a steep increase in all the selected countries, but the figures do not capture the rise in temporary labour migration from CEE countries (Figures 4.2). The UK offers a clear example. The data of the Workers Registration Scheme (WRS) – which does not include the self-employed – show that between May 2004 and December 2006, 328,000 Poles, 55,000 Lithuanians, 52,000 Slovakians and smaller groups from Latvia, the Czech Republic, Hungary, Estonia and Slovenia were registered (Bauere, Densham, Millar & Salt 2007).[4] These numbers do not seem to match the official inflow data.

Figures 4.2 *Inflows of nationals from CEE countries in Germany, Austria, the Netherlands and the UK, 2000-2008*

Germany

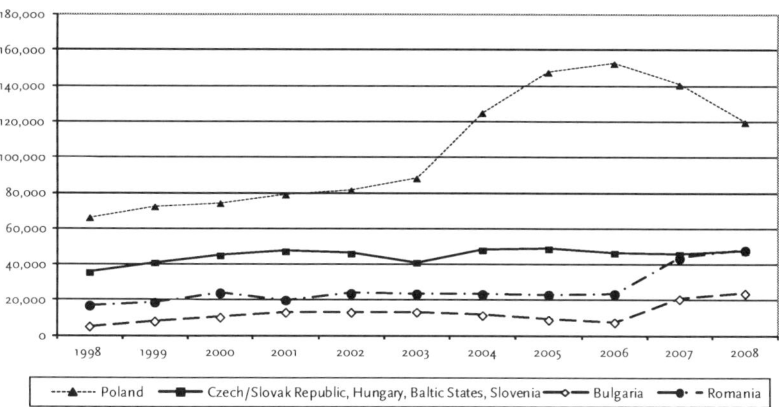

Austria

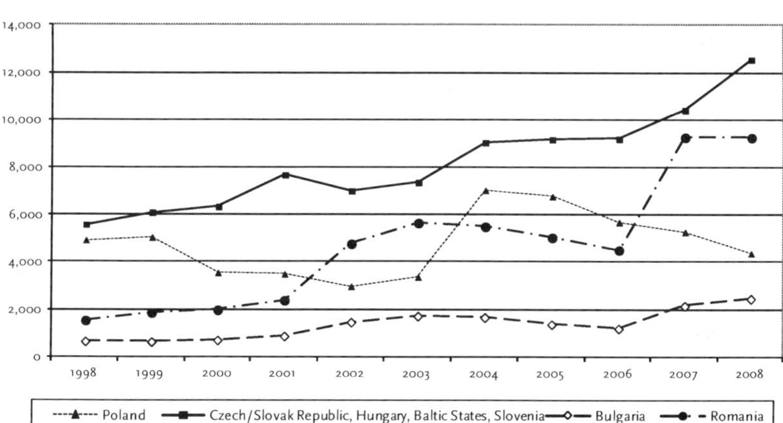

Source: Eurostat (http://epp.eurostat.ec.europa.eu/portal/page/portal/ population/data/database)

Moreover, the OECD data for Spain and Italy – two new immigration countries – do not provide reliable information on the inflow of migrants from Romania, though this is one of the largest migrant populations. According to OECD (2008: 278) sources, more than 500,000 Romanian migrants were in Spain in early 2007. Romanian sources state that there are about 968,000 legal Romanian migrants living in Italy, while in Spain that number is 770,000 (*Romania Libera* 5 April 2010) out of a total of roughly 2 million Romanians living abroad. The Spanish and Italian

Figures 4.2   *(continued)*

Netherlands

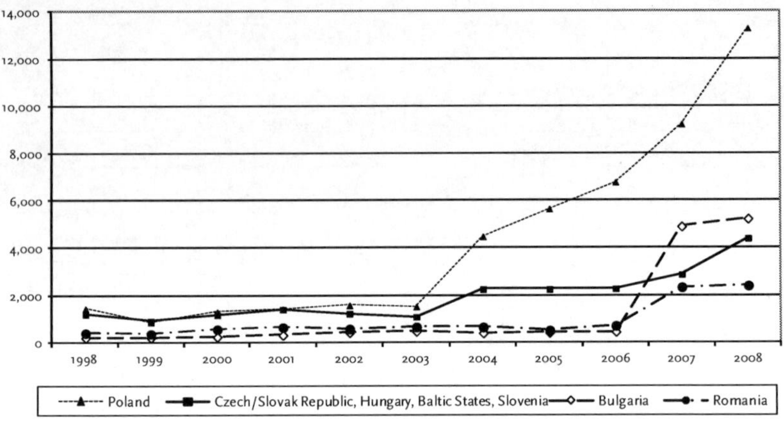

UK

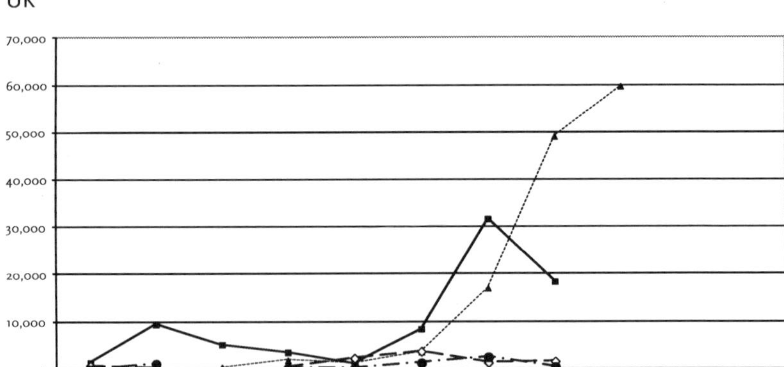

Source: Eurostat (http://epp.eurostat.ec.europa.eu/portal/page/portal/
population/data/database)

figures are rather low with respect to the inflow of Romanian migrants (see
Figures 4.3). The precise nature of contemporary forms of temporary migration is difficult to capture with the current measurements of flows.
Large groups of migrants are *unrepresented* or *underrepresented* in the
available migration statistics because they are not obliged to register if they
work and live for short periods of time in the destination country. This situation is a consequence of the current migration regimes involving open
borders for new EU citizens due to the EU enlargements in 2004 and

Figures 4.3 *Inflows of nationals from CEE countries in Spain and Italy, 2000-2008*

Spain

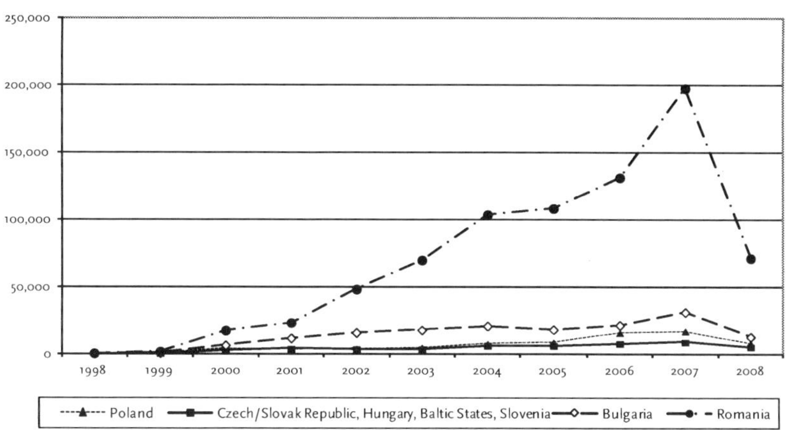

Italy

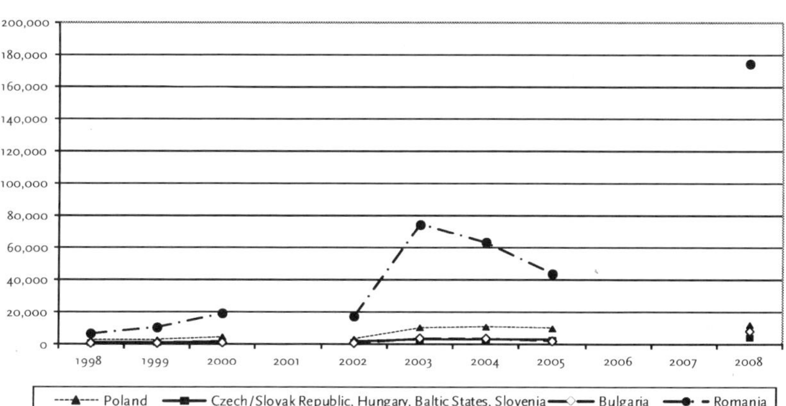

Source: Eurostat (http://epp.eurostat.ec.europa.eu/portal/page/portal/
population/data/database)

2007. The same is true for illegal migration. Irregular migrants are often absent from the official statistics. However, their absence is not a consequence of open borders, but of *closed* borders (Engbersen & Broeders 2009; Düvell 2006; CLANDESTINO 2009).

It seems crucial to take the *migration regime contexts* into consideration. The earlier migrant workers, the so-called guest workers, arrived in a period when national borders were still very real and significant. This is no longer the case for the labour migrants from CEE countries after the EU enlargements of 2004 and 2007. This disappearance of EU borders contributes strongly to contemporary forms of liquid migration. It is much easier to travel back and forth for labour migrants from CEE countries to Western European countries than in the past. The enlargement of the EU has led to a blurring of the boundaries between international and internal labour migration (King & Skeldon 2010: 1621).

4.4   Liquid migration

The concept of liquid migration is inspired by Zygmunt Bauman's work (1999, 2005) on liquid modernity (Engbersen, Snel & De Boom 2009). Central to the notion of liquidity is the idea that 'thick' and stable social institutions (class, family, labour, community, neighbourhood and nation-state) are transforming into more flexible, 'thin' institutions (see also Zijderveld 2000). Migration has always been strongly embedded in patterns of family, community, local labour markets and the nation-state (Portes & Sensenbrenner 1993; Portes 1995; Torpey 1998). These institutions are still crucial to understand the strategies and opportunities of groups of migrants. However, current labour migrants from Poland, for example, have more freedom and liberty to develop their own migration trajectories than in the pre-EU enlargement period with its restrictive West European migration regimes. The borderless zone created by the EU has weakened the monopoly of nation-states to regulate and prescribe movements of people. Another changing institution is the family. There is a well-documented literature on the importance of family networks and loyalties that explains the centrality of the family in the field of migration. However, today we also witness migrants from CEE who are able to develop rather individualised migration patterns. Their stay abroad is not aimed at supporting family members at home. They are strongly focused on their own careers. The first findings of a Dutch study show that more than 50 per cent of the 650 respondents from Poland, Bulgaria and Romania did not send any money to their relatives in their home country (Snel, Burgers, Engbersen, Ilies, Van der Meij & Rusinovic 2010; Burgers, Van de Pol, Snel, Engbersen, Ilies, Van der Meij & Rusinovic 2011). Individualisation processes have made the family less dominant as an 'engine of immigration' (Massey & Philips 1999). In other words, the transformation of institutions like the nation-state and the family, together with more advanced communication technologies, has changed migration patterns in contemporary European societies and has made labour migration trends less predictable. Liquid migration has six ideal typical characteristics (Table 4.1).

The first characteristic is the *temporary nature* of a stay abroad. Substantial numbers of migrants do not settle permanently, but move back and forth from their source country to receiving countries (circular and

Table 4.1 *Ideal typical dimensions of liquid migration*

---

1 Settlement: Temporality of migration and stay
– Temporary migration
– Temporary settlement; semi-integration in destination country

2 Type of migration: Labour migration
– Labour migrants
– Categories of asylum seekers, refugees, student migrants

3 Status: legal immigration status
– Regular migration
– Work permit holders (Romania and Bulgaria)

4 Destination: Multiplicity and multidirectionality of movements
– Multiple receiving countries
– New receiving countries

5 Family: Individualised life strategy
– Individualised forms of migration
– First-generation pattern

6 Migratory habitus: Intentional unpredictability
– No definite migration aspirations
– Open options

Source: Own design

pendulum migration) or move to other destination countries. Many stay very briefly, while others opt for a medium-term or longer-term stay. However, the temporary nature of residence – which often goes hand in hand with non-registration – contributes to the invisibility of liquid migration. The circularity of liquid migration resembles, to some extent, the circular forms of migration as described in the work by Douglas Massey on Mexican-United States migratory flows in the 1980s (Massey, Alarcon, Durand & Gonzalez 1986). However, there are also other migrant groups such as students and highly skilled migrants who develop forms of career migration. Their ambition is to capitalise on their foreign education, language proficiency and work experience in their home country to achieve upward social mobility. The temporary nature of migration means that many labour migrants reside in temporary accommodation settings (hostels, pensions, barracks, holiday camps) and that they occupy a marginal position in the receiving country.

A second dimension is that liquid migration is predominantly *labour migration*. Particular groups of 'economic' asylum seekers, refugees and students can also be regarded as labour migrants. All these groups aim to earn money or to invest in their education in order to better their economic position. Liquid migration is a typical first-generation phenomenon. However, some migrants will settle and may bring spouses over.

A third dimension is that migrants have a *legal immigration status*. Liquid migration is *regular* migration. However, some migrants that have legal residential status still need work permits in order to obtain access to the labour market. If they do not have a work permit, they become irregular workers. However, once the current 'transition period' ends – in which restrictions are currently imposed on workers from Bulgaria and Romania – these migrants will have free access to European labour markets. Another relevant category consists of students. Many of them are not allowed to stay in the country after completing their studies. If they do stay, they become illegal migrants. Thus, some categories of migrants have temporary legal residence status (students), while others may face the problem of irregular work. These categories show that legal status itself is a fluid classification that may change over time (Ruhs 2007).

A fourth dimension of liquid migration is that international migration flows have become more *unpredictable*. Some categories of labour migrants work and reside in well-established destination countries, while others have moved on to new destination countries. Liquid migration partly ignores the political and economic factors that shaped migration flows in the past. The Polish migration flows to Ireland and the United Kingdom – and then to the Netherlands – are a clear example of this. Labour migrants react and adapt to evolving opportunities in the labour markets of different European countries.

A fifth dimension of liquid migration concerns the role of *family*. International migration has always been encouraged and facilitated by family networks (Tilly 1990; Massey et al. 1986). Households develop strategies to maximise the household income. These classic forms of migration rely on the solidarity between generations and on extended family patterns. Grandparents take care of the children when one or both parents go abroad to earn money for the family. In addition to this classic pattern, however, new patterns emerge that are much more individualised. These more individualised patterns are the logical consequences of the changing nature of family ties (Beck & Beck-Gernsheim 2002). These ties are becoming looser, not only in Western but also in CEE societies (Ornacka & Szczepaniak-Wiecha 2005). Furthermore, people are postponing marriage and childbearing to a later age. Many contemporary labour migrants are unmarried and have few or no family obligations (Snel et al. 2011). They go abroad to try their luck and do not have specific obligations to support relatives in their home country (Eade, Drinkwater & Garapich 2006).

The relatively autonomous position of labour migrants is facilitated by the demand for their labour skills, especially in secondary labour markets and – in the case of CEE migrants – because of the disappearance of internal EU borders (free movement). Their social position and the migration field in which they strategically operate generate a specific *migratory habitus* of 'intentional unpredictability' (Eade et al. 2006). Some migrants have no clear ambitions or ideas concerning the future. Their options are wide open. They go to new destination countries without clear-cut aspirations of investing money in their home country or of settling in the receiving country. This migratory habitus reflects the more individualistic ethos of non-married labour migrants who are less bound by family obligations and also less restricted by borders and local labour markets than previous generations of migrants.

The fluid nature of East-West migration emphasises the contrasts between the so-called guest worker migration of the 1960s and 1970s and contemporary migrant workers from the CEE countries, who do not settle permanently in the receiving countries where they work but – at least until now – tend to return to their home countries. Workers go home when the job is finished and they return when necessary or are available on demand when certain work is to be done (Grabowska-Lusińska & Okólski 2009).

A crucial difference between both episodes of international migration is the *institutional context*. The earlier migrant workers, the so-called guest workers, arrived in a period when national borders were still very real and significant. When asked why the guest workers from this period stayed in the destination countries despite their often firm intention to return, migration researchers point out the significance of national borders. According to Saskia Sassen, there was a significant increase in the permanent foreign-resident population in Western Europe when borders were closed in 1973-1974. Sassen writes (1999: 143):

> [...] this growth might not have occurred if the option of circular migration had existed. Much migration has to do with supplementing household income in countries of origin; given enormous earnings differentials, a limited stay in a high-wage country is sufficient.[5]

Because it was impossible to move repeatedly between sending and receiving countries, many migrants decided not to return but instead to have their families come over. This was the beginning of the permanent settlement of the former guest workers who were consequently not 'guests' anymore.[6] The current labour migration from Eastern to Western Europe takes place in a different institutional constellation, that is, in a context in which national borders – at least within the EU – have lost their significance. East-West migration is strongly labour-motivated – like the guest worker migration trends in the 1960s and 1970s – but nowadays workers have more opportunities to come and go as they choose. However, the other factors continue to be of relevance.

4.5 An elective affinity between demographic-economic factors and migration control

The central point in our argument is that 'old' immigration countries in Europe are confronted with 'new' fluid forms of labour migration. There are indications that current migration patterns differ from the dominant migration patterns of the twentieth century. Several studies – quantitative as well as ethnographic and anthropological – indicate more fluid forms of migration that bear resemblance to the circular migration of the nineteenth century, but cover longer distances and go to more diverse destination countries (Moch 1992; Grabowska-Lusińska & Okólski 2009). To understand these forms of labour migration, the four main drivers of labour migration as discussed by Fassman and Reeger have to be taken into account: 1) demographic factors; 2) economic growth; 3) segmentation of developed labour markets into a primary and a secondary sector; and 4) modes of regulation concerning international migration. It is especially the specific interaction between these drivers that explains the rise of liquid migration. One could also speak of a *Wahlverwandtschaft* (an elective affinity) between demographic-economic factors and the fading of borders within the enlarged EU (Weber 2002). Unintentionally, this has contributed to the large flows of labour migration from the East to the West.

New research designs are needed to document these flows, because the current administrative data are inadequate. These flows may also require adoption of new policy by the state. The temporary stay of many new labour groups requires a new flexible structure (in terms of housing, healthcare, education and integration) that can deal effectively with new patterns of 'lasting temporality' (Grzymała-Kazłowska 2005). At present, in many European countries improvised solutions are being devised to accommodate labour migrants from CEE.

Notes

1   These figures are based on a count of Polish, Hungarian, Czech, Slovakian, Estonian, Latvian, Lithuanian, Slovenian, Bulgarian and Romanian nationals listed in the GBA. The number of CEE workers registered in the GBA greatly depends on the definition applied. Based on nationality, nearly 65,000 CEE nationals were living in the Netherlands on 1 January 2009. On the same reference date, the GBA contained 90,000 persons who had been born in one of the CEE countries. This means that the number of CEE workers when measured by country of birth is 25,000 higher than when measured by nationality. In particular, these are CEE workers who have lived in the Netherlands for some time and have acquired Dutch nationality.

2   Not all employees worked throughout the month of December, which means that the number of employees on a specific reference date is lower. Based on the not entirely reliable start and end dates, the number of CEE workers not registered in the

GBA for whom wage tax was paid as of 15 December 2008 has been calculated at 81,400.

3   Furthermore, there are CEE workers who are not listed in the GBA and do not appear on other registers, for instance, because they are working through mala fide agents. No reliable estimate can be given of the size of the latter group.

4   The WRS data give no indication of the duration of employment or if and when a return home might have occurred (Bauere et al. 2007: 8).

5   The same argument has been put forward by Alejandro Portes with respect to Mexico-US migration flows: 'Today, the U.S. Border Patrol is the second largest arms-bearing agency of the federal government, next to the armed forces themselves. The huge expenditure of dollars in this policy has not succeeded in topping the unauthorized flow, but has succeeded in keeping it bottled up on the American side of the border. Contrary to the prior pattern of cyclical migration, where Mexican workers commuted back and forth across the border, those who, at present, manage to cross into the United States do not return to their countries, given the difficulties of repeating the journey. Instead, they bring their families along. As a consequence of its supposedly rational policy, the United States now has in its midst an underground poor and vulnerable population numbering about twelve million' (Portes 2010: 46-47).

6   There were also other reasons, such as: i) changing plans of migrants as a consequence of the life cycle; ii) economic recessions in the home country; iii) the integration of migrant workers into welfare systems; iv) legal protection securing residence status and the right to live with families (Castles 2006).

References

Bauere, V., P. Densham, J. Millar & J. Salt (2007), 'Migrants from Central and Eastern Europe: Local geographies', *Population Trends* 129: 7-19.

Bauman, Z. (2005), *Liquid life*. Oxford: Polity Press.

Bauman, Z. (1999), *Liquid modernity*. Oxford: Polity Press.

Beck, U. & E. Beck-Gernsheim (2002), *Individualization: Institutionalized individualism and its social and political consequences*. London: Sage.

Black, R., G. Engbersen, M. Okólski & C. Panţîru (eds.) (2010), *A continent moving west? EU enlargement and labour migration from Central and Eastern Europe*. IMISCOE Research Series. Amsterdam: Amsterdam University Press.

Burgers, J., S. van de Pol, E. Snel, G. Engbersen, M. Ilies, R. van der Meij & K. Rusinovic (2011), *Arbeidsmigranten uit Polen, Bulgarije en Roemenië in West-Brabant: Sociale leefsituatie, arbeidspositie en toekomstperspectief*. The Hague: Nicis Institute.

Castles, S. (2006), 'Guest workers in Europe: A resurrection?', *International Migration Review* 40: 741-766.

CLANDESTINO (2009), 'Irregular migration: Counting the uncountable. Data and trends across Europe'. http://clandestino.eliamep.gr; http://irregular-migration.hwwi.net.

Cornelius, W., T. Tsuda, P.L. Martin & J.F. Hollifield (eds.) (2004), *Controlling immigration: A global perspective*. Stanford: Stanford University Press.

De Boom, J., A. Weltevrede & G. Engbersen (2009), *Migration and migration policies in the Netherlands 2008: Dutch SOPEMI report 2008*. Rotterdam: Risbo.

Drinkwater, S., J. Eade & M. Garapich (2009), 'What's behind the figures? An investigation into recent Polish migration to the UK', in R. Black, G. Engbersen, M. Okólski & C. Panţîru (eds.), *A continent moving west? EU enlargement and labour migration from Central and Eastern Europe*. IMISCOE Research Series. Amsterdam: Amsterdam University Press.

Düvell, F. (ed.) (2006), *Illegal immigration in Europe: Beyond control?* Houndmills: Palgrave Macmillan.

Eade J., S. Drinkwater & M. Garapich (2006), *Class and ethnicity: Polish emigrants in London*. Research Report for ERSC, CRONEM, University of Surrey.

Engbersen, G. & D. Broeders (2009), 'The state versus the alien: Immigration controls and strategies of irregular immigrants', *West European Politics* 32 (5): 867-885.

Engbersen, G., J. van der Leun & J. de Boom (2007), 'The fragmentation of migration and crime', in *Crime and justice: A review of research*, 389-452 (Special issue on crime and justice in the Netherlands). Chicago: Chicago University Press Crime and Justice Series.

Engbersen, G., E. Snel & J. de Boom (2009), ' "A van full of Poles": Liquid migration from Central and Eastern Europe', in R. Black, G. Engbersen, M. Okólski & C. Panţîru (eds.), *A continent moving west? EU enlargement and labour migration from Central and Eastern Europe*, 115-140. IMISCOE Research Series. Amsterdam: Amsterdam University Press.

Grabowska-Lusińska, I. & M. Okólski (2009), *Emigracja ostatnia?* Warsaw: Wydawnictwo Naukowe Scholar.

Grzymała-Kazłowska, A. (2005), 'From ethnic cooperation to in-group competition: Undocumented Polish workers in Brussels', *Journal of Ethnic and Migration Studies* 31 (4): 675-697.

King, R. & R. Skeldon (2010), 'Mind the gap! Integrating approaches to internal and international migration', *Journal of Ethnic and Migration Studies* 36 (10): 1619-1646.

Massey, D.S., R. Alarcon, J. Durand & H. Gonzalez (1986), *Return to Aztlan: The social process of international migration from Western Mexico*. Berkeley/Los Angeles: University of California Press.

Massey, D.S. & J.A. Philips (1999), 'Engines of immigration: Stocks of human and social capital in Mexico', *Social Science Quarterly* 81 (1): 33-48.

Moch, L. & P. Moch (1992), *Moving Europeans: Migration in Western Europe since 1650*. Bloomington & Indianapolis: Indiana University Press.

Muus, P. (2004), 'The Netherlands: A Pragmatic approach to economic needs and humanitarian considerations', in W. Cornelius, T. Tsuda, P.L. Martin & J.F. Hollifield (eds.). *Controlling immigration: A Global perspective*, 262-280. Stanford: Stanford University Press.

OECD (2009*), International migration outlook. Special focus: Managing labour migration beyond the crisis*. Paris: OECD.

Ornacka, K. & I. Szczepaniak-Wiecha (2005), 'The contemporary family in Poland: New trends and phenomena', *Journal of Family and Economic Issues* 26 (2): 195-225.

Portes, A. (1995), *The economic sociology of immigration: Essays on networks, ethnicity, and entrepreneurship*. New York: Russell Sage Foundation.

Portes, A. & J. Senssenbrenner (1993), 'Embeddedness and immigration: Notes on the social determinants of economic action', *American Journal of Sociology* 98 (6): 1320-1350.

Portes A. (2010), 'Reflections on a common theme: Establishing the phenomenon, adumbration, and ideal types', in C. Calhoun (ed.), *Robert K. Merton: Sociology of science and sociology of science*. New York: Columbia University Press.

Ruhs, M. (2007), *Changing status, changing fortunes? The impact of acquiring EU status on the earnings of East European migrants in the UK*, mimeo. Oxford: COMPAS.

Samers, M. (2010), *Migration*. London and New York: Routledge.

Sassen, S. (1999), *Guests and aliens*. New York: The New Press.

Snel, E., J. Burgers, G. Engbersen, M. Ilies, R. Van der Meij & K. Rusinovic (2010), *Arbeidsmigranten uit Bulgarije, Polen en Roemenië in Rotterdam: Sociale leefsituatie, arbeidspositie en toekomstperspectief.* The Hague: Nicis Institute.

Tilly, C. (1990), 'Transplanted networks', in V. Yans-McLaughlin (ed.), *Immigration reconsidered: History, sociology, and politics*, 79-95. New York: Oxford University Press.

Torpey, J. (1998), 'Coming and going: On the state monopolization of the legitimate "means of movement" ', *Sociological Theory* 16 (3): 239-259.
Vertovec, S. (2007), 'Super-diversity and its implications', *Ethnic and Racial Studies* 29 (6): 1024-1054.
Weber, M. (2002), *The Protestant ethic and the spirit of capitalism: New translation and introduction by S. Kalberg*. Los Angeles: Blackwell Publishers.
Zijderveld, A. (2000), *The institutional imperative: The interface of institutions and networks*. Amsterdam: Amsterdam University Press.

5 Immigrants, markets and policies in Southern Europe

The making of an immigration model?[1]

*João Peixoto, Joaquín Arango, Corrado Bonifazi,
Claudia Finotelli, Catarina Sabino, Salvatore Strozza and
Anna Triandafyllidou*

5.1 Introduction

Greece, Italy, Portugal and Spain have in common two long episodes of strong emigration – during the first period of globalisation and after World War II – and they now share comparable types of foreign immigration. During the first period of globalisation, in the second half of the nineteenth century and before World War I, these countries made an important contribution to intra-European migration and to settlement migration in North America and South America. After World War II, they were among the main suppliers of the growing economies of Western and Northern Europe. Currently, they are experiencing a significant inflow of foreigners. In a relatively short time span, Southern Europe underwent its migration transition, becoming one of the most important areas of attraction on the continent (Bonifazi 2008). According to the available statistics, the number of foreign immigrants in this area can be estimated as ranging from between 950,000 and 1.3 million in 1991 to between 8 million and 10 million in the period 2006-2007. This is a seven- to eight-fold increase in just fifteen years.

Despite some dissimilarities that stem from the different histories of these countries, their diverse social and economic characteristics and their specific cultural and colonial links to other geographical areas, many reasons for the growth of foreign immigration were similar across all four of them. It is worth mentioning several notable economic trends in recent decades: the improvement in living standards and educational levels of the native youth, both of which increased labour expectations; the persistence of significant informal economies and of segmentation processes in the labour markets; the effects of low fertility rates on labour supply; and the overall limitations of Mediterranean welfare systems, which are largely unable to provide for their populations' evolving needs, including those attributable to the ageing process. Furthermore, the political and economic transitions in Central and Eastern Europe (CEE) intensified the push forces into this area. While the gradual incorporation of most of those countries into the European Union migration system resulted in a relaxing of visa policies, labour migration from that area had been de facto tolerated even before the EU enlargement. This increased availability of foreign workers matched the growing needs of Southern European labour markets.

Engaging in a comparative analysis of immigration experiences in Southern European countries is not a novel exercise. Since the early 1990s, the many similarities in timing and other characteristics of immigration in these countries led to the frequent collaboration of researchers and policy-makers in order to discuss the common trends. During a period that culmi-nated at the turn of the century, numerous articles, books and special edi-tions of journals were released (see e.g. King & Rybaczuk 1993; Iosifides & King 1996; Baganha 1997; Baldwin-Edwards 1997; King & Black 1997; Baldwin-Edwards & Arango 1999; King, Lazaridis & Tsardanidis 2000; King 2002; Arango 2003; Ribas-Mateos 2004; Ritaine 2005; and, more recently, King & Thomson 2008[2] and González-Enríquez & Trian-dafyllidou 2009). Many of these works designated these new immigration experiences as a Southern European or Mediterranean 'model of immigra-tion' (King 2000), which differed in several ways from the model that pre-dominated in other European host countries during the second half of the twentieth century, when the Fordist type of capitalism was dominant.[3]

After the turn of the century, academic interest in drawing comparative analyses between the Southern European countries somewhat subsided. This is rather surprising, since the bulk of the inflows into Southern Europe occurred mostly after the late 1990s. Indeed, the framework and underlying immigration factors remained much the same as they had been before. But during the new century, some of the characteristics of the in-flows changed, several new policies were enacted and the overall outcomes of migration, including immigrant integration, varied. There thus exists a clear need to update the comparative exercises carried out previously. This is one of the objectives of this chapter.

Furthermore, it is important to understand the particular position of Southern European countries in the European international migration sys-tem when compared to the 'old' or 'mature' immigration countries in Northern and Western Europe and to the 'recent' or 'future' immigration countries in CEE. As discussed in chapters 1 and 2 in this volume, the dif-ferent timings of the migration transition – meaning the process by which countries change their migration status from net out-migration to in-migra-tion – depend on a broader economic and social framework, thus impacting differently over immigrants' modes of labour incorporation, social integration, public attitudes and immigration policy. In certain respects, the southern context has been unique, resulting from its specific moments of transition and structural similarity, whilst in other respects it shares the traits and dilemmas of its predecessors and, most probably, its followers.

The sections of this chapter are organised as follows. First, a detailed analysis of flows and stocks of foreign immigration will be set forth. Second, as a result of the centrality of labour demand variables in explaining immigration in this context, special attention will be devoted to immigrants' labour market incorporation. Third, the endemic presence of irregular migration in these countries will be described, together with its explanatory factors (including the informal economy and inadequate regulation) and policy attempts to regulate it. Next, other aspects of immigration policy will be examined, including labour recruitment, control and integration policies. Finally, some general considerations and final conclusions will be drawn, displaying the main similarities, explaining factors and overall position of Southern Europe compared to other European host countries.

5.2 Flows and stocks of foreign immigration

It is well known that data on international migration are collected in different statistical sources and that, even when they are taken from the same type of source, they are not always comparable over time and between countries. The specific features of national legal systems have a great impact on data. In the Southern European case, the endemic character of irregular migration adds to the difficulty of immigration's measurement.[4]

5.2.1 Flows and stocks of foreign immigration

At the beginning of the twenty-first century, according to the available sources, immigration exhibited a spectacular upsurge in Italy and above all in Spain (Figure 5.1). The Spanish trend is the most impressive. The data of the Padrón Municipal de Habitantes, the municipal population registry, which also include irregular migrants, show continuous and regular growth in foreign inflows since 1996. The volume of this growth is amazing, as in only twelve years the size of the inflow increased by a factor of 55: from 17,000 arrivals in 1996 to 921,000 in 2007.

The growing share of foreign immigration within the total inflow (foreigners and nationals) signals its increasing importance in the Southern European countries (Figure 5.1). In Italy, since 1996 this share has exceeded 80 per cent of the total inflow and is now estimated at 92 per cent; in Spain it has been over 90 per cent since 2000 and reached 96 per cent

Figure 5.1 *Immigration of foreign citizens from abroad: Italy, Portugal[1] and Spain,[2] 1990-2007 (absolute values and percentages of foreigners in the overall immigration)*

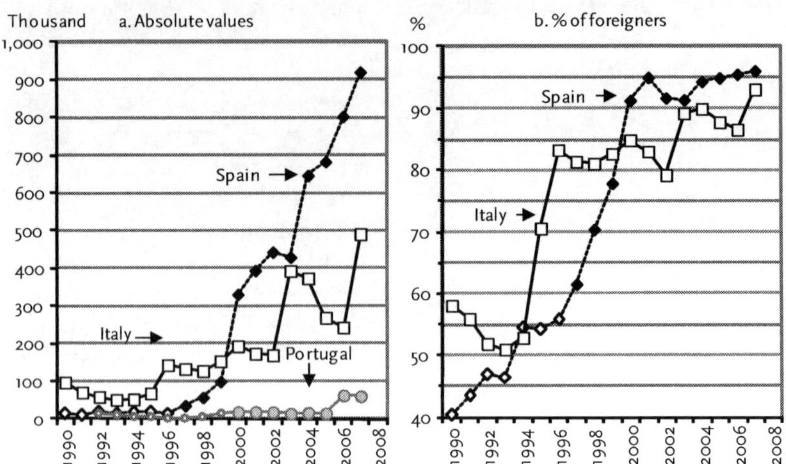

[1] Data refer only to *solicitacões de autorizacão de residência* (*autorizacões de permanência concedidas* and *vistos de longa duracão concedidos pelos postos consulares* are not considered).
[2] Data for 1996 are not perfectly comparable with those for earlier years due to a reform of the Padrón Municipal.
Sources: Italy: ISTAT, Anagrafi comunali; Portugal: Serviço de Estrangeiros e Fronteiras (SEF) – Ministério da Administração Interna; Spain: INE, Padrón Municipal.

in 2007. It is worth considering that, until the early 1990s, nationals were still almost half of the total inflow entering these two countries.

The evolution of the number of foreigners in the four countries since the 1980s can be evaluated using stock data from population censuses, population registers and permits to stay or residence permits (Table 5.1).[5] Regardless of technical differences, all the available information indicates that, between 1991 and 2007, the presence of foreign citizens has increased remarkably in all four countries. The pace of this growth, however, seems to be much more rapid in Italy and – above all – in Spain as compared to Greece and Portugal. In Italy, in particular, data indicate that the number of regular immigrants grew from some hundred thousand in 1991 to between 2.4 and 3.4 million in 2007. Consequently, the share of foreigners within the total population also increased from about 1 per cent to 4-6 per cent. The estimated number of foreigners reaches 4.3 million, or 7.2 per cent of the total population living in Italy, if non-resident regular immigrants and illegal immigrants are also taken into consideration (Blangiardo 2009).

Table 5.1 *Foreign population according to different sources in the Southern European immigration countries around 1991, 2001 and 2007 (absolute values in thousands and percentages of total population at the end of the year or the census data)*

Country/categories	Absolute values (in thousands)			% of total population		
	1991	2001	2007	1991	2001	2007
Italy						
Permits to stay holders[1]	649	1,448	2,415	1.1	2.5	4.1
Residents[2]	356	1,335	3,433	0.6	2.3	5.8
Estimate of total foreign population[3]	1,002	2,460	4,328	1.8	4.3	7.2
Spain						
Permits to stay holders[4]	361	1,109	3,979	0.9	2.7	8.6
Residents (census)[5]	353	1,572	...	0.9	3.8	...
Residents of Padrón (total foreign population)[6]	...	1,978	5,221	...	4.8	11.3
Greece						
Permits to stay holders[7]	149	...	696	1.5	...	6.3
Residents[8]	166	762	884	1.6	7.0	7.9
Estimate of total foreign population[9]	...	...	1,092	...	...	9.8
Portugal						
Legal residents and holders of visas[10]	...	351	446	...	3.4	4.2
Residents[11]	107	233	402	1.1	2.2	3.8
Estimate of total foreign population[12]	...	...	496	...	...	4.7

[1] Permits to stay collected by Ministero dell'Interno and revised by ISTAT; the last data is referred at the end of 2006

[2] Census data as of 24 October 1991 and 21 October 2001; 2007 municipal population registers data (Anagrafi comunali)

[3] For 1991 and 2001: our evaluations from ISTAT data and estimates of irregular migrants in Blangiardo and Tanturri (2006); for 2007: Blangiardo (2009)

[4] *Tarjeta o autorización de residencia*

[5] Census data as of 1 March 1991 and 1 May 2001

[6] Data of Padrón Municipal, including illegal foreigners

[7] Last data is end 2005

[8] Census data as of 14 March 1991 and 18 March 2001; 2007: Eurostat estimation

[9] Triandafyllidou and Maroufof (2008) estimation april 2008

[10] 2001 value is the sum of residence permits and permits to stay; 2007 value is the sum of residence permits, extended permits to stay (*autorizacão de permanência prorrogada*), granted long-term visas (*visto de longa duracão concedido*) and extended long-term visas (*visto de longa duracão prorrogado*)

[11] Census data as of 16 March 1991 and 12 March 2001; 2007 data on residence permits (*estatuto legal de residente – autorizacões de residência*)

[12] Legal residents, holders of visas and estimate of irregular immigrants (Lusa 2008)

Sources: Own elaboration from national statistical sources

The increase recorded for the stocks of foreigners in Spain is even more marked. Permit-to-stay holders and usual residents, who numbered less than 400,000, grew to almost 4 million and over 5.2 million, respectively. The latter value includes also illegal migrants. The percentage of foreigners in the Spanish population grew from less than 1 per cent in 1991 to 8.6 per cent and 11.3 per cent, respectively, for the two groups in question. High levels – in terms of percentage – of immigrants within the total population were recorded in Greece as well, with 7.9 per cent of residents and 9.8 per cent of total immigrants, including legal and estimated illegal presences. The number of regular foreigners in Greece's case was around 900,000, while the stock reached almost 1.1 million if irregular migrants are included. In Portugal, legal foreign immigration was almost 450,000, or around 4.2 per cent of the total population. These values would increase to 500,000 and 4.7 per cent, respectively, if an estimate of irregular immigrants was added.

By and large, labour migration and family migration have constituted the two main flows entering Southern Europe in the last 25 years. Southern European countries, generally speaking, do not seem to be countries of asylum and do not attract a large number of foreign students. Statistical evidence drawn from different sources, including the national census and registers of permits to stay and of residence permits, confirms these characteristics.

The main reasons for migration (work and family reunion) have a significant effect on the demographic structure of immigration flows. In fact, the first working-age cohorts (20-39 years old) generally accounted for the majority of all immigrants, while the share of the youngest population (less than twenty years old) usually fluctuated around 20 to 30 per cent of the total. The immigration of foreigners aged 60 or older accounted for a negligible share of total arrivals in Italy, while the percentages recorded in Spain and Portugal are higher, likely attributable to the relevance of retirement migration into these two countries.

The gender structure of foreign immigration flows has been relatively balanced in recent years. In Italy and Portugal, women have generally predominated in the current decade, while in Spain their share of the total has oscillated between 45 and 48 per cent. However, this statistic can reflect deep imbalances in the gender composition of the different national groups, in some cases in favour of men and in other cases in favour of women.

5.2.2 *Main nationalities and their evolution*

The evolution of foreign immigration in terms of area of origin is characterised by an increase in the size and proportion of immigration from CEE countries and from the Third World, and a corresponding reduction in the percentage from developed countries, despite its increase in absolute terms

(Table 5.2a, b). Alongside these two main common trends, the situation presents important and interesting differences between the Southern European countries. In fact, each country has a specific area of attraction, usually as a result of its geographical position, its history, its colonial heritage (if it exists) and its cultural and linguistic links with other countries.

Italy is probably the country where that collection of factors has been the least important. The proportion of foreigners from More Developed Countries (MDCs) fell from 32.7 per cent of the total in 1991 to 5.9 per cent in 2007. At the same time, immigration from CEE countries exhibited an extraordinary increase: from the period 1991-2007 it increased 30.2-fold, totalling more than 1.6 million and representing 47 per cent of the immigration total. There was also a strong but lesser-marked increase in immigration from developing countries, rising from 186,000 in 1991 to 1.6 million in 2007, and signalling a reduction from 52.3 to 47 per cent of the total. In the current decade, there is a clear prevalence of Romanians, Albanians and Moroccans, as well as a gradual stabilisation of many other previously numerous communities.

In Spain and Portugal, the level of immigration from MDCs has always been higher than in Italy, as a result of the greater significance of retirement migration. In 2007, it still accounted for 22.2 per cent of the total in Spain and for 24.8 per cent in Portugal. In these two countries, immigration from CEE is less significant than in Italy, although Romanians have become the biggest immigrant community in Spain, and Ukrainians constitute the third-largest immigrant community in Portugal. The main characteristic of the Spanish migration model is the large inflow from Latin America. The tightening of the United States' immigration policies after 9/11 probably contributed to directing the flows caused by the economic crises that troubled several Latin American countries to Europe (Pellegrino 2004). Linguistic and cultural bonds with the region due to Spain's colonial past probably constituted the main factors for migrants' choosing Spain as a preferred destination.

As regards Portugal, a marked increase in immigration from the CEE countries has appeared in the last decade. Until the end of the 1990s, immigration flows into the country were mostly reflective of its colonial past and had developed a specific migration 'system', unified by the Portuguese language.[6] The reasons for this 'Eastern revolution' are probably related to Portugal's EU membership and to the enlargement of the European migration system. The largest immigrant groups in the country are from Cape Verde, Brazil and Ukraine.

Some basic facts distinguish Greece's recent migratory trends from those observed in the rest of Southern Europe. First, a dramatic increase in the immigrant population has occurred despite a great number of 'administrative deportations' (2.2 million in the period 1992-2001), carried out with the intention of dissuading immigrant settlement. Forced circular migration

Table 5.2a Foreign resident population by geographical areas[1] and main countries of citizenship, Southern European immigration countries, 1991, 2001 and 2007 (absolute values in thousands and percentages by citizenship and of females) (Greece and Italy)

Main countries of citizenship	Greece			Main countries of citizenship	Italy		
	Number (thousands)	% by citizenship	% females		Number (thousands)	% by citizenship	% females
1991 Census				**1991 Census**			
Total	167.3	100.0	46.4	Total	356.2	100.0	47.1
MDCs	77.7	46.4	54.4	MDCs	116.5	32.7	59.3
CEE	49.8	29.8	37.8	CEE	53.5	15.0	48.9
LDCs	39.8	23.8	41.6	LDCs	186.2	52.3	38.9
Albania	20.6	12.3	29.7	Morocco	39.9	11.2	19.0
Cyprus	14.7	8.8	48.6	Germany	22.7	6.4	60.8
US	13.9	8.3	50.9	Former Yugoslavia	17.1	4.8	46.3
Russian Federation	12.9	7.7	49.5	Tunisia	16.7	4.7	21.9
Turkey	11.1	6.6	51.1	France	15.8	4.4	64.0
2001 Census				**2001 Census**			
Total	762.2	100.0	45.5	Total	1,334.9	100.0	50.5
MDCs	83.9	11.0	56.6	MDCs	180.9	13.5	63.9
CEE	577.4	75.8	45.2	CEE	436.7	32.7	50.9
LDCs	100.9	13.2	37.8	LDCs	717.3	53.7	46.9
Albania	438.0	57.5	41.3	Morocco	180.1	13.5	39.8
Bulgaria	35.1	4.6	60.4	Albania	173.1	13.0	43.7
Georgia	22.9	3.0	57.0	Romania	74.9	5.6	53.5
Romania	22.0	2.9	43.4	Philippines	54.0	4.0	61.1
US	18.1	2.4	51.5	Former Yugoslavia	49.3	3.7	46.8

2005 Permits to stay[2]				2007 Population registers (Anagrafe)			
Total	692.4	100.0	37.7	Total	3,432.7	100.0	50.4
MDCs	..	..	..	MDCs	201.1	5.9	59.9
CEE	605.0	87.4	38.5	CEE	1,614.9	47.0	54.4
LDCs	87.4	12.6	31.9	LDCs	1,616.7	47.1	45.3
Albania	481.7	69.6	31.4	Romania	625.3	18.2	52.9
Bulgaria	44.0	6.4	65.2	Albania	401.9	11.7	44.7
Romania	25.4	3.7	47.2	Morocco	365.9	10.7	40.8
Ukraine	19.8	2.9	81.7	China	156.5	4.6	47.3
Pakistan	15.8	2.3	1.2	Ukraine	132.7	3.9	80.4

[1] MDCs include North America, Japan, Israel, Oceania and other countries of Europe, excluding former socialist countries; CEE includes former socialist countries of Europe and Turkey; Less Developed Countries (LDCs) include Africa, Latin America and Asia (except Japan and Israel).

[2] Citizens of MDCs are not considered because of their strong underestimation (only 3,569). In addition, the register accounted for only 3,366 people under age fifteen (less than 0.5 per cent of the total).

Sources: Own elaboration from national statistical sources.

Table 5.2b *Foreign resident population by geographical areas[1] and main countries of citizenship, Southern European immigration countries, 1991, 2001 and 2007 (absolute values in thousands and percentages by citizenship and of females) (Portugal and Spain))*

Main countries of citizenship	Portugal			Main countries of citizenship	Spain		
	Number (thousands)	% by citizenship	% females		Number (thousands)	% by citizenship	% females
1991 Census				**1991 Census**			
Total	106.6	100.0	50.4	Total	353.4	100.0	51.1
MDCs	43.2	40.6	52.0	MDCs	219.8	62.2	52.5
CEE	2.3	2.1	50.7	CEE	4.0	1.1	48.0
LDCs	61.1	57.3	49.3	LDCs	129.6	36.7	48.9
Cape Verde	15.7	14.7	45.5	UK	53.6	15.2	52.5
France	13.7	12.9	53.6	Germany	34.0	9.6	53.2
Brazil	13.5	12.7	53.0	Morocco	31.4	8.9	38.7
Angola	9.4	8.8	54.8	Portugal	27.8	7.9	51.0
Venezuela	8.5	7.9	46.6	France	24.2	6.9	58.0
2001 Census				**2001 Population registers (Padrón)**			
Total	232.7	100.0	45.8	Total	1,977.9	100.0	47.0
MDCs	64.1	27.5	50.7	MDCs	541.3	27.4	49.4
CEE	20.5	8.8	23.5	CEE	187.8	9.5	44.8
LDCs	148.2	63.7	46.8	LDCs	1,248.8	63.1	46.3
Angola	37.0	15.9	49.1	Morocco	307.5	15.5	32.9
Cape Verde	33.1	14.2	48.7	Ecuador	259.5	13.1	50.7
Brazil	31.9	13.7	46.8	Colombia	191.0	9.7	57.6
Guinea-Bissau	15.8	6.8	37.3	UK	128.1	6.5	50.6
France	15.4	6.6	54.1	Germany	113.8	5.8	50.3

2007 Legal residents (SEF)				2007 Population registers (Padrón)			
Total	401.6	100.0	45.3	Total	5,220.6	100.0	46.8
MDCs	99.7	24.8	46.9	MDCs	1,160.0	22.2	46.8
CEE	79.2	19.7	41.9	CEE	1,180.3	22.6	47.3
LDCs	222.7	55.5	45.8	LDCs	2,880.3	55.2	46.6
Cape Verde	61.1	15.2	44.9	Romania	729.0	14.0	46.3
Brazil	55.7	13.9	52.8	Morocco	644.7	12.3	36.7
Ukraine	34.2	8.5	38.6	Ecuador	420.1	8.0	50.8
Angola	30.4	7.6	46.3	UK	351.9	6.7	49.2
UK	23.6	5.9	47.2	Colombia	280.7	5.4	55.6

[1] MDCs include North America, Japan, Israel, Oceania and other countries of Europe, excluding former socialist countries; CEE includes former socialist countries of Europe and Turkey; Less Developed Countries (LDCs) include Africa, Latin America and Asia (except Japan and Israel).

[2] Citizens of MDCs are not considered because of their strong underestimation (only 3,569). In addition, the register accounted for only 3,366 people under age fifteen (less than 0.5 per cent of the total).

Sources: Own elaboration from national statistical sources.

was a common pattern for Albanians. Second, one national group (Albanians) represent about 70 per cent of the whole foreign presence. No similar level of prevalence of nationals from a single source country is found in the other three Southern European countries considered here. More generally, the proximity of the sending countries distinguishes the Greek migration experience, as even other important immigrant groups (Bulgarians and Romanians) come from neighbouring countries. Finally, Greece is the Southern European country most often sought out by refugees (especially Iraqis and Afghans arriving from Turkey). Initially considered only as a country of transit, Greece has become more and more attractive to asylum seekers, especially as other EU countries restricted asylum policies.

5.3   Immigrants and the labour market

5.3.1   The strength of labour demand

Economic immigration has long been the main channel of entry and eventual residence of foreign immigrants in Greece, Italy, Portugal and Spain. Together with the age profile of immigrants, this contributes to the fact that the employment rate of foreign immigrants is high compared to other Northern and Western European host countries. According to OECD (2008) data for foreign- and native-born populations in 2006, immigrants in Greece, Italy, Portugal and Spain exhibit higher employment rates than natives. This is the case for both male and female immigrants. Generally, however, the unemployment situation for foreigners is relatively less favourable than it is for natives. Vulnerability to unemployment also seems to be lower for immigrant men than for women. Recent evidence suggests that the over-representation of immigrants in unemployment statistics mostly occurs in periods of economic recession (Martin 2009).

The strong association immigration has with the labour market in Southern Europe results from a number of factors. From an economic point of view, these include periods of rapid economic expansion (often resulting from an injection of EU funds); an economic fabric largely based in labour-intensive sectors; the seasonal character of many industries (such as agriculture and tourism); the non-transferability of many of the fast-growing industries (activities such as construction and services cannot be delocalised); the high segmentation of the labour market; the increase in flexible labour arrangements; and the importance of the informal economy. These factors correspond to a combination of country-specific characteristics and general traits of the post-Fordist context.

One of the most impactful factors is the informal economy. The extent of informal arrangements has been growing in all post-Fordist economies, but their longer histories in Southern Europe have made the region's economies more prone to informality. A study by Friedrich Schneider and Robert Klinglmair (2004) confirms that the relevance of the informal economy is a common characteristic of Southern European countries, where its volume far exceeds those of other OECD countries. The authors estimated that the size of the shadow economy in the period 2002-2003 was about 28.3 per cent of GDP in Greece, 26.2 per cent of GDP in Italy and 22.3 per cent of GDP in Portugal and Spain. Since foreigners are over-represented in this sector, it has typically provided a privileged route of entry for labour migrants, regular and irregular (Baganha 1998; Reyneri 1998; Mingione & Quassoli 2000; Fakiolas 2000).

From a social point of view, the native population's living standards and educational levels have increased in recent decades – largely coinciding with women's emancipation – and natives began refusing to work in less desirable jobs (King, Lazaridis & Tsardanidis 2000). In addition to fulfilling these roles, immigrants have been supplying services that have often not been available in the weak welfare regimes of Southern European countries. That is, their welfare systems provide little direct assistance and thus rely heavily on family members to care for the young, the elderly and others in need of assistance. To alleviate this burden, families have begun relying on immigrants to fulfil tasks such as housekeeping, babysitting and caring for the elderly (Sciortino 2004). In sum, constraints related to the welfare state have contributed to the strength of labour demand in these countries.

Demographic factors such as low fertility rates, high life expectancy and the related ageing of the population have also contributed to this situation. On the one hand, a shrinking population is linked to a diminished labour supply. On the other, the amount of care-related work is increasing as a result of the population's ageing. It can therefore be reasonably foreseen that quantitative labour shortages and the demand for care-related services not only will continue but will exhibit significant growth as well.

5.3.2 *Main occupational sectors and working conditions*

The economic incorporation of foreign immigrants in Southern Europe often occurs in low-skilled jobs and under precarious conditions. Immigrants are often employed in a few specific sectors, usually in less stable, less paid and less protected jobs (the so-called 3D jobs: dirty, dangerous and demeaning), which correspond to the least-protected parts of a highly segmented labour market (the secondary labour market, in dual labour market theory terms). For all Southern European countries, data for economic sectors indicate that immigrants are usually employed in the service sector (mainly domestic work, retail trade, hotels and restaurants), construction, manufacturing and agriculture.

According to OECD data on foreign-born employment in the period 2005-2006 (OECD 2008), the construction sector is quite important in all four countries, representing 29.1 per cent of the total foreign-born employment in Greece, 19.7 per cent in Spain, 14.8 per cent in Portugal and 14.2 per cent in Italy. Mining, manufacturing and the energy sector are particularly relevant for Italy, where they together represent 23.6 per cent of total foreign-born employment, known to be concentrated in the Central and Northern industrial regions. By contrast, the same sectors are less important in Greece (15.4 per cent), Portugal (13.8 per cent) and Spain (13.0 per cent). The service sector (mainly wholesale and retail trade, hotels and restaurants and domestic work) is also an important recruiter of immigrants in all four countries. Hotels and restaurants account for 14.2 per cent in Spain, 10.2 per cent in Greece, 8.7 per cent in Italy and 8.2 per cent in Portugal. Households (domestic services) account for 13.9 per cent in Greece, 13.3 per cent in Spain, 10.4 per cent in Italy and 4.9 per cent in Portugal (although these data are decidedly under-evaluated). Finally, employment in agriculture is also considerable, although its significance has been declining in recent years: data for the period 2005-2006 show that, of total foreign-born employment, the agriculture and fishing sector account for 6.2 per cent in Greece, 5.6 per cent in Spain, 3.5 per cent in Italy and 2.0 per cent in Portugal.

Immigrants' overqualification also seems to be a general trend in these countries. The lack of employment opportunities in their trades forces migrants to accept jobs that often do not correspond to their qualifications. Comparative ratios show that immigrant overqualification, as compared to that of the native population, is substantial in the countries of Southern Europe (OECD 2006). There are differences among immigrant groups, since educational levels vary by nationality. It is mainly in the case of Eastern European immigrants that there is a considerable mismatch between educational level and type of work.

Closely related to these employment patterns, the working conditions of most immigrants are poor. This applies to, among other factors, salaries and contractual arrangements. Immigrants tend to earn less than the native-born. In all countries, temporary work has been expanding over the years. The probability of getting a temporary job is also greater for immigrants than for the native population. Temporary work is often seen as one method for satisfying certain labour shortages, especially low-skilled ones, without admitting large numbers of workers into sectors that may eventually be subject to significant structural change. This reality reflects the greater precariousness that immigrants have to face in the labour market. According to OECD data, the share of temporary jobs among immigrants is nearly 45 per cent in Spain and almost 30 per cent in Portugal, i.e. respectively 20 and 16 percentage points more than for the native population (OECD 2006: 58).

Finally, as regards complementarity or substitution/competition with natives' employment, the former is by far the most prevalent. This has already been well established by former comparative studies on immigrants' insertion into Southern European labour markets. For example, Emilio Reyneri and Maria Baganha (2001: 49) stated that:

> [...] in segmented labour markets, such as those of the Southern European countries, migrant workers are in competition only with marginal sectors of the domestic labour supply and/or in narrow occupational areas [...]. Conflicts between migrants and the local population only seldom concern labour market problems.

5.4 Irregular migration and regularisation processes

5.4.1 The size and determinants of irregular stocks

The challenge of irregular immigration affects several countries in Europe. However, it is in Southern Europe that the number of irregular migrants is particularly high.[7] Since the 1990s, irregular migration has been perceived as a chronic disease of Southern European migration regimes. It would likely be no exaggeration if we affirmed that most foreigners now living legally in Southern European countries experienced a significant period of irregularity before getting their first residence permit. For this reason, estimation of the size of irregular migration became a priority for national governments and the European institutions. Admittedly, estimating irregular foreign population is not an easy task, though there have been efforts to provide reliable estimates of irregular foreigners. The frequent regularisation processes carried out in almost all Southern European countries, for instance, provide reliable figures about the presence of irregular migrants. In addition, various other research groups have provided additional estimates based on other available sources.

In Spain, based on information provided by the Padrón Municipal register, Joaquín Recaño and Andreu Domingo (2005) tried, quite successfully, to estimate irregularity before the regularisation of 2005.[8] Similar efforts have been made by other Spanish researchers such as, for instance, Alonso Pajares (2006), Lorenzo Cachón (2007) and Héctor Cebolla and Amparo Gonzalez (2008). Most of these researchers agreed that there had been about 900,000 irregular migrants before the 2005 regularisation. According to Cebolla and Gonzalez (2008), the irregularity rate reached its peak in 2003, when 53 per cent of the foreign population was estimated to be irregular. The percentage decreased after the 2005 regularisation and the entry of Romania and Bulgaria into the EU.

In Italy, there have been several attempts to estimate the number of irregular migrants (Table 5.3). The estimates provided by Gian Carlo

Blangiardo (2009) suggest a very high level of irregularity at the end of the 1990s and a decrease afterwards. Things changed significantly after the 2002 regularisation and the entry of Bulgaria and Romania into the EU in 2007. The impact of the European enlargement worked as a de facto regularisation in the case of Romanian immigrants. However, according to more recent figures, the number of irregular migrants has been increasing again.

Table 5.3   *Estimates of immigrants and irregular migrants in Italy*

Author[1]	Year	Immigrants	Irregular migrants	
		(thousands)	thousands	%
Natale (1986)	1985	523-725	97-299	19-41
Birindelli (1990)	1990	824	140	17
ISTAT (1991)	1990	1,144	623	55
Blangiardo (1997)[2]	1995	833-912	344-423	41-46
Natale and Strozza (1997)	1995	1,146	431	36
Blangiardo (1998)[2,3]	1998	982-1,101	176-295	18-27
Blangiardo (2006)[2,4]	2005	3,357	541	16
Blangiardo (2008)	2007	3,982	349	9

[1] Unless stated otherwise, values at beginning of year
[2] Only citizens of CEE and Third World countries
[3] 15 April
[4] 1 July
Sources: Strozza (2004) and some of the authors indicated in the table.

Recent estimates of the irregular migrant presence in Greece suggest numbers close to 200,000. More specifically, Anna Triandafyllidou and Michaela Maroufof (2008) estimate the number of irregular migrants to be at 167,000; Theodore Lianos and his co-authors (2008) suggest that irregular migrants in Greece range between 172,000 and 209,000; and Thanos Maroukis (2009) arrives at an estimate of 205,000 irregular migrants living in Greece in 2007. In Portugal, official institutions have recently provided an estimate of irregular migration levels, suggesting a number of 50,000 (Lusa 2008).

The presence of irregular migrants in Southern European countries has often been explained by the existence of weak external controls, by the countries' inexperience with immigration and by geographic positions that favour clandestine entries (Baldwin-Edwards 1999). A phenomenon like irregular migration, however, cannot be explained through unilateral cause-effect relationships. As a matter of fact, the question of irregularity is part of a more general analysis of the mechanisms of international migration. Irregularity is brought about, first of all, by the intersection of immigration regulations with large migration flows, and reflects what Douglas Massey (1999) has called the 'post-modern' paradox between global forces and restrictive policy rules. In this respect, irregular migration is the product of several factors, according to what could be summarised as an 'equation of irregularity' based on the intensity of the flows, restrictive regulations, the attractiveness of the informal economy, geographic proximity, the quality of controls and the activities of the smuggling industry (Arango 2005). All these aspects have been particularly important for the development of irregular migration systems in Southern Europe.

As will be elaborated in the next section, Southern European admission policies were characterised by a high degree of restrictiveness and inflexibility that hampered effective controls of the flows. As a consequence, they have been unable to craft or enforce efficient regulation, despite having acknowledged the necessity of foreign labour. The informal economy acts as a strong magnet for irregular migrants, and becomes an increasingly important element within the development of irregular migration systems (Reyneri 1998). That is why internal labour market controls are imbued with a particular significance in the struggle against irregular migration. As a matter of fact, the size of the informal economy corresponds to the weakness of labour market controls in all four of the Southern European countries.

Along with the pull factor posed by the informal economy, the presence of irregular migrants has clearly been bolstered by the geographic positioning of Southern European countries and their difficulties controlling their maritime borders. The increase of migration flows into Southern Europe coincided with the necessity of protecting common European borders after the coming into force of the Schengen Agreement.[9] Their relative lack of experience in dealing with inflows and exposed sea borders prompted a certain degree of mistrust of the Southern European member states, which was also encouraged by the media effect of 'boat people' arriving on their coasts. Smuggling also played a role. Smuggling networks in Spain have been very active and flexible. In the last couple of years, they have shifted their main routes from the Strait of Gibraltar to the Canary Islands, due to more intensive controls in the Mediterranean area. In Italy, networks seem to be particularly active on the Southern coasts, exploiting the Libyan route, because of the Spanish authorities' efforts to control the Moroccan channel. In the case of Greece, smugglers are active at sea and land borders, ranging from small informal networks to several more mafia-like organisations. Almost everywhere, smuggling networks seem to be flexible organisations that are able to adapt very quickly to the defensive strategies adopted by the nation-states (Pastore, Monzini & Sciortino 2006; Coslovi 2007; Carling 2007).

However, most evidence suggests that irregular immigration in Southern Europe usually begins with overstaying and not with a clandestine entry (see e.g. ENI-survey 2008 and Pastore et al. 2006). Where this is the case, several favourable visa conditions come into play. Today's visa policies and their effects are not a consequence of national decisions, but rather of

European policies, which identify the countries whose citizens need a visa to enter the Schengen space. However, visa policy is also embedded in the interests of each country and the migration systems in which they are involved. Some countries might thus be more generous or liberal than others because of economic and historical ties with a sending country. Most irregular migration systems in Portugal consist, for instance, of over-stayers proceeding from the PALOP countries, Eastern Europe and Brazil. Furthermore, the existence of the Schengen space allows 'false tourists' to move around Europe with a visa obtained by the foreign representation of one EU member state, a process often fuelled by smuggling networks. This was for example the case of Ukrainian immigrants who obtained their visas from Germany and subsequently moved to Italy, Spain and Portugal, where they could find a job in the construction and domestic service sectors (Finotelli & Sciortino 2006).

Finally, irregular migration in Southern Europe has been perceived favourably by the native population and administration. Indeed, living as an irregular is significantly easier in Southern than in Northern Europe. In most Southern European countries, irregular migrants have access to com-pulsory education and basic health services. Nevertheless, irregular mi-grants remain in a precarious position and represent a challenge to the con-trol capacity of the state.

5.4.2   Regularisations as ex post regulation instruments

The regularisation of irregular immigrants is, of course, not a Southern European peculiarity. Many European countries had to resort to a regular-isation at least once in their migration history. However, there are few doubts that the majority of such processes were carried out in Southern Europe (De Bruycker & Apap 2000).[10] For this reason, regularisations have often been considered proof of the Southern European 'public ambi-guity' towards irregular migration and for the Southern incapacity to con-trol migration (Brochmann 1993; Baldwin-Edwards 1999).[11] As a matter of fact, the lack of efficient recruitment procedures turned regularisations into the most useful way to 'repair' a posteriori the structural mismatches of most Southern European migration regimes (Arango & Jachimowicz 2005). Since the 1980s, six regularisation processes have been instituted in Spain, while the Italian and Portuguese governments carried out five regu-larisations in the same period.[12] In Greece, regularisations are a more re-cent phenomenon, since the first one was executed in 1998, followed by two others in 2001 and the period 2005-2006 (Table 5.4).

Regularisations have come to represent, both at the national and at the international level, a very controversial issue, one whose necessity is downplayed by the majority of the political parties. Nevertheless, in past years, regularisations were not linked to a particular government majority

Table 5.4 *Overview of regularisation dates in Southern European migration regimes, 1985-2007*

Spain	Italy	Greece	Portugal
1985	1986	-	1992-1993
1991	1990	-	1996
1996	1995	-	2001
2000	1998	1998	2003
2001	2002	2001	2004
2005	(2006)	2005-2006	(2007)

Source: Own elaboration

in all Southern European countries. Both left- and right-wing governments carried out various regularisations in all countries (González-Enríquez & Triandafyllidou 2009). Moreover, regularisation processes in each country exhibit a certain degree of periodicity, though all of them were touted as exceptional 'one-time-only' measures by the national governments. In the absence of effective recruitment systems, they soon became part of the regulation system, used to 'repair' the lack of an efficient migration policy.

Italy and Spain regularised the highest number of irregular migrants, not only in all of Southern Europe, but also as compared to other European countries (Table 5.5). In Spain, about 1.2 million foreigners have been regularised since 1986, and half of them after the regularisation of 2005 – which was, without a doubt, the most successful regularisation ever carried out in the country. Italy's case is similar. Irregularity increased after the surge in the inflows between 1998 and 2002 and the largest number of people was hence regularised in 2002.

Table 5.5 *Results of regularisation processes in Southern Europe*

Years	Italy	Spain	Greece	Portugal
1985-1990	322,626	34,832		-
1991-1995	244,492	109,135		39,166
1996-2000	217,124	221,748	370,000 (white card) 220,000 (green card)	35,082
2001-2007	634,728 (470,000)[1]	811,049		183,833[2]

[1] Number refers to the 'decree on flows' of 2006 that worked as a de facto or 'undeclared' regularisation of irregular immigrants who were already living in the country (Finotelli & Sciortino 2009).

[2] Data refer only to the 2001 regularisation, while data about the 2003 and 2004 regularisations and the 2007 ongoing process are very scarce.

Source: Own elaboration

Assessing the effects of regularisation processes is not a simple task, as there have not been enough empirical studies to provide an adequate answer. Nevertheless, some studies conducted in Italy and Spain uncovered some positive aspects. Given the restrictive and often inadequate effects of migration legislation, regularisations are likely to have allowed the legal inclusion and stabilisation of a large part of foreign residents, despite the inherent insecurity of the residence permits that were issued. Since 1986, 1.4 million immigrants received their residence permits through a regularisation process in Italy. According to Massimo Carfagna (2002) and Blangiardo (2004), the majority of immigrants regularised in Italy retained their legal status afterwards. Furthermore, it seems that the number of those who lost their residence permits and applied for several regularisation processes is rather insignificant. The case of Spain seems to be quite similar, as regularisations contributed to the inclusion of almost half of the foreign population (Arango & Finotelli 2009). Furthermore, recent studies carried out to assess the effects of regularisation processes in Spain demonstrate that such processes could serve to reduce the irregularity rate (Recaño & Domingo 2005; Pajares 2006; Cachón 2007; Cebolla & Gonzalez 2008; Arango & Finotelli 2009). There seem to be no analogous research results in Portugal and Greece. In Greece, however, the general assumption is that the number of reapplications in each process is rather high, since the legal status obtained in the various regularisations is lost rapidly.

Nevertheless, asserting that regularisations were able to 'stabilise' a large part of the foreign population in most Southern European countries does not mean they are a panacea against irregularity. All in all, regularisations do not substitute for an efficient immigration policy. They remain a regulation tool a posteriori, and there is no doubt that national governments cannot tackle the issue of irregular migration without seriously improving their migration policies. Real progress against irregularity can only be made if each national migration regime acts on the elements that factor heavily in the equation of irregularity. For this reason, both the Spanish and the Portuguese governments considered their most recent regularisations to be necessary and exceptional decisions to 'clean up the state' before carrying out wider legislative reforms of their migration regimes. In both countries, 'stigmatised' regularisation processes have been substituted by discrete and individual regularisation forms.[13] These important policy changes break with the mechanisms of the past and seem to be related to, among other factors, the improvement of the labour recruitment policies and control systems in recent years.

5.1 Admission and integration policies

5.5.1 Labour migration policies

During the first years of Southern European immigration history, Greece, Italy, Portugal and Spain developed a set of legislation more focused on administrative issues related to entry and residence than on the concept of effective regulatory instruments. The development and improvement of immigration laws of that type was one of the requirements that Greece, Portugal and Spain had to meet, like Italy at that time, for their European membership or prospects of membership in the EU. More sophisticated regulation and control mechanisms would mostly be enacted after the early 1990s, when massive inflows began to occur in some of these countries: first Italy and Greece, then Spain and Portugal.

The intensification of immigration flows, the awareness of an unmet demand for labour and the volume of irregular migration contributed to the development of several mechanisms of labour recruitment. As part of the broader objective of regulating the labour market, these mechanisms constituted an attempt to formulate an economic migration management policy that would allow for the legal admission of labour immigrants and the crackdown of irregular migration. As described above, these instruments paralleled the enactment of several regularisation schemes. Despite their tentative character and many failures, it can be argued that some of those policy initiatives were novel, especially in the EU context. In a sense, they were precursors of the EU's later statement on the need for immigration in the European economies. For example, it was only in 2000 that the then EU Commissioner for Justice and Home Affairs, António Vitorino, stated that 'the zero immigration policies of the past 25 years are not working', urging for 'new legal ways for immigrants to enter the EU' (quoted after Martin, Martin & Weil 2006: 74-75).

The legal channels of immigrants' labour recruitment differed across time and from country to country, though at least part of the rationale behind them could be considered similar. Whether they were invitation schemes, quota systems or shortage lists, they were designed to regulate future labour immigration and avoid the need for further regularisations. These systems were usually based on labour market needs (domestic skill and labour shortages) and on labour market tests (or checks), which gave preference to natives and other resident citizens to fill a job vacancy. As the recurrent increase of irregular immigration confirms, the regulating effect of these policies has been negligible.

When considered in detail in each Southern European country, the process of constructing labour admission policies is lengthy and cumbersome. In the early stages, a system of individual nomination or invitation of immigrants was coupled with the principle of labour market tests, whereby the native, the EU and the legal third-country nationals' resident workforce would be protected and given priority in employment. In the mid-1980s, Spain was the first to introduce a labour recruitment procedure coupled with a labour market test system. The Foreigners Bill of 1985 allowed the hiring of migrants who submitted a nominal request to the general regime known as the Regímen General. However, the bureaucratic procedure to hire a migrant was very complex and most employers preferred employing their workers irregularly. In 1986, Italy also introduced a nominal request procedure and a labour market test system – neither of which was successful. The rule soon turned out to be too restrictive to deal with actual inflows. A system based on an invitation scheme known as *metaklisi* has been in place in Greece since 1991, and the requirement to protect local workers has also been enacted (Emke-Poulopoulou 2007). This policy for labour migration, still in place today, is a rather complex one and its results have been far from initial expectations.

In a later stage, systems based on labour market quotas (or their equivalent) were common to all Southern countries. Italy (1990)[14] and Spain (1993) were the first to introduce this kind of system, followed by Greece (2001) and Portugal (2001). In Italy in 1990, a new law (Martelli law) introduced the principle of immigrant inflow control (the 'intended number', *numero programmato*) and, in 1995, a limited number of quotas was introduced. The Consolidation Act of 1998 on immigration and the status of foreigners (the Turco-Napolitano Law) and its amendment in 2002 improved the system. Every year, the Italian government, with one or more decrees, had to set the maximum quota of foreigners allowed to enter. The number was to be proportional to the needs of the Italian labour market (the necessary data was provided by the Ministry of Labour) and to the residence permits already issued for family reunification or for reasons of temporary social protection. The recruitment of foreign workers within this legal framework never worked properly. It was mainly used to regularise immigrants who were already living and working in the country.

In Spain in 1993, along with the system of nominal requests, the government introduced labour entry quotas known as *contingente*. The immigration quotas were published yearly by the Ministry of Labour, after consultations with the trade unions and employer associations. Again, the *contingente* never turned into an effective policy regulation instrument and came to be used to legalise irregular migrants already living in Spain. Other problems existed in the Spanish labour recruitment approach, such as poor communication between the central and the autonomic government (Aparicio & Roig 2006) and the fact that the *contingente* and the nominal request system constituted 'blind' recruitment tools that did not take into account that an employment relationship usually begins on the basis of trust and mutual knowledge.[15]

Greece and Portugal followed this 'quota trend' in 2001. The Greek Immigration Law of 2001 established an administrative procedure for the issuing of stay permits for the purpose of employment, based on a plan crafted each year by the Organisation for the Employment of the Labour Force (OAED), which outlined the domestic labour market needs per sector and area. The system was improved in 2005, although the underlying principle was the same. Nevertheless, the main problem of the Greek approach lay in the *metaklisi* system, a procedure that remained extremely complex and time-consuming. In particular, long waiting periods are disadvantageous to small firms, which, more than other businesses, need quick and flexible entry policies.[16] In Portugal in 2001, a system of quotas for immigrant recruitment following a report on domestic labour shortages was also created. The number of visas was to match the job vacancies detected in various economic sectors (the quotas), according to a report drafted annually by the Institute of Employment and Vocational Training (IEFP). The system was a complex, bureaucratic and largely ineffective procedure and has not helped in the fight against irregular immigration.

Taking all these labour recruitment policies together, it is clear that their degree of restrictiveness and their complex administrative requirements were unfit for dealing with the high demand for labour and vast immigrant supply, and they were overall ineffective at regulating inflows and limiting irregular immigration. Given these constraints, regularisation policies often became a type of last resort for regulating the immigrants' insertion into the labour market.

Because of the inefficacy of these systems, some countries have profoundly changed their labour immigration policies in recent years in order to develop more efficient systems to meet the labour market needs. Spain is the most advanced country in this respect. In 2004, concurrent with the announcement of the large regularisation of 2005, the Spanish government approved a new Regulation Act to make the recruitment procedure of labour immigrants more flexible. The regulation re-established de facto the possibility of hiring foreign workers in their countries of origin through a nominal offer in the Regímen General. As in all immigration host countries, the employment of a foreign worker following these kinds of procedures still depends on a previously conducted labour market test. To make the recruitment easier, every three months the 'Catalogo de trabajos de dificil cobertura' ('Catalogue of hard-to-fill positions') is published, specifying the types of jobs for which there are usually no available candidates (be they Spanish citizens or from other EU countries). For these jobs, no labour market test is required. If an employer is looking to fill a vacancy listed in this catalogue, he or she can immediately begin the recruitment procedure.

The *contingente* remains another important admission channel in Spain. Furthermore, new regulations have introduced the 'entry visa for job search'. The purpose of this type of visa was to promote further flexibility within the recruiting procedures. However, the ability to apply for such a visa was restricted to a limited number of sectors, such as the domestic sector. Very few visas have been issued for this purpose since the approval of the regulation. Finally, Spain is involved in a series of bilateral agreements with various sending countries, which are effective in providing long- or short-term workers to the Spanish labour market. However, the recent economic crisis affecting the country has not permitted a full testing of these measures.

5.5.2   Control policies

Migration control policies developed quickly in the Southern European countries in reaction to relatively massive initial inflows into Italy and Greece (in the late 1980s and early 1990s), followed by Spain and Portugal (from the late 1990s onward). Border and internal control policies developed to at least some extent due to pressure from the EU, which insisted that Southern European countries should stop being an easy route for irregular migrants to travel into Northern and Western Europe. There are other, more substantive factors, however, that have largely shaped the practices and policies of migration control in the region. These include the geographical morphology of these countries, their strategic position on Mediterranean migration pathways (and Portugal on the Southern portion of the European Atlantic coast), the operation of smuggling networks, the countries' lack of previous immigration experience and their large informal economies, which provide abundant irregular employment opportunities for immigrants.

Moreover, all four countries are important tourism destinations, which make strict border controls more difficult to implement – especially during peak tourism seasons. At the same time, some of these countries' prospective immigrants (in Spain and Portugal in particular) are or have been exempted from visa requirements because of their Latin American or Luso-speaking origins. Finally, vast amounts of irregular migration take place throughout the Schengen space. For example, as seen above, many Eastern European immigrants cross the continent using Schengen tourist visas in order to get through the Pyrenees to Spain and Portugal. These facts make border enforcement very difficult in practical terms.

Adding to the difficulties of any border control mechanism, Southern European countries have long sea borders along the Mediterranean. Tiny islands like Lampedusa between Sicily and North Africa, the Greek islands of Chios and Lesvos in the Aegean Sea and the Canary Islands in the Atlantic have become hubs for dinghies and other types of illegal small boat traffic, caused by desperate irregular immigrants from Asia and Africa. Despite the sophisticated technological equipment being used by border control authorities, intercepting all such arrivals poses significant difficulties. The importance of these particular migratory phenomena has been felt acutely since 2006, as there has been a dramatic and unexpected increase in irregular migrant arrivals from sub-Saharan Africa and Asia to the southern coasts of Europe.

The Canary Islands in the Atlantic, which are a part of Spanish territory, have long been a preferred target destination for thousands of irregular migrants sailing off the shores of Mauritania and Senegal for week-long journeys to Tenerife. Their numbers have fluctuated significantly, from 4,000 in 2001 to over 30,000 in 2006 (a so-called 'crisis year' for the Canary Islands-EU sea border) and falling again to approximately 12,000 in 2007 (Spanish Ministry of Interior data). During the same period (i.e. since 2000), the number of arrivals at the Strait of Gibraltar started at between 13,000 and 14,000 in the period 2001-2002, and then fell to half of that during the following years (thus fluctuating around 7,000 per year). The inversion of the trend at the Strait of Gibraltar is attributed mainly to the operation of the SIVE, the integrated border control system put in place by the Spanish government, as well as to the building of a militarised border around Ceuta and Melilla, the two Spanish enclaves in Morocco (Carling 2007).

The second most numerically significant destination in 2006 was the tiny island of Lampedusa, south of Sicily. Lampedusa receives between 15,000 and 20,000 irregular immigrants each year,[17] mainly sub-Saharan Africans setting off from the Libyan coast (and more recently from Algeria and Tunisia) aboard large fishing boats or other sea vessels. The relative success of sea border control by Italian authorities is well illustrated by the almost total cease in crossings of the Adriatic in the new century (Pastore et al. 2006).

Finally, the islands of the Aegean Sea near Greece are preferred target destinations for irregular Asian immigrants (Afghans, Iraqis, Syrians, etc.) who seek to enter Europe through Turkey. They cross the narrow straits from the Turkish mainland onto the islands of Mytilini (Lesvos), Rhodes, Samos, Chios, or even some smaller islands like Leros. The Greek coastguard and police forces intercepted nearly 9,000 people in 2007 and over 15,000 persons in 2008.

Migration across the EU's southern sea borders is, in total numbers, relatively small. Adding up the numbers referred to previously, in 2007 approximately 50,000 irregular migrants crossed the border, in 2006 it was 45,000, and in 2005 it was under 30,000. Considering that the EU-27 are home to some 2.8 million to 6 million irregular migrants,[18] that the EU-15 (excluding Greece) received a total of 2.6 million legal immigrants in 2004 (according to OECD data) and that the EU-27 have a total population of 486.5 million, it becomes evident that this amount of irregular migration is only a tiny fraction of overall irregular flows and stocks. It is indeed a rather small number in the overall population of the EU as well as in the overall immigrant population of the EU. The nature of migration across sea borders, however, imbues it with a sort of 'spectacular' news value: arrivals are dramatic, small boats sometimes capsize or sink near the shore and immigrants (including pregnant women and children) often die in their attempts to reach EU territory.[19]

Although the sea borders are a major concern for the Southern EU member states, the EU's external south-eastern land border is also a priority area. Land border controls mostly affect Greece and, to a lesser degree, Italy. The northern and north-eastern land borders have presented a major challenge to Greek migration control authorities since the early 1990s. Greece has been the target of irregular immigration flows because of its northern mountainous border with Albania, Bulgaria and Turkey. Italy experienced problems with the control of its border with Slovenia during the 1990s, including both irregular migration control and the management of visas (citizens of the former Yugoslavia or Albania would go to Slovenia and apply there for a visa to enter Italy as tourists). Nevertheless, land borders cannot be said to present too major a challenge for the Southern European countries, as they have largely internal EU borders and thus, increasingly, no borders at all (because of their participation in the Schengen no-internal-border area).

With regard to internal controls, all four Southern European countries have practised random public controls in efforts to stem irregular migration. In Greece, these controls were particularly frequent during the 1990s, and targeted mostly Albanian immigrants. In the early to mid-1990s, massive deportations – mainly of Albanian citizens – became common police practice. However, internal control policies in recent years have given more emphasis to actions targeting informal work. In Spain, since the regularisation of 2005, state authorities have prioritised labour inspections as a means of combating irregular migration. Spain's strategy has been three-pronged: border management has improved, irregular migrants who live in the country have been given the opportunity to legalise their stay and work and labour market inspections have been intensified. In Greece, Italy and Portugal, plans are in place to better control the informal economy and combat informal work, in general, but labour inspection mechanisms remain under-resourced and, to a certain extent, ineffective (Maroukis 2009; Pastore 2008). Moreover, in all four countries, dominant work areas like domestic services (cleaning and caring for families) are – by their very nature – hard to control and, as a result, it is improbable that informal work control policies can effectively regulate these sectors through labour inspections.

Finally, external control policies have been increasingly focused on cross-border cooperation with neighbouring countries. Readmission agreements have been signed between Greece and Albania, Bulgaria and Turkey (Protocol of Readmission), and there are local cooperation agreements on the Greek-Macedonian (FYROM) border. Spain and Italy have signed readmission and mutual cooperation agreements with several countries, including Morocco (Spain), Albania and Tunisia (Italy). The implementation of the Protocol of Readmission between Greece and Turkey is far from satisfactory, but Moroccan, Albanian and Tunisian authorities have been more cooperative.

Overall, the approach to enforcement of external controls has changed since the 1990s. Southern European countries do not seek to protect their borders from the inside – or rather not only from the inside. They aim to act in concert with major neighbouring sending or transit countries, providing programmes of seasonal migration and development aid in exchange.

In sum, there seems to be limited purposeful coordination between external and internal border controls as well as within the overall policy for managing migration flows and stocks. Border control efforts have been increasing throughout recent years, despite the fact that, within the last ten years, all these countries have enacted more than one large regularisation programme. While government authorities are aware that migration cannot be stopped as long as dramatic socio-economic inequalities persist between sending and receiving countries, they do not have an effective plan for managing migration. Their control policies appear to be, to a certain extent, detached from regularisation, management and integration policies, indeed seeking to accomplish a Sisyphean task.

5.5.3   *Integration and citizenship policies*

All the Southern European countries developed their integration policies in response to the arrival and settlement of relatively large numbers of migrants in a relatively short period of time. Although it is an exaggeration to claim that they are still 'new' host countries – since their experience dates back to the early 1990s – it is also important to note that migration to Southern Europe took place in the post-Cold War era, largely without planning and without a legal framework. Migrants did not arrive at a period of the manufacturing industry's expansion – they found jobs mainly in the service sector and, in particular, in the secondary labour market, notably at jobs that were underpaid and of low prestige and precarious conditions. These general socio-economic conditions framed the process of immigrant integration and the policies of integration that Southern European countries have since developed.[20]

Italy, the first Southern country to experience significant immigration in the late 1980s, developed its first integrated migration policy, which included issues of immigrant integration and political participation, in 1998. Greece and Portugal crafted their first comprehensive immigration laws including the issues of integration in 2001, and Spain did so in 2000.[21] During this last decade, all four countries have developed a set of integration policies tackling the issues of health, housing, education and socio-economic assistance to migrants.

There are important differences between the four countries as regards the public administration structures that manage welfare policies. In Spain and Italy, these policies apply to regions (*Comunidades Autonomas* in Spain) and municipalities, and there are hence different policies and practices in different regions. In Spain, migrants are concentrated in the two largest cities (Barcelona and Madrid), in the regions along the Mediterranean coast and in the two archipelagos. The regional and municipal authorities in the respective regions have, over time, developed plans for the social integration of migrants, and their social services have responded to the needs of these new populations as well. In Italy, too, regions with large immigrant populations in the north, north-east and in the centre are known for providing welfare assistance to legal migrants and their families, including housing, welfare allowances and other services (see Zincone 2000a, 2000b).

In Greece and Portugal, the national plans for integration are administered in a more centralised way than in Spain and Italy. In Greece, these plans for integration have often suffered from partial implementation and a lack of continuity. In Portugal, the early creation of the ACIME, later renamed ACIDI,[22] guaranteed some continuity within the policies and improved immigrants' integration prospects. This institution's role was to act as a go-between, facilitating communication between the government and immigrants and ensuring that the latter's rights were respected and their needs attended to. According to several sources, the role of ACIDI in structuring the civic sphere for migrant representation and participation and promoting socio-economic integration policies at the local and national level has been crucial (Teixeira & Albuquerque 2005; see also Niessen, Huddleston, Citron, Geddes & Jacobs 2007).[23]

In all four countries, EU initiatives and European Social Fund programmes have been valuable and given opportunity to immigrant organisations and other NGOs, as well as municipalities and universities, to promote the social and economic integration of immigrants. Indeed, European Social Fund programmes and the more recent European Integration Fund for the Integration of Third-Country Nationals have been instrumental in creating synergies, mobilising resources, even reorganising public administration offices, all with a view to providing services to migrant communities. On the whole, the outcome of these programmes has been positive, although their structural effect on the socio-economic integration of foreigners is limited. As seen in a previous section, migrants in Southern Europe mostly take on jobs in lower segments of the labour market. Moreover, they remain largely in poor housing and are often the targets of negative stereotyping by the media (King, Lazaridis & Tsardanidis 2000; Ribas-Mateos 2004).

With regard to citizenship policies, Southern European countries have generally restrictive approaches. In Spain, Italy, Greece and Portugal, until 2006 third-country nationals had to reside in the country for at least ten years in order to apply for naturalisation (six years now in Portugal; two years in Spain for some nationalities). In Italy and Greece, citizenship policies have been applied in a restrictive manner, leading to very low numbers of naturalised citizens (about 11,000 cases per year in Italy, mainly as a result of marriage to an Italian citizen, and about 50 cases a year in Greece). In the latter, applications from citizens of neighbouring countries have routinely been rejected during the past two decades, even when applicants satisfied all the requirements for naturalisation and even when they were married to a Greek citizen.

Naturalisation laws in all four countries are often contingent on ethnic descent. Naturalisation is easy if one has Greek, Spanish, Portuguese or Italian ancestors even two generations back (i.e. in a grandparent). By contrast, legally residing immigrants find it much harder to become naturalised even after ten years of residence. In most countries, preference is given to people who are of the same ethnic descent (Greece) or who can prove ancestry, as well as to individuals who come from former colonies (Latin American countries for Spain and Luso-speaking countries for Portugal).[24]

As regards the second generation, provisions vary. They are on the whole more generous than naturalisation policies in three out of the four countries (with the exception of Greece). However, second-generation provisions in Southern Europe fall short of becoming effective integration mechanisms for the children of immigrants. They often seem to perpetuate the distinction between 'native' and 'foreigner', without taking into account that children born in a country or who arrived at pre-school age in that country have completed all their education and have been socialised into the local and national norms and habits. It is thus questionable to treat them as foreigners.

All of these elements considered, the process of immigrant integration in Southern European host countries has taken place mainly through labour market insertion and at the personal or family level, through informal and personalised social networks, and with the help of third sector organisations. In other words, this slow process of piecemeal integration has had less to do with formal integration policies in these countries and related state structures, including welfare services, education services and other social agencies – Portugal being a partial exception. Although the importance of integration policies is not to be underestimated, a situation exists in Southern Europe whereby immigrants find their local niches in life and work, initially even without papers, and quickly adopt (or are forced to adopt) the local customs and, through personal relations with natives, manage to take part in the local networks of clientelistic relations. These networks generally structure both the labour market (e.g. the process of finding employment or improving one's work position) and interaction with the state in Southern Europe. The role of immigrants' associations and other NGOs, including ones linked to the Catholic Church, has also helped in the process. Immigrants' lives are of course made easier when appropriate integration policies (such as access to housing, health care, schooling) are provided in their cities and towns of residence.

Generally speaking, Southern European countries have developed a reactive, rather than proactive, framework for immigrant integration. Policies and practices have been more developed at the regional and local levels than the national level. The third sector, mostly involving immigrant associations and NGOs, has played an important part in assisting immigrants and integrating them in their chosen societies of settlement. However, formal policies of integration, including those for overall social and political integration and citizenship acquisition, have, to date, exhibited significant deficits that need to be addressed in the near future.

5.6   General considerations and concluding remarks

This comparative study of the Southern European countries – Greece, Italy, Portugal and Spain – and their immigration experiences confirms the existence of numerous similarities within this framework, which counterbalance the role of significant differences; a set of common explanatory factors; and a similar position within the broader context of the European migration system (see chapters 1 and 2 in this volume). As suggested in the initial chapters of this volume, there are reasons to believe that Southern Europe is the most homogeneous context regarding migration flows within Europe. The more relevant similarities and explaining factors are the following.

First, the evolution of migration flows has been quite similar in all four countries. Each one has had important emigration experiences to date. During the 1970s and 1980s, the migration transition took place. Emigration decreased, return migration increased (only to decline later) and foreign immigration rose as well. Over a short period of time, these countries went from net emigration to net immigration – though the timing and rhythm of inflows were not identical. Foreign immigration was manifest in all these countries during the 1980s, but the bulk of the movements varied, depending mostly on contextual factors. In Greece, most of the inflows occurred during the 1990s; in Italy and Portugal, during the early 2000s; and in Spain, throughout the new century until the recent economic recession. At the same time, emigration has not ceased completely. The most exceptional case is that of Portugal, where immigration decreased and emigration resumed in the first decade of the new century, almost reversing the previous migration balance. There is thus certainly an identifiable, long-term transition process that brings countries from situations of net emigration to net immigration in Southern Europe. However, as the volatility of inflows and the particular case of Portugal may confirm, any model of migration evolution with linearity prevailing – the best example of which being the 'mobility transition' model (Zelinsky 1971)[25] – would be both inaccurate and imprudent. A theory based on a rigid sequence of migration stages (see chapter 1 in this volume) thus warrants further scrutiny.

Second, despite a considerable variation in the national origin of immigrants, their demographic characteristics are very similar. Most inflows have comprised young adults who either directly targeted the labour market or came within the framework of family reunion (although many of the latter also inserted themselves rapidly in the labour market). This demographic profile explains why the immigrants' offspring are only now becoming visible. The most significant exception to this age profile – although not exceedingly significant, in relative terms – is the case of retirement migration coming mainly into Spain and Portugal from developed EU countries. In terms of gender, immigration is, in general, balanced – although some imbalances emerge upon closer inspection of certain flows and certain nationalities.

Third, the labour market insertion of immigrants exhibits many commonalities. In all four countries, both male and female immigrants have high employment rates – a fact that confirms the labour-oriented nature of most inflows. Immigrants are mostly concentrated in the same economic sectors: construction, manufacturing (mainly in Italy), hotels and restaurants, retail trade, domestic work and agriculture (except in Portugal). In many of these sectors, immigrants benefit from the seasonal nature of some activities – namely, tourism and agriculture. Data analyses confirm that newly arrived migrants are mainly absorbed into the least protected segments of the labour market, those that are normally rejected by natives. Migrants are also often overqualified for the jobs they perform, due to their relatively high educational backgrounds. Finally, they are commonly overexposed to precarious labour arrangements, including temporary contracts and unemployment risks.

Fourth, migration policies exhibit some similarities in terms of their general evolution and objectives, but many differences also result from differing institutional contexts. The core resemblances are attributable to the similar path adopted by most of their policy approaches. All four countries first began to deal with administrative norms related to the entry and residence of foreigners, mainly as a result of EU accession requirements in the cases of Greece, Portugal and Spain. They then sought stricter controls and rigorous enforcement when inflows began to increase. Over time, they devised ways to manage labour migration, especially when immigration became widespread, and used procedures that varied from invitation schemes to labour quotas. In later stages, they developed approaches to integration, whether at the national, regional or local level. And finally, in every case, the Southern European countries sporadically engaged in regularisation processes in order to regulate ex post what they were unable to regulate ex ante. The timing and concrete expression of these policy initiatives were, however, very different from country to country, and reveal specific institutional structures and a particular political context.

Fifth, integration outcomes are generally limited, although prospects vary from case to case. Substantial evidence confirms that, aside from rapid insertion into the labour market, much needs to be done in order to achieve successful integration. The labour insertion process itself is also confined to the least protected and least desired segments of the labour market, leading to what may be termed a situation of structural exclusion (Calavita 2005). However, increases in the duration of stays (many immigrants face harsh working conditions in earlier stages, only to later enjoy upward mobility (Chiswick 1978)), insertion into social networks (either of fellow foreign citizens, other foreigners or of nationals) and support from third sector organisations and other sources of political assistance have led and may continue to lead to situational improvement.

The questions to be asked are as follows: Why have all these processes evolved like this, and why did similarities arise so frequently among the Southern European countries? Moreover, why does the immigration experience in Southern Europe differ so markedly from the one of the 'old' European host countries? A set of explanatory variables can thus be added into the discussion.

The first factor has to do with the timing of inflows. Despite differences in rhythm and the inherent non-linearity of the migration process, it can be argued that all Southern European countries bear the same historical imprint in their immigration experience. To use other terminology, they are affected by the same 'generation effect' (see chapter 2 in this volume). They all have witnessed periods of strong immigration growth and have had to deal with their outcomes after the 1980s – a period characterised by deindustrialisation, liberalisation of the labour markets and deregulation of all advanced economies. This means that the regulation of migration – i.e. the enactment of effective recruitment and control policies – and the prevention of integration deficits would always be of utmost difficulty, as recent immigration trends within many other global contexts confirm.

The second factor is related to the migration cycle. In all Southern European cases, immigration flows are relatively recent and display a similar demographic pattern. Most of the inflows comprise young adults. Only now are the immigrants' offspring beginning to be statistically significant, either by means of '1.5 generation' immigrants (children who arrived early in their lives) or second-generation immigrants (children born in the host countries). In this way, Southern European countries are all affected by the same 'age effect' (see chapter 2 in this volume). The impacts of immigrants on the welfare system are still generally positive (they are net contributors, since they are mostly absorbed into the labour force, but this may change in the future) and the integration-related issues that pertain to second-generation immigrants are only now coming to the fore (and they will ultimately challenge the prospects for integration).

The third factor is labour demand. In all Southern European countries, low fertility and demographic ageing are responsible for a shortage of labour force, leading to diminishing emigration and increasing immigration (see chapter 1 in this volume). Moreover, a vast labour-intensive economic sector exists in these countries: it is sometimes linked to traditional activities or to new types of demand. This is the case of agriculture, construction, some manufacturing industries, hotels and restaurants (often related to tourism) and domestic work. In all these sectors, foreign manpower substitutes for native manpower – as is exemplified by the case of domestic work, a sector which has long been in existence, but which is now affected by a decreasing native labour supply. During recent decades, job creation in these sectors was vast, a phenomenon due to the high rates of economic growth during part of this period. The strong labour demand for immigrants is also related, in many ways, to the extent of the informal economy. Although informal arrangements are now part and parcel of all advanced economies, comparative studies show that Southern European countries are among those with higher levels of informality. This is a key contextual consideration to be made in explaining the endemic presence of irregular immigrants.

The fourth factor results from socio-economic structures or regimes (see chapter 2). One of the main variables is the type of welfare state. Although there is no consensus about what a 'Southern European' type of welfare entails, there are a number of commonalities. The 'conservative model' adopted by some authors (Esping-Andersen 1990; Sciortino 2004) attributes many welfare obligations directly to families, does not include the direct provision of all welfare services (using instead the principle of monetary transfers to the households) and protects the already employed extensively. The 'Southern European model' adopted by other authors (Ferrera 1996) stresses the importance of private-public partnerships and clientelism. All these traits, some of which are not specific to these countries, help explain the demand for immigration in some sectors (for example, given the rapid demographic ageing, caring for the elderly within the household is a fast-growing immigration recruitment sector) and the segmentation of the labour market (leading to the co-existence of protected and non-protected segments). If we add to all this the difficulties faced by law enforcement in Southern European states, we can also explain the widespread acceptance of informal and irregular situations that are common to natives and foreigners alike.

Another important element of the socio-economic regimes is the organisation of civil society. Again, this helps explain some immigration and policy trends. The growing presence of women in the labour market explains part of the immigrant recruitment trends for the domestic and care sector. Increased levels of education and, more generally, social expectations among the domestic youth explain their shunning of the bottom sectors of the labour market. The work of several NGOs demonstrates the support given to immigrants and the improvement of their integration prospects, even in the absence of adequate governmental policies. The importance of the Catholic Church in all countries, but Greece also, demonstrates the strength of the pro-immigrant coalition. The presence of active trade unions is a relevant variable, since it is directly related to the co-existence of well-protected sectors of the labour force and the comparatively less protected 'immigration jobs' (although unions have sometimes played a dual role, as they also have campaigned for immigrants' rights). The power of individual employers and employers' organisations explains the frequent use of irregular workforce, labour exploitation and lobbying for pro-immigration policies. All these elements are linked to the modes of immigrants' incorporation into society and, also, to the making of immigration policies (Zincone 2006). Last but not least, integration into the EU is an obvious factor directly constraining national immigration policies.

The fifth factor involves the dominant public perceptions and attitudes towards immigrants. Here again some similarities arise between the Southern countries, although differences seem to prevail. The importance of this factor is linked to the practical acceptance of immigrants in daily life, which affects their integration prospects, as well as to the role of political parties, which often makes immigration a decisive politicised element in modern democracies. Public opinion seems generally divided in Southern European countries. Some indicators confirm the public acceptance of immigration, while others suggest fear and concern. Past colonial and historical links, specific languages and culture, and various stereotypes add to the complexity already inherent in this field, making it impossible to generalise the situations of different countries and immigrant groups. All in all, perceptions and attitudes constitute a dependent and an independent variable – as occurs with other factors mentioned earlier. They evolve in a dynamic way, affecting and being affected by other variables.

In sum, it can be argued that a Southern European model of immigration does exist, as was supported by research during the 1990s and early 2000s (see e.g. King 2000). This model encompasses many similar traits, factors and outcomes, although specific national frameworks make a difference. Looking at the national level, for example, the various timings and characteristics of inflows have been accompanied by various timings and characteristics of immigration policies. A point that must be stressed is that this model is dynamic in the sense that new dimensions are continuously arising (for example, the second generation), new social frameworks are built (for example, evolving social attitudes) and new policies are enacted. An issue that merits further investigation is the effect of the current economic recession on migration trends (Martin 2009). It is well known that previous recessions have reshaped the world map of migration, and unexpected outcomes could now arise in the Southern European context. Another issue deserving scrutiny is the possibility of this model being enlarged to other newly expanding economies in Europe, such as Ireland and Finland (as well as other Southern European countries, including Malta, Cyprus and Slovenia (see King & Thomson 2008)).

Compared to the other groups of immigration countries examined in this book, the Southern European experience seems to be rather different from the 'old' immigration countries. The timing of inflows, the position in the migration cycle, the level and type of labour demand, the socio-economic structures, the public perception and the immigration policies are all significantly different in those contexts. Among other consequences, these differences seem to limit the prospects for a common policy approach, including a common EU policy – despite the long-term accumulated efforts in this direction (see chapters 11 and 12 in this volume). However, it may be argued that part of the framework in which immigration took place in the South is similar to the one involving the 'recent' or 'future' immigration countries in CEE. This is the case, for example, of the new type of inflows in the globalisation era and the overall trend for deregulation. In this sense, some traits of the Southern experience may replicate to the East, adding to the overall constraints that result from a common EU membership.

Notwithstanding national and contextual singularities, immigration has always constituted a major source of social change in Europe. This was also the case of Southern Europe. In recent years immigrants, native populations, civil society and governments have struggled to adapt to a new environment, which is now structural and will influence many years to come. Immigration became part and parcel of Southern European societies. While immigrants struggled to make a living in this new environment, local populations and institutions sought a way of dealing with immigration and its consequences. In a sense, it was not only immigrants who were looking for Southern Europe. It was also Southern Europe looking for itself.

Notes

1   This chapter results from the work carried out by the IDEA Southern European research teams in 2007 through 2009. The group benefited from the overall discussions of the project, intended to provide a comparison between North-Western, Southern and Central and Eastern European immigration experiences. Further work

was based on a detailed comparison between the Southern cases, which culminated in a workshop held in Lisbon in January 2009, where the first version of the current chapter was discussed. Most of the source information and further details about each country may be found in the national country reports elaborated during the project: Triandafyllidou and Maroufof (2009) for Greece; Bonifazi, Heins, Strozza and Vitiello (2009) for Italy; Sabino and Peixoto (2009) for Portugal; Arango and Finotelli (2009) for Spain. Most of the work was carried out before the advent of the global economic crisis in 2008.

2   The purpose of Russell King and Mark Thomson (2008) is to enlarge the scope of the analysis to other Southern European countries, namely, Malta, Cyprus and Slovenia.

3   The Fordist type of capitalism refers to the period characterised by mass production and mass consumption that predominated in Western economies between the end of World War II and the oil crisis of the mid-1970s. This period was characterised by high rates of economic growth, mostly due to the manufacturing industry, stable labour relations and state intervention in the welfare domain.

4   For the main sources on international migration in Southern Europe, see Cangiano and Strozza (2008).

5   Estimates of total foreign population, including the illegal component, are reported in some cases.

6   Most of the immigrants came from the former colonies in Africa (Países Africanos de Língua Oficial Portuguesa, PALOP) and from Brazil.

7   Recent research on this phenomenon demonstrated that countries like Germany, whose governmental authorities often denied the existence of irregular migration in their country, have also had to deal with a certain degree of irregular migration (Alt 1999; Schönwälder, Vogel & Sciortino 2004).

8   The data used for this estimate did not take into account the 'depuration' process of the municipal register and might contain a certain degree of overestimation.

9   The Schengen Agreement became operative in 1995 in Spain and Portugal and only in 1998 in Italy and Greece.

10   Estimates indicate that since 1973 Western European countries have regularised about 4 million immigrants, 3 million of them in Southern European countries (Papadopoulou 2005; MPG/Weil 2004).

11   In 2005, the German and the Dutch governments, for instance, sharply criticised the Spanish regularisation, fearing an 'invasion' of regularised immigrants from Spain to other European countries and blaming the Spanish government for not having informed the other EU member states in time about the process.

12   In Italy, we should add to the mentioned processes the special flows decree approved in 2006, which enlarged the quota for 2006 up to the number of applications received. The rationale behind this decision was a belief that most applications had been filed for workers already living irregularly in Italy, so that the increase of the contingent would work as a de facto regularisation programme. In Portugal, legislation approved in 2007 also allowed a special type of regularisation scheme, this time based on an ongoing individual approach.

13   The Spanish Regulation Act of 2004 assumes the risk of a certain volume of irregular migration, introducing the *arraigo*, which is an individual regularisation and an ongoing regularisation system. The Portuguese immigration law of 2007 contains some mechanisms allowing the legalisation of formerly irregular situations. These include, among others, stable labour activity and social integration indicators, such as the attendance of basic education by children of immigrants already born in the country.

14   The principle was set in 1990, although quotas would only be defined in 1995 and enforced in 1998.
15   This aspect is even more important in the case of domestic service, where trust is an essential condition for employment.
16   The agricultural sector seems to represent an exception.
17   Nearly 16,000 irregular migrants were apprehended upon arrival in Lampedusa in 2006. There were approximately 23,000 such arrivals during the first eight months of 2008, while numbers seemed to rise in early 2009 as 2,120 people were intercepted during the first two months of 2009, compared to 1,650 during the first two months of 2008.
18   This estimate is provided by the CLANDESTINO research project database, published on 20 February 2009 at http://clandestino.eliamep.gr/category/clandestino-database-on-irregular-migration.
19   Both media attention to irregular arrivals by sea and the rising numbers of such arrivals have led to the more active involvement of the FRONTEX agency in the patrolling of the southern EU borders. Following the European Council Meeting on 14-15 December 2006, FRONTEX, together with member states in the region, was invited to, as soon as possible, establish a permanent Coastal Patrol Network at their southern maritime borders.
20   The following paragraphs only describe integration policies, not integration outcomes. For a comprehensive view of immigrant integration patterns in Southern Europe, see e.g. King, Lazaridis and Tsardanidis (2000) and VV.AA. (2004).
21   The first national integration plan in Spain dates back to 1994. It was, however, barely effective.
22   The High Commissioner for Immigration and Ethnic Minorities was a governmental position created in 1996. It was the basis for the High Commission for Immigration and Ethnic Minorities (ACIME) in 2002, which in 2007 was designated as the High Commission for Immigration and Intercultural Dialogue (ACIDI).
23   www.integrationindex.eu.
24   The situation in Spain and Portugal is complex, since the law combines some traits of restrictiveness and permissiveness. In Spain, the application for citizenship for Latin Americans is possible after two years of legal residence. However, the two-year criterion is not clearly related to ethnic descent: besides Latin America, citizens from Portugal, Andorra, the Philippines and Equatorial Guinea may also apply after two years. In Portugal, the law was modified in 2006, easing the residence constraints for acquiring Portuguese citizenship by naturalisation and granting the same rights to citizens coming from Portuguese-speaking and other countries. This has produced notable results, since the number of valid requirements to get citizenship almost quadrupled between 2007 and 2008, increasing from approximately 9,000 to 35,000.
25   Referred to in the Introduction of this volume.

References

Alt, J. (1999), *Illegal in Deutschland: Forschungssituation zur Lage illegaler Migranten in Leipzig*. Karlsruhe: Von Loeper.

Aparicio Wilhelmi, M. & E. Roig Moles (2006), 'La entrada por razones laborales y el trabajo de los extranjeros: El progresivo desarrollo de un sistema ordenado de entrada laboral', in E. Aja & J. Arango (eds.), *Veinte años de inmigración en España: Perspectivas jurídicas y sociológica (1985-2004)*, 145-174. Barcelona: CIDOB.

Arango, J. (2003), 'Is there a Southern European model of immigration?', paper presented at the European Population Conference, Warsaw, August 2003.

Arango, J. (2005), 'La inmigración en España: Demografía, sociología y economía', in R. del Aguila (ed.), *Inmigración: Un desafío para España*, 247-273. Madrid: Pablo Iglesias.

Arango, J. & C. Finotelli (2009), 'Past and future challenges of a Southern European migration regime: The Spanish case', IDEA Working Papers 8 http://www.idea6fp.uw.edu.pl/pliki/WP8_Spain.pdf.

Arango, J. & C. Finotelli (2009), 'Spain', in M. Baldwin-Edwards & A. Kraler (eds.), *Regularisations in Europe: Study on practices in the area of the regularisation of illegally staying third-country nationals in the member states of the EU*, 443-457. Brussels: Pallas Publications.

Arango, J. & M. Jachimowicz (2005), 'Regularization and immigration policy reform in Spain', in F. Heckmann & T. Wunderlich (eds.), *Amnesty for illegal migrants?* 79-88. Bamberg: Europäisches Forum für Migrationsstudien.

Baganha, M.I. (ed.) (1997), *Immigration in Southern Europe*. Oeiras: Celta.

Baganha, M.I. (1998), 'Immigrant involvement in the informal economy: The Portuguese case', *Journal of Ethnic and Migration Studies* 24 (2): 367-385.

Baldwin-Edwards, M. (1997), 'The emerging European immigration regime: Some reflections on implications for Southern Europe', *Journal of Common Market Studies* 35 (4): 497-519.

Baldwin-Edwards, M. (1999), 'Where free markets reign: Aliens in the twilight zone', in J. Arango & M. Baldwin-Edwards (eds.), *Immigrants and the informal economy in Southern Europe*, 1-15. London: Frank Cass.

Baldwin-Edwards, M. & J. Arango (eds.) (1999), *Immigrants and the informal economy in Southern Europe*. London: Frank Cass.

Birindelli, A.M. (1990), 'Aspetti quantitativi della presenza straniera in Italia', in Labos (ed.), *La presenza straniera in Italia*. Rome: Edizioni Ter.

Blangiardo, G.C. (1997), 'La dimensione quantitativa', in ISMU (ed.), *Secondo rapporto sulle migrazioni, 1996*. Milan: Franco Angeli.

Blangiardo, G.C. (1998), 'Relazione di sintesi sugli aspetti quantitativi della presenza straniera irregolare', in Ministero dell'Interno (ed.), *Relazione sulla presenza straniera in Italia e sulle situazioni di irregolarità*. Centro stampa microfilm.

Blangiardo, G.C. (ed.) (2004), *L'immigrazione straniera in Lombardia: La terza indagine regionale, Rapporto 2003*. Milan: Franco Angeli.

Blangiardo, G.C. (2006), 'La presenza straniera in Italia', in ISMU (ed.), *Undicesimo rapporto sulle migrazioni 2005*. Milan: Franco Angeli.

Blangiardo, G.C. (ed.) (2008), *L'immigrazione straniera in Lombardia: La settima indagine regionale*. Milan: Osservatorio Regionale per l'integrazione e la multietnicità; Franco Angeli.

Blangiardo, G.C. (2009), 'Gli aspetti quantitativi della presenza straniera in Italia: Aggiornamenti e prospettive', in Fondazione ISMU (ed.), *Quattordicesimo rapporto sulle migrazioni 2008*. Milan: Franco Angeli.

Blangiardo, G.C. & M.L. Tanturri (2006), 'La presenza straniera in Italia', in G.C. Blangiardo & P. Farina (eds.), *Il Mezzogiorno dopo la grande regolarizzazione: Immagini e problematiche dell'immigrazione*, vol. III. Milan: Franco Angeli.

Bonifazi, C. (2008), 'Evolution of regional patterns of international migration in Europe', in C. Bonifazi, M. Okólski, J. Schoorl & P. Simon (eds.), *International migration in Europe: New trends and new methods of analysis*, 107-128. IMISCOE Research Series. Amsterdam: Amsterdam University Press.

Bonifazi, C., F. Heins, S. Strozza & M. Vitiello (2009), 'The Italian transition from an emigration to immigration country', IDEA Working Papers 5 http://www.idea6fp.uw.edu.pl/pliki/WP5_Italy.pdf.

Brochmann, G. (1993), 'Control in immigration policies: A closed Europe in the making', in R. King (ed.), *The new geography of European migrations*, 100-115. London: Belhaven.

Cachón, L. (2007), 'La experiencia internacional en regularizaciones extraordinarias de inmigrantes indocumentados: España en el modelo del Sur de Europa', Madrid (unpublished manuscript).

Calavita, K. (2005), *Immigrants at the margins: Law, race, and exclusion in Southern Europe*. Cambridge: Cambridge University Press.

Cangiano, A. & S. Strozza (2008), 'Foreign immigration in Southern European receiving countries: New evidence from national data sources', in C. Bonifazi, M. Okólski, J. Schoorl & P. Simon (eds.), *International migration in Europe: New trends and new methods of analysis*, 153-178. IMISCOE Research Series. Amsterdam: Amsterdam University Press.

Carfagna, M. (2002), 'I sommersi e i sanati: Le regolarizzazioni degli immigrati in Italia', in A. Colombo & G. Sciortino (eds.), *Stranieri in Italia: Assimilati ed esclusi*, 53-91. Bologna: Il Mulino.

Carling, J. (2007) 'Migration control and migrant fatalities at the Spanish-African borders', *International Migration Review* 41 (2): 316-343.

Cebolla Boado, H. & A. González Ferrer (2008), *La inmigración en España (2000-2007): Del control de flujos a la integración de inmigrantes*. Madrid: CEPS.

Chiswick, B. R. (1978), 'The effect of Americanization on the earnings of foreign-born men', *Journal of Political Economy* 86 (5): 897-921.

Coslovi, L. (2007), 'Brevi note sull'immigrazione via mare in Italia e in Spagna'. www.cespi.it/PDF/mig-mare.pdf.

De Bruycker, P. & J. Apap (2000), 'Les regularisations des étrangers illegaux dans l'Union européenne', Brussels.

Emke-Poulopoulou, I. (2007), *Η Μεταναστευτική Πρόκληση* (*The Migratory Challenge*). Athens: Papazisis.

Esping-Andersen, G. (1990), *The three worlds of welfare capitalism*. Cambridge: Polity Press.

Fakiolas, R. (2000) 'Migration and unregistered labour in the Greek economy', in R. King, G. Lazaridis & C. Tsardanidis (eds.), *Eldorado or fortress? Migration in Southern Europe*, 57-78. London: Macmillan.

Ferrera, M. (1996), 'Il modello sud-europeo di welfare state', *Rivista Italiana Di Scienza Politica* 26 (1): 67-101.

Finotelli, C. & G. Sciortino (2006), 'Looking for the European soft underbelly: Visa policies and amnesties for irregular migrants in Germany and Italy', in S. Baringhorst, J.F. Hollifield & U. Hunger (eds.), *Herausforderung Migration: Perspektiven der vergleichenden Politikwissenschaft*, 249-280. Munster: LIT Verlag.

Finotelli, C. & G. Sciortino (2009), 'The importance of being Southern: The making of policies of immigration control in Italy', *European Journal of Migration and Law* 11 (2): 119-138.

González-Enríquez, C. & A. Triandafyllidou (2009), 'Comparing the new hosts of Southern Europe', *European Journal of Migration and Law* 11 (2). Special issue.

Iosifides, T. & R. King (1996), 'Recent immigration to Southern Europe: The socio-economic and labour market contexts', *Journal of Area Studies* 6: 70-94.

Istat (1991), 'Gli immigrati presenti in Italia. Una stima per l'anno 1989', *Note e Relazioni* 1, Rome.

King, R. (2000), 'Southern Europe in the changing global map of migration', in R. King, G. Lazaridis & C. Tsardanidis (eds.), *Eldorado or fortress? Migration in Southern Europe*, 1-26. London: Macmillan.

King, R. (ed.) (2002), 'Migration into Southern Europe: New trends and new patterns', *Studi Emigrazione/Migration Studies* 39 (145). Special issue.

King, R. & K. Rybaczuk (1993), 'Southern Europe and the international division of labour: From emigration to immigration', in R. King (ed.), *The new geography of European migrations*, 175-206. London: Belhaven.

King, R. & M. Thomson (2008), 'The Southern European model of immigration: Do the cases of Malta, Cyprus and Slovenia fit?', *Journal of Balkan and Near Eastern Studies* 10 (3): 265-291.

King, R. & R. Black (eds.) (1997), *Southern Europe and the new immigrations*. Brighton: Sussex Academic Press.

King, R., G. Lazaridis & C. Tsardanidis (eds.) (2000), *Eldorado or fortress? Migration in Southern Europe*. London: Macmillan.

Lianos, T., K. Kanellopoulos, M. Gregou, E. Gemi & P. Papakonstantinou (2008), *Estimate of the size of foreigners residing illegally in Greece*. Athens: IMEPO. www.imepo.gr/documents/AENEAS_IMEPO_RESEARCH_.2008_GR_000.pdf.

Lusa (2008), 'Regularização ao abrigo da Lei de Estrangeiros "vai continuar"', 4 April 2008. www.acidi.gov.pt/modules.php?name=News&file=article&sid=2484.

Maroukis, T. (2009), 'Greece', research report prepared for the CLANDESTINO Project. http://clandestino.eliamep.gr/category/irregular-migration-in-the-eu/country-reports.

Martin, P. (2009), 'The recession and migration: Alternative scenarios', International Migration Institute Working Papers 13, Oxford.

Martin, P., S. Martin & P. Weil (2006), *Managing migration: The promise of cooperation*. Laham: Lexington Books.

Massey, D. (1999), 'International Migration at the dawn of the twenty-first century: The role of the State', *Population and Development Review* 25 (2): 303-322.

Migration Policy Group (MPG) (with the assistance of P. Weil) (2004), 'Managing irregular migration', *Policy Brief* 4.

Mingione, E. & F. Quassoli (2000), 'The participation of immigrants in the underground economy in Italy', in R. King, G. Lazaridis & C. Tsardanidis (eds.), *Eldorado or fortress? Migration in Southern Europe*, 27-56. London: Macmillan.

Natale, M. (1986), 'Fonti e metodi di rilevazione della popolazione straniera in Italia. Contributi del dibattito in corso e nuovi elementi conoscitivi', *Studi Emigrazione* 23: 82-83.

Natale, M. & S. Strozza (1997), *Gli immigrati stranieri in Italia: Quanti sono, chi sono, come vivono?* Bari: Cacucci Editore.

Niessen, J., T. Huddleston, L. Citron, A. Geddes & D. Jacobs (2007), *Migrant integration policy index*. Brussels: British Council and Migration Policy Group.

OECD (2006), *International migration outlook*, Annual Report. Paris: OECD.

OECD (2008), *International migration outlook*, Annual Report. Paris: OECD.

Pajares, M. (2006), *La inserción laboral de la población inmigrada en Cataluña: Efectos del proceso de normalización 2005*. Barcelona: Ceres (Estudis 15).

Papadopoulou, A. (2005), 'Regularisation programmes: An effective instrument of migration policy?', *Global Migration Perspectives* 33.

Pastore, F. (2008), 'Modes of migration regulation and control in Italy', in J. Doomernik & M. Jandl (eds.), *Modes of migration regulation and control in Europe*. Amsterdam: Amsterdam University Press.

Pastore, F., P. Monzini & G. Sciortino (2006), 'Schengen's soft underbelly? Irregular migration and human smuggling across land and sea borders to Italy', *International Migration* 44 (4): 95-119.

Pellegrino, A. (2004), *Migration from Latin America to Europe: Trends and policy challenges*. Geneva: International Organization for Migration, Migration Research Series 16.

Recaño, J. & A. Domingo (2005), 'Factores sociodemograficos y territoriales de inmigración irregular en España', paper presented at the XXV International Population Conference, Tours, 18-23 July 2005.

Reyneri, E. (1998), 'The role of the underground economy in irregular migration to Italy: Cause or effect?', *Journal of Ethnic and Migration Studies* 24 (2): 313-331.

Reyneri, E. & M. Baganha (2001), 'Migration and the labour market in Southern Europe', *IMIS-Beiträge* 17: 33-53.

Ribas-Mateos, N. (ed.) (2004), *Journal of Ethnic and Migration Studies* 30 (6). Special issue.

Ritaine, E. (ed.) (2005), *L'Europe du Sud face à l'immigration: Politique de l'Étranger.* Paris: Presses Universitaires de France.

Sabino, C. & J. Peixoto (2009), 'Immigration, the labour market and policy in Portugal: Trends and prospects', IDEA Working Papers 6 http://www.idea6fp.uw.edu.pl/pliki/WP6_Portugal.pdf.

Schneider, F. & R. Klinglmair (2004), 'Shadow economies around the world: What do we know?', *IZA Discussion Paper* 1043, Bonn: Institute for the Study of Labour.

Schönwälder, K., D. Vogel & G. Sciortino (2004), 'Migration und Illegalität in Deutschland', *AKI-Forschungsbilanz* 1, Berlin.

Sciortino, G. (2004), 'Immigration in a Mediterranean welfare state: The Italian experience in a comparative perspective', *Journal of Comparative Policy Analysis* 6 (2): 111-129.

Strozza, S. (2004), 'Estimates of illegal foreigners in Italy: A review of the literature', *International Migration Review* 38 (1): 309-331.

Teixeira, A. & R. Albuquerque (2005), 'Active civic participation of immigrants in Portugal', POLITIS Project Report. www.politis-europe.uni-oldenburg.de/9812.html.

Triandafyllidou, A. & M. Maroufof (with the collaboration of M. Nikolova) (2009) 'Immigration towards Greece at the eve of the 21st century. A critical assessment', *IDEA Working Papers* 4 http://www.idea6fp.uw.edu.pl/pliki/WP4_Greece.pdf.

Zelinsky, W. (1971), 'The hypothesis of the mobility transition', *The Geographical Review* 61 (2): 219-249.

Zincone, G. (ed.) (2000a), *Primo rapporto sull'integrazione degli immigrati in Italia.* Bologna: Il Mulino.

Zincone, G. (ed.) (2000b), *Secondo rapporto sull'integrazione degli immigrati in Italia.* Bologna: Il Mulino.

Zincone, G. (2006), 'The making of policies: Immigration and immigrants in Italy', *Journal of Ethnic and Migration Studies* 32 (3): 347-375.

6 The Southern European 'model of immigration'

A sceptical view

Martin Baldwin-Edwards

6.1 Introduction

Chapter 5 in this volume details a Southern European 'model of immigration' across Portugal, Spain, Italy and Greece with five empirical similarities and five structural or causal patterns. This line of theoretical thinking continues a tradition attempting to identify, variously, an immigration policy regime (Baldwin-Edwards 1991, 1997), immigrants' location within a 'southern' capitalist economy (King & Konzhodic 1995; King & Black 1997; Baldwin-Edwards & Arango 1999) or within southern societies (Iosofides & King 1999) or more generally a 'southern model' of immigration (Baldwin-Edwards 1999; King 2000). It is perhaps ironic that as one of the participants in these earlier analytic developments, I should now advocate scepticism about the utility or even validity of such a model. To this end, I adopt a critique of the specifications of the framework advocated by João Peixoto et al. in the previous chapter. I also suggest some missing variables that, in my view, should be central to such an explanatory framework. The inclusion of these variables not only reveals major differences across the Southern European region, but also casts doubt on some of the empirical assumptions underlying the common framework. I conclude with some thoughts on the relevance of the important hypotheses advanced by Joaquín Arango in chapter 2.

6.2 The explanatory framework

This section examines each of the five structural commonalities that make up the framework proposed for the common Southern European pattern.

6.2.1   Evolution of migration flows into the four countries

As countries of emigration in the post-war period, it is indeed true that all four had a 'migration turnaround', as originally identified in the model proposed by Russell King, Anthony Fielding and Richard Black (1997). What is not so clear is a similarity of migration flows. The ISOPLAN estimates of immigrant presence in the late 1980s had already put Greece as the leading per capita recipient at 2.8 per cent of total population, followed by Italy at 2.6 per cent and Spain at 2.0 per cent (Werth & Korner 1991). The year 1991 saw massive irregular inflows from Albania into Greece and, to a much lesser extent, Italy. It was not until the turn of the century that comparable flows arrived in the other countries; yet, Greece was the last of the four actually to pass an immigration law (1991) and to initiate regularisation of irregular immigrants (1997). The differences between the four countries have increased in recent years, with immigration into Portugal diminishing and emigration resuming, while Greece has had continued irregular inflows both from Albania and also via its eastern borders. Merely in terms of per capita immigration levels, it is now difficult to find comparability in the different national patterns, in contrast to the situation a decade ago.

6.2.2   Demographic characteristics of immigrants

Chapter 5's authors posit a similarity of the main demographic characteristics of immigrants, notwithstanding vastly differing nationalities: most notably, the prevalence of young adults is specified. An exception is noted in the case of European Union retirement migrants in Spain and Portugal. It is true that the Southern European countries show a younger age profile than those in the North, with more than 60 per cent of their known immigrant populations aged 15-44. Nevertheless, there are different trends: Italy has apparently had a decline in the young working-age bracket, from 70 per cent in 1991 down to 62 per cent in 2007. Greece, Portugal and Spain continue to increase their share of that age group, reaching around 65 per cent in the latest data. Italian data also show that its increasing immigrant age cohort of 45-59 is around 55 per cent female, unlike Spain and Portugal where it is under 50 per cent and Greece where it is 51 per cent. In the child age cohort 0-14, Italy has a very high proportion, amounting to 19 per cent of its immigrants, whereas Spain has only 14 per cent. These data suggest that Italy is in a more advanced phase of the migration transition, with family formation and the second generation appearing more prominently. This suggestion is reinforced by the observation of differing gender balances of immigrants, with Italy at 50.4 per cent female and the others at 46 to 47 per cent; this is also partially explained by the greater importance in Italy of older female migrants assisting with care of the elderly.

6.2.3   Labour market insertion

Although crude employment rates suggest that the southern countries are very different from the EU average, with very high participation of immigrants in the labour market, detailed data from the Labour Force Survey suggest more complex patterns. The role of immigrants in the different labour markets shows a rather different picture for Portugal, where traditionally high native participation rates – especially of women – are accompanied by lower levels of immigration and a smaller increase in the educational levels of younger age cohorts (Domingo & Gil-Alonso 2007). OECD data on employment also suggest a different pattern for Portugal, where immigrants are over-represented in several sectors (education, social services and administration) and not apparently in agriculture or manufacturing, as in the other three southern countries (OECD 2008a: Table I.10).

Looking at the phenomenon of 'overqualification', the OECD (using its 2000 census database) places Greece, Spain, Sweden, Italy and Denmark as the countries with the highest rates of overqualified immigrant workers (32% to 22%) with Portugal at 17 per cent (OECD 2008b: Chart 6.1). Ethnic entrepreneurship and self-employment also appear to have very different extents across the four southern countries, with similar rates between immigrants and natives in Spain and Portugal, but a very low rate in Greece and a high one in Italy (Baldwin-Edwards 2002: 14). Although there are some commonalities of labour market role and especially the significance of the informal economy, immigrants across the entire EU are concentrated in construction, services and domestic work: these are hardly defining features of the southern economies' utilisation of immigrant labour. In particular, Portugal appears not to fit the Mediterranean pattern well at all.

6.2.4   Evolution of immigration policies

Aside from a common pattern of dependence on post hoc regularisation of irregular migrants as the main mechanism for immigration recruitment (Baldwin-Edwards & Kraler 2009), it is not clear that there is so much resemblance in policy. The requirements of Schengen clearly shaped the legal texts of all southern countries, especially in the absence of traditions of immigration management (Baldwin-Edwards 1997), but the underlying objectives do not appear to have been identical. Spain and Portugal followed a fairly open policy towards immigrant recruitment; Italy from 1998 to 2002, had innovative policies on migration for job-seeking (Pastore 2008a); Greece passed its 1991 law explicitly to prevent migration flows and to facilitate mass deportations (Baldwin-Edwards & Fakiolas 1999). Subsequent developments saw some convergence towards restrictionism – which, in the Italian case, one commentator associates explicitly with centre-right governments (Pastore 2008b). Such a policy linkage did not occur in the case of Greece, where the 2001 law – despite the introduction of a theoretical labour invitation scheme by a centre-left government – had no practical consequences for the recruitment of labour migrants.

A more detailed examination of specific aspects of migration management is needed to assess 'immigration policy'. These sub-areas of policy include labour recruitment, management of political asylum, family migration and family reunification, regularisations, deportations and expulsions, residence permit policies, access to sub-areas of the labour market, policies for the integration of immigrants, access to citizenship, inter alia. Such an examination is rarely performed, yet is the only valid mechanism by which immigration policies can be compared. Without having the time or space here to carry out such a procedure, I feel confident in asserting that Greece is an outlier of the model proposed, that Portugal is also a poor fit, with some considerable similarities between Spain and Italy notwithstanding some important differences.

6.2.5 Integration outcomes

Despite several decades of immigration management, it is indeed the case that policies for the integration of migrants are poorly developed in Southern Europe (Vermeulen 2004; Baldwin-Edwards 2004a). Equally, measurement of outcomes is rarely made and policies are difficult to evaluate. Nevertheless, some patterns can be observed. First, where there is a tradition of local state management (as in Spain and Italy), policies for immigrant welfare and social integration are frequently to be found, although they are non-uniform and uncoordinated (Zincone 1999; Zincone & Caponio 2006). Such policies are only now being developed in Greece, and only in Athens. Secondly, the Migration Policy Group has repeatedly carried out evaluations of legislation and policies relevant to the integration of migrants, with fairly consistent results over a number of years (MPG 2007). The 2007 report ranked Greece at position 25 (out of 28), while Portugal is second, Italy seventh and Spain tenth. The 2010 report (MIPEX 2011) raised Greece to sixteenth place, leaving Portugal at second, Italy eighth and Spain tenth. However, MIPEX does not measure outcomes but policy developments, and Greece's higher ranking was achieved on the basis of legislation for voting rights and citizenship acquisition: these have now been blocked by the Supreme Administrative Court of Greece for alleged non-conformity with the constitution. In reality, little progress has been made.

Thus, again we can find Greece to be an outlier of the model, Portugal looking a little different from Spain and Italy, and fairly strong similarities between Italy and Spain.

6.3   The 'missing' variables

To interpret both commonalities and differences, Peixoto et al. offer five 'explanatory variables': timing of inflows, stages of the migration cycle, type of labour demand, socio-economic structures or regimes and indigenous perceptions of immigration. These variables actually partially repeat the points made in sections 6.2.1, 6.2.2 and 6.2.3, while offering structural differences across the region as an independent variable to account for national differences in policies and policy outcomes. I am not convinced of the intellectual validity of this approach: either there are enough structural similarities between the countries, or there are not.

Some specific structural differences are actually central to both policy creation and outcomes. Among these, I would include the points outlined in the following sections.

6.3.1   The role of local governance in policy development and implementation

This appears as a crucial factor, especially in managing access of both regular and irregular migrants to healthcare and social services. The highly devolved political structures of Italy and Spain have produced outcomes more able to facilitate the integration of immigrants, although with great regional variation across the country. Portugal and Greece are reliant on national political initiatives, with Portugal living up to the challenge and Greece essentially failing to implement any meaningful policy.

6.3.2   The lack of a common experience of immigration across the region

The relative magnitudes of this have already been discussed in section 6.2.1; here, I address some major qualitative differences. Spain and Italy show enough similarity to be taken together; Portugal, until 2002, had almost exclusively post-colonial immigrants (Baganha 2009) with very different implications for their reception. In the 1990s, Greece experienced several waves of Albanian mass irregular immigration, resulting in Albanians forming some 70 per cent of the immigrant population; this had serious implications relating to national identity and security, owing to Greece's difficult modern Balkan history (Baldwin-Edwards 2004b; Baldwin-Edwards & Apostolatou 2008). Thus, Portugal and Greece have had very different experiences of immigration from those of Spain and Italy.

6.3.3   The role of NGOs and civil society

Although there is a common short history of NGOs in Southern Europe, there is one major player – the Catholic Church. Along with CARITAS, this has had an important effect on both practical support and social legitimation of immigrants in Portugal, Spain and Italy. In Greece, on the other hand, the Orthodox Church has no support system for immigrants (despite its massive wealth) and has played almost no role in promoting social acceptance of immigrants. The little social support for immigrants in Greece comes mostly from international organisations such as Médecins du Monde, IOM, UNHCR, amongst others, or from self-help immigrant NGOs. Thus, Greece stands again as a complete misfit in the Southern European paradigm.

6.3.4   The role of political ideology and political parties in immigration policy development

As was pointed out in section 6.2.4, Italian immigration policies have exhibited innovation and openness during centre-left periods of governance, and closedness and increasing problems of irregularity during centre-right periods. The same observation might also be made of Spanish policy, particularly with its more recent innovative policies. In the case of Greece, policies passed under previous socialist administrations more closely resemble those of the centre-right administrations in Spain and Italy, reflecting the relatively minor role of political ideology in immigration policy and the more substantive one of bureaucratic traditions and interests (Baldwin-Edwards & Fakiolas 1999). The recent blocking (on putative constitutional grounds) of more progressive legislation in 2010 for the integration of immigrants confirms the unusual power of Greek bureaucracy and courts vis-à-vis both central and local government. Thus far, the evidence is clear that Greece is a misfit in the southern model on the basis of this criterion, too.

6.4   Some conclusions

It remains an open question as to how broad a model should be in order that it might have utility. The older literature naturally found the commonalities of Southern Europe to be a convincing framework of analysis; some of these are still pertinent, such as the size and weak regulation of (informal) employment. However, as Southern European countries have accumulated more experience and techniques for the management of migration, they have progressed from the relatively simple model that was implied in the older literature. With this progression, structural differences have become more important, with increasing dissimilarity of outcomes.

Arango in this volume (chapter 2, section 2.2.1) posits some important theoretical considerations concerning the grouping of countries. First, the 'age effect'. Here, he emphasises the major difference between a society composed of individual labour migrants and one consisting of families and communities. The evidence is clear that family grouping in Southern Europe has been extensive for over a decade. Thus, 54 per cent of immigrants in Greece were living in nuclear family arrangements according to the 2001 Census, with Albanians in Athens at 67 per cent (Baldwin-Edwards 2008: 12-14); in Spain in 2007, 56 per cent of immigrants were recorded as living in such arrangements, with another 33 per cent in various quasi-family units and only 11 per cent as individuals or in multi-member households (INE 2009: Table 2.7). Similar patterns seem to prevail in Italy and Portugal, although data are hard to find for any country. Thus, we can question the claim that immigration into Southern Europe is simple labour migration. Even data on the second generation are rarely collected, with one estimate for Greece of 220,000 (20 to 30 per cent of immigrant stocks) making newspaper headlines (Baldwin-Edwards 2008: 38).

The 'generation effect', hypothesis number two in section 2.2.2, focuses on the initial experience of immigration, leaving an imprint that shapes the dominant approach to migration management. Certainly, this is very relevant when examining the different experiences of immigration across the region. Another distinctive feature, not previously mentioned, is the traumatic 'exchange of populations' between Greece and Turkey of 1922: elsewhere, I argue that it is this that has shaped contemporary political and popular perceptions of migration in Greece (Baldwin-Edwards & Apostolatou 2008).

Hypothesis number three in section 2.2.3 suggests that the experience of forerunners exerts a marked influence on the behaviour of newcomers to the immigration phenomenon. This hypothesis is in line with much theory on policymaking – policy importation, policy imitations, transfers, etc. However, there is scant empirical evidence to sustain it in the case of Southern Europe. Certainly, the requisites of Schengen and the EU were adopted in all the countries under consideration (Baldwin-Edwards 1997): however, these are primarily legal in form and do not necessarily shape all policy. Indeed, there is no EU policy on labour migration and national management of that has been idiosyncratic and not derived from northern practices. Equally, regularisations have emerged apparently endogenously (Baldwin-Edwards & Kraler 2009), while those areas of EU weak regulation, by means of directives, have hardly been readily embraced. In particular, family rights and long-term residence permits are poorly managed across much of Southern Europe, although with Greece being the worst case.

Finally, hypothesis number four in section 2.2.4, looking at structural characteristics, may turn out to be the most important. This – along with hypothesis number two – actually explains the highly divergent grouping of the traditional receiving countries of Northern Europe. It seems that it will also explain, in a near-identical manner, the increasingly diverging patterns across Southern Europe. Despite the major differences between North and South, perhaps there is actually far more in common at an analytical level than we had at first imagined.

References

Baganha, M. (2009), 'Portugal', in H. Fassmann, U. Reeger & W. Sievers (eds.), *Statistics and reality: Concepts and measurements of migration in Europe*, 263-279. IMISCOE Reports Series. Amsterdam: Amsterdam University Press.

Baldwin-Edwards, M. (2008), 'Immigrants in Greece: Characteristics and issues of regional distribution', Mediterranean Migration Observatory Working Paper 10, Athens. www. mmo.gr.

Baldwin-Edwards, M. (2004a), 'Immigration, immigrants and socialisation in Southern Europe: Patterns, problems and contradistinctions', in C. Inglessi, A. Lyberaki, H. Vermeulen & G. J. van Wijngaarden (eds.), *Immigration and integration in Northern versus Southern Europe*, 11-24. Athens: Netherlands Institute in Athens.

Baldwin-Edwards, M. (2004b), 'Albanian emigration and the Greek labour market', *South-East Europe Review* 7(1): 51-66.

Baldwin-Edwards, M. (2002), 'Southern European labour markets and immigration: A structural and functional analysis', Mediterranean Migration Observatory Working Paper 5, Athens. www.mmo.gr.

Baldwin-Edwards, M. (1999), 'Where free markets reign: Aliens in the twilight zone', in M. Baldwin-Edwards & J. Arango (eds.), *Immigrants and the informal economy in Southern Europe*. London: Routledge.

Baldwin-Edwards, M. (1997), 'The emerging European immigration regime: Some reflections on implications for Southern Europe', *Journal of Common Market Studies* 35 (4): 497-519.

Baldwin-Edwards, M. (1991), 'Immigration after 1992', *Policy and Politics* 19 (3): 199-211.

Baldwin-Edwards, M. & J. Arango (eds.) (1999), *Immigrants and the informal economy in Southern Europe*. London: Routledge.

Baldwin-Edwards, M. & R. Fakiolas (1999), 'Greece: The contours of a fragmented policy response', in M. Baldwin-Edwards & J. Arango (eds.), *Immigrants and the informal economy in Southern Europe*, 186-204. London: Routledge.

Baldwin-Edwards, M. & K. Apostolatou (2008), 'Ethnicity and migration: A Greek story', *Migrance* 31: 5-17.

Baldwin-Edwards, M. & A. Kraler (eds.) (2009), *REGINE: Regularisations in Europe*. Amsterdam: Pallas.

Domingo, A. & F. Gil-Alonso (2007), 'Immigration and changing labour force structure in the Southern European Union', *Population* 4 (62): 709-727.

INE (2009), *Encuesta nacional de inmigrantes 2007*. Madrid: Institution Nacional de Estadística.

King, R. (2000), 'Southern Europe in the changing global map of migration', in R. King, G. Lazaridis & C. Tsardanidis (eds.), *Eldorado or fortress? Migration in Southern Europe*, 1-25. London: Palgrave Macmillan.

King, R. & I. Konzhodic (1995), 'Labour, employment and migration in Southern Europe', Research Paper 19, Geography Laboratory, University of Sussex.

King, R., A. Fielding & R. Black (1997), 'The international migration turnaround in Southern Europe', in R. King & R. Black (eds.), *Southern Europe and the new migrations*, 1-25. Brighton: Sussex Academic Press.

Iosofides, T. & R. King (1999), 'Socio-spatial dynamics and exclusion of three immigrant groups in the Athens conurbation', in M. Baldwin-Edwards & J. Arango (eds.), *Immigrants and the informal economy in Southern Europe*, 205-229. London: Routledge.

MIPEX (2011), *Migrant integration policy index.* www.mipex.eu/countries.

MPG (2007), *Migrant integration policy index.* Brussels: British Council and Migration Policy Group.

OECD (2008a), *International migration outlook 2008 edition.* Paris: OECD.

OECD (2008b), *A profile of immigrant populations in the 21st century.* Paris: OECD.

Pastore, F. (2008a), 'Report from Italy', in J. Doomernik & M. Jandl (eds.), *Modes of migration control and regulation in Europe*, 105-128. IMISCOE Reports Series. Amsterdam: Amsterdam University Press.

Pastore, F. (2008b), 'The Italian migratory laboratory: Promises, failure and lessons for Europe', paper prepared for the seminar 'Migration and European labour market transformations', Paris, 3 July 2008, Policy Network.

Vermeulen, H. (2004), 'Models and modes of immigrant integration... and where does Southern Europe fit?', in C. Inglessi, A. Lyberaki, H. Vermeulen & G.J. van Wijngaarden (eds.), *Immigration and integration in Northern versus Southern Europe*, 1-10. Athens: Netherlands Institute in Athens.

Werth, M. & H. Korner (1991), 'Immigration of citizens from third countries into the southern member states of the EEC', *Social Europe* supplement 1/91: 1-134.

Zincone, G. (1999), 'Illegality, enlightenment and ambiguity: A hot Italian recipe', in M. Baldwin-Edwards & J. Arango (eds.), *Immigrants and the informal economy in Southern Europe*, 43-82. London: Routledge.

Zincone, G. & T. Caponio (2006), 'The multilevel governance of migration', in R. Penninx, M. Berger & K. Kraal (eds.), *The dynamics of international migration and settlement in Europe.* IMISCOE Joint Studies Series. Amsterdam: Amsterdam University Press.

7 Framing the Iberian model of labour migration

Employment exploitation, de facto deregulation and formal compensation

Jorge Malheiros

7.1 Introduction

As mentioned in the Introduction to this volume and particularly in chapter 5, the two Iberian nations, Portugal and Spain, have experienced a transition from emigration to immigration countries since the 1980s. This process has occurred during a specific moment of the political and economic evolution of both countries, marked, on the one hand, by the consolidation of their democratic regimes and their integration with the European Union and, on the other hand, by significant economic growth. This growth cannot be dissociated from the dynamics of the construction and public works sectors, nor from the expansion of family consumption and investment, which (especially at the beginning of this period) benefited greatly from European funding. The status of 'immigration countries' was symbolically and de facto reached at the very beginning of the first decade of the twenty-first century, when the number of foreigners settled in both countries grew exponentially.[1]

The policy process framing this relatively rapid transition of the Iberian states to immigrant receiving countries has been considered casuistic and fragmented (Baganha & Marques 2001; Costa 2003) and has often been labelled as permissive and weakly regulated. As mentioned by Joaquín Arango (2005) and António Vitorino (2007: 23), for some Northern European politicians and public officials, their transition has even represented a danger for the whole EU due to the 'promotion' of irregular migration supposedly associated with the successive immigrant regularisations that took place in the second half of the 1980s. However, authors such as Martin Baldwin-Edwards (1999) remarked that the reactive and fragmented Southern European (and therefore Iberian) immigration policies were in line with the dominant local regulation scheme and its associated economic model, marked by an extensive informal economy and low wages in many sectors (Reyneri 1999; Baganha 1998).

Taking into consideration this last assumption, this chapter will try to demonstrate how Portugal and Spain have developed a low regulation immigration model that has contributed to supporting the relatively high levels of economic growth in both countries (1991-2001 in Portugal; 1995-2007 in Spain) and that was well adjusted to the specific features of the Iberian 'proxy' of neo-liberalism implemented in a society characterised by practices marked by familiarism, informality and traditionalism. This low regulation immigration model rests on three pillars that sustain immigration policy components using a sequential logic: i) strong imports of workers mostly for the unskilled labour market (involving irregular status and exploitation); ii) regularisation a posteriori (ex post adjustment); and iii) formal social compensation in terms of relatively extensive citizenship rights (according to European standards), particularly in the labour market domain.

Using both statistical and descriptive techniques, we will demonstrate how Spanish and Portuguese immigration flows and policy measures combined to produce this model that, despite sharing various features with the Italian and Greek cases, comprehends some distinctive characteristics. By emphasising these original elements, we assume that the Iberian model of labour migration is a specific variant of the Southern European migration model discussed in chapter 5.

7.2   Discussing the model's premises: International migration and the neo-liberal project

In an active market economy, labour migration tends to largely self-regulate. This is especially true where the accumulation regime incorporates principles of free market extension, limited state intervention and high international dependency and/or interdependency levels, understood within the framework of contemporary economic globalisation. The period between the early 1980s and the late years of the first decade of the twenty-first century has been dominated by a rationale that assumes 'open, competitive and unregulated markets, liberated from all forms of state intervention, represent the optimal mechanism for economic development' (Brenner & Theodore 2002: 2). This neo-liberal ideology was germane to the aggressive policies of Margaret Thatcher, Ronald Reagan and also Portuguese Prime Minister Cavaco Silva, which aimed to dismantle and replace Fordist-Keynesian elements in the early 1980s, but also to the softer projects of Tony Blair (in Britain), Adolfo Gonzaléz (in Spain) and José Sócrates (in Portugal), which assumed a sort of compromise between a somewhat regulated market and the maintenance of standards through social policies, often through strategies involving private-public partnerships.

In fact, even in the apparent sunset of neo-liberalism that has occurred with the international financial and real estate market crisis beginning in 2008, the anti-crisis strategies that have been implemented involve the pernicious use of the state-market relationship to support the regeneration (or at least the survival) of the neo-liberal accumulation regime. According to this logic, public finances should cushion the losses of private enterprises in the financial sector, but once equilibrium is re-established, the principles of broad free market rules, low regulation and supply-side economics should be reinstated.

Considering the neo-liberal framework of the 1980s and 1990s, with its signature of free markets and globalised economy, it would be no surprise to see a corresponding increase in the volume of international migration or some deregulation of migration flows. In fact, both processes have occurred, but their growth has been less than one would expect if the neo-liberal utopia had fully materialised. According to the United Nations, the estimated number of international migrants in the world grew from 82 million in 1975 to 155 million in 1990 and to 195 million in 2005, and the stock of international migrants in the world population reached a value of 2.6 per cent in 2000, after a period of systematic increase over the two previous decades (Özden, Parsons, Schiff & Walmsley 2001).[2] In addition, migrant trafficking attained an unprecedented scale and the number of irregular immigrants reached, in 2006, an estimated high of over 16 million in OECD countries, of which 11 million were in the United States (Passel 2006) and about 4 million in Europe (Malheiros 2009). However, over approximately the same period, the world stock of foreign direct investment increased seventeen-fold[3] and between 1985 and 2005, international trade experienced average annual growth of 7.5 per cent (UNCTAD).

These figures show that labour markets have internationalised less than capital markets, but have nevertheless increased their internationalisation levels in the neo-liberal period. During this period, developed nation-states have facilitated capital and goods circulation (through tax reduction, tolerance towards tax havens and subsidies to attract foreign capital), but have also imposed restrictions on human mobility. However, if neo-liberalism is more about capital and competitiveness than about people and solidarity, it still requires labour for economic accumulation.

Although we may identify some contradictions in capital interests between the free circulation of people and state policy measures imposing constraints on international migration, this is more apparent than real. On the one hand, the neo-liberal project incorporates contradictions that result from its construction within the nation-state matrix, namely, the need to protect the state and its nationals through mechanisms such as border control or the introduction of reserve schemes in the labour market to protect the recruitment of nationals. On the other hand, the success of the free market requires the introduction of coercive regulatory schemes capable of promoting competitiveness, privatisation and commodification, such as individual evaluation, highly bureaucratic assessment forms that feed the needs of financial and consultancy firms, the externalisation of former public services in crucial citizenship domains such as security and health and the demise of collective work contracts.

Due to the fact that labour market segmentation involving new gender (and ethnic) divisions of labour as well as temporary forms of recruitment, either formal or informal, is crucial to the functioning of the neo-liberal orthodoxy, an effective (or potential) systematic supply of foreign workers has become essential. Because the need for foreign workers in developed countries is segmented and responds to economic conjunctures, mechanisms aiming to regulate international migration tend to be selective, especially targeting highly skilled migrants (those who feed the specific needs of the speculative and 'creative' financial services and IT sectors of advanced economies). In addition to these, immigrants also fill gaps in low-skilled sectors, particularly those characterised by seasonality (e.g. agriculture) or by limited potential for geographical mobility (e.g. the leisure industry, tourism, construction and public works and domestic service). Due to the high mobility of capital compared to labour, most remaining low-skilled sectors are relocating towards less-developed economies, benefiting from abundant labour and low wages.

All things considered, the regulation of international migration contributes to ensure labour market segmentation and flexibility in developed countries, making possible the regular recruitment of a contingent of workers who are channelled into specific sectors, facilitating the reduction of production costs and weakening labour protection (recruitment is on a temporary basis, contracts are short-term or very short-term and citizenship rights are often limited). Nevertheless, this process is far from perfect. Frequently, state regulation of international migration does not match the needs of the free market due to factors such as the protection of national interests, pressure from religious and civil society institutions and issues of human rights in a post-national context (Soyzal 1996; Martiniello 2000). If this mismatch seriously affects the accumulation dynamics of some sectors, alternative processes assert themselves and phenomena such as irregular migration expand. Nevertheless, if the accumulation regime calls, immigrants tend to arrive regardless of regulatory constrains.

The Iberian variant

As Neil Brenner and Nik Theodore (2001) mention, neo-liberalism cannot be found in a pure and unique form. Instead, neo-liberal projects 'are always introduced within politico-institutional contexts that have been moulded significantly by earlier regulatory arrangements, institutional practices, and political compromises'.

The development of neo-liberal projects in Iberian countries has taken place in a specific political and economic context that, despite national differences, was marked in the 1980s by the consolidation of democratic regimes, adherence to the EU and the inflow of significant funds aiming to promote development through processes such as the expansion of infrastructure and vocational training. After the economic crisis of the 1970s and early 1980s, both countries experienced a high level of economic growth that, during the 1990s, was above EU and OECD averages (Table 7.1). In consequence, a process of convergence of the economies of Portugal and Spain with the EU average took place in this period: according to Eurostat, in 1997, their GDP per capita in PPS[4] was, respectively, 76.1 and 93.3 per cent of the EU average; in 2002, these values had risen to 77 and 100.5 per cent. Whereas in 2002 the Portuguese economy started to show signs of contraction that continued in following years, Spain sustained its growth until 2008, when it was hit by the financial and real estate market crisis (Table 7.2).

Table 7.1 *Yearly GDP per capita growth rate, 1991-2001*

Countries and regions	Yearly growth rate (%)
Spain	**2.2**
Portugal	**2.6**
Italy	1.4
Belgium	1.9
Germany	1.2
US	2.1
EU-15 average*	1.7
OECD countries	1.7
Highly developed economies	1.7

* Except Ireland and Luxembourg
Source: UNDP Human Development Report (2003)

Table 7.2 *Real GDP growth rate*

Country	Yearly growth rate (%)		
	2002	Average 2002-2008	2008
Spain	**2.7**	**3.0**	**0.9**
Portugal	**0.8**	**0.8**	**0.0**
Italy	0.5	0.8	-1.0
Belgium	1.4	2.0	1.0
Germany	0.0	1.3	1.3
US	1.8	2.3	0.4
EU-15	1.2	1.8	0.5
EU-27	1.2	2.0	0.8

Source: Eurostat

Throughout this period of expansion, immigration to Portugal and Spain has attained unprecedented levels through very significant growth rates (Figures 7.1 and 7.2), revealing the strong tie between immigration and economic dynamics in Iberian countries due to the labour market insertion of these immigrants mainly in low-skilled sectors such as construction and public works, commerce, domestic service and agriculture (the last more in Spain than in Portugal).

Figure 7.1   *Evolution of the stock of legal foreigners in Portugal, 1974-2008*

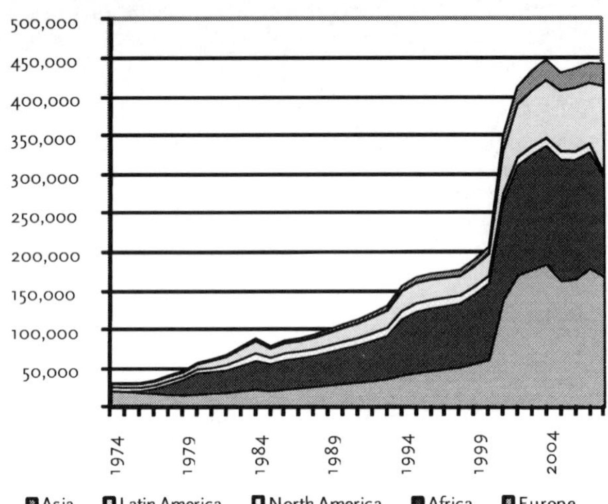

Sources: INE; Serviço de Estrangeiros e Fronteiras (various years)

Figure 7.2   *Evolution of the stock of legal foreigners in Spain, 1992-2006*

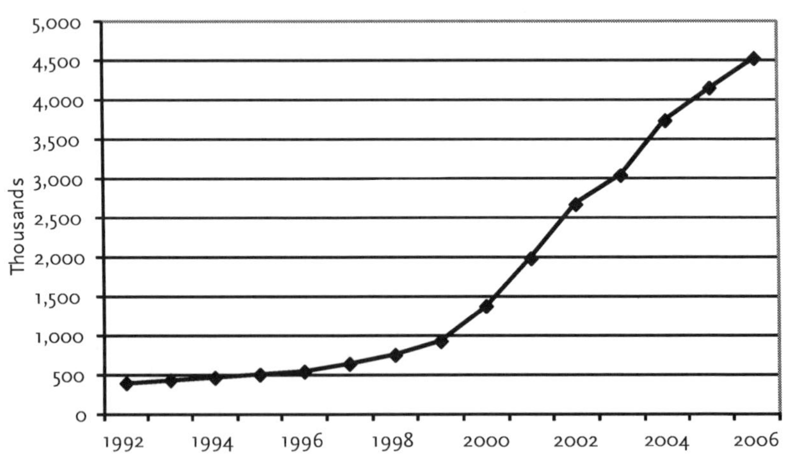

Sources: OECD Trends in International Migration (2003) and OECD International Migration Outlook (2008)

This strong external recruitment of immigrants, which involved new origin countries from the late 1990s to the early 2000s – namely, Ukraine, Romania, Bulgaria and Moldova – was crucial to remedy the labour deficits in the aforementioned sectors, a demand that could not be met by an ageing population with increasing education levels and corresponding social expectations that could only be satisfied by skilled jobs or, in the Portuguese case, by emigration.

However, this inflow of foreign workers, while crucial to cover specific labour market gaps, is also fundamental to the economic competitiveness of both countries, within the principles of their specific variant of the neo-liberal project.

It is important to underline that the economic growth of Portugal and Spain in the 1990s and early 2000s was supported by, among other things, the expansion of the speculative financial sector and its engagement with public works and the *filière* of construction (production-promotion-final consumption), two sectors with high profitability. The first has benefited from the modernisation process of the two countries that received significant inflows of EU funds in the 1980s and the 1990s, and the second from the expansion of consumption levels among families stimulated, partly through public policies, to invest in assets such as home ownership. Growth rates in housing construction in Portugal and Spain in the 1980s and 1990s were among the highest in Europe, despite the relative slowdown between the 1980s and 1990s (IHRU 2001). As a result of this process, which continued in Spain in the first decade of the twenty-first century, a value of 10.41 new dwellings built per 1,000 inhabitants was registered in this country in 2000, the second highest in the EU, after Ireland (Alonzo 2002). Although qualitative housing shortages for deprived families, including immigrant ones, can be identified in both countries, in 2001, Portugal and Spain registered a number of dwellings per family (including vacant dwellings and second homes) of 1.38 and 1.44, respectively, well above the European average (IHRU 2008). This expansion in the consumption of new houses, involving a high proportion of second homes,[5] has been supported by public policies geared towards home ownership (through public support for mortgages and the removal or reduction of new housing taxes) that accompanied the orientation of the banking sector towards real estate and housing.[6] This process, which increased debt levels in the construction sector to around 70 per cent of GDP in both countries in 2005 (IHRU 2008), is related to the patrimony-based traditions of Iberian societies, which display, together with Ireland and Greece, the highest percentages of home ownership in Europe (over 70 per cent). While in the past, access to real estate and housing was achieved via fragmented semi-informal and informal strategies such as the acquisition of land lots in the informal market of the urban peripheries, in the 1960s and 1970s such an access progressively became the domain of the formal market in the subsequent decades, where financial institutions play a major role.

The constant influx of foreign workers into the construction sector made an important contribution to its profitability and success in the two decades previous to the structural crisis that began in 2008. In addition, it also fuelled the family-conscious and heritage-based Iberian traditions, facilitating the deregulation of the housing market, contributing to increase the financial responsibilities of young families and limiting the direct intervention of public authorities in the social housing sector. This was kept at a relatively residual level by targeting only the most deprived groups through the promotion of re-housing processes, as in the case of the Portuguese slum clearance programme PER, launched in 1993. Immigrants ensured the necessary labour supply and contributed to sustaining salaries in the construction sector (Pereira 2010), a situation that has facilitated the accumulation of gains particularly in Spain, where housing prices rose significantly between the mid-1990s and the mid-2000s. In addition, swift growth in the number of immigrants in the first years of the twenty-first century in both countries, but particularly in Spain, has increased housing demand and may help to soften the negative impacts – such as the pressure to reduce prices – of the present housing and real estate crisis.

Public works and construction are not the only sectors where the presence of immigrants has played a key role. In market agriculture (especially in Spain) as well as in the hospitality and service industry and retail trade, a sector dominated by small enterprises that, according to OECD data, has seen greater growth than in other advanced economies, the entry of immigrant workers, often irregularly, helps to circumvent the stringency of work regulations and also to sustain an accumulation process based on labour, i.e. low wages.

Finally, the high rate of participation by female immigrants in the Iberian domestic sector – the other side of the gender segmentation process that has been observed in the construction/public works sector – (Ribas-Mateos 2000; Pereira 2010) enables the control of reproduction costs and facilitates the maintenance of 'welfare society' systems based on family and kinship networks and services (Santos 1995) that contribute to the reduction of public investment in domains such as care for the elderly and young children.

7.3 A three-step model of labour migration: Features and implications

Having clarified the role of immigrants in the development of the Iberian form of neo-liberalism in the 1990s and 2000s, it becomes fundamental to understand how economic interests and immigration policies work together to produce a specific model of recruitment, labour incorporation and integration of foreign workers.

As we previously mentioned, Spain and Portugal, especially, have labour markets characterised by relatively low wages compared to the former EU-15 countries (Figure 7.3). In addition, labour-intensive and capital-intensive sectors coexist (King, Fielding & Black 1997), a situation that has helped to polarise wages in societies with high levels of inequality (particularly Portugal) when compared to other developed countries. Because the transition to advanced service societies took place later in these nations, and particularly in Portugal, the issue of polarisation is not just the result of the symbiotic labour relation between highly skilled services (e.g. software creation, banking, design) and undifferentiated occupations (e.g. industrial cleaning, retail trades sellers, call centre assistants) in the context of the post-Fordist society, as Saskia Sassen (1996) and other researchers have shown. It is also a consequence of the slow modernisation of certain segments of industry and service, where employers continued to adopt defensive strategies, often based on low-skilled work and labour exploitation.

Figure 7.3 *Minimum wages in selected countries*

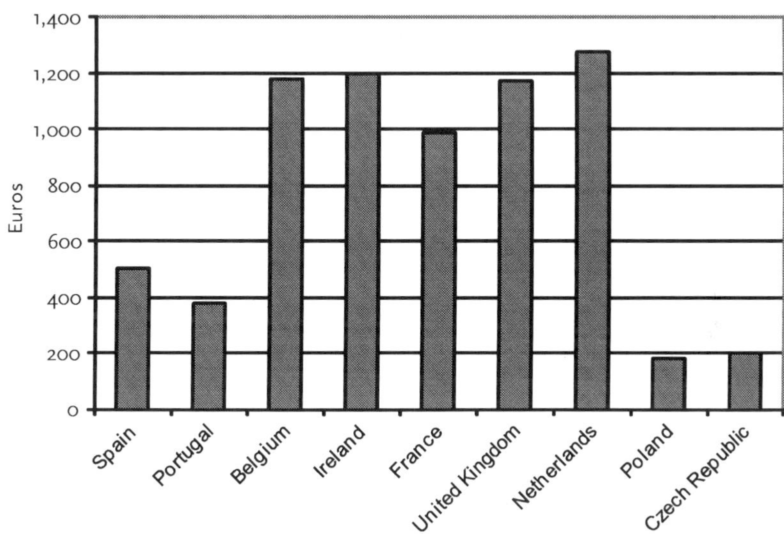

Source: Venn (2009)

Low wages and inequality have to be understood in the framework of a labour market characterised by a high level of formal rigidity. In effect, the late transition to democracy in the 1970s, along with corporatism and legal support based on the French tradition, explains this formal inflexibility (Figure 7.4) in terms of the difficulty of hiring and firing as well as rigidity in terms of working hours. Despite the evolution towards greater flexibility and precariousness introduced by recent changes in labour regulations, the Iberian nations were still among the OECD members with the highest levels of employment protection in 2009 (Venn 2009).

Figure 7.4 *Rigidity of employment index (0-100) in selected countries, 2009*

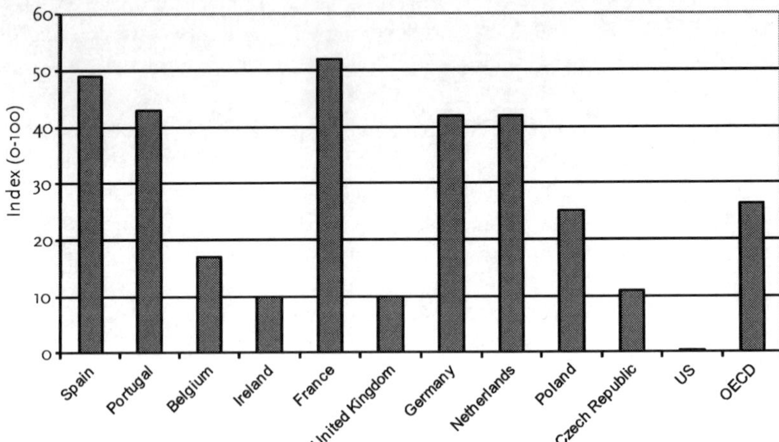

Source: www.doingbusiness.com (World Bank Group 2009)

Because progressive changes towards flexibility have been slow, Iberian entrepreneurs have developed different strategies to affect labour protection and weaken labour market ties. These include the increase of temporary contracts, a limited transition from fixed-term contracts to permanent employment (OECD 2004) and the wide use of informal employment. In fact, Portugal and Spain share with other Southern European countries relatively large informal economies, both in terms of employment and GDP (Figure 7.5).

Thus, in this specific and somewhat contradictory context, common elements of neo-liberalism such as limited direct public intervention (as in the case of the housing sector), transfer of activities to the private sector and progressive labour market deregulation and flexibility are combined with features of the tradition of Latin Europe that involve formal rigidity anchored in corporatism and the French legal tradition, and patrimony-based practices that facilitate the affirmation of free markets and a culture of economic informality. Labour immigration here plays a particular role, assuming specific contours that may be summarised in a three-step model involving irregular migration and labour market exploitation, followed by ex post regularisation and finally formal compensation in terms of citizenship rights.

Figure 7.5 *Percentage of shadow economy in the GDP of selected countries, 2001-2002*

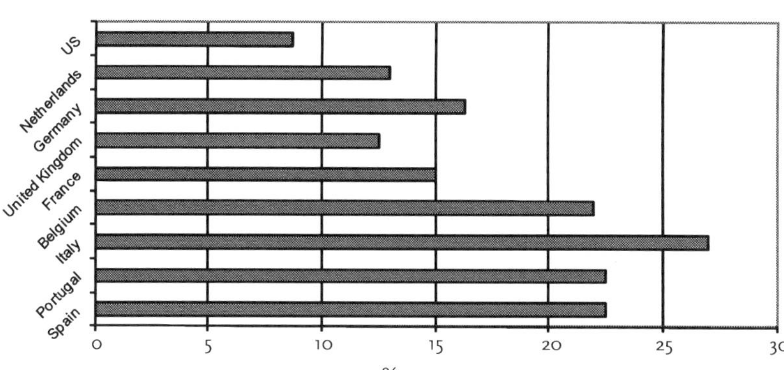

Source: Schneider (2002)

In concrete terms, a very significant number of the labour migrants who entered Portugal and Spain between the early 1990s and the mid-2000s have done so irregularly (Table 7.3). This form of recruitment made it possible to overcome the lengthy formal immigration processes in both countries[7] as well as the application of restrictive immigration laws based on mismatched quota systems in the early 2000s. In addition, irregular migration has ensured the existence of a large contingent of workers available for unskilled work in various sectors, whose vulnerability supports the flexibility and precariousness that established local workers avoid through formal regulations and collective bargaining. Despite various changes in the immigration laws of both countries since the early 1990s, we agree with Antonio Izquierdo-Escribano (2002) that the immigration panorama in Spain is basically the result of the needs and actions of private entrepreneurs, sustained a posteriori by public regulation. In the case of Portugal, the changes introduced in the law in 1993, following the first extraordinary

Table 7.3 *Regularisations of immigrants in Portugal and Spain*

	Year of regularisation	*Number of concessions of authorisation* *
Portugal	1992/1993, 1996, 2001, 2003 and 2004	275,000
Spain	1986/1987, 1991, 1996, 2000, 2001 and 2005	1,100,000

* These concessions do not correspond to regularised people because in several cases the regularised people return to irregularity (because the permits attributed become out of date or the job that justified the permit attribution is lost) and have to regularise themselves again in the next regularisation process.

Sources: Izquierdo (2002); Arango and Jachimowicz (2005); Levinson 2005

regularisation, still incorporated a paradigm of 'zero immigration' (Carvalho 2009) in contrast with the Portuguese economy's growing need for low-skilled labour. Despite the influence of the securitisation lobby over immigration regulations, the implementation of a restrictive policy did not prevent the entry of an increasing number of irregular migrants into Portugal, ensuring both the availability of labour and the conditions required by entrepreneurs.

After the changes introduced in the Portuguese immigration act of 1998, immigration policy followed an economic trend, progressively attempting to incorporate entrepreneurs' interests. Although bureaucratic recruitment procedures were kept intact by the 1998 and 2001 legal reforms, exceptional mechanisms of regularisation were introduced that were particularly comprehensive in the later reform. Throughout this period the government did not increase the systems of control over irregular migration and froze the volume of expulsions at a relatively low level, and the procedures were in line with the interests of economic agents, particularly in the growing construction and public works sector (Carvalho 2009). Even the legal reform introduced in 2003, which expressly incorporated the rhetoric (and the practice) of integrationism, did not challenge the association between the flow of irregular immigrants and national labour market needs (Carvalho 2009).

All things considered, the inflow of immigrants to Spain and Portugal was clearly generated by the needs of the labour markets not only in quantitative terms, but also in qualitative ones. The immigrants' irregularity enabled a quick entrance in the labour market – namely, in its informal segments – and ensured the necessary flexibility to overcome stringent work regulations and helped to sustain low wages. Within this framework, irregularity and potential labour market exploitation are linked, with massive ex post regularisations as a mechanism that ensures (temporary) rights to immigrant workers, responding to the demands of certain sectors of society (Catholic organisations, left-wing parties, immigrants' associations) and acts as a necessary release of social tension.

The uncontrolled growth of irregular immigrant workers in the labour market has two potentially negative social and political consequences. Internally, if unsatisfied labour market needs are met by irregular immigrants who then continue to arrive and start to compete effectively with national workers, particularly with established ones, anti-immigrant and xenophobic feelings tend to grow to levels that disturb social peace and political order, and institutions such as trade unions tend to increase pro-regularisation claims. Externally, as far as EU member states are concerned, the excessive number of irregular migrants in Iberia has been seen as a danger because they could then easily enter – due to the reduction in internal border controls – the societies and labour markets of most developed European countries. It may be argued that extraordinary regularisations have actually been explicitly criticised by the politicians and civil servants of some Northern and Central EU countries based on the argument that these procedures were stimulating irregular migration, a process that could have impacts all over Europe. However, we can interpret these declarations more on the side of political rhetoric than effective politics, not only because the circulation of non-EU Eastern European citizens (e.g. Ukrainians, Moldavians or Romanians previous to 2007) who migrated to Spain or Portugal has been facilitated by countries such as Germany, but also because effective EU principles and legislation on the promotion of case-by-case regularisations,[8] forced return[9] and increasing workplace inspections[10] were only approved in 2008 and 2009. This means that only when evidence of the economic downturn had started to show clearly in Southern European countries, including Portugal and Spain, did the EU promote legislation aiming to harmonise procedures fighting irregular migration and make public recommendations against extraordinary massive regularisations. In other words, while the first two steps of the model (irregular entry and massive ex post regularisations) served the economic interests of the Iberian countries and also of Greece and Italy within its specific version of neo-liberalism, the EU and even some Northern European politicians continued to criticise them for their incomplete rhetoric of statements and principles. Once the neo-liberal project started to present signs of crisis, mechanisms to restrict the entry of irregular foreign workers, to prohibit extraordinary regularisations and to send back those made redundant were actively promoted.

In addition to the two aforementioned pillars, it is important to mention that this migration model includes a third element: the attribution of extensive formal citizenship rights within the rubric of immigrant integration. In fact, Portugal and Spain have developed, since the second half of the 1990s, integration policies based on an extensive 'equal rights' principle that has been provided through legal devices that tend to award foreigners rights identical to those of nationals in the majority of citizenship domains, with the partial exception of the political ones. In order to implement some of these rights, integration services have been created at the national, regional and local levels, under the responsibility, the supervision or the guidance of the High Commission for Integration and Intercultural Dialogue in Portugal and the General Directorate for the Integration of Immigrants in Spain.

As a result of these active integration policies, Portugal and Spain have risen to top positions in the Migrant Integration Policy Index (MIPEX),[11] particularly in the labour market domain, where immigrants are eligible for most jobs soon after their arrival, can start businesses on their own and are offered a relatively large range of training and language courses (especially in Portugal) (Table 7.4). In addition, workers' security and employment rights are fully ensured to immigrants in both states (Nissen, Huddleston, Citron, Geddes & Jacobs 2007).

Table 7.4 *Value of MIPEX index and position of selected countries in the EU-27 group, 2006-2007*

Country	MIPEX global	MIPEX labour market
Portugal	79/100 (2nd)	90/100 (2nd)
Spain	61/100 (10th)	85/100 (4th)
Italy	65/100 (7th)	90/100 (2nd)
EU-15 average	60/100	64/100

Source: MIPEX (2006-2007)

Despite the positive character of these measures, empirically confirmed by the position of Portugal and Spain in the MIPEX, they somehow play a compensatory role in the Iberian immigration policy. On the one hand, these measures compensate immigrants for the vulnerability and exploitation they have undergone during their period of irregularity and also for the potential de facto labour market exploitation they still can face after their regularisation (it is important to remember that control mechanisms and bureaucratic procedures tend to be less effective than some ex ante regulatory devices, such as diversification of migration channels or the introduction of visas for work searching in destination countries). On the other hand, public authorities ensure, through this policy, fundamental citizenship rights to immigrants, respecting the principles of a democratic state and alleviating some potential social tension. However, these positive integration mechanisms are only seen in response to the 'irregularity route', and often only ensure de jure and not substantive rights.

7.4   Final considerations

As mentioned in the previous two chapters, the scientific arguments for the existence of a distinct Southern European migration model were presented to academia in the second half of the 1990s and stress a set of common factors that supposedly explain the immigration landscapes of Greece, Italy, Spain and Portugal, as well as the mechanisms responsible for the transition from emigration to immigration observed in these four countries (King & Iosifides 1996; King, Fielding & Black 1997; Baldwin-Edwards 1999; King 2000). Among these, the existence of internally unsatisfied labour demand in several labour-intensive sectors such as construction, hospitality and service industry, domestic work and agriculture, as well as the significant dimension of the informal sector, emerged as explanatory elements for the need for foreign labour. The less regulated migration context of these countries and its post-industrial character contrasted with the North-Western European migration model of the 1950s and 1960s, framed by Fordist-Keynesian principles (see chapter 2 in this volume). Finally, issues such as the similarity of the socio-demographic features of the immigrants (young adults oriented towards the unskilled segments of the labour market) or of policy responses to the management of flows (tolerance towards irregular entry, the importance of ex post mass regularisations, and the prevalence of reactive policies), are also underlined in the Southern European immigration model.

If the common patterns identified, as well as the explanatory power of their logical combination, has led some authors to consider that the model continues to be valid (Arango, Bonifazi, Finotelli, Peixoto, Sabino, Strozza & Triandafyllidou 2009; chapter 5 in this volume) and others to use it as a reference for other cases (King & Thompson 2008), the arguments presented in this text highlight two caveats.

First, beneath the general similarities identified, a set of specific elements have to be considered, such as the over-representation of construction and public works both in the economic dynamics and in the labour market incorporation of immigrants in Spain and Portugal. In addition, similar policy options may correspond, in some cases, to different policy strategies in the matter of migration. For instance, when Spain and Portugal introduced, in the period 2004-2007, a set of mechanisms enabling case-by-case regularisations in their immigration laws,[12] these had the purpose of better controlling migration through the adjustment between entry processes and access to a formal legal status. In the case of Italy, the introduction of an identical mechanism has been conceived as part of a more restrictive immigration policy. Finally, if we incorporate in the immigration model the third pillar regarding the nature of integration options, differences between Southern European countries become even clearer. For instance, the compensation strategy resulting from the extension of citizenship rights in the cases of Italy, Spain and particularly Portugal is not applicable in the situation of Greece.[13] Distinct political cultures, perceptions of identity and notions of 'us' and 'the other' may contribute to explain the different evolutionary paths of migrants' integration regimes.

Second, the Southern European migration model is largely the product of a specific variant of neo-liberal regimes, characterised by familiarism, patrimony-based traditions and informal relations that developed between the 1980s and the first decade of the 2000s in Iberia and eventually in Italy. Thus, the proposed model is only applicable if the features supporting a given accumulation regime are dominant in that particular historical moment. In other words, the Southern European migration model and its Iberian variant are structurally dependent on specific variants of the neo-liberal regime.

Given this, we should now ask what will happen to this three-stage immigration model, where economic interests are followed by reactive policy-making, now that several elements that used to sustain neo-liberal regimes are threatened by the present economic crisis. No single and clear answer can be provided to this question. However, the need to import unskilled labour will continue to decline or at least will maintain its 2009 level, well below that of the early 2000s given several structural changes in the economy, such as the likely end of the construction/public works engine; the continuing diffusion of technologies even in the service sector; and the contraction of some labour-intensive segments of manufacturing and agriculture due to firm relocation to cheaper regions or increased technology available for 'soil renewal' and international production transfer. On the contrary, the need for immigrant care workers will continue and eventually increase due to the swift ageing process of Portugal and Spain. Because the care sector is highly feminised, this process may change the gender balance of immigration, leading to a predominance of women migrants. In exceptional periods of strong public works growth (e.g. the construction of the new Lisbon Airport around the period 2015-2020), temporary recruitment of male foreign workers may take over women's predominance.

If this reduction in the need for immigrants and recomposition of flows effectively occur in Iberia, two extreme regulation routes could result. The first corresponds to an adjusted version of the three-stage immigration model, but with a stronger and more effective restrictive approach that privileges security, migration control and the eventual loss of the rights already achieved. The tolerance towards irregular entry will be more limited, but will continue, particularly at times of higher need for low-skilled workers. Regularisations will be more discrete (an adjustable and somehow flexible case-by-case perspective), eventually discretionary, and forced return will be the option pushed by governments.

The second approach involves a diversification of flows based on a continuous and efficient dialogue with labour market actors (entrepreneurs, trade unions, some immigrant organisations), an assumed reduction in ordinary migration costs (in terms of bureaucracy, length of procedures, etc.) and the development of positive international cooperation in matters of migration. In this case, the orientation of immigrants towards regular channels would potentially help reduce irregular migration, and forced return processes as well as the withdrawal of immigrants' rights would become complementary elements of the policy and not central issues. Naturally, due to the embeddedness of these immigration models in the framework of different accumulation regimes, this second hypothesis could only materialise if the present type of Iberian neo-liberalism evolved towards a different regime, one that effectively counters real estate speculation, property-based traditions and labour exploitation, and which, moreover, champions more efficient forms of public regulation. Eventually, the nation-state scale may not be sufficient to sustain a new and fairer immigration policy based on cooperation and respect for the rights of immigrant workers and their families. Demands for a more global regulation of financial circuits and markets, put forward by some heads of state of the G7 and the G20 in the past two years, should effectively be put into practice and clearly be extended to the regulation of international migration flows.

Notes

1   In Portugal, the number of legal foreigners grew from approximately 190,000 in 1999 to about 350,000 in 2001; in Spain the values changed from 800,000 in 1999 to more than 1.6 million in 2003.
2   It is worthwhile to mention that the increase in the volume of international migrants in the 1960s and 1970s was rather modest when compared to the values of subsequent decades and has even led to a reduction in the weight of the stock of international migrants in the total world population (Ozden et al. 2001).
3   According to UNCTAD *Handbook of Statistics 2009*, the world FDI stock passed from USD 705 billion in 1980, to 1,942 billion in 1990 and to 12,404 billion in 2005. Although these values are in current prices, their enormous increase clarifies the trends of globalisation of financial markets.
4   PPS stands for purchasing power standard.
5   In 2001, the percentage of secondary homes in the total volume of dwellings was placed between 15 and 20 per cent in both countries, the highest values of the EU (IHRU 2008; Alonzo 2002).
6   For instance, in the period 1997-2004, the percentage of housing loans in the total volume of credit attributed by Spanish banks had risen from 40 to 54 per cent (Alonzo 2002).
7   According to Jorge Malheiros (2008), the legal recruitment of a foreign worker could take more than four months in Spain and in Portugal.
8   Only in the European Pact on Immigration and Asylum of 17 June 2008 has the European Council explicitly recommended the use of case-by-case regularisations instead of general regularisations.
9   Directive 2008/115/EC, approved on 16 June 2008 and published on 16 December of the same year.
10   Directive 2009/52/EC, approved on 19 February 2009 and published on 18 June of the same year.
11   MIPEX, developed under the responsibility of the Migration Policy Group and the British Council, comprehends a set of indicators that measure the integration policies of EU-27 countries, Switzerland, Norway and Canada in six domains: labour market access, family reunion, long-term residence, political participation, access to nationality and anti-discrimination.
12   Royal Decree 2393/2004 of 30 December, published on 7 January 2005, which establishes the regulation of the Organic Law no. 4/2000 of 20 November (Foreigners' Law), changed by the Organic Law no. 14/2003 of the 20 November (Spain) and Law no. 27/2003 from 4 July (Portugal).
13   As far as MIPEX is concerned, Greece occupies one of the last positions, clearly below the EU-25 average. This shows that integration of foreign citizens in Greece, measured by the extension of formal citizenship rights, is much less accomplished than in the cases of Italy and the two Iberian countries (Nissen et al. 2008).

References

Alonzo, R.R. (2002), 'La política de vivienda en España desde la perspectiva de otros modelos europeos', *Boletin Ciudades para un Futuro mas Sostenible* 29. Madrid: Instituto Juan de Herrera. http://habitat.aq.upm.es/boletin/n29.

Arango, J., C. Bonifazi, C. Finotelli, J. Peixoto, C. Sabino, S. Strozza & A. Triandafyllidou (2009), *The making of an immigration model: Inflows, impacts and policies in Southern Europe*, IDEA Working Papers 9, www.idea6fp.uw.edu.pl/pliki/WP_9_Southern_countries_synthesis.pdf.

Arango, J. & M. Jachimowicz (2005), *Regularizing immigrants in Spain: A new approach.* Washington, D.C.: Migration Policy Institute.

Baganha, M.I. & J.C. Marques (2001), *Imigração e Política: O caso português.* Lisbon: Fundação Luso-Americana.

Baganha, M.I. (1998), 'Immigrant involvement in the informal economy: The Portuguese case', *Journal of Ethnic and Migration Studies* 24 (2): 367-385.

Baldwin-Edwards, M. (1999), 'Where free markets reign: Aliens in the twilight zone', in M. Baldwin-Edwards & J. Arango (eds.), *Immigrants and the informal economy in Southern Europe*, 1-15. London: Frank Cass.

Brenner, N. & N. Theodore (2002), 'Cities and the geographies of actually existing neoliberalism', in N. Brenner & N. Theodore (eds.), *Spaces of neoliberalism: Urban restructuring in North America and Western Europe*, 2-32. Oxford: Blackwell Publishing.

Carvalho, J. (2009), *A política de imigração do estado Português entre 1991 e 2004.* Lisbon: ACIDI.

Costa, P.M. (2004), *Políticas de imigração e as novas dinâmicas da cidadania em Portugal.* Lisbon: Instituto Piaget.

Iosifides, T. & R. King (1996), 'Recent immigration to Southern Europe: The socioeconomic and labour market contexts', *Journal of Area Studies* 6: 70-94.

Izquierdo-Escribano, A. (2002), 'Panorama de la inmigración en España en al alba del siglo XXI', *Mediterrâneo Económico* 1: 247-264.

King, R. (2000), 'Southern Europe in the changing global map of migration', in R. King, G. Lazaridis & C. Tsardanidis (eds.), *Eldorado or fortress? Migration in Southern Europe*, 1-26. London: Macmillan.

King, R., A. Fielding & R. Black (1997), 'The international migration turnaround in Southern Europe', in R. King & R. Black (eds.) *Southern Europe and the new immigrations*, 1-25. Brighton: Sussex Academic Press.

King, R. & M. Thomson (2008), 'The Southern European model of immigration: Do the cases of Malta, Cyprus and Slovenia fit?', *Journal of Balkan and Near Eastern Studies* 10 (3): 265-291.

Malheiros, J. (2008), 'Irregular migration in OECD member states: Nature, profiles and policies: An overview', unpublished research paper.

Martiniello, M. (2000), 'Citizenship of the European Union', in T.A. Aleinikoff & D. Klusmeyer (eds.), *From migrants to citizens*, 342-380. Washington, D.C.: Carnegie Endowment for International Peace.

Nissen, J., T. Huddleston, L. Citron, A. Geddes & D. Jacobs (2007), *Migrant integration policy index.* Brussels: British Council and Migration Policy Group.

Özden, Ç., C. Parsons, M. Schiff & T. Walmsley (2001), *The evolution of global bilateral migration, 1960-2000.* http://siteresources.worldbank.org.

Passel, J.S. (2006), *Estimates of the size and characteristics of the undocumented population.* Washington, D.C.: Pew Hispanic Center.

Pereira, S. (2010), *Trabalhadores de origem africana em Portugal: Impacto das Novas Vagas de Imigração.* Lisbon: Colibri.

Ribas-Mateos, N. (2000), 'Female birds of passage: Leaving and settling in Spain', in F. Anthias & G. Lazaridis (eds.), *Gender and migration in Southern Europe: Women on the move*, 173-195. New York: Berg.

Reyneri, E. (1998), 'The mass legalization of migrants in Italy: Permanent or temporary emergence from the underground economy?', in M. Baldwin-Edwards & J. Arango (eds.), *Immigrants and the informal economy in Southern Europe*, 83-104. London: Frank Cass.

Santos, B.S. (1995), 'Sociedade-Providência ou Autoritarismo Social?', *Revista Crítica de Ciências Sociais* 42: I-VII.

Sassen, S. (1996), 'New employment regimes in cities: The impact on immigrant workers', *New community* 22 (4): 579-594.

Schneider, F. (2002), *The size and development of the shadow economies of 22 transition and 21 OECD countries*. Bonn: IZA.

Soysal, Y. (1996), 'Changing citizenship in Europe: Remarks on postnational membership and the national state', in D. Cesarani & M. Fulbrook, *Citizenship, nationality and migration in Europe*, 17-29. London: Routledge.

Venn, D. (2009), *Legislation, collective bargaining and enforcement: Updating the OECD employment indicators*, OECD Social, Employment and Migration Working Papers no. 89. Paris: OECD.

Vitorino, A. (2007), 'Intervenção', in *Seminarios Palhavã, La inmigración en Europa: Una visión ibérica*, 23-24. Lisbon: Embajada de España.

8 Patterns of immigration in the Czech Republic, Hungary and Poland

A comparative perspective[1]

Dušan Drbohlav[2]

8.1 Introduction and conceptual framework

International migration in the countries of Central and Eastern Europe (CEE) is not a new phenomenon. Nevertheless, as late as the beginning of the 1990s, it began evolving into a more important topic for scientists and researchers, who started to look at international migration movements from various angles and perspectives. A missing key component, however, was a more systematic comparative perspective that could anchor the issue within a broader conceptual and theoretical framework (see also the Introduction in this volume). These very aspects were a primary focus of the IDEA project, which sought to compare the migratory experience of three groups of countries – Western European, Southern European and CEE – using the perspective of the IDEA conceptual framework and its key concepts within the European migration cycle (see chapters 1, 2 and 3 in this volume). By making use of the historical experience Western Europe has had in migration developments, one can more aptly identify the positioning of the CEE countries within the migration cycle and, more specifically, within its transition phases. It then becomes possible to make detailed observations of similarities and differences, both within the region and relative to the concept.

The underlying premise of the migration cycle concept is that, in the course of time, and in step with modernisation processes overall, European countries undergo a migration transition process from countries of emigration to countries of immigration. During this cycle, countries experience specific phases (see chapter 3). The main drivers of these developments are perceivable in the demographic and economic developments of both sending and receiving countries, as well as in the paradigms of migration and migration control policies (Fassman & Reeger 2008). A general condition sine qua non is that of a democratic regime (with open borders and free market economy), under which a migration transition can freely take place. The transition from an emigration country to an immigration country is typically composed of several characteristic stages. These stages differ in the features of the migration flow itself, by the socio-economic circumstances in the sending and receiving countries and by the transformation of the dominant migration regime (see chapters 1 and 3; also Fassman & Reeger 2008). Furthermore, there is an additional assumption that 'young' – meaning more recent – immigration countries go through more or less similar phases or stages within the migration cycle as did the 'old' immigration countries two or three decades previously. The migration cycle's three different phases follow the chronology of a preliminary phase, a transition phase and an adoption phase (see chapter 3); or in another possible understanding, a preliminary stage, a take-off stage, a stagnation stage and a mature stage (Fassman & Reeger 2008).

So, at what point in the migration cycle are the CEE countries (with their past and current migratory patterns) – represented here by Poland, Hungary and the Czech Republic – and what conditions apply to their positions? What common features do they share and, on the other hand, in which aspects do they differ? Can one 'coherent trajectory' be identified for the given CEE countries and their going through the migration cycle? Put forward here is the question of uniformity or particularity of CEE countries' migration characteristics vis-à-vis others. These are the main questions and issues that are tackled in this chapter, which is based on an extensive synthetic report for Poland, Hungary and the Czech Republic[3] (see Grabowska-Lusińska, Drbohlav & Hars 2011). An essential component of the approach adopted here is not only to provide a descriptive comparison, but also to give an explanation of what causalities factor in a given country's position within the migration transition process.

As compared to the two other European regions evaluated in this book (chapters 3 and 5), CEE countries lag significantly behind in their passage through the migration cycle – in other words, in their shift from emigration to immigration status. We depart from the presumption that the CEE countries, despite having entered the migration transition phase at the same time in the early 1990s (thus having in common the age and generation effects, as defined in chapter 2), exhibit significant differences, for many reasons which will be described in the following parts of this chapter. These differences are apparent in their migration patterns, as they have assumed slightly different positions within the transition phase. Nevertheless, the CEE countries still fit the pattern of early migration transition. They seem to be, for a variety of reasons, positioned along the path from very early migration transition stages (as is the case of Poland) to proper transition stages (as is the case of Hungary and the Czech Republic, especially).

What makes the CEE countries unique vis-à-vis other European regions is their shared heritage of enduring more than 40 years of communist rule

(CEE communist governments constructed very restrictive migration regimes). This period instilled in the societies many negative tendencies that affected, in addition to many other areas, that of migratory conditions (e.g. tolerance of undeclared work, corruption) (see 'features of an economy of shortage' in Kornai 1980). Another characteristic shared by these countries, which, importantly, has a noticeable impact on the generation effect (see chapter 2) they experience, is that in 1989 they underwent revolutionary changes reintroducing them into the 'continental migration system' from which they had been previously isolated by the Iron Curtain (Bonifazi, Okólski, Schoorl & Simon 2008).

The current democratic period began with a profound transformation process, from centrally planned economies to prosperous democratic systems – coupled with free-market economies. Overall migratory behaviour was quickly normalised vis-à-vis the developed democratic world. Thus, the CEE countries opened their borders and soon received both transitory migrants and migrants who decided to remain for longer periods. The transformation from communist regimes to democratic systems appears to have had a crucial impact on migration patterns in the CEE countries.

There was, however, no universal pattern and no specific mechanism underlying that complex transformation. Due to their different histories, varied economic heritages – which they acquired during the communist era – and the various policies they developed during their respective transformation processes, the outcomes of each transformation are different, at least to some extent. In the past, the CEE countries followed different models of centrally planned economies. Whereas the economy of (what was at that time) Czechoslovakia was very close to a classical centrally planned model, Hungary and Poland's economies represented particular kinds of free-market and command-type economy amalgamations. This especially became the case with the introduction, in Hungary, of market-oriented reforms in the late 1960s, and in Poland with the development of a 'natural' economy, limited instances of entrepreneurship and the early introduction of market-oriented reforms (Dorenbos 1999).

Thus, at the inception of their deep societal transformations (and before they entered the migration transition period), the three countries differed in terms of their economic situations. Whereas in Hungary and, to a lesser extent, the Czech Republic, the final decade of the socialist era and centrally planned economy could be characterised as a period of stagnation, in Poland there was decidedly a period of significant economic crisis (especially after martial law was introduced in 1981), with a rapid decline in real wages, high rate of inflation, a reduction in social benefits and imports and a decrease in consumption. All the countries, however, embarked on transformation processes with their labour markets in a rather confusing state characterised by full employment, labour misallocation and pseudo-labour shortages.

Robust changes in the economic system during the transformation period led to a shift from an excess demand for labour and over-employment to surpluses of labour and job shortages. Unemployment emerged as a new phenomenon and started growing, while newly functioning market forces contributed to a selection of workers. Simultaneously, the transformation brought about a reallocation of labour across enterprises, occupations, sectors and regions (with high regional variance) (Dorenbos 1999). In the course of the transformation (depending on which stage was reached) 'new spaces' (new attraction poles) in the CEE countries and their economies appeared. These spaces served as important destinations for new labour migrants and new inflows of workers from third countries – mainly from less-developed Eastern European countries (mostly Ukraine or Romania) or those located farther east (chiefly Vietnam and China). In these source countries, modernisation processes that led to intensive economic transition and transformation processes were delayed, and labour markets were unable to absorb redundant local labour forces.

All in all, the results of the complex transformation period in each of the CEE countries have been equally significant and far-reaching. They are also related to a period of rapid economic growth in the 1990s and those CEE countries' incorporation into western political, economic and security institutional structures.[4]

8.2   Historical experience: Migration patterns up to 1990s

When describing existing migration patterns, an overview and explanation of historical contexts becomes necessary. There are two main kinds of processes that have significantly influenced current migration patterns: geopolitical shifts (accompanied by administrative redrawing of state borders) and population migration. Accordingly, both the commonalities and the particularities of the countries within this region were, to some extent, already cultivated long before revolutionary changes of the late 1980s.

Prior to World War I, migration processes in the three CEE countries discussed here had many similar features, stemming mainly from the following two factors: relative delays in European-style modernisation and the multiethnic character of political entities to which those countries belonged. In fact, since the middle of the nineteenth century, all the CEE countries saw huge emigration losses – despite efforts to control the outflow. The main destination countries were located throughout Western Europe and Northern America, but varied according to who was on the move (see e.g. Nugent 1995).[5]

After World War I, the development of migration patterns in the CEE countries can be separated into four specific periods:[6] a) up to 1939 (dismantling of the Austro-Hungarian monarchy, establishment of new independent states, economic emigration combined with some return migration); b) 1945-1989 (the post-World War II rearrangements and the rule of the communist regime); c) 1990-2004 (a period of democratisation and incorporation into western institutions); and d) after 2004 until now (accession to the EU). For a more detailed overview of migration in the period 1945-2004, see chapter 1. This sort of division is particularly suitable because of the fact that the time periods differ significantly from each other in socio-economic, political and geopolitical ways and, perhaps as a result, in migration mobility patterns. One of the key factors differentiating these periods, which at the same time contributes to the similarities shared by the CEE countries (at least in the first two periods), is precisely that of net migration patterns. Obviously, during the first two periods all three countries experienced emigration rather than immigration. As late as 1989, after more than 40 years under communist rule, revolutions erupted and brought relative freedom to the societies – new political and, consequently, economic structures and regimes were established. For migration movements, this meant that the three countries quickly began deviating from the old communist model characterised by almost complete isolation. They slowly became transit and migration destination countries, and Hungary and the Czech Republic, especially, evolved into net immigration countries.

The following sections will describe selected migration patterns related to the first two periods (until 1989), the impacts of which can still be seen today. As far as geopolitical and administrative changes are concerned, Czechoslovakia[7] and Poland[8] were established as sovereign political entities in 1918 (freeing themselves from the Austro-Hungarian monarchy and, in the case of Poland, also from the German Empire and the Russian Empire). Hungary also became a sovereign state but, as a result of the peace Treaty of Trianon in 1920, its territory was significantly reduced as compared to that belonging to the Hungarian kingdom. Consequently, more than 30 per cent of ethnic Hungarians found themselves outside of Hungary (mainly in Romania, Slovakia, Serbia and Ukraine), which was an important influencing factor for the post-1989 immigration patterns into Hungary (Drbohlav 2011).

Some other historical events and contexts – important for understanding the entirety of the situation in the field of migration and ethnic composition – are worth elaborating. First, massive involuntary population movements continued after the end of World War II, particularly in Poland, and ended in 1948. They resulted in population resettlements (mostly forced movements based on ethnic grounds) and returns of prisoners or fugitives of war. Nevertheless, in 1948, with the advent of the Cold War, most or all of these movements were interrupted. This abrupt discontinuation of compatriots' resettlements led to renewed eruptions of these movements later (e.g. massive family reunion migration in Poland in the mid-1950s). Secondly, at the very end of the 1940s – when migration movements in the

Communist bloc were heavily controlled and restricted – a widespread ethnic homogenisation took place. It was exacerbated by policies of ethnic cleansing between 1945 and 1947[9] (e.g. nearly all Germans living in CEE countries were deported to Germany; and population exchanges occurred between Hungary and Czechoslovakia as well as Poland and the Soviet Union). Thirdly, political upheavals – which took place in Hungary in 1956, in Czechoslovakia in 1948 and 1968 as well as in Poland in the period 1980-1981 – led to huge waves of emigration. As a result, large diasporas were established or significantly strengthened in key destination countries (chiefly in Western Europe and North America) (Grabowska-Lusińska & Okólski 2009; Drbohlav 2011).

Differences between Poland, Hungary and the Czech Republic also existed during the communist era. In contrast to Czechoslovakia and, to a lesser extent, Hungary, which both suffered from a shortage of labour, Poland exhibited a continuous excess of labour. Shortly after World War II, the regions of the present Czech Republic that were heavily hit by deportations of the German ethnic minority were partly resettled, mostly via internal immigration (specifically of the Czechs and Slovaks). Moreover, after 1960, the Czech lands received a steady influx of temporary migrant workers from Poland, Vietnam[10] and other socialist countries. On the other hand, Poles (unlike the Czechs and Hungarians) were involved not only in labour migration related to temporary employment (e.g. in Czechoslovakia or Hungary), but also, especially in the 1980s, in petty trade activities performed under the guise of tourism. Both Czechoslovakia and Hungary were major destinations for circulating Polish petty traders (Drbohlav 2011).

8.3   Current migration patterns

As already mentioned, since the late 1980s, all three countries have undergone a deep political and socio-economic transformation, which has been accompanied by a profound transformation of migration patterns – albeit of different pace and volume. The dismantling of communist regimes resulted in the opening of formerly closed and heavily controlled state borders, which led, in turn, to a reshaping of European migration patterns. International mobility between 'Eastern' and 'Western' Europe increased significantly, though the previous predictions of massive immigration movements to Western Europe were not fulfilled. This is due to many simultaneously occurring factors. They include stringent migration regulations and controls; limited labour market opportunities in Western European countries; rapid improvement in the socio-economic situations of certain post-communist countries; and an overall increase in migration between the CEE countries themselves (Zlotnik 1999; Wallace & Stola 2001; Kaczmarczyk & Okólski

2005). As a result, a new international migration space emerged in CEE, characterised by its own sending and receiving countries, specific categories of migrants and particular dynamics and directions of flows. The Czech Republic and Hungary were quickly transformed to transit and destination areas. Poland, on the other hand, has been characterised by high rates of emigration, accompanied by the circular mobility of foreign nationals and only modest immigration levels (e.g. Korys 2004).

Before making academic use of migration figures, the reliability of migration statistics must be discussed. Generally speaking, there tends to be a marked under-registration of migration movements, as well as an incompatibility of migration-related definitions over time[11] and across the countries in question. The overall quality of statistical data seems to be, in many instances, related to the volume of immigration. Thus, Czech migration statistics are thought to be better developed than Polish statistical data on migration – which is, by contrast, perceived as highly unreliable and incomplete (Hars 2011). In all likelihood, the most important data-related shortcoming (common to all three CEE countries) is the under-registration of emigration flows, a reality that seriously limits the possibility of further analysing net migration as an integral variable.

The problem of low-quality emigration-related statistics is of special importance in the case of Poland, which has recently been an important source country for many other EU receiving countries (see e.g. Triandafyllidou 2006). The official emigration statistics suggest that only 20,000 to 25,000 emigrants have left the country each year since 2000 (with the exception of some 47,000 in 2006 (see Kępińska 2007). However, a more accurate and realistic picture, one of an entirely different scale, is provided by Izabela Grabowska-Lusińska and Marek Okólski (2009), who determined that, within the period 2004-2006, about 950,000 persons left Poland (for a stay abroad of more than two months).

Due to the various data-related deficiencies so far described, and in accordance with the analytical focus being placed on the immigration side of the 'migration coin', only immigration statistics will be discussed (see Figure 8.1).

Although drawing an apt comparison is somewhat problematic, since the early 1990s, a continuous inflow of long-term immigration – albeit of different 'rhythms' – has been observable in each country. Whereas immigration to Hungary already peaked in 1990, when thousands of ethnic Hungarians (mainly from Romania) came into the country (Hars 2009), a rapid decline ensued in the period 1992-1994. A steep increase in immigration from 2001 onwards clearly separates the Czech Republic from the other two countries. This boom, aside from the aforementioned statistical changes, was triggered mainly by a favourable economic situation and growing labour demand, which was chiefly supplied by immigrants from post-Soviet countries (Ukraine, Russia, Moldova), Slovakia, Vietnam or

Figure 8.1 *Migration inflows to the Czech Republic, Hungary and Poland, 1989-2007*

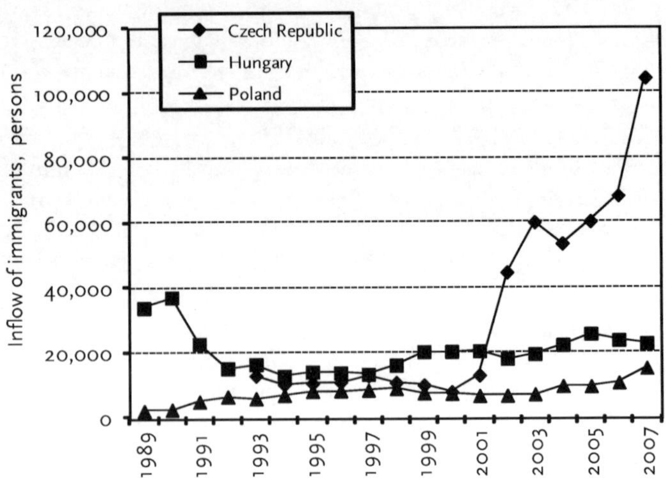

Notes: In 2001, there was a change of statistical definition of population. Besides foreigners with permanent residence on the Czech territory, the Czech statistics started to also include asylum seekers and foreigners staying in the country with a visa for more than 90 days whose length of stay exceeded one year.
Hungary: Data include foreigners holding a long-term residence permit (valid for up to one year), foreigners who have been residing in the country for at least one year and who currently hold a long-term permit; data are presented by actual year of entry (whatever the type of permit when entering the country).
Poland: Data include the number of permanent and 'fixed-time' residence permits issued.
Source: Hars (2011)

Mongolia (Drbohlav, Lachmanova-Medova, Cermak, Janska, Cermakova & Dzurova 2009; Drbohlav, Medova, Cermak, Janska, Cermakova & Dzurova 2010). Immigration to Poland has been quite stable over time, although a slight growth was recently observed. This could be attributed to favourable economic developments, which could be, in turn, the result of an increase not only of foreigners (from Ukraine, Germany or Belarus), but also of Polish return migrants (Górny, Grabowska-Lusińska, Lesińska & Okólski 2009). In the case of Poland, a particular type of short-term migration (which is not reflected in Figure 8.1), known as 'incomplete migration' (Okólski 2001, 2004), has also arisen and, for a long time, even dominated as a type of labour mobility. These short-term movements (usually lasting only several weeks) are typical of post-Soviet (namely Ukrainian) migrants engaging in irregular economic activities (petty trade and/or employment) in Poland, while maintaining their family lives in their home country (Grzymała-Kazłowska & Okólski 2003, 2010).

The trends described are partly reflected by migrant stocks (see Figure 8.2). This time, the Czech data series is without major disruption (or changes in definition). The number of registered foreigners in the Czech Republic has gradually grown over time (with the exception of 2001, when a worldwide economic crisis, beginning in the late 1990s, along with application of restrictive migration measures, seemed to derail growth). Since 2004, migration growth has even accelerated: in the new millennium, the number of foreigners has almost doubled. In 2007, it reached 394,000, representing more than 3 per cent of the population (Drbohlav et al. 2009). There is, unfortunately, no data series on migrant stocks in Poland – the only reliable information comes from the 2002 Census and predicts about 75,000 foreigners (who remained in Poland more than two months).

Figure 8.2   *Migrant stocks in the Czech Republic, Hungary and Poland, 1993-2007*

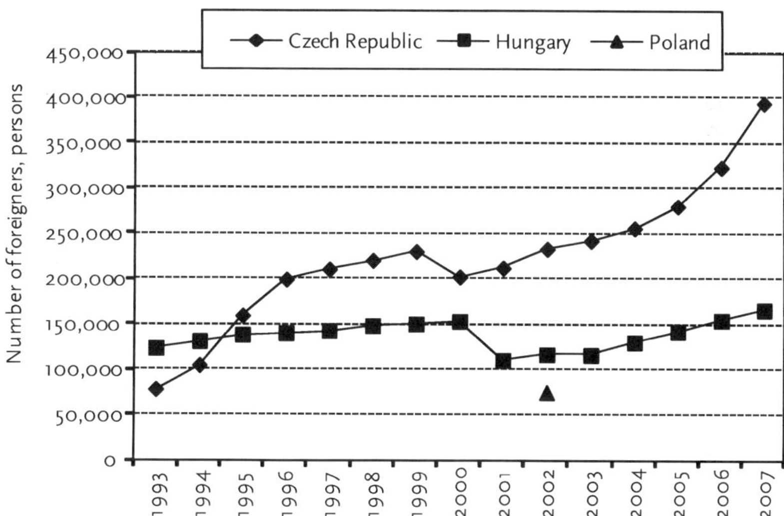

Notes: Czech Republic: Foreigners with permanent residence permits (until 2006: permanent residence gained after ten years of residence, however shorter for family members; since 2006: after five years); foreigners with long-term residence (prior to 2000: foreigners with permits for a stay of over 180 days; since 2000: generally meaning foreigners with visas for a period exceeding 90 days and with long-term residence permits).
Hungary: Settlement permit prior to 2002: after five years; following 2002: after three years of stay (with proof of residence and subsistence, shorter for family reasons) and for up to one year (drop in Hungarian data between 2000 and 2001 due to data correction).
Poland: Only 2002 Census data are available. Polish residence permit databases do not allow for the differentiation between the stocks and flows of the migrant population at any given time.
Source: Hars (2011)

A recent increase in migrant stock is also visible in Hungary (in 2007 it was some 175,000 persons). In sum, especially in the years following their EU accession, the Czech Republic and Hungary entered a new period of intense migrant population growth.

Migrant populations in Poland, Hungary and the Czech Republic come mainly from neighbouring and/or former post-Soviet republics. Some long-distance migrants – namely, those from China and Vietnam – also factor among the most numerous migrant groups in these countries. In all three countries, an important segment of citizens from the developed EU-15 states and the United States (Hars 2011) is also present.

Since the mid-1990s, the most sizable migrant groups in the Czech Republic are those comprising citizens of Ukraine, Slovakia, Vietnam, Russia and Poland. Whereas the numbers of Slovak and Polish citizens have not changed much since the mid-1990s (in 2007 they reached 68,000 and 21,000, respectively), figures of those from Ukraine (127,000 in 2007), Vietnam (51,000 in 2007) and Russia (23,000 in 2007) increased twofold as compared to levels in the mid-1990s. The largest 'Western' migrant groups originate from Germany and the US (Drbohlav et al. 2009). The main source country of migrants in Hungary is neighbouring Romania (with the majority of migrants being ethnic Hungarians). Romanian migrants clearly outnumber other foreign communities (in 2007 they represented nearly 50 per cent of the migrant stock figure). Other significant groups are migrants from Ukraine, Serbia, Germany and China (Hars 2009). According to the 2002 Census results, the largest migrant groups in Poland came from Ukraine (some 12,000 persons), Germany, Russia, Belarus and Vietnam (Górny et al. 2009).

Clearly, the main purpose of immigration to the CEE countries is for work (or economic activities, in general) and the related family reunification. In 2006, work and opening small businesses were the main migration purposes of nearly 50 per cent of the migrant stock in the Czech Republic (according to the reasons provided on residence visas and permits) (Drbohlav et al. 2009). Similarly, a high share (50 to 60 per cent) of new and renewed resident permits issued between 2002 and 2006 in Hungary stated purposes of employment. The share of self-employment – including entrepreneurship – fluctuated around 1 to 10 per cent, and family reunification reasons were also around 13.8 per cent (Hars 2009). The main purpose of immigration to Poland was structurally somewhat different, with family reasons topping the list (40 per cent of migrants). About 30 per cent of migrants indicated work-related reasons, and some 20 per cent came for educational reasons (Górny et al. 2009).

Consequently, the age structure of migrant populations in the CEE countries skews rather young, and resembles a traditional labour migrant model with a dominant 'productive age' cohort (see also chapter 5). About 85 per cent of the migrant populations in all three countries are younger than 65 years of age. When we compare migrant population's age structure with the structure of total population in the given countries, the proportion of children as well as persons aged 65 or more is much smaller than that of the total population. While in the Czech Republic and Hungary migrants aged between 25 and 40 dominate the migrant stock, the Polish migrant population is slightly older, with the main age groups ranging between 40 and 64 (Hars 2011). The migrant population in the Czech Republic is dominated by men (they amounted to about 60 per cent in the period 2001-2007), which is another characteristic of the traditional labour migrant model. The share of women in Hungary and Poland is equal to that of men (Hars 2011).

Although foreign workers dominate the migrant stocks, they represent a rather small segment of the total labour force in Poland (0.1 per cent) and Hungary[12] (1.5 per cent), and are slightly more numerous in the Czech Republic (3.6 per cent),[13] demonstrating a high growth dynamic (see Figure 8.3).

What is the migrants' labour market position? Despite varying levels of labour demand and/or migrant labour supply among the countries in question, their structures seem to be similar in all three. In Hungary and the Czech Republic, legally employed migrants work mainly in the construction services and manufacturing sectors. There is also a rather small but important segment of labour migrants – professionals who arrive from other developed countries (mainly the EU-15) and who are chiefly involved in more intellectually demanding jobs. By contrast, legal migrants in Poland are mostly concentrated in this 'more qualified' sector (trade, education, etc.). This difference in types of migrant employment between the CEE countries is somewhat deceptive, however, as in Poland the construction, agriculture, trade and service sectors are also 'migrant labour sectors', but these migrant workers are typically irregular (Drbohlav 2011). Indeed, irregular migrant labour is a common migration feature of all three countries, in fact, of the whole EU, too (chapter 5 in this volume or Düvell 2006). As is the case in Poland, irregular migrant workers in Hungary and the Czech Republic are also employed in the secondary labour market, which is characterised by labour-intensive, poorly paid jobs[14] (see Cermak & Dzurova 2008). Especially since the 1990s, Poland has become known for the short-term mobility of post-Soviet foreigners, accompanied by irregular, cross-border petty trade (see incomplete migration mentioned earlier in this section) (Okólski 2001, 2004). This is a phenomenon that has never arisen in the Czech Republic, and only to some extent in Hungary (Drbohlav 2011). The irregular employment of foreigners and, generally, the size of the irregular migrant population in CEE countries is considered significant, although estimates do differ (from some 40,000 to 300,000 in the Czech Republic, about 100,000 in Hungary and from 80,000 to 200,000 in Poland) (Drbohlav et al. 2009; Hars 2009; Górny et al. 2009). Typically, irregular labour migrants in the CEE countries arrive (usually

Figure 8.3a   *Employment of foreign workers in the Czech Republic, Poland and Hungary, 1993-2007: Stock of foreign workers 1990-2007*

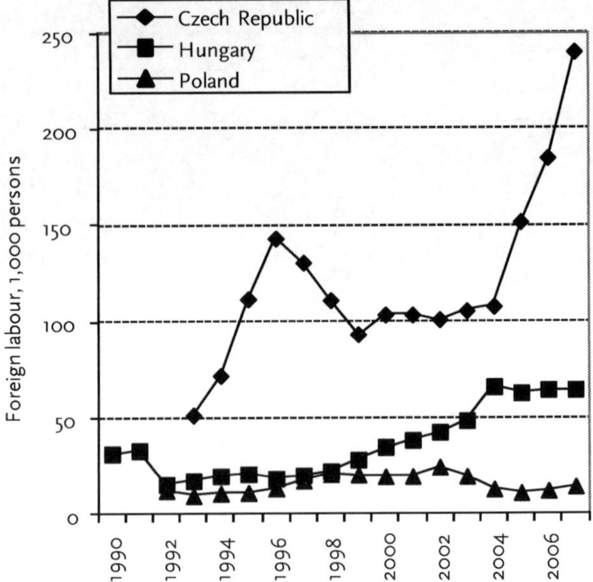

Notes: Czech Republic: Work permit holders and registered Slovak workers until 2003; as of 2004, foreigners registered at labour offices (i.e. third-country employees usually with a work permit obligation versus EU, EEA and Switzerland nationals with no work permit obligation). Data excludes trade licence holders. Hungary: Work permit holders until 2004; as of 2004, work permits, green card holders and registrations.
Poland: National Labour Office and Ministry of Labour and Social Policy.
Source: Hars (2011)

with tourist visas) from the same sending regions as legal migrants (from economically less developed countries, for the most part). Although a significant number of irregular migrant workers participates in the shadow economy, the 'grey labour market' in CEE countries is, to a much larger extent, occupied by the domestic labour force (Drbohlav 2011).

There is an additional and very specific segment of the foreign population: asylum seekers. Since the early 1990s, asylum seekers have used the CEE countries – especially the Czech Republic and Hungary – as primary destinations to submit an application. Until the early 2000s, their numbers fluctuated from between 5,000 to 10,000 a year in Hungary and the Czech Republic, though have as of late dropped significantly to some 2,000 or 3,000 annually (Hars 2011). Poland, on the other hand, has experienced a growth only recently, with numbers ranging from 7,000 to 8,000, mainly comprising Chechens (Górny et al. 2009). The share of 'successful' asylum

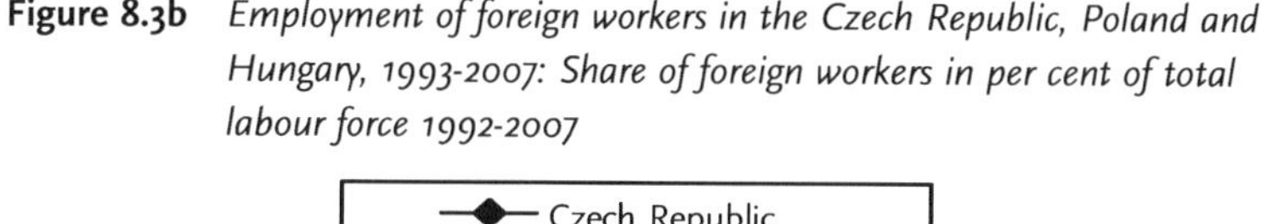

Figure 8.3b *Employment of foreign workers in the Czech Republic, Poland and Hungary, 1993-2007: Share of foreign workers in per cent of total labour force 1992-2007*

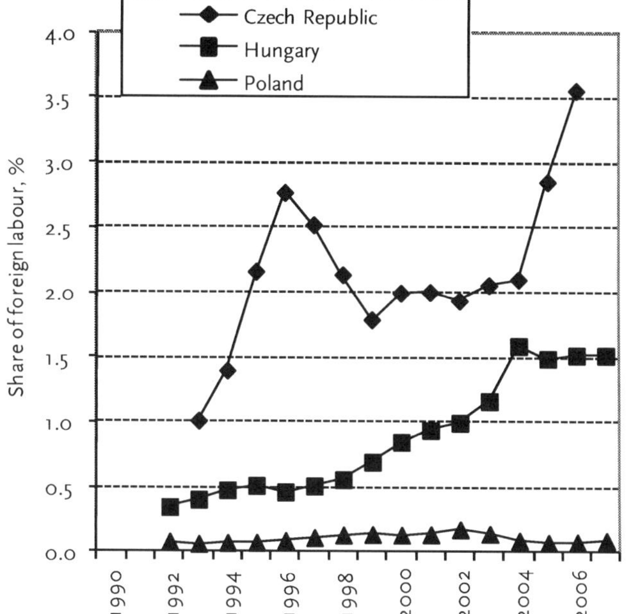

Notes: Czech Republic: Work permit holders and registered Slovak workers until 2003; as of 2004, foreigners registered at labour offices (i.e. third-country employees usually with a work permit obligation versus EU, EEA and Switzerland nationals with no work permit obligation). Data excludes trade licence holders. Hungary: Work permit holders until 2004; as of 2004, work permits, green card holders and registrations.
Poland: National Labour Office and Ministry of Labour and Social Policy.
Source: Hars (2011)

seekers – that is, those given asylum – in all three CEE countries has been very low (e.g. some 2.5 per cent in the Czech Republic for the period 1994-2007 (see Horakova 2008)), presumably due to many unfounded applications for asylum, submitted by economic migrants (mostly in transit).

8.4   Determinants of migration

This section focuses on migration drivers: key factors that impel the migration transition process. These drivers were identified (and subsequently tested) based on the experience of Western European countries – the so-called mature immigration countries within the migration cycle (chapter 3). Discussed here are step-by-step, structural factors including geopolitical, economic and demographic variables, along with other contextual factors (including historical patterns of migration, etc.). Most of the attention will be devoted to economic factors, which seem to be decisive in explaining immigration patterns in the CEE region. The economy and, more specifically, the demand for labour have also been confirmed as the most important migration drivers for 'old' immigration countries such as Germany or Austria (see chapter 3).

The role of economic transformation processes in the 1990s was a particularly crucial factor in triggering immigration flows to the CEE countries. We attempt to identify here the specific economy-related factors that are the most important for explaining immigration to the countries in question. A direct relationship between the economic situation (at a macro-level) and immigration has already been proven in the Czech Republic (see more in Drbohlav et al. 2009). In fact, it is only in the Czech case that the demand side matched the foreign supply side – a circumstance that seems to be a key precondition for robust immigration. In Poland, this 'demand-supply harmony' arose only recently (after Poland joined the EU). To some extent, these conditions have been the result of the continuous and intensive emigration of Poles abroad.[15] Under these conditions, the demand for foreign labour force has increased significantly. Even this synergy, however, has not been enough to trigger massive immigration into the country – immigration levels into Poland are still rather low. In Hungary, due to its somewhat different economic path and structure, the demand for labour has been rather low; the growth of the economy in Hungary can in fact be characterised as a jobless growth.[16]

There are also important labour market deficiencies in CEE that function as strong ('pull') factors to attract a foreign labour force. Among these deficiencies are: mismatches between the demand and supply of domestic labour; natives' low motivation to take on certain jobs; high labour costs; limited occupational and geographical (internal spatial) mobility; and, of chief significance, the widely tolerated practice of undeclared work. It appears that all these pull factors play an important role in all three countries (see more in Drbohlav 2011).

To further elucidate the role of undeclared work, one must take stock of the fact that there has been a persisting tolerance of informal business practices and undeclared work in the CEE countries since the time of the communist economic system (e.g. Renooy, Ivarsson, Van der Wusten-Gritsai & Meijer 2004; Fassmann 2008). This tolerance goes hand in hand with existing robust informal economies (chiefly composed of domestic workers) that consequently incentivise irregular migration into CEE countries (see also Reyneri 2002; Arango, Bonifazi, Finotelli, Peixoto, Sabino, Strozza & Triandafyllidou 2009). Previous estimates have put the extent of undeclared work (as a percentage of GDP) in the CEE countries at 9 to 10 per cent in the Czech Republic, 14 per cent in Hungary and 18 per cent in Poland at the turn of this century (see Renooy et al. 2004). More noteworthy than the figures themselves is the fact that the phenomenon of undeclared work and its social tolerability are widespread throughout all social strata and regions of the CEE countries (Drbohlav 2011).

The demographic situation of the CEE countries constitutes another major migration driver (see the Introduction and chapter 3), although its importance has only recently been acknowledged. In recent years, like many other developed European countries, the CEE region has suffered from several demographic problems. They originate in the ageing process (low fertility levels, growing life expectancy), diminishing population levels and gradually declining economically active segments of population (see Eurostat 2009). In contrast to past developments, the role of migration in shaping the demographic situation (vis-à-vis fertility and mortality patterns) will probably increase in significance in the CEE region. Thus the most important effects upon labour markets remain to be seen[17] (see e.g. Eurostat 2009; Bijak, Kupiszewska & Kupiszewski 2008). All in all, the demographic situation has become – and will likely continue to be – an important factor that triggers immigration in a variety of ways. For example, this may happen directly through growing demand for labour and spontaneous migration movements and indirectly through various state recruitment policies that seek to saturate the weakening pool of domestic human resources. In all likelihood, these new challenges will cause countries to reassess their established economic and social policies, such that they will seek to resist such developments. The Czech Republic was the earliest of the CEE countries to launch programmes for recruiting foreign labour force: the first was instituted as early as 2003, followed by a second in 2009 (see Drbohlav et al. 2009, 2011). Poland and Hungary have also recently started engaging in such activities, at least in the form of public proclamations and debates (see Lesińska, Stefańska & Szulecka 2011).

Two major events (and important additional migration drivers) have also significantly changed the geopolitical situation in the three CEE countries and had a tremendous impact upon migratory realities. The first was the breakdown of the entire eastern Communist bloc at the very end of the 1980s. The second was the accession of the CEE countries to the EU on 1 May 2004. Other important country-specific geopolitical developments have also influenced migration realities. Poland has been demonstrating its national interests by trying to maintain special close and friendly relationships with eastern neighbouring countries (Ukraine, Russia and Belarus)[18] (Górny et al. 2009). Particular historical developments (as described in the previous section) have led to a situation in which large pools of co-ethnics reside in countries bordering Hungary; these pools serve as dominant sources of Hungarian immigration. These ethnic patterns have had an important impact on the migratory situation and policies of contemporary Hungary (Hars 2009). The Czech Republic also has very special geopolitical links to Slovakia. More than 70 years of shared history within one Czechoslovak state – as well as significant cultural and linguistic similarities – have been key factors driving the liberalisation of migration admission and labour policies towards Slovakian migrants in the Czech Republic between 1993 and 2004 (Drbohlav et al. 2009).

Migration policies are an important contextual factor within the migration cycle (see chapter 3); the rest of this section includes a discussion of their relevance.

Last but not least, there are other (perhaps less important) contextual migration factors of note as CEE countries move through their respective migration cycle phases. Namely, historical backgrounds, historical migration patterns and migrants' own social networks have all served to frame the migration transition process. Due to heavily controlled migration movements during the communist era, the previously established migration networks and family or community-specific systems were disrupted. On the other hand, some trainees, workers and students who arrived in the CEE countries during the socialist era became 'embryos' of further immigrant inflows in the 1990s (e.g. the Vietnamese community in the Czech Republic and Poland). In Hungary, as previously indicated, ethnic ties were a key factor behind Hungarian immigration patterns (Drbohlav 2011).

Interestingly, public attitudes towards migration issues and immigrants – which might have been thought to wield influence as another contextual migration factor – have not played a significant role in influencing migration flows. To date, that is, no evidence in the CEE context has been found.

Finally, factors lying behind state borders cannot be overlooked. Certain 'push' factors – namely, political and socio-economic conditions in surrounding or otherwise significant migration source countries are of particular importance (Fassmann & Reeger 2008). Of note are recently modernising eastern regions – countries of the former Soviet Union and some Asian countries such as Vietnam and China – that have been sending out their labour forces to the CEE region.

8.5   Migration policies

Migration policies constitute an important contextual factor within the migration cycle and the migration transition process (chapter 11 in this volume). Their impact upon migratory realities and trends in the CEE region is illustrated by two key examples. First, especially in the first half of the 1990s, it was not migration policies, but the lack thereof ('migration nonpolicies', as it were, which were typical of very liberal approaches) that contributed significantly to large immigration inflows, especially in the case of the Czech Republic. Second, a common pattern for all three countries is that gaps in migration policies have served as pull factors used flexibly by migrants, e.g. by 'masked' asylum seekers or 'hidden employment' engaged in by holders of trade licenses (more on this in Grabowska-Lusińska et al. 2011).

Obviously, there are other common features shared by these countries, especially in the post-revolutionary era of the last two decades. Migration policy development is one such area. At the beginning of the 1990s, all the countries in the CEE region missed out on the experience of natural labour immigration[19] and its management. Although they started from scratch and were situated in different contextual environments, the migration policies of the countries in question gradually developed in similar ways. There are three main stages of migration policy development in Poland, Hungary and the Czech Republic (based on Lesińska et al. 2011). The first stage, from 1989 to the early 1990s, is that of institutionalisation and the birth of the legal system. The second stage, from the late 1990s to 2004, is characterised by stabilisation and harmonisation with EU standards. The third stage, since 2004, is one of consolidation of the migration regime.

An analysis of Polish, Hungarian and Czech migration policy developments reveals that policymakers from CEE states followed the traditional process (developed by the EU and Western countries) of conceptualisation and subsequent implementation of migration policies. In other words, all three countries drew inspiration from the more mature and experienced immigration countries, both in terms of perceptions of immigration as well as management models for migration inflows (a sort of learning process has occurred, as specified in hypothesis 3 in chapter 2 by Arango this volume); moreover, 'the paradigms of migration and control policies' are considered to be among the most important drivers within the migration transition process (see Fassman & Reeger 2008). Of the three countries, Czech migration policies have evolved into the most 'mature' in terms of the formulation of a migration doctrine, the implementation of particular policies to encourage the inflow and settlement of foreigners (Lesińska et al. 2011). There is also one pattern characteristic of policymaking principles in all three countries (and, to some extent, one which is still valid in the present-day) – that can be described as the 'power of discretion'. This means that the administration, rather than precisely formulating rules that require compliance, set forth policies that enable officials to use their own discretion.

Another aspect shared by the CEE countries is the Europeanisation of their respective migration policies, as the EU exerted significant influence in many migration policy areas (except for naturalisation and repatriation policies) (chapter 11). Moreover, a similar institutional reality developed in all three countries over time: namely, institutional responsibilities for immigration issues are divided among several bodies, with a key coordinating role played by the Ministry of the Interior. This body alone plays the dominant role in migration policymaking. The institutional system is highly centralised: only a rather marginal influence is exerted at the lower level (regional and local) by the administration on migration or integration issues. With the exception of the Czech Republic, the same is valid for the role of NGOs. Special bodies (such as inter-ministerial committees or interdepartmental groups), dealing exclusively with the migration issue or related areas, have only recently been established. Their main goal is to declare and formulate long-term strategies for migration policies (migration doctrines) and to coordinate the activities of a variety of institutions that focus on immigration and the integration of immigrants into their host societies (Lesińska et al. 2011).

Another common aspect is the low importance, or even the non-existence, of a state integration policy (especially in Poland and Hungary). Krystyna Iglicka and Okólski (2005) characterise integration measures instituted in the CEE countries as catering only to small, specific immigrant groups, or else as applying only to limited aspects of integration. It seems clear that the integration of immigrants is still not perceived as a top priority for states in the CEE region, although relevant policies have recently begun being implemented (in the Czech Republic) or drafted (in Poland and Hungary).

Indeed, the issue of immigration comes up very rarely in political or public discourse in the CEE countries in question (chapter 11), which is one clear symptom of a rather immature transition phase within the whole migration cycle (see chapter 3). Many challenges involving migration or immigration are either not discussed or else discussions remain highly bureaucratic, without engaging the broader public. Neither the process of drafting legal acts concerning migration, nor establishing related institutions are, with few exceptions, accompanied by any extensive political debate. On the contrary, political debates seem to be confined to technicalities and have historically taken place exclusively within the state's administration. In particular situations, selected interest groups – including NGOs, employer or labour unions – have publicly announced their points of view on immigration – but, generally speaking, there appear to be low levels of politicisation of the migration topic, with only 'bureaucratic' concerns prevailing (Lesińska et al. 2011).

Although the three countries share many similar aspects in terms of migration policy development, as previously noted, crucial differences also exist. More specifically, Czech migration policies seem to be distinct from the policies of Poland and Hungary in that the country has achieved a more mature policymaking stage (Lesińska et al. 2011). So, what are the key differences among the three countries or rather, what separates the Czech Republic from the other two?

It would appear that the Czech migration policy was the only one in existence when quickly changing migratory realities began stimulating progress in the migration policy field. In other words, internal impulses were crucial for migration policymaking. By contrast, in Hungary and Poland, migration policies have developed in response to external pressures. That is, policies have mostly followed the EU harmonisation process. To some extent, it is a logical consequence of the more modest immigration inflows into Hungary and the very small inflows into Poland (as well as their characteristics, including fluidity and circularity). These sorts of realities do not create the necessary push for policymakers to be especially active in the field of migration management. It only happened, to some extent, to be the case in the Czech Republic, which hosts hundreds of thousands of immigrants (Lesińska et al. 2011; Drbohlav et al. 2010).

The Czech Republic also clearly represents the 'most mature' case in our comparative CEE framework in terms of formulating its migration doctrine. The basic policy principles and objectives related to international migration were already announced by the Czech government in 2003.[20] Although they are criticised by some experts as being very general and vague and as having no real impact upon migration policy, the process of their conceptualisation is still more developed as compared to Poland and Hungary. The Czech government also launched proactive migration recruitment measures and, consequently, implemented specific activities to encourage the inflow of immigrants (and their admission to the labour market as well as, to some extent, their settlement. The country has also been active in developing its integration policy. Overall, more systematic and more goal-oriented approaches are characteristic of migration policies in the Czech Republic. It is worth mentioning here, however, that Poland and Hungary also engage in more 'systematic' activities in terms of migration management: policies towards co-ethnics and their repatriation systems are two such examples. Still, neither Hungary nor Poland has a single document in which a migration doctrine is clearly set forth. These countries' migration strategies could be only deduced from other sources, such as various (mostly unpublished) documents and policymakers' statements (Lesińska et al. 2011).

While the Czech Republic has more proactively encouraged labour and settlement migration (even through small-scale programmes), Poland and Hungary opted for different strategies. They accepted rather short-term immigration from neighbouring countries and supported the settlement of narrowly defined groups – of co-ethnics, above all. In recent years, the situation has changed slightly; the issue of actively recruiting foreign labour has begun being debated in all three countries. In addition, some more liberal rules of admission of foreigners to national labour markets have recently been introduced. These activities seem to be propelled by the desire to fill gaps in labour markets, where there is a growing demand for foreign labour. The Czech Republic again leads the group with the launch of two projects, i.e. a 2003 pilot project for attracting skilled migrant workers and encouraging them to settle in the country and a 2009 green card project for recruiting new labour. Each of these targeted both high- and low-qualified immigrants from selected countries (Drbohlav et al. 2009). Poland and Hungary appear to have a long way to go in order to catch up with the Czech Republic's activities in this field.

There is one final difference worth identifying: whereas, in Poland and Hungary, small-scale regularisation programmes for selected groups of irregular migrants have already been instituted, the Czech Republic has so far never accepted such an idea (Lesińska et al. 2011).

8.6   Immigration impacts

Immigration is a complex phenomenon, one having both positive and negative impacts upon a host society. These impacts can, in turn, significantly influence migration policy measures along with public attitudes towards immigrants (chapter 2). They must therefore be elaborated further here. This, however, is a deceptively complicated task. Many important impacts are difficult to measure in terms of both a set of defined characteristics and available data or statistics. Most importantly, though, only a short amount of time has elapsed since significant volumes of international migrants began arriving in the CEE countries. The impacts of this kind of immigration have not yet had enough time to develop and crystallise. The sheer number of temporary and circular migration movements (especially in Poland) also limits the integration of immigrants in the CEE countries in question. Since these countries are currently going through a particular transition phase within the migration cycle, it can be argued that their patterns of immigrant integration are still in the making.

The economic impacts of immigration are generally the most important in all three countries. This reality springs from the fact that immigration into the CEE countries is based predominantly on economic motives – most migrants are workers who stay temporarily while becoming intensely involved in the host country's economy. Migrant populations' common characteristics include high economic activity rates – which typically outrank the average levels of the domestic population – along with below-average unemployment (Medova 2011).[21] Consequently, immigrants in the CEE countries evaluated here also exhibit only limited levels of consumption of public services and welfare benefits. Finally, the foreign labour force in all three countries also seems to constitute a supplement, rather than competition, vis-à-vis native workers (Drbohlav et al. 2009; Hars 2009; Górny et al. 2009).[22]

Like many other developed European countries, the CEE countries have also recently begun facing a process of population ageing (see e.g. Grant,

Hoorens, Sivadasan, Van het Loo, DaVanzo, Hale, Gibson & Butz 2004), which will likely have serious economic and social impacts upon all societies. As has been shown many times in different regional contexts, however (see e.g. Bijak, Kupiszewski & Kupiszewska 2008), immigration as such is not and cannot be a remedy for demographic ageing and for the weakening of the labour force potential.[23] Immigration inflows can only contribute to the stabilisation of the total population size of individual countries, provided that they are of a long-term or permanent nature.[24]

So far, the mostly temporary and recent migration movements into and out of CEE countries have not yet led to immigrants' integration, at least not in ways and volumes known to mature immigration countries. Both the integration processes of migrant populations and state integration policies are still in infancy stages. Immigrants' integration has thus far not posed any major problems for the three societies, which is also probably why no proper integration monitoring takes place in any of these countries. As a matter of fact, it is only recently that immigrants' second generations have begun appearing: at the moment, this only being true for the Czech Republic and partly also for Hungary (Medova 2011).

Some studies in the Czech Republic have suggested that the successful inclusion of migrants into the Czech society is strongly connected to assimilation models of integration (e.g. typically rejecting close ties of immigrants to their home countries and their adoption of the Czech lifestyle and language). Accordingly, assimilation to the Czech lifestyle seems to be the option preferred by the Czech public, as suggested by national opinion polls (Drbohlav et al. 2009, 2010).

Integration outcomes in Hungary and Poland are even harder to assess, as smaller immigration volumes and more short-term migration movements occur in both countries. In Poland, temporary patterns of mobility prevail (especially within the groups of post-Soviet citizens and 'Westerners') and the traditional settlement and integration patterns are observable only in the case of Vietnamese immigrants (Górny 2010). The integration of immigrants in Hungary is somewhat different, as the Hungarian ethnic origin of most immigrants is a crucial factor. More specifically, the integration of immigrants of ethnic Hungarian origin seems to be smoother than that of other groups, especially due to their knowledge of the Hungarian language. For other migrants, the distinctiveness of the Hungarian language represents a significant integration barrier (Medova 2011).

In all three CEE countries, the spatial distribution of migrants is uneven, albeit with no large separated or segregated spatial concentrations of migrant populations within cities or towns, as has been the case for mature European immigration countries, not to mention the US. Nevertheless, some 'embryonic zones' of these concentrations began appearing in Prague and Budapest (Drbohlav et al. 2009; Hars 2009). Spatial distribution patterns also seem to differ by individual immigrant ethnic groups and by migrants' statuses (meaning long-term or temporary versus permanent migrants). It has been shown that capitals represent the most important centres in which migrants are concentrated (Medova 2011). More specifically, Prague hosts about one third of all legally staying foreigners in the Czech Republic, and the concentration of foreign permanent settlers in Budapest has reached about 40 per cent (Drbohlav et al. 2009; Hars 2009). On the other hand, the spatial concentration of migrants and permanent settlers in Warsaw amounts to about 16 per cent (Górny et al. 2009). The dominance of the capital city in migrant settlement patterns is thus lower in Poland, which could be attributed to the overall character of the Polish settlement structure, in which the dominance of the capital city (Warsaw) is suppressed or subdued (see e.g. Weclawowicz 2001).

Finally, let us briefly touch upon the issue of immigrant naturalisation, the host country's granting of citizenship. For the three CEE countries examined here, it is evident that the numbers of naturalised immigrants (Figure 8.4) mirror the state naturalisation policy more than anything else. This is apparent, for example, in the Hungarian case (see Figure 8.4), where the number of naturalised immigrants is manifold times higher than it is in the Czech Republic, even though the Czech Republic received many more immigrants in the same time period. The reason for this imbalance is that most of the individuals naturalised in Hungary are immigrants

Figure 8.4 *Naturalisations per year in the Czech Republic, Poland and Hungary, 1993-2006*

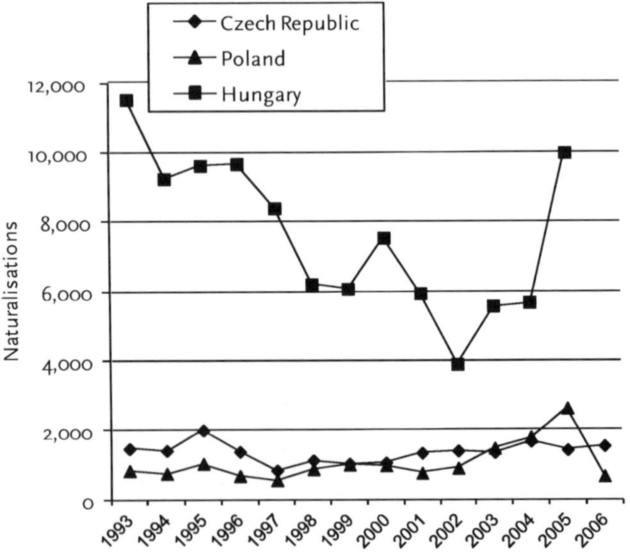

Source: Medova (2011)

of Hungarian origin who can be made citizens on preferential terms (Hars 2009). However, in recent years the stock of naturalised persons in Hungary has become more heterogeneous in terms of country of former citizenship (or rather of ethnic origin). In addition, in the Czech Republic, the stock of naturalised individuals also became more heterogeneous over time as regards the former country of citizenship of naturalised migrants (Medova 2011).

8.7   Conclusions

This chapter has mapped contemporary and historical migration patterns, determinants of migration transition – including migration policies – and the impacts of immigration in the Czech Republic, Hungary and Poland. All these were evaluated using a comparative perspective and in accordance with the conceptual framework suggested in chapters 1 through 3 of this volume.

During the 1990s, all three countries underwent deep political, economic and social transformation processes, from communist systems with planned economies to democratic systems with free-market economies. Since the mid-1990s, Poland, Hungary and the Czech Republic have joined various Western political, economic and security institutional structures. Simultaneously, transformations in migratory patterns have also taken place – the CEE countries shifted from strict regimes with closed borders to standard migration models. Although many similarities exist among them, the three countries have nevertheless each had unique experience of international migration process.

The resulting situation can be briefly summarised as follows: the Czech Republic has high immigration levels and, at the same time, low levels of native emigration, and is apparently the most attractive migration destination country of the CEE countries (see e.g. Drbohlav 2004a; Drbohlav et al. 2010). Hungary also experiences positive net migration with low levels of emigration. By contrast, Poland is characterised by high native emigration levels, rather low long-term immigration levels and frequent short-term types of migration patterns. All three countries seem to be in the same phase of the migration cycle or transition (chapter 1). They nevertheless fall into different categories or stages within the transition phase. Whereas Poland still seems to be in the very early stages, Hungary and the Czech Republic, especially, have progressed much further along in the transition process to becoming an immigration country. The differences among these countries have their roots in historical patterns, different levels of socio-economic development at the beginning of societal transformation periods, the structure of the overall economy (including sectoral and educational structures) and in the outcomes of the complex societal transformation process.

The migration transition process by which countries shift into countries of immigration is impelled by several important migration drivers. Economic pull factors are by far the most important. Without successful economic (and political) transformations – leading to developed free-market economies – there would be no immigration. More specific economic drivers include mismatches between the demand and supply of domestic labour, the natives' reluctance to take on certain jobs, high labour costs, low internal spatial mobility and, most importantly, the tolerated practices of undeclared work. In order to trigger considerable immigration inflows there must be, among other things, an apt convergence between demand and supply (a condition that the Czech Republic has already exhibited). In Poland, this harmony between demand and supply has only recently begun to materialise and, to some extent, could be attributed to the continuous and intensive emigration of Poles abroad (Anacka & Okólski 2010). Along with a strong economic performance, this harmony contributed to an increase of demand for foreign labour in Poland. On the other hand, the Hungarian economic structure features a rather low demand for migrant workers.

The demographic characteristics of the three countries (e.g. very low fertility levels and growing life expectancies leading to population ageing) are important migration factors whose impact and significance is certain to grow. Even today they have begun influencing some of the migration policy measures aimed at recruiting a foreign labour force to make up for the diminishing pool of domestic human resources.

The most important moment for all three countries – and not only from a geopolitical perspective – was, first of all, the breakdown of the Communist bloc in 1989 and, secondly, their accession to the EU in 2004. Within existing migration patterns, countries' particular geopolitical interests are manifest in their preferential attitudes towards certain countries (e.g. that of Poles towards selected former post-Soviet countries, Hungarians towards Romanian compatriots and the Czechs towards Slovakia).

Other important contextual determinants were also identified in this chapter. Specifically, these included historical experience, migrant social networks and migration policies. From a historical perspective, the three countries were emigration countries until the onset of the 1990s transformation period. Since the conclusion of World War II, all three countries have been ethnically homogeneous (Hungary even after World War I). This homogeneity was further strengthened during the communist era, due to the states' very restrictive regimes (no 'standard' international migration movements occurred). Despite this fact, a sort of labour immigration (including workers, trainees and students) from distant developing communist countries (under the pretext of 'international aid') took place, especially in Czechoslovakia and, partly, in Hungary. The early immigration of the

Vietnamese to Czechoslovakia led to the subsequent establishment of a strong migrant community after 1989.

Migration policies – or the lack thereof – also played an important role in shaping migration patterns in the 1990s. The development of migration policies was propelled by EU legislative harmonisation requirements, and led to the creation of very similar institutions in each country: migration policy management is thus centralised, with very limited involvement by regional and local institutions. Another common feature is that migration issues have not been visible to the government, political parties or the public. Recently, though, more proactive and systematic approaches to migration policies have emerged – especially in the Czech Republic. Indeed, only the Czech Republic (unlike Poland and Hungary) has designed a coherent migration policy framework, involving legal regulations, standard practices and a well-defined organisational environment. The involvement of NGOs in migration and integration issues also seems to be much more extensive in the Czech Republic than in the other two countries.

All of the foregoing circumstances (determinants) have led to the creation of unique immigration realities for each of the CEE countries. As previously mentioned, the Czech Republic hosts the largest pool of immigrants: in 2007, there were some 394,000 legally residing migrants, followed by Hungary with some 175,000 migrants in the same year and finally Poland, which appears to be the least attractive immigration destination country with about 75,000 migrants counted in the 2002 Census.

Current immigration inflows into the CEE countries are predominantly labour-motivated. Legal labour migrants in the Czech Republic and Hungary are mainly employed in the construction, service, hotels and restaurant and manufacturing sectors. These branches are also typical areas for irregular migrants to work (in all the three countries). There is also a rather rare but important type of legal labour migrants – that is, professionals who arrive from other developed countries (mainly the EU-15) and who are involved in more intellectually demanding jobs. Interestingly, in Poland, it is these migrants who dominate the pool of legal foreign labour. A very important conclusion can thus be drawn: namely, that foreign labour in all three countries is complementary rather than competitive vis-à-vis domestic workers.

Gainful employment as a principal motive and a common core of migratory source countries (the CEE and post-Soviet countries, Vietnam and China) are two features shared by the CEE countries being examined. By contrast, one can find important differences in terms of immigrants' lengths of stay. Significant numbers of migrants stay for a long time (several months) or permanently in the Czech Republic and Hungary, whereas in Poland short-term stays (often related to circular mobility) are more prevalent.

The impacts of immigration on the three countries have so far been most apparent in the economic sphere, and have apparently not seriously affected social and cultural relationships. Immigrants generally display higher economic activity rates and lower unemployment rates as compared to domestic populations. In demographic, social, cultural and geographic areas, the impact of immigration has so far been rather marginal. It has been shown, however, that the capital cities of the Czech Republic, Poland and Hungary are the major immigration hubs.

The integration of immigrants has not yet become a social problem, likely because of the still rather low shares of immigrants and the temporariness of their migration patterns. Integration measures are limited in the CEE countries, though much more has been done in this field in the Czech Republic than in the other two countries.

In sum, we have shown that, from a socio-economic, political, cultural and migratory perspective, Poland, Hungary and the Czech Republic all belong to one distinctive group of countries: they exhibit more similarities to one another and, at the same time, differ significantly from the other two groups of Western and Southern European countries (see chapters 3 and 5). The CEE countries seem to have already entered the second phase of the migration cycle, i.e. migration transition. Within this transition phase, the countries each fall into unique transition stages, depending on their net migration patterns, volume of immigration, prevailing types of migration (short-term versus long-term or permanent), the maturity of migration policies and practices and, finally and overall, their migration impacts. If all these factors are considered together, one inevitably arrives at the conclusion that the Czech Republic, followed by Hungary, are further along on the path to becoming mature immigration countries, while Poland lags significantly behind. One cannot derive other far-reaching conclusions from this analysis of the given three CEE countries. However, this analysis alone clearly indicates that right now it is rather difficult to justify one 'more coherent transition model' through which CEE countries go from their emigration to immigration eras. Only time will tell whether some important differences will be washed down and CEE will finally appear as a more homogeneous migratory region, sharing more similar and apparent migratory features than it does now.

Notes

1   The IDEA project's Czech team is grateful for support from the Ministry of Education, Youth and Sports of the Czech Republic, project no. MSM0021620831 'Geographic Systems and Risk Processes in the Context of Global Change and European Integration'.

2   This chapter could not have come together without the input of various people whom I would like to recognise here as co-authors in a sense: Marek Okólski, Agata

Górny, Izabela Grabowska-Lusińska, Magdalena Lesińska, Ágnes Hárs, Lenka Medova, Zdeněk Čermák, Eva Janská, Dita Cermakova and Dagmar Dzurova.

3   Preliminary work on this synthesis report was done for the IDEA national reports (see Drbohlav et al. 2009; Hars 2009; Górny et al. 2009).

4   Namely the OECD – the Czech Republic in 1995, Poland and Hungary in 1996, NATO in 1999, the European Union in 2004, and the Schengen zone in 2007.

5   Poles, besides arriving in metropolitan areas such as Berlin, St. Petersburg, Kiev, Moscow, Vienna and Paris, headed in great numbers for both Americas and industrial centres of Germany. Hungarians mainly left their mother country for the US. Czechs headed chiefly to metropolitan areas of the monarchy (Vienna), heavy industrial centres of Western Europe located in France and Germany; North America; and western parts of the Russian Empire.

6   The World War II period is not taken fully into account – migration processes were heavily influenced by the war (for more on this, see e.g. Kosiński 1975).

7   Until 1938, Czechoslovakia was composed of the Czech lands, Slovakia and Carpathian Ruthenia. After World War II, Carpathian Ruthenia was incorporated into the USSR.

8   Poland was composed of parts of present-day Lithuania, Belarus and Ukraine, but was missing its present northern and western lands, which still belonged to Germany at that time.

9   Poland continued ethnic displacement under the label of repatriation (or family reunion) in the 1950s and 1970s.

10   Vietnamese trainees and workers who came during the socialist era established a community that, after the Velvet Revolution, became a nucleus of a newly entrenched, strong Vietnamese immigrant group in the Czech Republic.

11   For example, in the Czech Republic, the definition of 'immigrants' (flow statistics) has been significantly broadened since 2001. Earlier, only permanent movements were counted. Since 2001, however, foreigners staying more than one year in the country have been included in the flow statistics.

12   Unfortunately, Hungarian data fails to cover the EU-15 citizens who need neither permits nor registration.

13   Besides foreign employees in the Czech Republic, there is also an important segment of foreign entrepreneurs (holders of trade licences). In 2007, there were some 69,000 of them (mostly Vietnamese retail traders). The total of economically active migrant population hence represented 5.6 per cent of the total economically active population in the Czech Republic (Drbohlav et al. 2009). Unfortunately, no data on foreign trade licence holders are available for the other two countries.

14   The secondary labour market is generally characterised by comparatively low wages, unstable and difficult working and living conditions, and a lack of reasonable prospects for advancement (see e.g. Piore 1979).

15   There was, however, also a boom in infrastructural and other direct investments that contributed to creating many new jobs.

16   The Hungarian economy has a job structure that resembles a more productive economy. Low-wage small enterprises or self-employed jobs are missing or have a character of provisory, non-increasing family-based ones. The economy highly relies on multinational firms with limited freedom of activity (Laki 1998; GKM 2007). Kristof Tamas and Rainer Münz (2006) give a similar example for Sweden, explaining its relatively low immigration despite the liberal immigration regime towards the EU-8.

17   For example, following again Eurostat (2009) data: in 2060, the ratio of persons aged 65 and over to the number of persons aged 15 to 64 will grow almost four times in the case of Poland, almost three times in the Czech Republic and a bit less so in Hungary.

18   For example, Poland successfully delayed the date of introducing visas for its eastern
      neighbouring countries' citizens, which is clear evidence that not only EU require-
      ments, but also national interests shape migration policy (Kicinger 2005).
19   Immigration in the communist era was directed and quite specific as compared to
      what one could find in developed Western societies.
20   Nevertheless, the basic philosophy of integration policy was already formulated in
      the very late 1990s and it was even preceded by basic integration measures regard-
      ing refugees and compatriots, which were implemented in the beginning of the
      1990s (Drbohlav et al. 2009).
21   One has to realise, though, that strict legal regulations often do not allow long-term
      migrants who were made redundant to stay in the host country.
22   This is illustrated by the case of the Czech Republic, where foreign labour immigra-
      tion in districts grows as unemployment falls and vice versa (see Drbohlav 2004;
      Cesky statisticky urad 2006; Horakova 2006).
23   The replacement migration concept (United Nations Secretariat 2000) clearly shows
      us, however, that immigration as such cannot stop demographic ageing (see also
      Grant et al. 2004; Burcin, Drbohlav & Kucera 2005).
24   It is still a question, though, whether a sort of a traditional pattern of transformation
      of temporary labour migration into permanent settlement (see e.g. Martin & Taylor
      1995) will prevail in the CEE region, or a stabilisation and even strengthening of the
      circular character of immigration flows in the context of migratory transnationalism
      (e.g. Portes, Guarnizo & Landolt 1999) will take place.

References

Anacka, M. & M. Okólski (2010), 'Direct demographic consequences of post-accession mi-
    gration for Poland', in R. Black, G. Engbersen, M. Okólski & C. Panţîru (eds.), *A conti-
    nent moving West? EU enlargement and labour migration from Central and Eastern
    Europe*, 141-164. IMISCOE-AUP Research Series. Amsterdam: Amsterdam University
    Press.
Arango, J., C. Bonifazi, C. Finotelli, J. Peixoto, C. Sabino, S. Strozza & A. Triandafyllidou
    (2009), 'The making of an immigration model: Inflows, impacts and policies in Southern
    Europe'. IDEA Working Papers 9, www.idea6fp.uw.edu.pl/pliki/WP_9_Southern_
    countries_synthesis.pdf.
Bijak, J., D. Kupiszewska, & M. Kupiszewski (2008), 'Replacement migration revisited:
    Simulations of the effects of selected population and labour market strategies for the
    aging Europe, 2002-2052', *Population Research and Policy Review* 27 (3): 321-342.
Bonifazi, C., M. Okólski, J. Schoorl & P. Simon (eds.) (2008), *International migration in
    Europe: New trends and new method of analysis*. IMISCOE-AUP Research Series.
    Amsterdam: Amsterdam University Press.
Burcin, B., D. Drbohlav & T. Kucera (2005), 'Czech Republic population prospects in the
    mirror of replacement migration concept', *Acta Universitatis Carolinae – Geographica
    XL* 40 (1-2): 47-67.
Cermak, Z., D. Dzurova (2008), 'Pracovni a zivotni podminky nelegalnich migrantu v Cesku',
    in D. Drbohlav (ed.), *Nelegalní ekonomicke aktivity migrantu: Cesko v evropskem kontex-
    tu*, 130-149. Prague: Karolinum.
Cesky statisticky urad (2006), *Cizinci v regionech CR*. Prague: Cesky statisticky urad/
    Ministerstvo prace a socialnich veci CR.
Dorenbos, R. (1999), *Labour market adjustments in Hungary and Poland*. Groningen:
    Graduate School in Systems, Organization and Management.

Drbohlav, D. (2011), 'Determinants of migration', in I. Grabowska-Lusińska, D. Drbohlav & A. Hars (eds.), *Immigration puzzles: Comparative analysis of the Czech Republic, Hungary and Poland before and after joining the EU*, 38-76. Saarbrücken: Lambert Academic Publishing.

Drbohlav, D. (2004a), *The Czech Republic: The times they are a-changing*. European Commission's series 'Migration trends in selected EU applicant countries'. Vienna: International Organization for Migration.

Drbohlav, D. (2004b), 'Migration trends in selected EU applicant countries, Volume II – The Czech Republic, the times they are a-changing', in European Commission, *Sharing experience: Migration trends in selected applicant countries and lessons learned from the new countries of immigration in the EU and Austria*. Vienna: IOM.

Drbohlav, D., I. Grabowska-Lusińska, L. Medova, A. Hars & M. Lesińska (2011), 'Conclusions', in I. Grabowska-Lusińska, D. Drbohlav & A. Hars (eds.), *Immigration puzzles: Comparative analysis of the Czech Republic, Hungary and Poland before and after joining the EU*, 128-132. Saarbrücken: Lambert Academic Publishing.

Drbohlav, D., L. Medova, Z. Cermak, E. Janska, D. Cermakova, D. Dzurova (2010), *Migrace a (i)migranti v Cesku: Kdo jsme, odkud prichazime, kam jdeme?* Prague: SLON – sociologicke nakladatelstvi.

Drbohlav, D., L. Lachmanova-Medova, Z. Cermak, E. Janska, D. Cermakova & D. Dzurova (2009), 'The Czech Republic: On its way from emigration to immigration country', IDEA Working Papers 11, www.idea6fp.uw.edu.pl/pliki/WP11_Czech_Republic.pdf.

Düvell, F. (ed.) (2006), *Illegal immigration in Europe. Beyond control?* New York: Palgrave Macmillan.

Eurostat (2009), *Main tables*. http://epp.eurostat.ec.europa.eu/portal/page/portal/population/data/main_tables.

Fassmann, H. & U. Reeger (2008), ' "Old" immigration countries: Synthesis report', IDEA Working Papers 3, www.idea6fp.uw.edu.pl/pliki/WP3_Old_countries_synthesis.pdf.

Fassmann, M. (2008), 'Charakter trhu prace na cerno a situace v Cesku', in D. Drbohlav (ed.), *Nelegalní ekonomicke aktivity migrantu: Cesko v evropskem kontextu*, 68-81. Prague: Karolinum.

GKM (2007), *A kis- es kozepvallalkozasok helyzete 2005-2006*. Budapest: GKM.

Górny, A. (2010), 'Conclusions', in A. Górny, I. Grabowska-Lusińska, M. Lesińska & M. Okólski (eds.), *Immigration to Poland: Policy, employment, integration*, 194-196. Warsaw: Wydawnictwo Naukowe Scholar.

Górny, A., I. Grabowska-Lusińska, M. Lesińska & M. Okólski (eds.) (2009), 'Poland: Becoming a country of sustained immigration', IDEA Working Papers 10, www.idea6fp.uw.edu.pl/pliki/WP10_Poland.pdf.

Grabowska-Lusińska, I. (2011), 'Introduction and conceptual framework', in I. Grabowska-Lusińska, D. Drbohlav & A. Hars (eds.), *Immigration puzzles: Comparative analysis of the Czech Republic, Hungary and Poland before and after joining the EU*, 5-21. Saarbrücken: Lambert Academic Publishing.

Grabowska-Lusińska, I., D. Drbohlav & A. Hars (eds.) (2011), *Immigration puzzles: Comparative analysis of the Czech Republic, Hungary and Poland before and after joining the EU*. Saarbrücken: Lambert Academic Publishing.

Grabowska-Lusińska, I. & M. Okólski (2009), *Emigracja ostatnia?*, Warsaw: Wydawnictwo Naukowe Scholar.

Grant, J., S. Hoorens, S. Sivadasan, M. van het Loo, J. DaVanzo, L. Hale, S. Gibson & W. Butz (2004), *Low fertility and population ageing: Causes, consequences, and policy options*. Santa Monica: The RAND Corporation.

Grzymała-Kazłowska, A. & M. Okólski (2010), 'Amorphous population movements into Poland and ensuing policy challenges', in U.A. Segal, D. Elliot & N.S. Mayadas (eds.),

Immigration worldwide: Policies, practices, and trends. New York: Oxford University Press.

Grzymała-Kazłowska, A. & M. Okólski (2003), 'Influx and integration of migrants in Poland in the early 21st century', CMR Working Papers 50, www.migracje.uw.edu.pl/obm/pix/050.pdf.

Hars, A. (2011), 'Immigrant flows and stocks in Central and Eastern Europe: The Czech, Hungarian and Polish experience', in I. Grabowska-Lusińska, D. Drbohlav, A. Hars (eds.), *Immigration puzzles: Comparative analysis of the Czech Republic, Hungary and Poland before and after joining the EU*, 22-37. Saarbrücken: Lambert Academic Publishing.

Hars, A. (2009), 'Immigration countries in Central and Eastern Europe: The case of Hungary', IDEA Working Papers 12, www.idea6fp.uw.edu.pl/pliki/WP12_Hungary.pdf.

Horakova, M. (2008), 'Mezinarodni pracovni migrace v CR', *Bulletin VUPSV* 20. Praha: Výzkumny ustav prace a socialnich veci VUPSV.

Horakova, M. (2006), *Zahranicni pracovni migrace v Ceske republice dva roky po vstupu CR do EU*. Prague: Výzkumny ustav prace a socialnich veci VUPSV.

Iglicka, K. & M. Okólski (2005), 'A Central European perspective', in R. Süsmuth & W. Weidenfeld (eds.), *Managing integration: The European Union's responsibilities towards immigrants*. Gütersloh: Bertelsmann Stiftung.

Kaczmarczyk, P., M. Okólski (2005), *International migration in Central and Eastern Europe: Current and future trends*. United Nations Expert Group Meeting on International Migration and Development. New York: United Nations, Population Division.

Kępińska, E. (2007), 'Recent trends in international migration: The 2007 SOPEMI report for Poland', CMR Working Papers 29, www.migracje.uw.edu.pl/obm/pix/029_87.pdf.

Kicinger, A. (2005), 'Between Polish interests and the EU influence: Polish migration policy development 1989-2004', CEFMR Working Paper 9/2005.

Kornai, J. (1980), *Economics of shortage*. Amsterdam: North-Holland.

Korys, I. (2004), *Volume III – Poland: Dilemmas of a sending and receiving country*. European Commission's *Migration trends in selected EU applicant countries* series. Vienna: International Organization for Migration.

Kosinski, L.A. (1975), 'Interregional migration in East-Central Europe', in A. Kosiński & R. M. Prothero (eds.), *People on the move*. 277-291. London: Methen and Co.

Laki, M. (1998), *Kisvallalkozas a szocializmus utan*. Budapest: Kozgazdasagi Szemle Alapitvany.

Lesińska, M., R. Stefańska & M. Szulecka (2011), 'Development of migration policies of the Czech Republic, Hungary and Poland – on the way towards maturity', in I. Grabowska-Lusińska, I., D. Drbohlav & A. Hars (eds.), *Immigration puzzles: Comparative analysis of the Czech Republic, Hungary and Poland before and after joining the EU*, 77-115. Saarbrücken: Lambert Academic Publishing.

Martin, P.L. & J.E. Taylor (1995), *Guest-worker programs and policies*. Washington, D.C.: The Urban Institute.

Medova, L. (2011), 'Migration impacts', in I. Grabowska-Lusińska, D. Drbohlav & A. Hars (eds.), *Immigration puzzles: Comparative analysis of the Czech Republic, Hungary and Poland before and after joining the EU*, 116-127. Saarbrücken: Lambert Academic Publishing.

Nugent, W. (1995), 'Migration from the German and Austro-Hungarian empires to North America', in R. Cohen (ed.), *The Cambridge survey of world migration*, 103-108. Cambridge: Cambridge University Press.

Okólski, M. (2004), 'Migration patterns in the Central and Eastern Europe on the eve of the European Union expansion: An overview', in A. Górny & P. Ruspini (eds.), *Migration in the New Europe: East-West revisited*, 23-48. Houndmills/Basingstoke/Hampshire: Palgrave Macmillan.

Okólski, M. (2001), 'Mobilność przestrzenna z perspektywy koncepcji migracji niepełnej', in E. Jaźwińska & M. Okólski (eds.), *Ludzie na huśtawce: Migracje między peryferiami Polski i Zachodu*, 31-61. Warsaw: Wydawnictwo Naukowe Scholar.

Piore, M.J. (1979), *Birds of passage: Migrant labour and industrial societies*. Cambridge: Cambridge University Press.

Portes, A., L.E. Guarnizo & P. Landolt (1999), 'The study of transnationalism: Pitfalls and promises of an emergent research field', *Ethnic and Racial Studies* 22 (2): 217-237.

Renooy, P., S. Ivarsson, O. van der Wusten-Gritsai & R. Meijer (2004), *Undeclared work in an enlarged Union. An analysis of undeclared work: An in-depth study of specific items. Final report*. Brussels: European Commission.

Reyneri, E. (2002), 'Migrants' involvement in irregular employment in the Mediterranean countries of the European Union', ILO International Migration Paper 41. Geneva: ILO International Labour Organization.

Tamas, K. & R. Münz (with a contribution by E. Hönekopp) (2006), *Labour migrants unbound? EU enlargement, transitional measures and labour market effects*. Stockholm: Institute for Futures Studies.

Triandafyllidou, A. (ed.) (2006), *Contemporary Polish migration in Europe: Complex patterns of movement and settlement*. Washington, D.C.: The Edwin Mellen Press.

United Nations Secretariat (2000), *Replacement migration: Is it a solution to declining and ageing populations?* New York: Population Division, Department of Economic and Social Affairs, United Nations Secretariat.

Wallace, C. & D. Stola (eds.) (2001), *Patterns of migration in Central Europe*. Houndmills/ New York: Palgrave.

Weclawowicz, G. (2001), 'Transformation of large cities and urban centres in Poland: Selected issues', in J. Kitowski (ed.), 'Spatial dimension of socio-economic transformation processes in Central and Eastern Europe on the turn of the 20th century', in *Rozprawy i Monografie Wydziału Ekonomicznego Filii UMCS w Rzeszowie* 22, 337-364. Rzeszów: Wydział Ekonomiczny Filii UMCS w Rzeszowie.

Zlotnik, H. (1999), 'Trends of international migration since 1965: What existing data reveals', *International Migration* 37 (1): 21-61.

9   An uncertain future of immigration in Europe

Insights from expert-based stochastic forecasts for selected countries

Arkadiusz Wiśniowski, Jakub Bijak, Marek Kupiszewski and Dorota Kupiszewska

9.1   A research paradigm for the uncertain world
(Kupiszewski and Kupiszewska)

The theoretical underpinning of this volume is the analysis of changes in migration patterns over time, discovering regularities and formulating a theory describing the observed migration processes. Marek Okólski offered such a theory in chapter 1. Migration forecasting allows for the extension, albeit with a degree of uncertainty, of migration patterns into the future. In an ideal and reasonably predictable world, it would be possible to use forecasts to identify the moment of transition from an emigration to an immigration country for those countries that are in the transition phase. To do so, the IDEA project team (see note 9 in Introduction) tried to introduce some quantitative measure of the stage in the migration cycle and to develop some kind of 'trajectory' on which each country could have been located, depending on its migration system characteristics. However, operationalising the theory turned out to be an impossible task due to its long-term perspective. Also posing a challenge were the irregularity of the migration processes involved, complexity and inherent differences in the historical changes in migration observed in various countries (see chapter 2) and uncertainty embedded in forecasting (see later in this section). Substantial impact of historical and political processes (for example, the demise of communism in Central Europe and the 2010-2011 revolts sweeping Arab World countries), which have profound impact on migration flow counts, is impossible to account for in a theoretical framework, although it is very apparent in statistics. This failure is not a surprise: Sture Öberg and Babette Wils (1998) and Marek Kupiszewski (2002) noted that theories of migration are always difficult, and very often impossible, to operationalise and use for forecasting purposes.

Apart from purely theoretical considerations, migration forecasting serves utilitarian purposes by supporting the formulation of migration policies. The authors of this chapter feel strongly that migration policies are often formulated without a firm base of factual support and are rather predicated on qualitative information only. While chapters 3 through 8 present data on past trends, this forecasting exercise is done in an effort to provide some quantitative insight into the future and thus provide a better factual basis for policymaking. The Bayesian forecasting method, implemented in the IDEA project, allows for combining qualitative information with statistical data. Moreover, it has an added bonus: very clearly showing how much uncertainty is involved in the forecasts. As a consequence, it allows for the formulation of alternative policies in case some extreme scenarios are realised.

One of the central methodological problems of forecasting in general and of demographic forecasting in particular is how to handle forecasting error. In population forecasting, Nico Keilman (1990) specified several types of possible sources of errors in deterministic population forecasts. If we shift from thinking in terms of deterministic forecasts and forecasting errors calculated ex post to considering some measure of forecasting uncertainty[1] calculated ex ante, as posited by the proponents of the stochastic approach, the sources of forecast errors listed by Keilman could be interpreted as the sources of uncertainty of a forecast.

Even though the methodology of migration forecasting is much less developed than the methodology of population forecasting – as is clearly demonstrated by Jakub Bijak's (2010) study – we can attempt to create a similar, but not identical list of sources of uncertainty in migration forecasting. The forecasts of migration are uncertain because:

– We cannot uniquely define the migration phenomenon.
– We cannot measure migration precisely.
– We do not know how migration depends on explanatory variables or how to quantify the relationship.
– We do not know how migration, or the determinants of migration, will change in the future.

The key problems with the definitions of international migration include, but are not limited to, the lack of international harmonisation and the changes of definitions over time (see Kupiszewska & Nowok 2008; Nowok, Kupiszewska & Poulain 2006; Nowok & Kupiszewska 2005). The differences between the IDEA countries involve, among others, the duration of stay criterion used to determine which individuals are included in the migration flow count. In particular, the following categories of migration flow statistics can be observed: changes of permanent residence (e.g. in Poland), long-term migration for one year or more (e.g. the immigration of non-European Economic Area citizens to the Czech Republic and

Hungary), short-term and long-term migration for more than *x* months (e.g. three months in Austria) or changes of usual residence irrespective of the duration of stay (e.g. in Spain).

The second source of uncertainty is the measurement of migration. The problems related to measurement include, among others, underestimation due to registration avoidance. This is probably the largest source of uncertainty in migration statistics (for legal flows, especially emigration) and applies to all the countries where population registers are the source of migration flow statistics. In addition, illegal migrants in the IDEA countries are usually not included in official statistics, with the exception of Spain. In France, immigration flow data are available for non-EEA citizens only, while data on emigration flows are not available at all. Greece started to provide data on immigration flows to Eurostat in 2007 (data on residence permits issued in 2006). In the countries where data on total immigration flows are available, some disaggregated statistics are sometimes missing, for example, there is no data on immigration by country of previous residence in Hungary and France and no data until 2005 on immigration by citizenship to Poland. Even if such disaggregated data are produced, there is sometimes a problem of a large value in the 'unknown' category (e.g. a large number of immigrants with unknown country of previous residence in Austria).

Other problems include the delays in the production and publication of statistics, differences in data published in various secondary sources and the lack of relevant metadata. The numbers published in various sources may be provisional or final, may or may not include administrative corrections, may be produced using different methodologies or may cover different categories of migrants (Kupiszewska & Nowok 2008; Nowok et al. 2006).

In explanatory models, where migration is modelled as a function of exogenous variables, the randomness of the parameters of a forecasting model itself or the uncertain relationship between the migration and exogenous variables constitute a separate source of forecast uncertainty. In addition, problems with definitions and the measurement of the exogenous variables can be very similar to those specified above with respect to migration.

Finally, we have to deal with the last source of uncertainty, which is closely linked with the lack of knowledge of future migration processes. Migration is very volatile and can rise to extremely high levels or drop very quickly, as shown by migration from Poland to Germany at the turn of the 1980s and 1990s and post-enlargement migration from new EU member states to the United Kingdom and Ireland. These changes are dictated by external factors, not usually accounted for in the forecasting models, such as wars, significant political changes and modification of migration policies. If we look back to 1980 and inspect the forecasts of migration between the European states 25 years on (around 2005), we would – firstly –

have an incorrect set of states; no one at that time predicted the fall of the Soviet Union and the creation of an independent Latvia, Lithuania, Estonia, Ukraine and Moldova, not to mention the Central Asiatic Republics, and the dissolution of Czechoslovakia and Yugoslavia – the latter in a violent manner. Second, at that time nobody, expected the 2004 and 2007 enlargements of the European Union to accept, among others, ten new countries formerly in the Communist bloc and such large-scale flows from new to selected old EU member states after 2004. The discontinuity of demographic processes is one of the main problems for migration forecasters.

The above considerations lead us to the conclusion that, as far as migration is concerned, we live in a very uncertain world and uncertainty is a key factor shaping the development of migration processes. However, many researchers and policymakers are under the illusion that the world is predictable. In economics, Roman Frydman and Michael Goldberg (2007) noted in their influential book that we are unable to precisely understand and describe the future; therefore, forecasting error is a natural phenomenon. The authors made a plea for recognising the limitations of economic knowledge. In demography, in parallel to economics, similar thinking has developed, which aims to incorporate uncertainty – both as a concept and as a quantifiable variable – into research, and in particular into forecasting. Philip Rees and Ian Turton (1998) offered a simple classification of possible ways of dealing with uncertainty in population forecasting.

– To ignore it by constructing a single variant population forecast and pretending that uncertainty does not exist.
– To incorporate it by constructing a multi-variant population forecast (typically with central, high and low variants).
– To create a stochastic forecast which allows for the provision of some ex ante measures of uncertainty.

The solution to depart from deterministic population forecasts and devise a forecast where the uncertainty of the results could be somehow quantified – that is, stochastic forecasts of population – has been considered for well over a decade. The methodology of such forecasts has been proposed by Ronald Lee and Shripad Tuljapurkar (1994), Wolfgang Lutz, Warren Sanderson and Sergey Scherbov (1996), Juha Alho and Bruce Spencer (1997) and many others. Stochastic forecasts have been prepared for many developed countries, but they are not yet part of the standard toolkit of national statistical institutions and international organisations. However, the development of the new sub-field was advanced enough to allow pioneers to write a monograph-cum-textbook (Alho & Spencer 2005).

Interestingly, the development of stochastic approaches in population forecasting has led to a change in professional self-identification. Alho and Spencer (2005: 3), quoting other prominent demographers, describe this change in the following way: James Vaupel, they say, defined a demographer as 'someone who knows Lexis [diagram]'. Joel Cohen defined a demographer as 'someone who forecasts population wrong'. Finally, Alho and Spencer (2005) themselves define a statistical demographer as 'someone who knows Lexis, forecasts population wrong, but can at least quantify the uncertainty'. While somewhat anecdotal, this change of definition shows the evolution of modern demography; perhaps a similar process will arise in the future in other social sciences.

The development of stochastic population forecasting had quite a limited impact on the way the components of population change have been forecasted. As Bijak (2010) demonstrated, there were some attempts at modelling and forecasting migration using probabilistic and stochastic methods, but this was not in existing mainstream research. Bijak (2010) proposed a new methodology, in which Bayesian statistics was applied to produce forecasts of international migration flows between Germany and three European countries: Italy, Poland and Switzerland.

A methodology similar to the one proposed by Bijak, extended through the application of the Delphi method to complement information on immigration reported by national statistical offices, was used in the current study. The forecasts were prepared for seven European countries: Austria, the Czech Republic, France, Hungary, Italy, Poland and Portugal.[2] The forecasts concerned total immigration flows (nationals and foreign citizens together), except for France, where immigration of foreigners was forecasted (in line with the data availability). In all cases, the definitions used by national statistical offices in their demographic statistics were applied.

There were four reasons why immigration, rather than net migration, was forecasted. First, the data concerning emigration (required to calculate net migration) are less reliable than data concerning immigration, mainly because people often do not report their departure, even if they register their arrival at the destination. Second, the elicitation of knowledge through the Delphi method was deemed to be easier when the questions referred to immigration rather than to net migration. Moreover, it was expected that using a variable referring to unidirectional flows (rather than a difference of two flows, as is the case for net migration) would reduce the uncertainty, which was expected to be (and was indeed) very large. Finally, from the policy point of view, immigration is the variable that policymakers are keen to look at, whereas net migration somehow blurs the picture from the perspective of the receiving country. The methodology and results of this study, presented in subsequent sections of the current chapter, are described in more detail and in more technical terms in Bijak and Wiśniowski (2009, 2010).

9.2 Bayesian forecasting of migration: A methodological outline
(Wiśniowski and Bijak)

9.2.1 Why forecast migration?

Forecasting migration is a very difficult research task for the reasons outlined above, in particular, due to the lack of comprehensive migration theories and the lack of data, including short time series (Willekens 1994; Kupiszewski 2002). On the other hand, migration forecasts with suitable uncertainty assessments are crucial for obtaining credible population predictions, as well as for other policy and planning purposes.

It has to be noted that, in general, the primary aim of socio-economic forecasting is not to predict the future with 100 per cent accuracy, as this is impossible. The forecasters' goal is rather to provide input in order to guide the political decision-making process. Therefore, the key issue in the forecasting process is not to offer a (what is improbable) point estimate of the future values of some variables, but rather to provide a reliable, quantitative assessment of the related uncertainty span. In the current study, this was attempted by estimating predictive probability distributions (i.e. probability distributions of the future volumes of immigration flows). Such distributions are a way of illustrating how probable particular immigration scenarios are in our view.

With these considerations in mind, we sought to provide forecasts of immigration into seven European countries up to the temporal horizon of 2025. To do so, we relied both on quantitative data and on knowledge of country-specific migration experts.

9.2.2 Forecasting methodology

Frans Willekens (1994) noted that the problems with the migration predictions mentioned above call for including expert knowledge in the forecasting exercise. The methodology that allows for a combination of subjective expertise and hard data in a coherent and structured manner is the so-called Bayesian approach, dating back to the theorem proposed by an eighteenth century English statistician, Rev. Thomas Bayes (1763). This approach allows for combining expert judgements or opinions, treated as 'prior' knowledge, with data.

The variables forecasted in the current study were immigration inflows, both total and from up to three of the most important sources of immigration (countries of previous residence or – in the case of immigration to France and Hungary – countries of citizenship). It should be noted that no harmonisation of migration data was envisaged for the project. As a result, the predictions of flows obtained for various countries were virtually incomparable. Rather than providing comparisons of the flows forecasted for different countries, we concentrated on the consistency of the forecasted immigration volumes and population stocks for a given country, within its own demographic balance equation.

9.2.3 Statistical models

The statistical tools employed included the following simple time series models.

- For the total immigration flows: the autoregressive model (AR) of order 1, stationary (i.e. exhibiting stable characteristics over time) and, for the sake of comparison, the so-called random walk with drift (not stationary). The models also allowed for the capture of the changing variability of migration (known as stochastic volatility).
- For modelling the most important sources of immigration: vector autoregressive (VAR) models of order 1 were applied to log-ratio transformed variables, ensuring the summation of the shares to the total.
- Additionally, for assessing the impact of the selected demographic and economic variables, VAR models of order 1 were used.

In general, the AR models assume that the number of immigrants in a given year depends on their number one year before and on some purely random change that reflects all the uncertainty (on average, this change is assumed to be zero). Generally, in an AR process, the number of immigrants in a given year is the sum of all these random components from the very beginning of the process (in practice, it is the first observation in the series). This specification allows us to describe three different patterns of behaviour: stationary, non-stationary (random walk) and explosive.

In the case of a stationary AR process, the older the random component, the less influence it has on today's immigration flow. The expected value of the immigration flow is then constant, which means that the process is, on average, stable over time. Any shock (e.g. radical liberalisation of the immigration policy) will change the number of immigrants only temporarily (say, for a few years) and, in the long run, this number will return to the average observed before the shock. Hence, the forecasting based on an AR model is relatively precise. The addition of a trend term (e.g. linear, logistic or logarithmic) introduces an increasing (or decreasing) deterministic tendency along which the process develops.

In a random walk model (which is a special case of AR), all random components have equal influence on today's value. As a result, the process is non-stationary, which means that it is unstable in time and the precision with which we are able to predict the number of immigrants becomes smaller with the forecasting horizon (e.g. such a model may be used to describe a situation where we are unable to predict the behaviour of immigration flows after a liberalisation of the policy in the long-run). A drift term (i.e. a constant value added in each step) introduces increasing (or decreasing) tendencies along which these characteristics hold.

The last possibility, as far as AR models are concerned, is the 'explosion' of the process under study. In this scheme, the more distant the past changes are, the more influence they have today. In the current application, this would lead to the number of immigrants growing exponentially to achieve very large values. After some period of time, the predicted values would become simply implausible.

Finally, the VAR models are multidimensional generalisations of the AR model, including not only the variable of interest (here, migration flow or share of flow from a specified country), but also other variables, such as the considered migration determinants or shares of flow from other countries. In the VAR models, the potential instantaneous and lagged relationships among all the variables under study are analysed jointly.

9.2.4 Prior expert knowledge elicitation

Prior knowledge, a very important element of analysis in the Bayesian framework, was obtained by means of a Delphi survey from country-specific migration experts selected by the national teams participating in the IDEA project.

The Delphi survey is a technique that acquires anonymous opinions and judgements from selected respondents and provides a means of reaching an informed consensus among them. Originally, the usual applications of the Delphi survey involved forecasting. In the current study, we used it as a tool for obtaining expert knowledge that served only as part of the input into the model that produced the forecasts. One of the most important characteristics of the Delphi survey is that the answers are obtained iteratively. After each round, an anonymised statistical summary of the preceding round is provided to the respondents. In the consecutive rounds, they can reformulate their judgements and views and reach an agreement.

There are two major issues that require attention during preparation of the Delphi survey: proper formulation of the questions and the selection of the experts. The questions should take into account the hints provided by cognitive psychology, so as to ensure correct interpretation and unambiguous answers. Apart from this problem, two additional problems were identified in this study.

First, the questions relate to the characteristics of the immigration process, and were then transformed into the characteristics of the models that served as forecasting tools. It could have been the case, however, that the underlying experts' model – which led them to formulate such an opinion – was different and could have brought about inconsistencies. The second issue relates to the survey questions, which contain subjective probabilities. The literature on the subject (see e.g. Kadane & Wolfson 1998; Rowe &

Wright 2001) points out that the respondents tend to perceive probabilities as frequencies, and are also overconfident with respect to their beliefs. As a result, they tend to provide exceedingly narrow uncertainty spans. Inconsistent answers can be given to differently formulated questions. Yet another issue is that the group of experts can sometimes comprise specialists untrained in statistics and hence unfamiliar with the terms and concepts used for model formulation.

As far as the selection of experts is concerned, in order to avoid complications, their joint knowledge should be heterogeneous and should cover various aspects of the problem. The group of experts should not be too large or too small, according to J. Scott Armstrong (1985) and Gene Rowe and George Wright (2001).

The anonymous survey in question here was made up of two stages. Answers were obtained from between six and fourteen experts per country. The survey was given to those with various professional backgrounds – from demography, economics and sociology, to political science and law, and public administration – thereby ensuring the heterogeneity of their joint knowledge on migration. The questions focused on the characteristics of immigration processes in the period between 2007 and 2025: namely, trends, types of processes and variability, as well as the uncertainty of the processes' future developments. It should be stressed that there was no explicit question concerning the stage of the migration cycle of a particular country, which was meant to largely emerge from the qualitative analysis of the results.

The experts were also asked about the impact of economic variables (GDP per capita growth and unemployment rates in the receiving countries) and demographic variables (natural population growth rate and share of the productive-age population in the receiving countries) on immigration. Additionally, they were asked to identify three (in the case of Poland, two) of the most important sources of immigration to their countries in the future.

The answers were transferred to a form required by the model (e.g. expressed as prior probability distributions or deterministic trends) and then combined with data on immigration flows produced by the national statistical institutions (mostly available in the Eurostat database) in order to produce forecasts.

9.3   Bayesian forecasting of immigration: Results
(Wiśniowski and Bijak)

A key aim that accompanies the interpretation of Bayesian forecasting results is measuring the change in expectations, as formulated in subjective expert knowledge, due to quantitative and objective, yet still inherently flawed data.

As far as the underlying forecasting model is concerned, the data exhibited a clear preference for the non-stationary – and thus hardly predictable – random walk process in most of the countries. This conclusion is in line with that of several other studies (for more discussion, see e.g. Pijpers 2008).

The predictions are presented in terms of central tendencies (medians) with uncertainty spans, which are based on symmetric quantiles of predictive distributions. Hence, the 50 per cent ranges are based on the predictive quantiles (lower and upper), the 80 per cent ranges on the quantiles of rank 0.1 and 0.9, and the 90 per cent ranges on the quantiles of rank 0.05 and 0.95. These uncertainty assessments reflect our conclusions, based on expert knowledge and statistical data, that future migration inflows will fall within a given interval with a pre-defined probability. Of special note is the fact that the probability of migration not being higher than the upper values of the 50 per cent, 80 per cent and 90 per cent intervals is 0.75, 0.90 and 0.95, respectively.

9.3.1   Forecasting total immigration flows

Examples of quantile-based ex ante assessments of predictive uncertainty for Poland and Italy are illustrated in Figure 9.1. The forecasts for Italy are characterised by a relatively large level of uncertainty. The median expectations of immigration flows follow historically increasing tendencies: from 305,000 in 2005, to 370,000 in 2016, to 434,000 in 2025. Broad 50 per cent intervals indicate large uncertainty levels inherent in the expected future flows. The upper bound amounts to 839,000 people in 2016 and 1.4 million in 2025. These values should be thought of as only barely plausible. We thus advise forecast users to interpret such extreme values only as an indication of orders of magnitude. There are two main reasons for such high levels of uncertainty: first, the steadily increasing inflows of immigrants in the past; second, prior input into the models based on experts' expectations of the explosive patterns of future immigration to Italy. These factors, together with the data that were affected by regularisations in the past, suggest that these outcomes should be considered an indication of the extremely high levels of uncertainty surrounding future immigration inflows.

Compared to Italy, the inflows forecasted for Poland are relatively moderate and stable. The predictive median tendency indicates an increase in permanent immigration to Poland from an initial 15,000 people in 2007, to 28,000 in 2016, to 53,000 people in 2025. The 50 per cent intervals are relatively narrow, yet exhibit an increasing predictive uncertainty: between 16,000 and 54,000 people estimated to immigrate in 2016 and between 21,000 and 158,000 in 2025.

Figure 9.1   *Immigration to Italy and Poland*

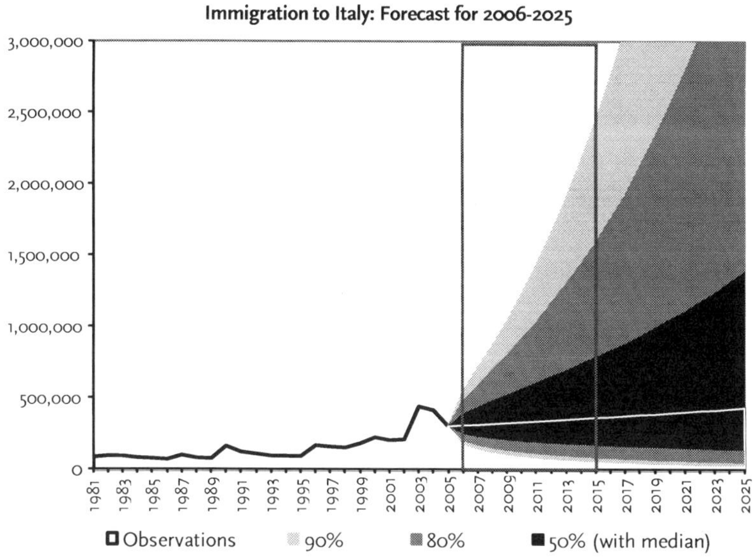

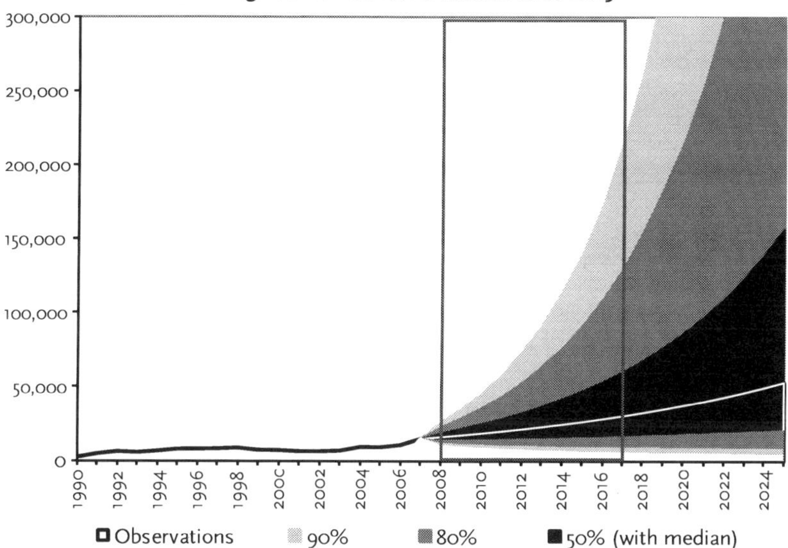

Note: The frame indicates a ten-year forecast horizon.
Source: Data until 2006 (Italy) or 2007 (Poland): Eurostat and NSIs with own re-calculations; forecast: own computations

The forecasts for the rest of the countries are presented later (left-hand side, Figure 9.3). The general conclusion is that immigration flows are expected to increase in all the countries (in terms of the median variant). Although uncertainty appears to be growing over time in all the cases, its magnitude differs among different countries. The widest uncertainty spans are observed for Austria, the Czech Republic and Italy, whereas the narrowest ones are visible for France and Hungary. In all the cases – including Italy and Poland though with the exception of Portugal – incorporating expert knowledge increased the uncertainty of the forecasts. This result may stem from the fact that experts were knowledgeable about past events not reflected by the data and, based on that knowledge, they formulated their opinions and judgements for the future and thereby increased data-based uncertainty.

9.3.2   Forecasts for the top source countries of immigration

Figure 9.2 presents the median forecasts of cumulative source country shares (cumulative shares of migrants from countries of previous residence within immigration totals), again for Italy and Poland. For the sake of clarity, the uncertainty spans were omitted here. However, the predictive uncertainty of the shares appeared to be so high that the analysis of different combinations of quantile-based predictions became meaningless. The forecasted numbers of migrants coming from major source countries are conditional upon the median values of the predicted shares (presented in Figure 9.2) and overall immigration volumes (presented in Figure 9.1).

For Italy, the three most important immigrant countries of origin were Romania, Albania and Morocco. The available data series were very small, covering only ten years (1995-2004). During the last observation year, out of the total registered inflow of 415,000 people, 15 per cent came from Romania (64,000), 9 per cent from Albania (37,000) and 7 per cent from Morocco (31,000). According to the median forecasts, the share of inflows from Morocco is projected to remain stable, at just below 8 per cent, throughout the forecast horizon – which would correspond to 28,000 immigrants in 2015 and 34,000 in 2025. At the same time, the share of inflows from Romania would rapidly decline to about 10 per cent and remain relatively constant; while the inflow from Albania is thought likely to stabilise at just around 12 per cent starting in 2008. In absolute terms, however, these inflows would follow an increasing trend: from Romania, 38,000 people in 2015 and 45,000 in 2025; from Albania, 44,000 in 2015 and 52,000 in 2025.

For Poland, experts identified two of the most important sources of future inflows as Ukraine (immigration) and the UK (return migration). In 2007, out of 15,000 immigrants newly registered for permanent residence, 777 people (5 per cent) came from Ukraine and 3,900 (26 per cent) from

Figure 9.2 *Immigration to Italy and Poland, cumulative source country shares, median forecasts*

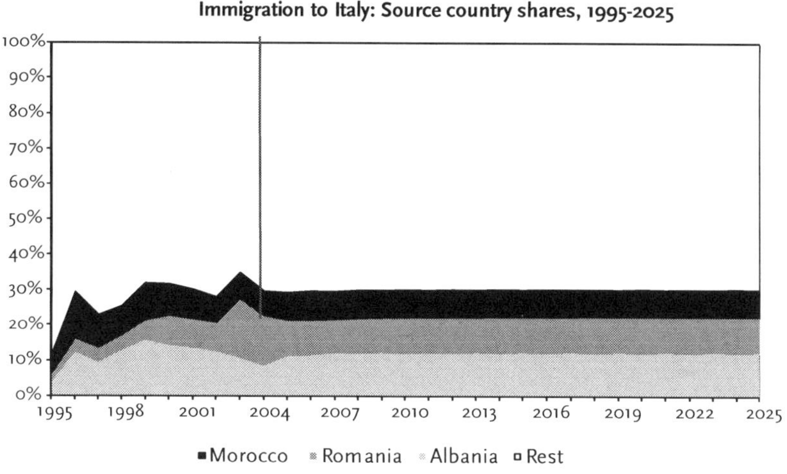

Notes: Italy data until 2004, forecast for 2005 to 2025
Rest refers to the rest of the world.
Source: Data until 2004 (Italy) or 2007 (Poland): Eurostat and NSIs with own recalculations; forecast: own computations

the UK. The median forecasts, prepared on the basis of 1990-2007 data, indicate that the share of immigrants from Ukraine would first increase to 10 per cent in 2008 and then exceed 11 per cent in 2013, only to decline below 10 per cent in 2016 and to ultimately 6 per cent in 2025. Return migration from the UK would follow a similar pattern: from below 15 per cent in 2008, to a peak of over 18 per cent in 2014, to below 17 per cent in 2016, down to below 10 per cent in 2025. Both these trajectories are the result of including experts' opinions in the forecast. The shares for 2016 would correspond to 2,800 immigrants from Ukraine and 4,800 thousand return migrants from the UK or around 28,200 immigrants altogether. For 2025, the respective numbers would amount to 3,300 for Ukraine and 5,100 for the UK, out of the total 53,100 permanent immigrants.

Figure 9.3 (see right-hand side) presents the forecasts of cumulative source country shares for the other countries. As mentioned earlier, the predictive uncertainty levels were too high to draw any meaningful conclusions from them. The forecasted shares are aligned with the trends suggested by the experts. For instance, in Austria the future shares of

Figure 9.3 *Immigration (left) and cumulative source country shares (right) for Austria, Czech Republic, France, Hungary and Portugal*

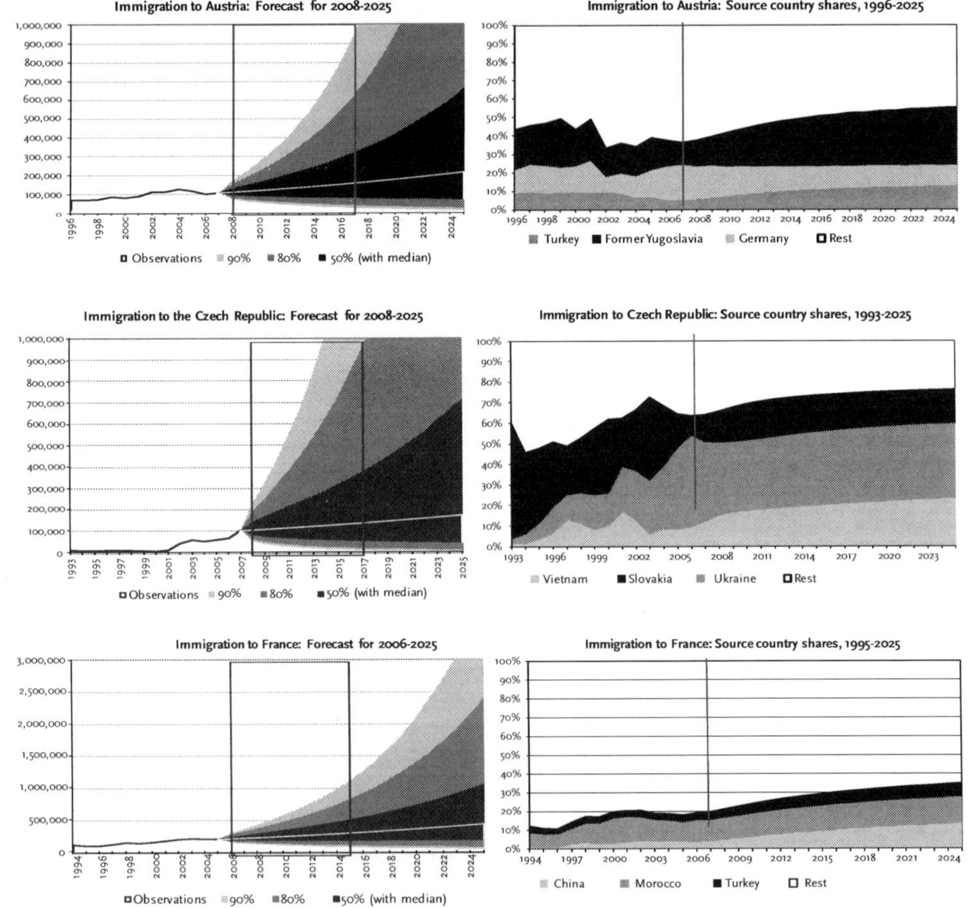

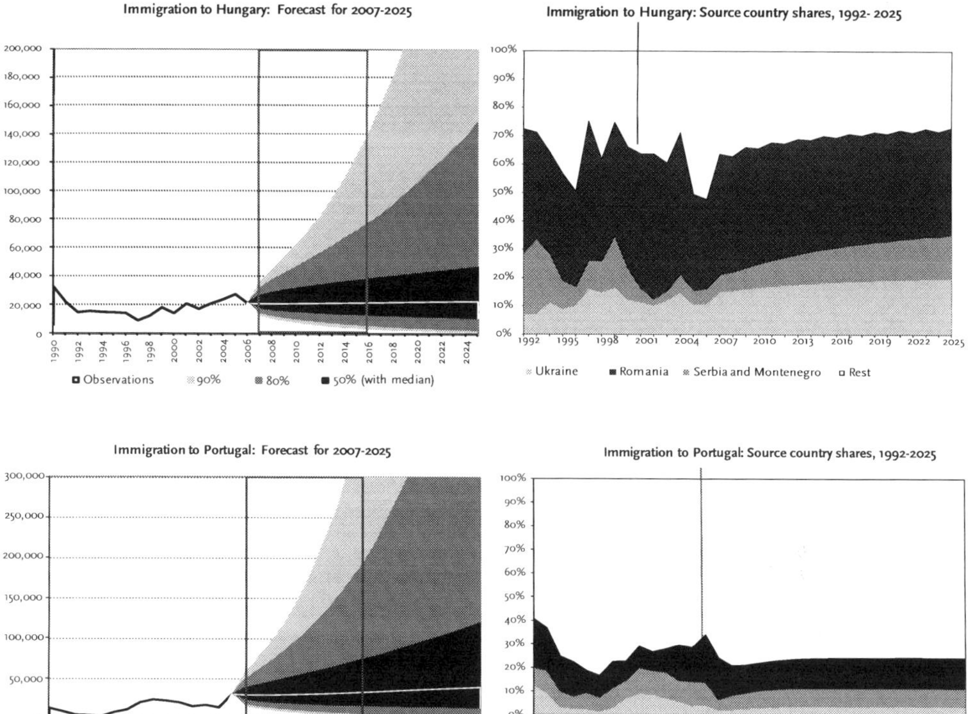

Notes: The frame indicates a 10-year forecast horizon (left), and the vertical lines mark the end of the data series (right).
Sources: Eurostat and NSIs with own recalculations; forecast: own computations

immigrants arriving from former Yugoslav countries and from Turkey are expected to increase. For France, an increase in the share of Chinese immigrants is predicted, as is the share of natives of Serbia and Montenegro in inflows to Hungary.

9.3.3   *Impact of economic and demographic variables*

An analysis of the impact of additional economic and demographic variables demonstrates the emergence of a clear pattern. The two macroeconomic covariates examined (GDP growth rates and unemployment rates in the receiving countries) appeared to have hardly any influence on migration, even when data were supported by expert judgement. The only exceptions were economic growth in France (instantaneous impact) and Portugal (a one-year time lag). That result does not confirm the hypotheses of Heinz Fassmann and Ursula Reeger, put forward in chapter 3. However, it should be emphasised that our analysis concerned total immigration, not net migration, which was assumed to be influenced by GDP growth. Secondly, unemployment rate was used in the forecasts as a proxy covariate for a labour market situation and it might have not reflected the overall situation of a given country. Alternatively, the impact of the labour market situation could have been already captured by the demographic covariates, especially the productive-age population in the destination country. A tentative conclusion might also be that the available data generally do not allow for formal inferences to be drawn about the interrelations between immigration and its two most important (e.g. according to Jennissen 2004) economic determinants.

The impact of the two demographic variables (natural population growth rates and the share of the productive-age population in the destination countries) was significant in most cases, except for Portugal. For Austria, significance applied to the lagging share of the productive-age population only, while for the five remaining countries various combinations of lagging and/or instantaneous influence of both demographic covariates were found. A tentative conclusion is thus that the two demographic factors indeed play some role in shaping immigration flows.

Despite the explanatory potential of the demographic migration determinants in this study, the conditional forecasts they helped generate remain unsatisfactory from a policymaking point of view. In cases with the 'best' test results (France and Italy), the forecasts quickly reached implausible values with high uncertainty spans. It thus seems that, even if the demographic covariates have a significant impact, the price to pay for including them in the forecasts is extremely high predictive uncertainty.

In many cases, despite the variables' significant impact on migration inflows, the interpretation of the model parameters was counterintuitive. This means that the positive outcomes of significance tests alone do not guarantee reliable scenario-based predictions and that the latter need to be considered with all due scepticism.

9.3.4 *Migration cycle in the light of the forecasting exercise*

It is difficult to draw a meaningful conclusion concerning confirmation or disproval of the migration cycle stage of a given country, as put forth in previous chapters, just by looking at the results of the forecasting exercise presented above. There are two main reasons for that. The first and most important is the exclusion from the analysis of the emigration flows from the countries under study due to reasons described in section 9.1, primarily the lack of data or their poor, even worse than for immigration, quality. This automatically precludes using immigration forecasts alone for falsifying or validating the migration cycle theory outlined in previous chapters. Hence, all results should be examined with caution, only as potential symptoms indicating the possible position of a given country in the cycle. Secondly, the differences between definitions of migrants in the countries under study, the quality of the available data and their scarcity, as outlined in section 9.1, additionally hampered comparisons between the analysed countries.

Let us consider, for example, the case of Austria, an 'old' immigration country. In chapter 3 of this volume, Fassmann and Reeger state that since 1994 Austria has been in the last stage of the cycle, i.e. the adaptation phase. However, the results of the forecasting exercise do not seem to support that thesis unequivocally. The median trend of immigration is increasing, reaching more than 200,000 migrants by 2025, with a very wide uncertainty span. Should the adaptation phase hypothesis hold, this would have to be balanced with increasing outflow (due to e.g. increased mobility within Europe) in order to maintain the predicted stable net migration. Another speculative explanation is a return to the initial stage of migration, as suggested by Godfried Engbersen in chapter 4 in this volume.

The comparison of the four Southern European countries is hindered by not having Greece and Spain in the analysis. For Italy and Portugal, median tendencies and uncertainty spans (relative to the migration levels) are similar. However, these two countries are distinct in their migration context, as they apply different definitions of migrants and duration-of-stay criteria, use different migration policies and have different colonial histories, as described in chapters 5 through 7. This further obstructs the comparison of their position in the migration cycle.

In the case of 'future' immigrant countries – the Czech Republic, Hungary and Poland – the results are ambiguous. All three share the same source country of immigrants suggested by the experts: Ukraine. It may be expected that flows from Ukraine will be largely comprised of labour migration. This would be in line with the historic experiences of the 'old' migration countries, as stated by Okólski in chapter 1 and Joaquín Arango in chapter 2 of this volume. On the other hand, there are many differences between the results for these three countries, which show that there is a considerable heterogeneity of migration patterns within this group.

In chapter 8 in this volume, Dušan Drbohlav concluded that the Czech Republic and Hungary are in their transition period of the cycle, yet considerably further on the path to becoming mature immigration countries than Poland. This seems to be supported for Hungary, whose median tendency is only slightly increasing with comparatively very narrow uncertainty, suggesting the stability of future migrant inflows and relative 'maturity' of the migration cycle. On the other hand, immigration to the Czech Republic is characterised by increasing tendency and very wide uncertainty. However, it should be noted that the data for this country were subject to definitional change in 2001. Drbohlav's conclusions concerning Poland being at the early stage of the transition period of the migration cycle seem to be approved by the experts. They suggested that flows would start to increase even faster until around 2016, when the increase would start to slow down and immigration will stabilise. It must be kept in mind that forecasting for Poland was carried out using official data based on the permanent duration of stay criterion. This might have precluded from the analysis all temporary stay and labour migrants, i.e. liquid migration as outlined by Engbersen in chapter 4 and Drbohlav in chapter 8. Moreover, interpolation of the recent post-enlargement emigration patterns, as presented by Okólski in chapter 1, may prevail over even increasing immigration and further aggravate the positioning of Poland in the migration cycle.

9.4 Conclusions
(Wiśniowski and Bijak)

The outcomes of the forecasting exercise carried out within the IDEA project can be summarised as follows (for details, see Bijak & Wiśniowski 2009, 2010). First, migration appears to be a hardly predictable demographic process, strongly in accordance with previous research findings (see e.g. Pijpers 2008). Moreover, assuming stationarity of immigration, which is in fact a non-stationary variable, seems reckless from a methodological standpoint, as it can bring about very serious forecasting errors and lead astray forecast users. A recent example is the study prepared for the British Home Office (Dustmann, Casanova, Fertig, Preston & Schmidt 2003), in which the stationarity of the underlying model was assumed explicitly (Dustmann et al. 2003: 28, 68). The forecasted volumes of immigrants to the UK after the 2004 EU enlargement were underestimated by more than an order of magnitude (see IPPR 2008).

Second, precise forecasting of the exact values of immigration flows is virtually impossible, especially in light of the above. Predictive uncertainty, however, can be accounted for by using the stochastic approach (Keilman 1990; Lutz et al. 2004). The randomness can then be quantified and expressed in probabilistic terms. It should be stressed that the stochastic methodology of migration forecasting does not impact the nature of the process itself. It simply addresses the fact that migration is difficult to predict. Consequently, the use of deterministic models is not a wholesale solution. Without an appropriate warning, it serves only to blur the picture, giving forecast users and decision makers the false impression that migration can be predicted.

As for the subjective information obtained using the Delphi survey – which served as an input for the forecasting models in the current study –

its impact on final outcomes was diverse. Expert knowledge appeared to play a very important role in the estimation of the model parameters, especially with respect to the forecasts' precision. Model selection, and thus determining the very nature of the process, seemed almost completely unaffected by the experts' opinions. Given the prevailing selection of random walk models – often independent from experts' expectations – we argue that the uncertain and barely predictable character of migration flows is not just characteristic of a particular forecasting model, but also a fundamental feature of migration. Again confirming earlier suggestions (e.g. Holzer 1959 or Keyfitz 1981), this implies that migration should be forecasted for only a relatively short period: five to ten years at most. The uncertainty and inherent unpredictability of migration flows grows over time, mainly due to its non-stationary characteristics. Using horizons of more than a decade into the future will necessarily lead to very broad uncertainty spans, which will ultimately constitute a meaningless piece of information for policymakers.

Finally, the impact of migration covariates proved to be difficult to quantify. Due to the brevity of the time series and hardly predictable nature of migration itself, the economic variables' impact, if any, was very limited. On the other hand, despite the significant impact of demographic covariates, in many cases the counterintuitive results of the parameter estimation and subsequent largely meaningless forecasts rendered the interpretation of the outcome dubious at best. It should be borne in mind that these results may stem from the usage of an inexhaustive series of data or from the narrow scope of measures chosen for the study. That is, the uncertainty of the forecasts had at least three sources of uncertainty: of the migration processes, of the covariates and of the interactions and interrelations among them. These outcomes support earlier suppositions that additional, theory-based determinants of migration – although extremely helpful in explaining the processes ex post – are of very limited use when it comes to forecasting (see Kupiszewski 2002). The results of the current study seem to indicate that, while demographic factors play a significant role in shaping migration processes, they simultaneously fail to contribute to more meaningful and precise migration forecasts – even despite the very important support of expert judgement.

The most important implication of the above conclusions for would-be users of forecasting models is that migration is indeed a vastly uncertain phenomenon. This may be seen as an undesirable feature. However, the degree of uncertainty can nevertheless be quantified and evaluated using statistical data and additionally enhanced by expert knowledge. This sort of assessment is in itself an important piece of information for policymakers.

Migration forecasts such as the ones presented in the current study may serve as an informational basis for political leaders and for informed and rational migration policymaking, as outlined by Magdalena Lesińska in chapter 11 in this volume. Their actions will strongly depend on the nature, strategic objectives and constraints of a particular decision-making problem, as well as on their own preferences and views. A proper assessment of the consequences of possible underestimation or overestimation of future migration flows is crucial.

Our results should be viewed through the lens of the overall findings of the IDEA project. In particular, and with respect to interpreting forecast results, the phase of the migration cycle in a particular country, as described in chapters 1 and 2, along with the specificities of the countries belonging to one of the three groups ('old', 'new' and 'future' immigration countries), should all be taken into account. However, it must be emphasised that the forecasting concerned only immigration flows, which shows only half of the picture of future migration, thus all results can only serve as symptoms indicative of a country's position in the migration cycle. Data-related issues, such as differences in definitions and collection schemes, regularisation programmes and the unending problem of estimating the number of illegal immigrants (see chapter 5), should also be acknowledged. Moreover, identification and quantification of the migration cycle in the forecasting exercise is affected by the definition of migrants in the specific country, as well as the country-specific characteristics, economic and demographic. Thus, formal comparisons between, for instance, 'old' and 'future' immigration countries were hardly possible.

As far as the impact of social, economic and demographic variables is concerned, it should be borne in mind that their influence upon migration may be subtle and not immediate. The ambiguous results and data-related shortcomings described above, along with the uniqueness of the experiences of the particular countries (e.g. in Central and Eastern Europe; see chapter 8) indicate that the detection of these impacts and interrelations can be strongly hampered, as, of course, can be future implications for migration movements.

Finally, the authors strongly recommend that forecast-based, mature migration policies should be crafted with extreme caution. The central tendency (median) trajectories are well suited only for situations in which an underestimation of future migration would entail the same costs as an overestimation of the same amount; they may not work well at all for other decision-making scenarios or to inform other subjective priorities of migration policymakers. In some cases, the underestimation of future migration inflows could be more costly than their overestimation, as, for example, in assigning budgets to migrant integration programmes. In such cases, it would seem rational to use the above-median variants, if only in order to err on the side of caution. In other instances, however, overestimation can be more problematic – as in the case of the inflows required to fill local labour market shortages. The use of below-median forecast variants would be recommended in these cases. Irrespective of which variants are used, however, the level of predictive uncertainty must always be kept in mind. Above all, researchers and policymakers, alike, must remember that simply using the median (or any other) trajectories and treating them as universal, deterministic predictions is both unwise and imprudent. They will almost certainly never come true.

Notes

1   In this chapter, uncertainty will be understood as a state of not having enough knowledge about a process or phenomenon now or in the future.
2   Forecasting migration was impossible for Greece, where no adequate migration data exists. For Spain, the unavailability of a second round of the Delphi questionnaires also rendered the forecasting exercise impossible.

References

Alho, J.M. & B.D. Spencer (2005), *Statistical demography and forecasting*. New York: Springer.

Alho, J.M. & B.D. Spencer (1997), 'The practical specification of the expected error of population forecasts', *Journal of Official Statistics* 13: 203-225.

Armstrong, J.S. (1985), *Long-range forecasting* (2nd edition). New York: John Wiley.

Bijak, J. (2010), *Forecasting international migration in Europe: The Bayesian approach*. Springer Series on Demographic Methods and Population Analysis 24. Dordrecht: Springer.

Bijak, J. & A. Wiśniowski (2009), 'Forecasting of immigration flows until 2025 for selected European countries using expert information', IDEA Working Paper 7. www.idea6fp.uw.edu.pl/pliki/IDEA_Working_Paper_No.7.pdf.

Bijak, J. & A. Wiśniowski (2010), 'Bayesian forecasting of immigration to selected European countries by using expert knowledge', Forthcoming in *Journal of the Royal Statistical Society, Series A* 173.

Bayes, T. (1763), 'An essay towards solving a problem in the Doctrine of Chances', *Philosophical Transactions of the Royal Society* 53: 370-418.

Dustmann, C., M. Casanova, M. Fertig, I. Preston & C.M. Schmidt (2003), 'The impact of EU enlargement on migration flows', Home Office Report 25/03. London: Home Office.

Frydman, R. & M.D. Goldberg (2007), *Imperfect knowledge economics: Exchange rates and risk*. Princeton: Princeton University Press.

Holzer, J.Z. (1959), *Prognoza demograficzna Polski na lata 1960-1975 wg województw* [Demographic forecast for Poland for 1960-1975 by voivodships]. Warsaw: PWG.

IPPR (2008), *Floodgates or turnstiles? Post-EU enlargement migration flows to (and from) the UK*. London: Institute for Public Policy Research.

Jennissen, R. (2004), *Macro-economic determinants of international migration in Europe*. Amsterdam: Dutch University Press.

Kadane, J.B. & L.J. Wolfson (1998), 'Experiences in elicitation', *The Statistician* 47 (1): 3-19.

Keilman, N. (1990), *Uncertainty in national population forecasting: Issues, backgrounds, analyses, recommendations*. Amsterdam: Swets & Zeitlinger.

Keyfitz, N. (1981), 'The limits of population forecasting', *Population and Development Review* 7 (4): 579-593.

Kupiszewska D. & B. Nowok (2008), 'Comparability of statistics on international migration flows in the European Union', in J. Raymer & F. Willekens (eds.), *International migration in Europe: Data, Models and Estimates*, 41-71. Chichester: John Wiley and Sons.

Kupiszewski, M. (2002), 'Modelowanie dynamiki przemian ludności w warunkach wzrostu znaczenia migracji międzynarodowych' [The role of international migration in the modelling of population dynamics], *Prace Geograficzne* 181. Warsaw: Institute of Geography and Spatial Organization, Polish Academy of Sciences.

Lee, R. & S. Tuljapurkar (1994). 'Stochastic population forecasts for the United States: Beyond high, medium, and low', *Journal of the American Statistical Association* 89: 1175-1189.

Lutz, W., W.C. Sanderson & S. Scherbov (1996), 'Probabilistic population projections based on expert opinion', in W. Lutz (ed.), *The future population of the world: What can we assume today? Revised edition*, 397-428. Laxenburg: IIASA; London: Earthscan.

Lutz, W., W.C. Sanderson & S. Scherbov (eds.) (2004), *The end of world population growth in the 21st century: New challenges for human capital formation & sustainable development*. London: Earthscan.

Nowok, B. & D. Kupiszewska (2005), 'Official European statistics on international migration flows: Availability, sources and coverage', CEFMR Working Paper 5/2005.

Nowok, B., D. Kupiszewska & M. Poulain (2006), 'Statistics on international migration flows', in M. Poulain, N. Perrin & A. Singleton (eds.), *THESIM: Towards Harmonised European Statistics on International Migration*, 203-231. Louvain-la-Neuve: Presses Universitaires de Louvain.

Öberg, S. & A.B. Wils (1992), 'East-West migration in Europe: Can migration theories help estimate the numbers', *Popnet* 22: 1-7.

Pijpers, R. (2008), 'Problematising the "orderly" aesthetic assumptions of forecasts of East-West migration in the European Union', *Environment and Planning A* 40 (1): 174-188.

Rees, P.H. & I. Turton (1998), *Investigation of the effects of input uncertainty on population forecasting*. Paper for the 3rd International GeoComputation Conference, Bristol, UK, 17-19 September.

Rowe, G. & G. Wright (2001), 'Expert opinions in forecasting. Role of the Delphi Technique', in J.S. Armstrong (ed.), *Principles of forecasting: A handbook of researchers and practitioners*, 125-144. Boston: Kluwer Academic Publishers.

Willekens, F. (1994), 'Monitoring international migration flows in Europe: Towards a statistical data base combining data from different sources', *European Journal of Population* 10 (1): 1-42.

10 Comments on 'An uncertain future of immigration in Europe' by Wiśniowski et al.

Leo van Wissen

10.1 Introduction

Forecasting is not in the first place a technical exercise; rather, it involves thinking methodically about the future. In so doing, we need to strategically leverage our knowledge and expertise of the migration process and assess how our experiences in the past will (or will not) carry over into the future. We have our own theories and models – sometimes intuitive, sometimes explicit – for doing so. In the end, we are obliged to quantify our beliefs about the future – an undertaking that is, by its very nature, technical. In order to make this task of 'projecting' a scientific one, a framework that integrates beliefs about the future with empirical evidence about the past is necessary. The Bayesian approach advocated by Wiśniowski and co-authors in chapter 9 of this volume is an example of an appropriate framework for migration forecasting. The Bayesian method is intimately related to forecasting. In fact, Bayesian forecasting is something of a mild redundancy because forecasting is at the core of the Bayesian approach to just about anything (Geweke & Whiteman 2006). Still, its application to the complex undertaking of immigration forecasting is relatively new (for one of the first attempts, see Gorbey, James & Poot 1999). Bijak (2008) also provides a good introduction. The authors have covered new areas with their approaches, and have set the stage for a fruitful new line of thinking about forecasting in migration research. Without an abundance of academic precedents, they sought to invent new ways of dealing with multiple complexities in the application. They have done so successfully, and have tried to document these steps as diligently as possible. Nevertheless, migration forecasting remains a difficult exercise involving many different steps, including a series of Delphi rounds among country experts, statistical modelling, interpretation, adjustments and forecasting.

For all these reasons, this is not just another forecasting exercise, but an innovative new step. Its main innovative qualities can be found in the way expert views and empirical evidence are combined to produce an 'optimal' forecasting model. It is an important contribution to the discussion of whether and how to integrate expert opinions about the future into quantitative trend-type models. The Bayesian method may be viewed as a fundamental alternative approach or even as an epistemological shift in statistical reasoning and forecasting. Bayesian forecasting involves applying conditions to what is known in order to make statements about what is not known (Geweke & Whiteman 2006). It is a very elegant but at the same time somewhat controversial and – as already noted above – undeniably complex approach.

It is elegant because it explicitly acknowledges that subjective beliefs about the process under study are important. In a way, it begins by asking: What do you think a priori about the migration process? It then uses historical data to adjust these a priori beliefs and to estimate the key features of the migration process: it is thus a mix of subjective beliefs – expert views – and objective data. It is somewhat controversial, as the traditional statistical view is based exclusively on data: the frequentist approach. This approach claims complete objectivity and distances itself from subjective elements in the analysis. The Bayesian view, by contrast, is explicitly subjective (Lancaster 2004).

Despite my esteem for the approach taken by Wiśniowski et al. and my admiration for the way they have handled the many difficulties that crossed their path, I have one serious objection to their approach: I do not agree with the main statement that migration is hardly predictable. In my view, it is too early to draw such a conclusion. I have a few doubts regarding this point in their current application, and I have many serious doubts about the aforementioned statement when it is intended as a general assessment with wider applicability. In the next section, I make a number of objections that call into question its validity.

10.2 Translating expert views into prior distributions regarding the parameters of the forecasting model

Experts hold widely different views about the future developments of migration. In the Delphi questionnaire included as part of the methodology of Wiśniowski et al., experts are asked various questions that need to be translated into beliefs about model parameters. These models will, in all likelihood, not reflect the underlying theory or model of the expert. The translation of expert opinions into relevant prior beliefs in the form of probability distributions of the parameters is not a trivial task. Although the researchers found innovative means of making this translation, it remains questionable whether this method allowed all relevant information about future migration trends to be solicited from the experts. This is a difficult issue and by no means one that is easily resolved, but it remains an important consideration: if the measurement instrument is not valid, then the output of the Delphi method will indeed increase forecast uncertainty rather than decrease it. It is clear that much work remains to be done in this field in the future. Nevertheless, I am convinced that there is still a world to win in this matter. In my view, this strategy should lead to reducing forecasting uncertainty.

As a first step, it might be a good idea to confront the experts with the first round of results, and ask them: Was this what you meant? They might rethink their beliefs and – perhaps – a second round would lead to adjusted views and more informative inputs (a learning exercise), which, all together, could lead to less uncertainty in the predictions.

10.3   Beliefs about parameter distributions are correlated

A related, more technical point asks: Can separate distributions for each of the parameters be constructed without taking account of the values of another? The value or interpretation of one parameter may depend on that of another. Expert opinions about the future are often shaped by a few leading latent causal factors that determine a set of coherent and correlated parameters. It appears as though the authors have treated them as independent. By not taking into account the covariance structure among the parameters, the variance of the prediction will necessarily be inflated.

10.4   The limited role of explanatory variables

I find it intriguing that economic variables do not come up as significant factors driving immigration. There is a large body of literature that suggests otherwise (see e.g. Jennissen 2004) and the authors are no doubt aware of and familiar with this literature. It is possible that this literature is more based on the North-Western European experience (the 'old' or 'mature' migration countries in IDEA's terms) and uses longer time series as a result. In this case, of course, we have a different set of countries and a shorter time series. But it is my conviction that economic forces in relation to long-term demographic trends are quite important in the long run. I also believed, until recently at least, that including information about driving forces in the forecast would result in better conditional forecasts – but this is apparently not true here. I have two possible explanations for this: the short length of the time series and the choice of countries in combination with the time periods. In the chosen period, the countries in the project underwent significant transitions: for the Eastern European countries, from centralised to market economies, followed by their introduction into the EU; for Southern and Western European countries, there were the consequences of the Balkan Wars. It is therefore not a surprise that the common structural driving factors of migration do not reveal themselves as very important. By including longer time series and other countries, different results would have been likely. For instance, what would have been the result if one had done this exercise for the Western European countries, where the relation between economic determinants and immigration has been firmly established? Is the inclusion of CEE countries into the EU not a strong trigger of some form of economic convergence towards a Western European economic model and therefore, in some sense, easier to predict? This convergence issue is important, and certainly a necessary additional consideration to make in this approach. Convergence of Eastern European countries' migration pattern to the Western European one certainly involves a shift from emigration to immigration countries, a prediction firmly grounded in the earlier chapters of the present volume.

10.5   The choice of the optimal model

In view of the empirical evidence, prior beliefs about models are changed. The model is then chosen for the forecast that has the highest posterior probability. In general, non-stationary models were favoured over stationary ones. In lay terms: models that show explosive growth or decline of immigration are more the rule than models that show well-behaved trends over time. Again, that could be due to the choice of countries in this particular period of time, which indeed revealed non-stationary trends. This need not be universally true, however. Maybe migration is not easily predictable in the short term, but it is in the long term.

Moreover, one of the points of criticism is that the Bayesian approach and the use of the Bayes factor to choose between models generally favour simpler models – such as the random walk model – over models that provide better explanations. If one opts for a random walk model, then the large uncertainty in outcomes is almost a given by definition, because it is cumulative.

10.6   The data problem

A final note about data. We all know that migration data have serious problems. The authors, who are specialists in this area, are well aware of them. Nevertheless, the limited reliability of the data is a very serious problem for arriving at accurate outcomes. Comparing matrices based on emigration statistics and on immigration statistics reveals, for instance, that the number of reported migrants from Poland to Germany differs by a factor of twenty to 30, depending on whether you retrieve the data from Germany or Poland. In the short term, nothing can be done about this, but it may be a significantly influencing factor in drawing the conclusion that migration is unpredictable. Let us first see if we can define and measure it consistently.

10.7 Final remarks

The main conclusion – that migration is hardly predictable – in my view, is drawn too early. In this chapter, I have given a number of arguments for why the situation is potentially not so bleak. The statement that migration is hardly predictable is conditional on the choices that were made in this analysis, yet the choices to make are not yet exhausted. Longer time series, other countries, better explanatory models and perhaps alternate modes of extracting useful information from experts are all necessary before this conclusion can be drawn definitively.

Nevertheless, the study is a very important contribution to this discussion. If it remains a true conclusion after my reservations have been dealt with and discarded, then the implication is not only about migration forecasting, but also about population forecasting. Obviously we cannot expect good population forecasts without good migration forecasts – so there is a lot at stake here.

References

Bijak, J. (2008), 'Bayesian methods in international migration forecasting', in J. Raymer & F. Willekens (eds.), *International migration in Europe: Data, models and estimates*, 255-288. New York: Wiley.

Geweke, J. & C. Whiteman (2006), 'Bayesian forecasting', in G. Elliott, C. William, J. Granger & A. Timmerman (eds.), *Handbook of economic forecasting*, vol. 1, 4-73. Amsterdam: Elsevier.

Gorbey, S., D.S. James & J. Poot (1999), 'Population forecasting with endogenous migration: An application to trans-Tasman migration', *International Regional Science Review* 22 (1): 69-101.

Jennissen, R. (2003), 'Economic determinants of net international migration in Western Europe', *European Journal of Population* 19 (2): 171-198.

Lancaster, T. (2004), *An introduction to modern Bayesian econometrics.* Malden: Blackwell Publishing Ltd.

11 Migration policy matters

A comparative analysis of policy recommendations

Magdalena Lesińska

11.1 The logic of policy recommendations based on research projects

The process of formulating policy recommendations is based on the main assumption that, among the main factors having an impact on migration processes – including the labour market, development gaps, demographic factors or international situations – a state's migration policy falls among the most influential. In other words, there exists a view that migration flows could be to some extent regulated through political measures (Brochmann & Hammar 1999; Boswell 2007; Cornelius, Tsuda, Martin & Hollifield 2004; Hollifield 2000).

In order to improve our understanding of the creative role of the state and its policies, a thorough analysis of the past and present status of migration processes in Europe is needed – one which includes their logic, course and consequences. Every immigration country has its own unique characteristics. What distinguishes one from the other is the country's history and tradition of immigration, the qualitative and quantitative characteristics of its inflows and also the way the state reacts to the entry and settlement of newcomers. Moreover, every country is part of a regional, European and worldwide migration system. This means it is not only the national milieu that has to be taken into account, but also the wider international context (Gosh 2003; Lahav 2004).

Although the patterns of migration flows in Western, Southern and Eastern Europe in 'old', 'new' and 'future' immigration countries (see the Introduction and chapters 1 and 2 in this book) are hardly comparable in a direct way, all the countries experience similar challenges and face similar dilemmas related to controlling, managing and integrating newcomers. Exchanging national experiences improves common knowledge and historical understanding of the migration cycle with an internal logic. Since the cycle is experienced by every country, this information set is of priceless value for all states, especially those at the preliminary stages of the cycle.

Policy recommendations, as a relevant component of scientific knowledge, play a vital role in developing research-policy partnerships. Scientific analyses should supply some value added, not only by providing reliable data and expertise, but also by inspiring and supporting certain policy developments. Researchers' role is not only to shed a light on social processes, but also to provoke critical reflection among policymakers and to propose alternative resolutions. Especially in the case of such an intensively debated issue as immigration, the broad dissemination of knowledge via open dialogue and using all available communication tools is more than desired. Scientific results should be distributed broadly, including to non-academic audiences (policymakers, civil society actors, public opinion leaders) in the most accessible way and using direct channels of communication.

11.2 Background of formulation of migration policy

The formulation of migration policy requires, first and foremost, the conceptualisation of a given state's interests related to immigration. This means submitting a set of key questions and finding a commonly accepted response to at least some of them.
– Does the state need or not need immigration (and why or why not)?
– What kind of immigration is desired?
– How can the desired inflows be recruited and how can undesired ones be constrained?
– How should the immigrants who are already in the country be dealt with?

Political recommendations are formulated mostly for policymakers (representing, generally speaking, the state's government and administration), thereby putting the centre of gravity on the state and its functions. The recommendations presented here are the result of a thorough analysis of migration processes in nine countries, representing three diverse levels of maturity in the European immigration cycle and involving migration policy and the management of human mobility.[1] Immigrants, however, are not one consistent or coherent group. To the contrary, innumerable typologies describing particular migrating groups can be identified in the literature. Injecting some order into analysing the logic and content of these migration policy recommendations, this chapter identifies two main groups of immigrants that require action from the state, as follows:
– Potential (expected) immigrants, including two different types: desired (those who the state wants to come) and undesired (those who the state does not want to come).

– Real immigrants (who have already come), including two different types: wanted (those who the state wants to stay) and unwanted (those who the state does not want to stay).

These two groups require different approaches from states. The first requires mechanisms of encouragement (such as special entry and recruitment schemes) or discouragement (strict visa policies, restrictive rules of admission to labour market). A similar set of policies applies to the second group; according to the state's categorisation of who is wanted and who is unwanted, the first type is encouraged to stay, and the second is encouraged to leave the country.

The main aim of migration policy can thus be succinctly defined as regulating and controlling international migration flows according to state interests. These are the imperatives in the formulation of migration policy. However, any definition would be incomplete without taking into account other points of view and interests of actors who take part in the entire process: immigrants themselves, as well as transit or sending countries. This suggests that policymakers constructing migration policies must also take into consideration a wide set of factors, both internal (the national political system, labour market, population characteristics, public opinion) and external (international law, geopolitical situations, relations with neighbouring countries).

Following this line of reasoning, at least three main concerns should be highlighted here as guidelines in migration policy development:

– The interests of the host state (and its citizens) versus the interests of newcomers.
– The interests of the state versus the interests of other political entities, such as neighbouring countries, source countries and the European Union; indeed, the ability of the state to manage migration flows has always been limited by many factors that are, in fact, independent of and uncontrollable by the state, including political crises or war and the mass asylum inflows that can result.
– Idealism versus pragmatism; this is especially noticeable in the case of asylum integration policies, when consensus between the so-called human rights approach and other types of practical approaches (usually advocated by policymakers) is sometimes difficult to achieve.

These also pose dilemmas that policymakers have to confront, but could be treated as rationales for migration policy formation.

11.3 Immigration as a challenge

There are several commonalities within the logic underlying migration policies in every country, regardless of the level of maturity they may already have reached. All destination countries are necessarily confronted with the same migration-related challenges: they can be broken down into categories of pre- and post-immigration challenges.

The pre-immigration challenges are related to potential immigrants. They most significantly affect the state's interests related to labour market needs, economic development, demographic situations, etc. Policymakers attempt to respond to these challenges by implementing effective mechanisms of admission and recruitment of selected groups, including high-skilled or seasonal workers. The pre-immigration challenges also comprise undesired migration inflows (first and foremost irregular ones) and the state's response via stricter border controls.

Post-immigration challenges, on the other hand, arise from the direct and indirect effects of immigrants' inclusion into, and functioning within, the labour market and social fabric of a given destination country. Integration policies are the key to counteracting the discrimination, marginalisation and social exclusion of newcomers, as well as weak social cohesion, ethnic and cultural tensions and the irregular employment of immigrants.

11.4 Towards mature migration policies

In accordance with the migration cycle concept dictating that particular countries move forward from states of emigration to immigration – ultimately evolving into 'mature' immigration states – the question for migration policy is: what do 'mature' migration policies entail? Insofar as it is a final goal, what could 'younger' countries – those at a preliminary stage, on their way towards maturity – learn from the 'older' and more experienced states?

Following traditional approaches, an ideal policy should be:
- Predictive and well-planned (based on a widely accepted long-term strategy that defines the state's interests and aims to achieve them via migration policy).
- Well-organised and coherent (supported by a legal framework that serves as a normative basis and an appropriate bureaucratic structure that ensures successful implementation).
- Rational (based on a thorough analysis of all available data and information sources, as well as the experiences of other countries).

– Efficient (there should be a consistency between the intended objectives and final outcomes of a given migration policy), which is the most challenging criterion.

It is a difficult task (if it is possible at all) to evaluate migration policy according to these 'ideal' characteristics. From a more practical point of view, a basic condition seems to be of utmost importance – namely, whether migration policy corresponds well with the actual state of affairs and whether the demand for state intervention in regulating migration flows is sufficiently met. Mature migration policy requires a broader context analysis; geopolitical situation, other countries' interests and influence, international commitments have to be taken into account by policymakers.

A key pre-condition for designing 'mature' migration policies is having access to reliable data on past and present immigration flows and stocks, as well as certain immigration forecasts. Although there is a serious 'forecasting uncertainty' (see chapter 9 in this volume), this knowledge is necessary to create a long-term political strategy in many areas: the economy, labour market and demography, in particular. It is closely related to the issue of developing research-policy partnerships in the field of migration, as introduced at the beginning of this chapter.

11.5 Overview of policy recommendations

If a migration cycle is also to be considered a cycle of influencing via teaching and learning processes, a key question is what countries at different stages of development could learn from each other?

11.5.1 General lessons from western and southern countries

Immigration is an unavoidable and indispensable phenomenon, mostly for demographic and economic reasons. However, there are two different perspectives for handling immigration: as a solution (to economic or demographic needs) and as a problem (as a threat to social cohesion, national identity and security and welfare systems). Depending on which perspective prevails, the formulation of migration policy can be influenced significantly.

The economic imperative rules migration policy dictates not only how the state reacts, but also whether this reaction takes place at all. As Mirjana Morokvasic observed, 'most workers arrived not via the official recruitment channels, but as tourists, as workers under "nominal contracts", and the authorities closed their eyes as long as the workers responded to the immediate needs of the labour market' (IDEA Policy Brief no. 2: 3).

The importance of the demographic argument is growing. Immigration is necessary, or at least desirable, for stabilising labour forces and population sizes in times of negative natural growth, low fertility and, as a consequence, ageing and shrinking societies. It is not a time to question whether we need immigrants at all, but rather the type and number should be considered.

Qualified immigrants and demand-oriented proactive migration policies should be given top priority as a result of the common awareness of the competition for 'qualified, talented and motivated' immigrants (IDEA Policy Brief no.1: 2). At the same time,

> attracting the best should not be to the detriment of the countries of origin, depriving them of their 'brains'; neither should it imply 'de-skilling', non-recognition or inadequate recognition of the credentials and know-how of immigrants. (IDEA Policy Brief no. 2: 2)

Integration has to be treated as an issue of significant concern. Immigration has to be accepted as a permanent process, not as a temporary phenomenon, and one with long-term consequences that very often lead to settlement. The number of immigrants who have stayed in France, according to various sources, is estimated to between 50 and 60 per cent. This might mean that, for approximately half of all incoming immigrants, temporary migration has transformed into long-term settlement (IDEA Policy Brief no. 2). This requires offering 'a clear life perspective for immigrants' within the destination country (IDEA Policy Brief no. 1: 2). Moreover, integration activities should be targeted not only at regular migrants, but also at irregular ones, who are the most vulnerable to social exclusion and marginalisation (that is, irrespectively of their legal status, free access to basic health care services and education for minors should be provided) (IDEA Policy Brief no. 4 and 6).

The number of immigrants should be kept under control. Migration policy should define upper limits for immigration for certain periods of time. These limits should depend on economic needs and the social acceptance of immigrants (IDEA Policy Brief no. 1).

There is no interdependence between more restrictive policy and less immigration. The example of western countries is clear evidence that restrictive policies are largely ineffective and:

> transform migration flows into business opportunities for traffickers and smugglers. Illegal entries have not been stopped in spite of the measures taken – rather, migrants tend to rely more and more on professional intermediaries. (IDEA Policy Brief no. 2)

Immigration as well as migration policy need certain social acceptance by the native population. There is a common fear against immigration in receiving societies, especially in times of economic crisis, which effectively influences migration policy. To achieve societal consensus and public support, an information policy and a broad public debate is necessary; it requires open and regular communication with the public opinion via a variety of channels, including the media.

Irregular immigration and illegal employment require a complex approach and tackling root causes. The effective promotion of channels for legal immigration is required in order to cope with economic demand and counteract the complications posed by irregular inflows.

A few key issues enumerated above will be presented in detail in a later section of this chapter.

11.6 Three key questions constituting the pillars of migration policy

11.6.1 Question one: How should labour migration be managed?

Finding more flexible and effective admission rules and recruitment schemes is the best response here. Immigration represents a long-term solution to unmet labour and skill needs in a national economy and, at the same time, supports state development. The main challenge could be articulated as follows: how should policies be designed in order to meet the real demands of the labour market for foreign labour and match the demand with immigration flows? This dilemma is also widely discussed at the EU level.[2]

As mentioned previously, in all the countries there has been a demand, albeit to varying degrees, for short-term labour migration. These types of immigrants enter the country for limited periods of time in order to fulfil labour shortages that usually result from economic growth. As was described by Heinz Fassmann and Ursula Reeger in their analysis of the case of western countries:

> foreign workers were supposed to behave like spinning tops on the domestic labour market. They should come and go, if possible alone and without families, and be very flexible both occupationally and geographically. This would bring maximum benefits to Austrian and German businesses while relieving society from fundamental questions of integration, which were inevitable when labour migrants began to settle. (IDEA Working Paper no. 3: 21)

However, the situation that arises when circular and short-term type immigration transforms into settlement is usually out of state control – the example of western countries in the 1960s and 1970s illustrates this convincingly.

Over time, several mechanisms have been designed for legal recruitment: quota systems (setting up labour quotas per economic sector followed by a process of granting of work visas), a point system or shortage lists. All of them, however, have some limitations and operate with questionable efficiency.

A commonly recurring recommendation is a call for effective monitoring of labour market in order to overcome mismatches between market demand and state regulations. The monitoring system should be well-grounded institutionally (not dependent on the political cycle), cohesive in task assignments, effective in maintaining the flow of information between involved partners/institutions, multi-level and systematic. The most important aim of this sort of system would be not only to monitor the demand for a foreign labour force in terms of its dynamics of inflow, scale and structure, but also the fluctuations of the number of foreigners in the labour market and the role of foreign workers – that is, whether they complement or substitute the domestic labour. It thus would require an adequate, up-to-date and detailed database of the shortages of and, consequently, the demand for foreign workers. The monitoring system should involve all the sectors of the labour market, including domestic services.

As the example of the Southern European countries illustrates, recruitment is an important but not sufficient migration control activity. The main weakness of recruitment systems is that hiring procedures are very complex and time-consuming (usually lasting several months), which is unacceptable for seasonal employment in agriculture or small companies, where quick and flexible rules of entry and recruitment are necessary. Additionally, there is the need to check on the availability of the local workforce (in order to protect local workers), which also prolongs the time needed for recruitment and makes the system more restrictive and inflexible. Some employers thus prefer an easier option and employ workers irregularly.

Again, the southern countries' experiences are worth discussing here. The nominal request system introduced in the mid-1980s in Spain and Italy turned out to be unsuccessful. In Greece, the invitation scheme was implemented beginning in 1991

> allowing immigrants to work in Greece, for a specific employer and performing specific type of work, only if there is an available position for them which cannot be filled by the Greek labour force or the immigrant labour force that already resides in Greece. (IDEA Working Paper no. 9: 37)

Moreover, the scheme was criticised for its restrictiveness. Similarly, systems based on labour market quotas, introduced as pioneering solutions involving a system of annual quotas for economic migrants at all skill levels, that were implemented in the beginning of the 1990s in Southern European countries (such as the 'programmed number' or *numero programmato* in Italy or *contingente* in Spain) have never functioned as effective labour channels.

Quota systems were also criticised.

> The large number of immigrants working in the low-paid, low-skilled segments of the labour market in Italy are meeting a demand for labour that the quota system has difficulty quantifying. This means that the demand for labour is underestimated, specifically as regards new migration flows, and so the maximum quota for annual entries is also underestimated [...]. Also considering that the directions and dimensions of the new immigration flows are constantly changing, any predetermined estimate of the maximum quotas for new entries that is used as a tool in planning and managing the flows must take into account various new factors. In this way, the quota mechanism should be a flexible instrument that can be corrected as and when it is necessary. (IDEA Working Paper no. 5: 58)

The lesson to draw from the attempts to create an effective recruitment system could be articulated as follows:

> Taking all these labour immigration policies together, it is clear that their degree of restrictiveness and their complex administrative requirements were unable to deal with high labour demands and vast immigrant supplies, thus being incapable of regulating inflows and limiting irregular immigration. Moreover, it was the cause of the continuity and large volume of irregular inflows. (IDEA Working Paper no. 9: 40)

There is no ideal system; serious loopholes could be found in each of them. In reality, employers officially recruit foreign workers and declare hiring them in a particular occupation, then employ them in other roles once the recruitment procedure has been concluded. Also worth noting is that, very often, legal channels of entry have served to legalise irregular migrants already staying in the country, rather than acting as a measure to recruit new immigrants.

To overcome the weaknesses thus described and to improve the system of legal recruitment, a few recent, rather successful initiatives are elaborated here:

- The list of vacant positions. In Spain, in order to facilitate the recruitment process, every three months the Catalogo de trabajos de dificil cobertura is released. It contains information on positions that are not
  filled by available workers (nationals or citizens of other EU countries).
  The system allows an employer looking to fill a vacancy listed in this
  catalogue to start a recruitment procedure immediately. Then the system
  allows for 'eluding the priority check of the labour market and represents, thus, a step forward in the conception of workable immigration
  policies' (IDEA Policy Brief no. 6: 2).
- The system of an entry visa for 'job search'. The aim of this type of
  visa is to promote flexibility in the recruitment procedures. However,
  the possibility to apply for such a visa is limited to a certain number of
  employment sectors, such as the domestic sector. However, the visa for
  job searches (according to Spanish experts) still has something of a
  symbolic character, as it has been issued to a very limited number of
  immigrants since its introduction.
- 'Global contingent' of labour needs (the report of total labour needs,
  published every year) introduced in 2007 in Portugal. The system
  includes an announcement of job vacancies abroad and the subsequent
  issuance of visas.

This new framework represents an attempt to improve and make effective the issuance of residence and temporary visas for work purposes. Foreign citizens have direct access to job offers through the
IEFP website, and there is also the possibility of direct contact between the potential candidates and the recruiters. (IDEA Working
Paper no. 9: 40)

Quota regulations need to be flexible and open for modification, according
to the necessities of the labour market during a given year.
- Recruitment schemes based on bilateral agreements with sending countries to establish an effective system for providing long- or short-term
  workers to the national labour market via specialised agencies.

11.6.2 Question two: How should irregular immigration be addressed?

The answer here is by controlling, regularisation and addressing root
causes. In all the countries, albeit to a different extent, irregular immigration has become a structural feature of migration regimes. It represents one
of the most important challenges for national governments. What system
factors rooted in the state's regime reinforce irregular migration? A conclusion drawn from a variety of analyses is clear on this point, singling out
the most important as follows: the existence of a shadow economy and a
common acceptance of its existence; the lack or excessive restrictiveness

of legal entry and recruitment procedures; weak administrative structures; ineffective systems of labour market control; and the lack of transparent regularisation schemes.

Taking migration histories into account, the best cases by which to analyse the problem of irregular immigration are the Southern European countries. Since the 1980s, there has been a dynamic increase in immigration flows into these countries. Although the demand for foreign workers was recognised by the state, legislation did not adapt to this trend and was still characterised by 'a high degree of restrictiveness and inflexibility, which hampered effective programming of the flows' (IDEA Working Paper no. 9: 28). Cumbersome admission rules, along with weak external controls, a large informal economy (according to recent estimates around 20 per cent of GDP, even more in Greece) and widespread social acceptance of informal employment are all factors that have contributed to a growing number of irregulars in Southern European countries.

Special attention should be given here to the role of the informal economy, which serves as a magnet for irregular employment. Its relatively large size and particular structure facilitate immigrants' flexibility and 'invisibility' in the labour market. The attractive qualities of unregistered employment are reinforced by widespread societal acceptance, relatively high non-salaried costs of work and the time-consuming and complex administration procedures required to register. The size of the shadow economy also corresponds to the weakness of labour market controls.

Irregular immigration is also one of the unintended consequences of excessively restrictive immigration policies. As the case of Italy and other Mediterranean countries demonstrates, when a rather liberal system of entries is restricted (as happened in response to pressure from Western European countries that perceived the southern states as the backdoors for entry into the EU) and there is high demand for foreigners' work, more and more immigrants will begin to use illegal means of accessing the territory and the labour market. The lesson seems to be that if the entry channels for labour migration underestimate the real needs of the national economy, irregular migration will increase.

There is a well-known catalogue of state actions taken against migration irregularity. They can be divided into external (border controls, cooperation with countries of origin) and internal (labour market controls, regularisation).

The role of, and problems with, effective border control (especially in the case of Spain, Greece and Italy) are well known. However, they cannot be separated from an active presence in the countries of origin and ongoing cooperation with their institutions. The case of the southern countries shows that a traditional approach, based on a prioritisation of strict external border control, must be modified in light of its inefficiency and, moreover, completed with the addition of cooperation with neighbouring sending or transit countries.

Especially valuable in migration control is the role of bilateral agreements with sending countries. They represent a condition sine qua non for reducing irregular immigration successfully. The state should provide a legal alternative to illegal entries. Through bilateral agreements, privileged entry quotas could be offered as compensation for the introduction of a visa system. Bilateral agreements, as the Spanish example illustrates, have to be connected with broader public campaigns against irregular migration, as well as with the formation of an institutional framework of interstate cooperation (e.g. working groups with relevant authorities from destination and sending countries). In 2006, the Spanish government introduced the two-year Africa Plan. Its objective was to create a close system of cooperation with several African countries in order to improve management of migration flows from Africa to Europe. The recent initiative of the Portuguese government to open the Support Centre for Migrants in the Sending Country in Cape Verde is also a good example. Bilateral agreements have also been shown to be a precondition for effective expulsion processes (most of the expulsions in Spain have been carried out via readmission agreements) as well as voluntary returns.[3]

The immigration issue should be an integral part of neighbouring states' policies at the national and the EU levels. Close cooperation between the Mediterranean EU countries and Northern Africa Region on the migration issue – within the framework of the EU neighbourhood policy – is another example of good practice here. The immigration issue should also be high on the political agenda in the eastern EU countries' neighbourhood policies.

Another important activity is internally controlling the labour market. In recent years, in all the countries analysed, the number of inspections has increased significantly, as actions are more frequently taken against informal employment. The effectiveness of such actions is questionable, though, especially in the case of sectors traditionally recognised as immigrants' niches (agriculture, petty trade and especially domestic work). It is implausible indeed that any country could effectively regulate these sectors through labour inspections. In the Southern European countries, an interesting shift towards somewhat different incentives has taken place: for instance, a tax relief for those who officially employ a babysitter or an elderly person's caregiver; or the introduction of flexible insurance schemes for cleaners, construction workers and domestic servants who have more than one employer. 'They are able to register with the dependent employee welfare fund under special conditions and hence both have affordable insurance and retain their legal migration status' (IDEA Working Paper no. 9: 47). These solutions could lead to the emergence of this sector from the shadow economy. Overall, however, labour market inspections should be also accompanied by wide public campaigns against informal work.

Regularisation programmes have become a measure used regularly by Southern European countries (even if every subsequent regularisation programme has been presented as an exceptional 'one-time-only' remedy). 'The lack of efficient recruitment procedures turned regularisations into the most useful way to 'repair' a posteriori the structural mismatches in migration policy' (IDEA Working Paper no. 9: 30).

The structural weaknesses of regularisation processes are evident in the case of Southern European countries. A high recognition rate is not a result of success in stabilising and integrating the legalised population. The main criticism was related to the short amount of time (usually one year) that a residence permit obtained as a result of regularisation permitted – especially one that had to be renewed soon afterwards. As a consequence, many of the regularised immigrants fell back into illegality as soon as their residence permits expired. Another weak point stressed by the experts is that mass regularisations can sometimes produce a 'pull' effect that, rather than reducing the rates of irregularity, further attracts irregular migration inflows.

The main conclusion to be drawn from analyses of mass regularisations is that they are not an appropriate or effective instrument to be used in the fight against irregular immigration (IDEA Policy Briefs no. 3, 5, 6). In Spain and Portugal they have been substituted by a more discrete, individual and ongoing regularisation system. The introduction of individual and permanent regulation schemes should be taken into consideration in all the countries – but they should not be considered as a main tool, rather as a correction mechanism to use alongside active policies and more effective controls.

11.6.3 Question three: How can the eternal problem of integration be solved?

Despite their manifold differences, in every country of immigration integration is treated as a priority, or at least is declared as such. There is, however, a disconnect between countries with active and developed integration policies (most of the western and southern states; the Czech Republic also could be included in this group), and those where integration policies are just a set of initiatives limited to selected groups, such as refugees and repatriates, and have not even been the subject of any considerable debate (the cases of Poland or Hungary) (IDEA Policy Briefs no. 8, 9).

Worth noting is that integration policy is significantly influenced by several systemic characteristics of a state. Integration policy is focused mainly on the areas of health services, housing, welfare schemes, education and the labour market. It is therefore related to, and dependent on, the national welfare system, which varies from country to country. Moreover, in federal countries with high levels of decentralisation, as in Spain or Italy, the regional and even municipal authorities have significant independence in the implementation of particular policies. Overall, it seems to be a positive solution for integration policies, in accordance with the principle of subsidiarity (which assumes that a political decision-making system should be taken as close as possible to the governed to ensure that the decisions be indispensable and respond well to their needs) and taking into account diversity and the strong territorial dispersion of immigrants. Regional authorities typically possess better knowledge about immigrants' needs and are thus better prepared to frame successful plans for social integration and design a more appropriate structure of services. 'The integration of immigrants is a policy area where a local approach is critical' (IDEA Policy Brief no. 2: 5). Moreover, 'more attention should be paid to "organizational structures" that could deal with immigrants' integration at regional and local levels' (IDEA Policy Brief no. 7: 3).

No one should be excluded from basic integration activities, even irregular immigrants. This group is even more vulnerable to social exclusion, discrimination and marginalisation than others and cannot be deprived of basic needs and rights. In this sense, the Southern European countries have introduced a somewhat innovative approach: irregular migrants in Spain or Italy have access to primary school and health provisions, just like nationals.

> The law also recognizes that the rights to healthcare and education are fundamental human rights that must be guaranteed regardless of a person's legal status. Consequently, urgent hospital or other medical treatment is also available for foreigners without permits to stay, as is the right to compulsory schooling for foreign minors. (IDEA Working Paper no. 4: 6)

In order to plan integration initiatives more effectively, a solid understanding of immigrants' situations is required, along with facilitated communication between authorities and immigrants. The encouragement and assistance of self-organising processes, as well as wide support of immigrants' organisations, should also be one of the priorities of integration policy. Here the role of European funds cannot be overestimated.

> Indeed, European Social Fund programmes and the more recent European Integration Fund for the Integration of Third Country Nationals have been instrumental in creating synergies, mobilising resources, even reorganising public administration offices with a view to providing services to migrant communities. (IDEA Working Paper no. 9: 50)

> Information policy is also a key part and has a powerful impact on integration processes, first and foremost by increasing national citizens' abilities to deal with diversity.
> Stereotypes about migrants are often an obstacle to the implementation and success of immigration policies and integration programmes. An ever closer cooperation between the political agenda and the media [...] should be emphasized, as well as awareness-raising campaigns for media on immigration issues. Furthermore, a deeper knowledge on migration should be increased in order to avoid disseminating false and negative images of immigrants. (IDEA Policy Brief no. 5: 11)

Taking into account that immigrants, especially those of the first generation, appear trapped in the low-skill, low-paying sectors of the labour market and are vulnerable to discrimination and inequality in wages, special attention to anti-discriminatory measures should also be paid.[4] A new system of data collection pertaining to foreigners employed by companies should be created, tasked also with serving as a system of monitoring discriminatory practices towards foreigners. Such a system, which would allow for gathering and managing data on foreigners' presence on the labour market and on any unlawful or reprehensible practices towards foreign workers, would constitute a basis for the creation and implementation of adequate anti-discriminatory measures.

> One of the most important anti-discriminatory measures is the availability and clarity of the information on what labour discrimination means, what the consequences of it are, how to respond to it, where to report cases of discriminatory acts, how to apply for compensation, where to find a competent legal advisor and support, etc. Therefore, a proper information campaign addressed to employees as well as employers is also required. Such a campaign should be based on multicultural and human rights issues and would have educational, informative and preventive character. (Lesińska, Stefańska & Szulecka 2010: 206)

Taking into account that freedom from labour discrimination is granted only to those foreigners who possess the legal entitlement to work, activities aimed at detecting and solving the problems of serious discrimination of foreigners working partly or fully in contradiction to immigration rules should also be initiated. The introduction of anti-discriminatory measures may make legal employment more desirable for immigrants.

11.7 What can be learned from migration policy analysis: Some final thoughts

Several conclusions worth highlighting arise from this chapter's analysis. They mostly constitute a continuation of the catalogue of problems to cope with on the way towards mature migration policies. For, despite the level of maturity already reached by particular states in the migration cycle, the conclusions presented below seem to be common to all of the countries examined. Many of these issues have their own rationale and accompanying controversies, which I will describe briefly in turn.

11.7.1 Europeanisation of policy and its influence

The last several decades have marked a time of building the EU as a legal and political entity. The process commonly called 'Europeanisation' refers to the convergence of EU and national approaches in numerous areas. Migration is also one of them, and the process of reorienting the direction and shape of migration policy into a European one is currently taking place. The chance for a real Europeanisation of migration policy is rooted in the fact that all states share the same basic logic, which is based on community interests. As the analyses included in this book demonstrate, each state has similar interests and concerns related to immigration. Each state faces the same set of challenges presented above. Pragmatism, not idealism – namely, of being one European community – should be a push factor towards greater cooperation.

Undoubtedly, one of the consequences of the whole process of Europeanisation is the creation of a common general legal and political framework, based on an obligatory acquis and a collection of recommendations and best practices – which all countries should follow (via an open method of coordination introduced by the EU). For the new member states, accession to the EU was a powerful determining impulse and brought about an acceleration in the evolution of national migration policies. Institutions and measures designed by more mature immigration countries have been transposed, during the process of harmonisation with the EU, to the newly acceding states. Initiatives related to integration have been very much triggered by the recent developments in the EU 'soft law', particularly the Common Basic Principles of Integration and the Commission's communication on the proposed Common Agenda for Integration of Third-Country Nationals in the European Union, supported by the INTI (European Fund for the Integration of Third Country Nationals as a financing instrument) and the Network of National Contact Points on Integration (as an institutional structure established for exchanging and discussing best practices). The role of Annual Reports on Migration and Integration, which monitor the process of policy developments as well as provide a full package of information on the establishment of the EU framework in these matters, is also worth highlighting.

Also of note is a kind of synchronisation of ways of perceiving immigration. Western European states, as mature immigration regimes, have emerged as the primary reference points for policymakers in other countries, especially the eastern ones. There, the public imagery of immigration is perceived in a very 'mature' way, as a highly problematic issue. The focus is, first and foremost, on the problem of integration, potential conflicts or the protection of state security and public order – even though none of these phenomena has appeared in reality.

There is also a cost to Europeanisation. Even if a particular country wishes to preserve its national interests and introduces innovative or independent activities, the limits of self-determination established by the EU always have to be taken into account. Standardisation of rules has positive sides, but could also restrain innovation: it is much easier to follow the common tracks – checked and tested ones – than to experiment with new paths and solutions. This trend is most noticeable in the case of the new member states, which, first and foremost, analyse the political recommendations of more mature countries. However, it must be emphasised once more that Eastern European countries do not necessarily follow the same paths within the migration circle.

11.7.2 *Immigration as more of a public and less of an administrative issue*

Mature migration policy – to be effective – requires legitimisation through social consensus and public support. Immigration should be a subject of broad debate, including not only representatives of administration, scholars and experts, but also a wide range of social actors and the media.

There is a common negative image of immigration, which is noticeable in western countries.

> In the public imagery in France, the focus is more on immigrants as social problems, on the 'failure of their integration', rather than on positive outcomes of migration and on immigrants' multiple and outstanding contributions to social, cultural, economic, scientific and political life. (IDEA Policy Brief no. 2: 4)

Therefore, there is an urgent need to combat negative myths resulting from ignorance, visible also among policymakers. The 'discourse of fear' present in many countries of Europe should not be the only driver influencing public opinion. Immigration should be recognised and presented in a more balanced way, not only as a threat, but also as a value and opportunity. It must be stressed that human mobility is 'a value in itself which corresponds to an increase in personal freedom' and 'with a migration and integration policy conceptualised in a methodological, scrupulous way, the benefits of migration will prevail' (IDEA Policy Brief no. 1: 3).

In more mature countries, the immigration issue is picked up regularly in times of political instability or public elections by politicians. As a result, it has become a major debated issue, very often highly polarising public opinion. On the contrary, in the case of Eastern European countries, immigration is rarely visible in public discourse and, due to the rather small scale of immigration, it is not a controversial issue at all.

What is also worth noting is that, if migration is not an issue of public interest and a minor subject in political debates, it could have an important effect on the way policy is implemented. The fact that migration is not a controversial topic means, in practice, that there will be a lack or a very limited number of public debates around the legal and political actions undertaken by policymakers in this field. In the countries examined, the process of wider consultation with representatives of the non-governmental and academic sector on migration policy is rather limited. As a consequence, the process of policy implementation could be easier and quicker; however, it does not necessary mean that it would be more effective.

11.8   What kind of migration policy in the era of circular and fluid migration? Lessons from Poland

> Before they settle in another country, most people tend to circulate between their place of origin and the country or countries of residence. Others, for different reasons, never settle, but commute for a considerable portion of their lifetimes ('settle in mobility') before 'returning' or starting another move (multiple migrants). (IDEA Policy Brief no. 2: 6)

The term 'fluid migration' was recently proposed to describe the phenomenon of inflow of the foreign nationals to Poland (see Górny, Grabowska-Lusińska, Lesińska & Okólski 2010). The fluidity of migration means 'being here and there' and, at the same time, 'deliberately keeping various options open' (mostly with respect to the labour market) (Engbersen, Snel & de Boom 2010). Such migrants are characterised by a high level of flexibility to change their country of residence and employment.

> Many of those migrants live in transnational social spaces, sustaining strong ties with both the country of origin and the country of residence. Circulation, involving earning money in Poland and spending it in the home country, seems a rational choice for migrants originating from the neighbouring countries [...]. At present,

> the migrants' social context – social relations and networks, which
> migrants already have established in Poland – and migration policy
> facilitate the development of a temporary, chiefly circular form of
> immigration. (Lesińska, Stefańska & Szulecka 2010: 197)

Facilitating this kind of mobility – back-and-forth movements reinforced
by a modern economy and characterised by post-industrial flexibility and
insecurity – will be the greatest challenge for immigration states. Its management would require interstate and/or regional cooperation and could
imply multiple entry or long-term visas. It could also mean the free movement of persons within the framework of regional integration processes or
that of their development of the regions of origin. It would also require
going beyond the traditional approach, understood as the state being able
to control migration via strict rules, and accepting the fact that the state is
only one body among a variety of actors in the process of human mobility.
As such, it has only limited power to influence modern mobility's directions, patterns and numbers. The final lesson is that migration policy
should be more flexible than ever before in order to successfully respond
and to cope with the effects of contemporary immigration.

Notes

1   Policy recommendations included in this chapter are mainly based on content from
    the IDEA project's final products (2007-2009), comprising policy briefs, national
    and regional reports and working papers prepared by eleven participating teams.
    They are available on the project website (www.idea6fp.uw.edu.pl).
2   See the 'Green Paper on an EU approach to managing economic migration' (COM/
    2004/0811 final) or the 'Policy Plan on Legal Migration Policy Plan on Legal
    Migration' [SEC(2005)1680], a search for the EU approach to labour migration and
    the most appropriate form of common rules for admitting economic migrants from
    third countries, as well as the Council Directive (2003/109/EC) concerning the sta-
    tus of third-country nationals who are long-term residents.
3   See also Directive 2008/115/EC on common standards and procedures in member
    states for returning illegally staying third-country nationals, which was very recently
    adopted by the European Parliament and the Council of the European Union.
4   A strong legal foundation on anti-discrimination measures has been adopted at the
    EU level; see Council Directive 2000/43/EC implementing the principle of equal
    treatment between persons irrespective of racial or ethnic origin and Council
    Directive 2000/78/EC establishing a general framework for equal treatment in em-
    ployment and occupation.

References

Boswell, C. (2007), 'Theorizing migration policy: Is there a third way?', *International
    Migration Review* 41 (1): 101-126.

Brochmann, G. & T. Hammar (1999), *Mechanisms of immigration control: A comparative analysis of European regulation policies*. Oxford/New York: Berg Publisher.

Cornelius, W., T. Tsuda, P.L. Martin & J.F. Hollifield (eds.) (2004), *Controlling immigration: A global perspective*. Stanford: Stanford University Press.

Engbersen, G., E. Snel & J. de Boom (2010), ' "A van full of Poles": Liquid migration from Central and Eastern Europe', in R. Black, G. Engbersen, M. Okólski & C. Panţiru (eds.), *A continent moving West? EU enlargement and labour migration from Central and Eastern Europe*, 115-140. IMISCOE-AUP Research Series. Amsterdam: Amsterdam University Press.

Górny, A., I. Grabowska-Lusińska, M. Lesińska & M. Okólski (eds.) (2010), *Immigration to Poland: Policy, employment, integration*. Warsaw: Scholar.

Gosh, B. (ed.) (2003), *Managing migration: Time for a new international regime*. Oxford: Oxford University Press.

Hollifield, J. (2000), 'The politics of international migration: How can we "bring the state back in?" ', in C. Brettell & J. Hollifield (eds.), *Migration theory. Talking across disciplines*, 137-185. New York/London: Routledge.

IDEA Policy Brief no. 1 (2008), 'Policy oriented executive summary: The Austrian contribution' (http://www.idea6fp.uw.edu.pl/pliki/POES_Austria_PB_1.pdf).

IDEA Policy Brief no. 2 (2008), 'Policy oriented analysis: France' (http://www.idea6fp.uw.edu.pl/pliki/POES_France_PB_2.pdf).

IDEA Policy Brief no. 3 (2009), 'Migration and migration policy in Greece. Critical review and policy recommendations' (http://www.idea6fp.uw.edu.pl/pliki/POES_Greece_PB_3.pdf).

IDEA Policy Brief no. 4 (2009), 'Policy oriented executive summary: Italy' (http://www.idea6fp.uw.edu.pl/pliki/POES_Italy_PB_4.pdf).

IDEA Policy Brief no. 5, (2009), 'Policy oriented executive summary: Portugal' (http://www.idea6fp.uw.edu.pl/pliki/POES_Portugal_PB_5.pdf).

IDEA Policy Brief no. 6 (2009), 'Policy recommendations: Spain' (http://www.idea6fp.uw.edu.pl/pliki/POES_Spain_PB_6.pdf).

IDEA Policy Brief no. 7 (2009), 'Policy oriented executive summary: The Czech Republic'(http://www.idea6fp.uw.edu.pl/pliki/POES_Czech_PB_7.pdf).

IDEA Policy Brief no. 8 (2009), 'Policy oriented executive summary: Poland' (http://www.idea6fp.uw.edu.pl/pliki/POES_Poland_PB_8.pdf).

IDEA Policy Brief no. 9 (2009), 'Policy oriented executive summary: Hungary' (http://www.idea6fp.uw.edu.pl/pliki/POES_Hungary_PB_9.pdf).

IDEA Working Paper no. 3 (2008), 'Old' immigration countries: Synthesis report' by H. Fassmann & U. Reeger (http://www.idea6fp.uw.edu.pl/pliki/WP3_Old_countries_synthesis.pdf).

IDEA Working Paper no. 5 (2009), 'The Italian transition from an emigration to immigration country' by C. Bonifazi, F. Heins, S. Strozza & M. Vitiello (http://www.idea6fp.uw.edu.pl/pliki/WP5_Italy.pdf).

IDEA Working Paper no. 9 (2009), 'The making of an immigration model: Inflows, impacts and policies in Southern Europe' by J. Arango, C. Bonifazi, C. Finatelli, J. Peixoto, C. Sabino, S. Strozza & A. Triandafyllidou (http://www.idea6fp.uw.edu.pl/pliki/WP9_Southern_countries_synthesis.pdf).

Lahav, G. (2004), *Immigration and politics in the New Europe: Reinventing borders*. Cambridge: Cambridge University Press.

Lesińska M., R. Stefańska & M. Szulecka (2010), 'Migration policy considerations', in A. Górny, I. Grabowska-Lusińska, M. Lesińska, M. Okólski (eds.), *Immigration to Poland: Policy, employment, integration*, 197-209. Warsaw: Scholar.

12 The evolving area of freedom, security and justice

Taking stock and thinking ahead

Dora Kostakopoulou

Justice and Home Affairs cooperation in the European Union has evolved in increasingly variable and unpredictable environments. Evolution and altered conditions more often than not represent both an opportunity and a need for initiating observations, reflection about the past and thinking ahead and bettering what exists. This is, indeed, the case with the Area of Freedom, Security and Justice (AFSJ) – that is, the institutional architecture that emerged following the partial Communitarisation of the Justice and Home Affairs pillar of the Maastricht Treaty (1993), which was agreed during the 1996 Intergovernmental Conference and which culminated in the Amsterdam Treaty (in force as of 1 May 1999). A moment of reflection is needed not only because the AFSJ is ten years old, but also because The Hague Programme, successor to the Tampere Programme[1] that laid down the policy priorities in this domain and was agreed by the European Council in November 2004, is about to expire.[2] Preparations for its new five-year successor, the Stockholm Programme, have been made and, in anticipating the European Council's meeting in December 2009, the European Commission published a communication on 'An Area of Freedom, Security and Justice serving the citizen' in June 2009 (Commission Communication 2009). The communication seeks to make the policy priorities of justice and home affairs cooperation more balanced by stating explicitly that 'the priority now has to be to put the citizen at the heart of this project' (Commission Communication 2009: 2).

Although the new 'citizen-oriented' approach is a welcome development in light of the restrictive and security-based focus of discourse and policy that prevailed since the adoption of The Hague Programme, the absence of references to 'Europe's Others' – that is, migrants, third-country national border crossers, asylum seekers and refugees – is puzzling. In any case, the communication outlines what the European Commission perceives to be the major successes of member state cooperation during the last ten

years: the removal of controls at internal borders; the management of the
EU's external borders in a coherent fashion; progress towards a common
policy on immigration – that is, the existence of 'rules that make legal
migration fairer and easier to understand'; the adoption of an EU framework on migrant integration; 'stronger action being taken against illegal
immigration and human trafficking'; the establishment of partnership
agreements with third countries, mainly readmission and visa facilitation
agreements, designed to make 'circular migration' a reality (Commission
Communication 2009: 2-3); progress towards the establishment of a common European system of asylum; and the development of a common visa
policy. At the same time, the European Commission recognises that ensuring the proper implementation of community law by the member states
remains a significant challenge.

It is true that the modus operandi of the AFSJ as well as the ensuing policy output have been successful, particularly if one takes into account the deficiencies of the previous intergovernmental institutional framework (1993-
1999). Namely, the ineffectiveness of policymaking due to the prevalence of
unanimity, convention law-making and the unduly cumbersome five-tier decision-making structure, the absence of clearly defined objectives, effective
parliamentary involvement and judicial supervision and the lack of enforcement mechanisms (for a detailed discussion, see Kostakopoulou 2007).

But it is equally true that success is not merely a measure of juridico-
political output and of deepening member state cooperation in areas that
have traditionally been regarded as bastions of state sovereignty. Successful
cooperation cannot be measured only by its results; it must also be tested
on the merits of what has been agreed. In other words, success is also a matter of ensuring a policy's conceptual coherence with the existing normative
framework as well as with other, equally important, policies. It also means
its capacity to provide credible and effective solutions to the problems at
hand. In assessing success in more substantive terms, one must identify
qualitative differences between the present and the past and indicators of
better regulation in the service of human needs. Measured against such an
ambitious yardstick, one cannot but conclude that the alleged successes in
the past ten years of the AFSJ have been relative. For instance, Frontex op-
erations have given rise to a number of concerns about the agency's ac-
countability and the compatibility of its actions with human rights obligations under international and EU law and the directives that have been
adopted in the field of legal migration: namely, Directive 2003/86 on family
reunification; Directive 2003/109 on the status of long-term residents;
Directive 2004/114 on the conditions of admission of students, pupils, unre-
munerated trainees and volunteers; Directive 2005/71 on the admission of
third-country national researchers; and Directive 2009/50 on highly skilled
migrants. All these now need modification. It is widely acknowledged that
– despite the advantages of securing agreement on EU-wide minimum

albeit uniform standards (the United Kingdom, Ireland and Denmark have secured opt-outs) – the migration directives nevertheless contain a number of restrictive clauses and fall short of the Tampere objective of 'near equality' for third-country national residents (European Council 1999).

The developing EU framework on integration, on the other hand, which commenced with the establishment of National Contact Points on Integration in 2003[3] and the adoption of the Common Basic Principles on Integration in 2004,[4] has been shaped by the member states in ways that accommodate not only their own migration rules and policy priorities in this area, but also national conceptions of integration and neo-national narratives seeking to preserve social cohesion and the societies' 'national' values (Carrera 2009). Predominant national approaches have managed to disconnect the issue of migrant integration from the principle of equal treatment in socio-economic spheres, non-discrimination in the workplace, society and service delivery and easy access to citizenship (Kostakopoulou, Carrera & Jesse 2009).

In so doing, they have aligned integration with migration control, restrictions in the admission and settlement of third-country nationals and the preservation of the alleged homogeneity of national societies. Migrants' entry, residence, settlement and access to citizenship are now conditional on meeting integration requirements in almost all 'old migration countries' (Van Oers, Erboll & Kostakopoulou 2010). Naturalisation is premised on successful performance in civic orientation tests (Belgium and France are exceptions), and pre-existing language requirements have been tightened and reinforced. Migrants are also required to attend language and civic orientation courses and, in most cases, to sit integration tests in order to enter and/or obtain permanent residence in the Netherlands, Austria, Denmark, France, Germany, Luxembourg and the UK. Non-attendance of integration courses affects their access to social benefits in Germany, the Netherlands, Belgium, Sweden, Finland, Denmark, France and the UK. More controversially, since 2006, integration requirements and tests have 'migrated' abroad – that is, to (non-European) states of origin – as the Netherlands, France, Germany, Denmark and the UK require third-country national spouses seeking reunification to have adequate knowledge of the national language and societal values. In Austria, France, Denmark and Luxembourg, integration requirements are contained in integration contracts that migrants have to sign in order to obtain a secure residence status (Van Oers et al. 2010). Finally, the notion of circular migration gives rise to fears that old guest worker programmes are being resurrected and that, despite the emphasis on migrant integration and promoting 'a Europe of rights' (Commission Communication 2009: 7), third-country nationals are prevented from settlement and are merely submitted to utilitarian calculations and labour market needs.

In sum, one cannot overlook the fact that the EU is at a crossroads as far as migration and integration laws and policies are concerned. Further work remains to be done in designing and implementing common juridico-political frameworks that are coherent, normatively sound and effective in policy terms. At this juncture, the IDEA project is envisaged to make a timely and important contribution. It imports historical understanding and conceptual coherence into the frames of regular and irregular migration and supplies empirical rigour and policy recommendations that can be implemented. Among its recommendations is the development of 'a more innovative, flexible and pro-active migration policy and responding to the phenomenon of "fluid" migration as part of the EU *acquis communautaire*' (chapter 4). An innovative and proactive migration policy would have to be based on an alternative frame for migration. For, to arrive at a new vision, one often needs to alter the ways in which an issue has been perceived. This is not simply an issue of challenging hegemonic narratives and establishing a counter-hegemony. The issue is rather one of choice, and choice is a matter of reflection upon alternatives, upon their strengths and weaknesses. As Heinz Fassmann and Ursula Reeger have argued in this volume (chapter 3), it is perhaps time to view migration as a permanent element – and not as an exception – in a globalising world. After all, even before their transformation into homelands in the nineteenth century, lands have always been receptors of people. In the nineteenth century, there was an exodus of people from Europe to North and South America. And, as Marek Okólski has noted in this volume (chapter 1), in the second part of the twentieth century, Europe witnessed considerable migration: post-war adjustment migration, migration related to labour recruitment, migration related to new globalisation, post-community migration and post-enlargement migration. Furthermore, as Southern European countries have become immigration countries and Central and Eastern European countries are in 'migration transition', migration needs to be seen as a normal issue – not a problem or a security threat to be dealt with through restrictive admissions policies and a law-enforcement approach. Acknowledgment of the 'ordinary' or 'normal' nature of migration, coupled with the abandonment of the incorrect expectation that it is controllable (see chapter 3 in this volume), can lead to qualitatively different migration policies. It will certainly reduce the incoherence characterising the regulation of third-country nationals' entry into the EU using the existing category-by-category approach[5] and will simplify the administrative requirements for both migrants and their employers.[6]

It may also expose the artificial boundaries between regular and irregular ('illegal' in member states' discourses and policies) migration and prompt the readjustment of the sanctions-oriented approach pertaining to the latter. As Elspeth Guild and Sergio Carrera (2009: 8) have recently argued:

> [...] in the term 'illegal' itself we can perhaps find an answer. What
> is needed is to change laws so that people do not fall into undocu-
> mented statuses. If we analyse the legal measures that lead to people
> being categorised as 'illegal' or undocumented, we may find a more
> helpful approach.

João Peixoto et al. (chapter 5 in this volume) have also commented on
Southern European states' willingness to remove undocumented migrants
from the artificially constructed domain of 'illegality' and to relax the
weight that traditionally has been attributed to states' consent (or the lack
of it) in favour of more pragmatic considerations and individuals' de facto
social membership due to their residence and ('irregular') employment in
the informal economy. However, as Peixoto et al. observe, regularisations
are 'used to "repair" the lack of an efficient migration policy'. It is true that
irregular migration is a multi-variable phenomenon (Baldwin-Edwards &
Arango 1999). Magdalena Lesińska (chapter 11 in this volume) has succinctly noted them: the existence of a shadow economy and its generalised
acceptance by the population and the state, restrictive entry and recruitment
procedures, weak administrative structures and ineffective labour market
controls and the lack of a transparent regularisation scheme. As she ob-
serves with respect to 'the new migration countries', 'special attention
should be given to the role of the informal economy which serves as a
magnet for irregular employment', as well as to other relevant institutional
factors that create social realities. Understanding migration patterns better
and the role of the historical links between sending and receiving societies
and migrant networks (see, in particular, Drbohlav as chapter 8 in this volume) will also assist us in overcoming the simplicity of push-pull explanations. Guild and Carrera (2009) have made this point convincingly. On the
basis of Eurostat's statistics in December 2008, they show that although
unemployment was at 2.7 per cent in the Netherlands and 14.4 per cent in
Spain and statutory minimum wages were under € 300 per month in
Bulgaria and about € 1,570 per month in Luxembourg, the respective
movements of Spanish nationals to the Netherlands and Bulgarian nationals to Luxembourg were minimal.

In light of the foregoing, European migration law and policy require readjustment. There is an urgent need to rethink the existing political frames
of migration and integration and to devise a coherent framework of migration governance that de-securitises migration, reflects international and
European legal commitments and takes sufficiently into account the specificity of migration patterns in the 'old', 'new' and 'future' migration countries. In the quest for a new conceptual frame, the EU would have to promote the merits of a paradigm shift – namely, away from perceiving and
framing migration as a problem and/or a threat, to viewing it as a resource.
And it would also have to convince national electorates of the error of past

approaches in this domain. To convince of error is simply to assist people not only in understanding and valuing the past and present contributions of non-national migrant labour to economic productivity, service delivery and the vibrancy, innovation and dynamism of societies. It is also a matter of recognising the facticity of human mobility – both inward and outward – and the necessity of devising pragmatic, coherent and principled responses to it in the twenty-first century.

Similarly, migrant integration should not be seen as a matter of imposing additional conditions to entry and settlement, testing individuals' resolve and knowledge, imposing sanctions, causing hardship and placing hurdles on the path to citizenship. Instead, it should be a matter of developing partnerships, fostering mutual respect and dynamic learning among citizens, residents and newcomers, and promoting intercultural dialogue and pluralism in action.

The quest for coherence, on the other hand, might lead to the transcendence of the multiple, variegated and conflicting conceptual and legal frames with respect to intra- and extra-EU migration and integration. The contrast between the template of internal mobility for the community nationals, which is based on rights, non-discrimination and equal opportunities, on the one hand, and the migration template, which has been based on restriction, discrimination on the grounds of third-country nationality and less-than-equal opportunities, on the other, sheds ample light on the benefits of inclusiveness, equal treatment and the making of migrant EU nationals into the union's citizens (Kostakopoulou 2001). The basic traits of the former are rights, uniform and equal treatment irrespective of nationality and protection; the basic traits of the latter are restriction, control, conditionality, national variations and law enforcement. The narrowing of the artificial difference between internal mobility and migration would make migration law and policy more inclusive and rights-based. Its impact on integration law and policy in the EU and the member states would also be significant; it would require a non-discrimination-based and citizenship-driven approach to migrant integration akin to that applying to the community nationals.

The European Commission's communication has recognised the importance of treating existing obstacles as challenges to remaking European migration and asylum policy, setting out a clear vision in this field and promoting dialogue among all stakeholders at local, national and European levels. Promoting a more integrated society – a Europe of solidarity – features among the political priorities of the new Stockholm Programme. To this end, the European Commission calls for a dynamic and comprehensive migration policy which consolidates the global approach to migration and displays responsibility and solidarity (see priority 5 in Commission Communication 2009: 23ff.):

> Immigration policy must be part of a long-term vision that empha-
> sises respect for fundamental rights and human dignity. This policy
> must also be designed to deal with increased mobility in a globalis-
> ing world through emphasis on social, economic and cultural rights.
> (Commission Communication 2009: 23)

In this respect, the European Commission wishes to see the consolidation of a global approach to migration by making migration issues part of EU external policy, promoting cooperation and dialogue with third-world countries and laying the foundations for additional initiatives on migration and development as well as the development of 'an innovative and coherent framework' (Commission Communication 2009: 23-24). A skeleton of the latter has been furnished. It includes, among other things, 'a common framework in the form of a flexible admission system that will enable it to adapt to increased mobility and the needs of national labour markets'; a better analysis and assessment of migration issues (compare Lesińska's policy recommendation in chapter 11 of this volume); establishment of a European platform for dialogue; and a 'proactive policy based on a European status for legal immigrants' (Commission Communication 2009: 24-25). With respect to the last point, the resurrection of the Tampere mandate is clear:

> [...] to maximise the positive effects of legal immigration for the
> benefit of all – the countries of origin and destination, host societies
> and immigrants – a clear, transparent and equitable approach that re-
> spects human beings is required. To do this, an Immigration Code
> should be adopted to ensure a uniform level of rights for legal immi-
> grants, comparable with that of Community citizens. (Commission
> Communication 2009: 25)

An immigration code will bring to an end the present uneven, piecemeal approach to legal migration and will be accompanied by the revision of the family reunification directive and the support of member states' integration efforts through a joint coordination mechanism. Although, in my opinion, the latter proposed initiative does not go far enough in the direction of re-thinking integration law and policy, it is nevertheless the case that the majority of the communication's proposals, coupled with its overall approach to migration issues, are more consistent with the Tampere agenda. As such, they represent a rupture from the restrictive, security-oriented and law-enforcement approach of The Hague Programme.

In light of the preceding discussion, it seems to me that – given the fact that mobility is an integral part of the European integration project and the importance the EU has attributed to encouraging border crossings and transborder relations – perceiving third-country national migration in negative terms and erecting impermeable borders to discourage border crossings are counterproductive strategies. True, one cannot underestimate the political obstacles that stand in the way of reform in the migration field. However, the review of member states' policies in this domain, as undertaken by IDEA project participants, and evidence drawn from the evolving AFSJ over the last ten years indicate that national executives' fears about uncontrollable migration and its negative impact have been greatly overblown. Such narratives have served as electoral devices for eliciting public support and as ideologically driven excuses for the maintenance of the status quo. But they have hardly offered any compelling reasons to oppose the design of 'a dynamic and fair migration policy' in the twenty-first century (Commission Communication 2009: 32). Hopefully, the Stockholm Programme will lay down firm foundations for such policy. The conundrum, of course, is how to reform migration regulations and practices in ways that treat migrants and refugees as partners and promote the positive effects of migration while working with and within national statist systems that themselves are built on the exclusion and subordination of outsiders. Fortunately, the European integration project contains the conceptual and normative resources required in order to furnish a clear vision for migration law and policy in the twenty-first century and to provide solutions to the conundrum. After all, it has successfully done so with respect to intra-EU mobility and the development of EU citizenship over the last 50 years.

Notes

1   The Tampere Programme was adopted by the heads of state and government on 15-16 October 1999. It was based on four policy priorities, namely, partnerships with migrants' countries of origin, the creation of a common European asylum system, fair treatment of third-world country nationals and the management of migration flows.
2   The Hague Programme set the objectives to be implemented in the AFSJ for the period 2005-2010.
3   Council Meeting 2455, Luxembourg, 14-15 October 2002.
4   Justice and Home Affairs Council Meeting 2618, 14615/04, 19 November 2004.
5   See Directives 2005/71 on the admission of third-country national researchers ([2005] OJ L289/15) and 2009/50 on highly skilled migrants ([2009] OJ L155/17).
6   See the commission's proposal for a directive on a single application procedure for a single permit for third-world country nationals to reside and work in the territory of a member state and on common set of rights for third-world country workers legally residing in a member state, COM (2007) 638 final, 23 October 2007.

References

Baldwin-Edwards, M. & J. Arango (eds.) (1999), *Immigrants and the informal economy in Southern Europe*. London: Frank Cass.

Carrera, S. (2009), *In search of the perfect citizen? The intersection between integration, immigration and nationality in the EU*. The Hague: Martinus Nijhoff.

Commission Communication (2009), 'An Area of Freedom, Security and Justice serving the citizen: Wider freedom in a safer environment', COM (2009) 262/4, Brussels, 10 June.

European Council (1999), 'Presidency conclusions Tampere 15 and 16 October 1999', SN 200/99, Brussels, 16 October.

Guild, E. & S. Carrera (2009), 'Towards the next phase of the EU's Area of Freedom, Security and Justice: The European Commission's proposals for the Stockholm Programme', CEPS Policy Brief.

Kostakopoulou, D. (2001), *Citizenship, identity and immigration in the European Union: Between past and future*. Manchester: Manchester University Press.

Kostakopoulou, D., S. Carrera & M. Jesse (2009), 'Doing and deserving: Competing frames of integration in the European Union', in E. Guild, K. Groenendijk & S. Carrera (eds.), *Illiberal, liberal states: Immigration, citizenship and integration in the EU*, 167-186. London: Ashgate.

Van Oers, R., E. Erboll & D. Kostakopoulou (2010), *A redefinition of belonging? Language and integration tests in Europe*. The Hague: Martinus Nijhoff.

Europe, a continent of immigrants

A conclusion

Marek Okólski

This volume has offered a comprehensive description of migration processes that take place in various parts of Europe. In particular, it has attempted an in-depth inquiry into the phenomenon of European immigration.

Analyses presented in the foregoing chapters have explicitly or implicitly referred to a common conceptual framework that implies the existence of a pattern of migration typical of European countries, whose major characteristic has been assumed to be the change of migration status from net emigration to net immigration. It has also been assumed that such change – concomitant with the relatively high intensity of international movements of population – occurred (or was supposed to occur) independently in individual countries in various periods of time. Thus, the processes related to mass inflows of people to European countries, which are the main focus of the volume, have been embedded in a very long-time perspective.

The volume has explored three basic hypotheses. The principal hypothesis concerns the existence of a Europe-specific migration cycle. In one variant of that cycle, it is assumed that European countries are subject to a change from a predominance of the mass outflow of people ('emigration countries') to a predominance of the mass inflow ('immigration countries'). It follows from the very nature of that hypothesis that, over a very long period of time, in both types of countries international migration above all reflected, if not responded to, the prevailing regime of vital movement/reproduction of the population.

Another variant of the migration cycle (called interchangeably, and more precisely, the 'immigration cycle') has been analysed more extensively. This one implies the passing by 'immigration countries' of Europe through different stages of immigration reality (characterised by, among other things, different sizes and forms of inflows, a varying socio-demographic and economic composition of immigrants, changing perceptions and attitudes towards immigration and different immigration-related policies). With each consecutive stage, the 'immigration country' becomes more mature in terms of the cycle. The flows are more orderly. The composition of migrants tends to converge with that of the native population. The immigrants more closely integrate into the host society. The mainstream of migration policy shifts from preventive or restrictive measures to the comprehensive and sophisticated programmes that promote integration. In addition, the hypothesis assumes that countries that attain the status of 'immigration country' later (e.g. 'new' immigration countries) imitate, at least to some extent, experiences of the forerunners (e.g. 'old' immigration countries). This, in turn, would facilitate the convergence of immigration cycles that individual European countries undergo.

It should be recalled that the first of cycle variants offered a very long-time and rather general perspective, in which migration experiences of practically all European countries could be accommodated. Its second variant provided the authors with a tool suitable for an in-depth cross-country analysis that would reveal both similarities and differences in becoming a mature immigration country. Needless to say, the latter concept proved to be especially useful for Europe's 'old' immigration cases and of limited use for 'future' immigration countries.

The second hypothesis directly stems from the first one. Its message is that in order to become 'immigration countries', European countries had to experience the migration transition. The transition was conceived as an intermediate phase between the situation where the mass outflow overwhelmed immigration and the situation which was characterised by a growing preponderance of the inflow of people relative to the outflow. This has served as a frame for this volume's comparative analysis of factors that shaped the process of becoming an 'immigration country', the factors that were either country-specific or typical (similar) for all European countries.

Finally, the third (and rather implicit) hypothesis, which has supplemented the analyses of real migration phenomena in this volume, suggests that, in addition to similarities observed among European countries concerning their transition into an 'immigration country', in the background there emerged a process of convergence of migration policies, called 'Europeanisation'. That process was believed to enhance similarities in migration transition.

What major conclusions ensue from the empirical verification of the hypotheses carried out by the authors in the consecutive chapters? In answering this question, I will try to be concise and, by necessity, selective.

The main hypothesis – concerning the historical change of the migration status of an individual country from net emigration ('emigration country') to net immigration ('immigration country') – was only partly confirmed. A large majority of countries have already attained the status of immigration country. In some European countries, as has been evidenced in the case of Hungary and Poland, the change of the migration status is an ongoing and largely unfinished, if directed, process. Moreover, while in the long run the tendency is clear, in the short run it displays divergences and strong sensitiveness to shocks in the social milieu, mainly of a political and economic nature. It is by no means a deterministic process and probably not a universal one. It suffices here to bring forward the example of Central and Eastern European countries, where between 1950 and 1990 severe administrative controls imposed strong and lasting perturbations on the secular pattern of migration. They, in turn, caused a counter-reaction and, in fact, a further disturbance (albeit in the opposite direction) in the following years, when migration ceased to be forcefully restricted. Another example is a recent breakdown of the immigration trend and migrant integration policy in several Western and Southern European countries under the influence of economic crisis, which signalled a warning: the migration transition should not be perceived as irreversible. The notion of the European pattern of migration – which assumes a clear linear tendency and predicts that latecomers will follow in the footsteps of those countries that paved the way to the status of mature immigration countries – should therefore be viewed with caution. It should be considered a useful model, rather than a reflection of reality.

The analyses presented in this volume, while to a large degree confirming the general tendency – the European migration cycle or pattern – viewed from a very long-time perspective, shed new light on intra- and inter-group differences. Those analyses reveal a great deal of diversity across Europe, especially when it comes to a not-so-lengthy perspective and when the stages of the immigration cycle are in focus.

'Future' immigration countries, those of Central and Eastern Europe, on their way to completing the migration transition seem to deviate in many ways from the pattern followed earlier by 'new' immigration countries. The most striking difference is the former's application of relatively severe regulatory measures with respect to the inflow of foreign citizens and in fact a striving towards suppression of immigration. From this follows another significant dissimilarity – a seemingly relatively high proportion of circular and short-term migrants in the total volume of inflow.

On the other hand, the southern ('new') immigration countries display several distinctive features in their migration pattern relative to 'old' countries, i.e. those that belong to Western and Northern Europe. One of the most important of them seems to be a relatively high level of irregularity of the immigrants arriving or staying in the southern destinations. It manifests itself most characteristically in a widespread irregular employment. This, inter alia, stems from two specific and interplaying factors. Firstly, the extent of the informal economy in those countries is generally greater and, so to speak, socially more widely accepted than in western and northern countries. Secondly, the recruitment of migrant workers in the South was, as a rule, poorly institutionalised compared to 'old' immigration countries. The high degree of irregularity of the immigrants' stay and employment prompted the southern countries to introduce vast and recurrent programmes of regularisation that became a trademark of migration policy common to that group of countries.

A relatively high proportion of female migrant workers constitutes another distinctive feature of the southern countries. Unlike in the West and North, the onset of mass immigration here coincided with a strong activisation of the native female workforce (which was very small relative to the western standard). Due to this, and a specific model of welfare state that levies many welfare obligations on the family (and/or household), an increased demand for predominantly female labour in the household sector (e.g. related to elderly care) encouraged a relatively higher proportion of women among the immigrants.

Not only does each of the three groups of European countries display its own substantive specificity in following the European pattern of migration, but prominent differences have also been observed between individual countries within each group. Among 'old' immigration countries, Austria, for instance, significantly differs from France. Whereas in the group of the four 'new' immigration countries, Greece in many respects presents a distinct exception. Portugal and Spain, forming the 'Iberian model', visibly differ from Italy. Among the 'future' immigration countries, the Czech Republic differs strikingly from Hungary and Poland, which, in addition, are both equally inexperienced in hosting immigrants and focus on different migration concerns (and migration realities). Poland confronts the mass post-EU accession outflow of people, while Hungary tackles the delicate matter of the Hungarian minority living in neighbouring countries. Still, all countries within each group possess most of the group-specific characteristics.

At the regional level within countries, we would certainly notice a number of important internal (intra-regional) differences in migration patterns. In other words, the deeper we go in our analysis, the more diversity we notice across the social space. Is this really surprising? Of course not. By their very definition, social settings and social processes differ and, if they are grouped or clustered, their variance is of both an inter-group nature and an intra-group nature. By the same token, the inter- and intra-group variation noted in this volume does not impair the validity of the European migration pattern as a tendency common and specific to countries of the continent.

Irrespective of the assessment of similarities among the European countries with regard to the migration pattern and particularly to their experience of the immigration cycle, it might be argued that the degree of similarity tends to be higher at the symbolic level and lowest at the level of real phenomena. In all three groups of countries we observed the following: a strong convergence concerning ways to prevent illegal immigration and to protect migrants against discrimination; decisions on the kind of foreigner inflow to European countries that should be preferred; methods to manage immigration; and a choice of models of immigrant integration that should be recommended. This is reflected in ever more systematic and orderly public debate and in manifestos and policy documents produced in individual countries and by international organisations addressing the phenomena in question. The convergence of migration patterns of different countries seems to reflect a long-run process of learning and imitating. It has been considerably accelerated and reinforced by the activities of EU institutions. Less resemblance was noticeable in the sphere of migration-related institutions and their activities (not to mention, the effectiveness of those activities) in the immigrant-receiving European countries. Above all, this was manifested in divergences, instability and inconsistencies of migration policy. As already suggested, the least degree of similarity is displayed by actual migration phenomena: specifically, their intensity, forms and types of flows, the characteristics of migrants (country of origin, social and demographic features) and their activities in host countries.

The inter- and intra-group differences in the migration pattern are deeply embedded in historical contexts of immigration. As this volume has made evident, those contexts vary across European countries and change over time. The 'cohort effect' – the time of initiation of the migration transition and circumstances specific to that time – proves of particular importance here. Using the terminology of the present volume, 'old' countries began the transition when their economies were overwhelmed by the Fordist organisation of production. The post-Fordist system was blossoming at the time of initiation of the transition in 'new' countries. Presently, the 'future' countries of immigration are entering their transition under circumstances of the IT revolution. In addition, the historical contexts logically also bore heavily and in a country-specific way on migration pattern characteristics at each consecutive stage of the immigration cycle. The coincidence of the initiation of the migration transition (and the first stage of the immigration cycle) in Central and Eastern European countries and the IT revolution (besides other reasons) meant that a considerable part of the early inflow of foreigners to those countries took the form of liquid/fluid migration. Such form was hardly observed when other groups of European countries experienced immigration at that stage. Of importance here is that migrants adhering to that form of movement are believed to be less prone to stable behaviours and settlement in the host country. On the other hand, the flows typical for liquid migration appeared in 'old' countries at the very final stage of the immigration cycle, which within the cycle concept might have undermined or delayed the expected maturity of their migration regime.

The great complexity of the European migration pattern – so evident in this volume – was highlighted by the inclusion of several viewpoints on the same problem. This especially pertains to the analyses of the immigration cycle's distinctness and pattern in southern countries, which were the main geographical focus. In effect, despite some controversies and different emphases between authors of the various chapters, the analytical outcomes were comprehensive and provided a wide comparative perspective. The variety of analytical angles and scopes and the pluralism of interpretations may be this book's greatest asset.

All in all, this volume has not only contributed to the growing body of knowledge on contemporary European migration, but in a systematic manner it has also revealed and discussed the complexity of that phenomenon. In its final chapters, focus fell on the limited manageability and even lesser predictability of immigration. That part is far from conclusive; it was rather meant to open new threads of thought and to fan scientific debate.

Last but not least, a short comment of a methodological nature seems worthwhile. In this volume, a great number of facts or opinions have been presented that are not consistent with the main hypothesis concerning the European migration cycle or which might even be viewed as contradicting it. According to one of cognitive stands, this might lead to the rejection of the hypothesis. That, however, would have been the case if the present authors aimed at its falsification.

It should be recalled, first of all, that the approach adopted in this volume is based on the methodology of *longue durée*, which deals with the social processes in their complexity and entire 'life'; a very lengthy, wide contextual perspective was thus called for. Such is the conceptual framework sketched in the Introduction chapter of the volume. However, the empirical analyses in subsequent chapters referring to that framework do not take a long view because the authors' ultimate goal was a pragmatic one. We hope to have provided other researchers and, most of all, policymakers with useful clues – if not solutions – that could enhance further research and promote understanding of contemporary European immigration and possibly its more effective regulation.

In pursuing this task, we have striven to strengthen the evidence supporting the very existence of a European migration pattern as a very long-term tendency. To our best judgment, we have accomplished that.

Contributors

Joaquín Arango, Center for the Study of Migration and Citizenship (IUIOG), Complutense University of Madrid, Spain
  arango@cps.ucm.es

Martin Baldwin-Edwards, Mediterranean Migration Observatory (MMO), Panteion University, Athens, Greece
  baldwin-edwards@migrationresearch.info

Jakub Bijak, Central European Forum for Migration Research (CEFMR), Warsaw, Poland
  j.bijak@soton.ac.uk

Corrado Bonifazi, Institute for Research on Population and Social Policies (IRPPS), Rome, Italy
  c.bonifazi@irpps.cnr.it

Dušan Drbohlav, Faculty of Science, Department of Social Geography and Regional Development (DSG), Charles University in Prague, Czech Republic
  ddrbohlav@quick.cz

Godfried Engbersen, Sociology Department, Erasmus University Rotterdam, the Netherlands
  engbersen@fsw.eur.nl

Heinz Fassmann, Regional Research and Spatial Planning Institute, University of Vienna, Austria
  heinz.fassmann@univie.ac.at

Claudia Finotelli, Center for the Study of Migration and Citizenship (IUIOG), Complutense University of Madrid, Spain
  cfinotel@cps.ucm.es

Theodora Kostakopoulou, Centre for European Law (CELS), University of Southampton, United Kingdom
   dora.kostakopoulou@manchester.ac.uk

Dorota Kupiszewska, Central European Forum for Migration Research (CEFMR), Warsaw, Poland
   d.kupisz@twarda.pan.pl

Marek Kupiszewski, Central European Forum for Migration Research (CEFMR), Warsaw Poland
   m.kupisz@cefmr.pan.pl

Magdalena Lesińska, Centre of Migration Research (CMR), University of Warsaw, Poland
   m.lesinska@uw.edu.pl

Jorge Malheiros, Institute of Geography and Regional Planning, University of Lisbon, Portugal
   gatomaltes@netcabo.pt

Marek Okólski, Centre of Migration Research (CMR), University of Warsaw, Poland
   moko@uw.edu.pl

João Peixoto, Research Centre on Economic Sociology and the Sociology of Organizations (SOCIUS), Lisbon, Portugal
   jpeixoto@iseg.utl.pt

Ursula Reeger, Institute for Urban and Regional Research (ISR), Austrian Academy of Science, Vienna, Austria
   ursula.reeger@oeaw.ac.at

Catarina Sabino, Research Centre in Economic Sociology and the Sociology of Organizations (SOCIUS), Lisbon, Portugal
   socius@iseg.utl.pt

Salvatore Strozza, Institute for Research on Population and Social Policies (IRPPS), Rome, Italy
   strozza@unina.it

Anna Triandafyllidou, The Hellenic Foundation for European Foreign Policy (ELIAMEP), Athens, Greece
   anna.triandafyllidou@iue.it

Leo van Wissen, Netherlands Interdisciplinary Demographic Institute (NIDI), The Hague, the Netherlands
l.j.g.van.wissen@rug.nl

Arkadiusz Wiśniowski, Central European Forum for Migration Research (CEFMR), Warsaw, Poland
awisniowski@gmail.com

Corrado Bonifazi, Marek Okólski, Jeannette Schoorl, Patrick Simon, Eds.
*International Migration in Europe: New Trends and New Methods
of Analysis*
2008 (ISBN 978 90 5356 894 1)

Maurice Crul, Liesbeth Heering, Eds.
*The Position of the Turkish and Moroccan Second Generation in
Amsterdam and Rotterdam: The TIES Study in the Netherlands*
2008 (ISBN 978 90 8964 061 1)

Marlou Schrover, Joanne van der Leun, Leo Lucassen, Chris Quispel, Eds.
Illegal Migration and Gender in a Global and Historical Perspective
2008 (ISBN 978 90 8964 047 5)

Gianluca P. Parolin
Citizenship in the Arab World: Kin, Religion and Nation-State
2009 (ISBN 978 90 8964 045 1)

Rainer Bauböck, Bernhard Perchinig, Wiebke Sievers, Eds.
Citizenship Policies in the New Europe: Expanded and Updated Edition
2009 (ISBN 978 90 8964 108 3)

Cédric Audebert, Mohamed Kamel Doraï, Eds.
Migration in a Globalised World: New Research Issues and Prospects
2010 (ISBN 978 90 8964 1571)

Richard Black, Godfried Engbersen, Marek Okólski, Cristina Pantîru, Eds.
*A Continent Moving West? EU Enlargement and Labour Migration from
Central and Eastern Europe*
2010 (ISBN 978 90 8964 156 4)

Charles Westin, José Bastos, Janine Dahinden, Pedro Góis, Eds.
Identity Processes and Dynamics in Multi-Ethnic Europe
2010 (ISBN 978 90 8964 046 8)

Rainer Bauböck, Thomas Faist, Eds.
Diaspora and Transnationalism: Concepts, Theories and Methods
2010 (ISBN 978 90 8964 238 7)

Liza Mügge
*Beyond Dutch Borders: Transnational Politics among Colonial Migrants,
Guest Workers and the Second Generation*
2010 (ISBN 978 90 8964 244 8)

Peter Scholten
Framing Immigrant Integration: Dutch Research-Policy Dialogues in Comparative Perspective
2011 (ISBN 978 90 8964 284 4)

Albert Kraler, Eleonore Kofman, Martin Kohli, Camille Schmoll, Eds.
Gender, Generations and the Family in International Migration
2011 (ISBN 978 90 8964 285 1)

Michael Bommes, Giuseppe Sciortino, Eds.
Foggy Social Structures: Irregular Migration, European Labour Markets and the Welfare State
2011 (ISBN 978 90 8964 341 4)

Giovanna Zincone, Rinus Penninx, Maren Borkert, Eds.
Migration Policymaking in Europe: The Dynamics of Actors and Contexts in Past and Present
2011 (ISBN 978 90 8964 370 4)

Blanca Garcés-Mascareñas
State Regulation of Labour Migration in Malaysia and Spain: Markets, Citizenship and Rights
2012 (ISBN 978 90 8964 286 8)

Julie Vullnetari
Albania on the Move: Links between Internal and International Migration
2012 (ISBN 978 90 8964 355 1)

Bram Lancee
Immigrant Performance in the Labour Market: Bonding and Bridging Social Capital
2012 (ISBN 978 90 8964 357 5)

Maurice Crul, Jens Schneider, Frans Lelie, Eds.
The European Second Generation Compared: Does the Integration Context Matter?
2012 (ISBN 978 90 8964 443 5)

Christina Boswell, Gianni D'Amato, Eds.
Immigration and Social Systems: Collected Essays of Michael Bommes
2012 (ISBN 978 90 8964 453 4)

Ulbe Bosma, Ed.
Post-Colonial Immigrants and Identity Formations in the Netherlands
2012 (ISBN 978 90 8964 454 1)

Marek Okólski, Ed.
European Immigrations: Trends, Structures and Policy Implications
2012 (ISBN 978 90 8964 457 2)

IMISCOE Reports

Rainer Bauböck, Ed.
Migration and Citizenship: Legal Status, Rights and Political Participation
2006 (ISBN 978 90 5356 888 0)

Michael Jandl, Ed.
*Innovative Concepts for Alternative Migration Policies: Ten Innovative
Approaches to the Challenges of Migration in the 21st Century*
2007 (ISBN 978 90 5356 990 0)

Jeroen Doomernik, Michael Jandl, Eds.
Modes of Migration Regulation and Control in Europe
2008 (ISBN 978 90 5356 689 3)

Michael Jandl, Christina Hollomey, Sandra Gendera, Anna Stepien,
Veronika Bilger
*Migration and Irregular Work In Austria: A Case Study of the Structure
and Dynamics of Irregular Foreign Employment in Europe at the
Beginning of the 21st Century*
2008 (ISBN 978 90 8964 053 6)

Heinz Fassmann, Ursula Reeger, Wiebke Sievers, Eds.
Statistics and Reality: Concepts and Measurements of Migration in Europe
2009 (ISBN 978 90 8964 052 9)

Karen Kraal, Judith Roosblad, John Wrench, Eds.
*Equal Opportunities and Ethnic Inequality in European Labour Markets:
Discrimination, Gender and Policies of Diversity*
2009 (ISBN 978 90 8964 126 7)

Tiziana Caponio, Maren Borkert, Eds.
The Local Dimension of Migration Policymaking
2010 (ISBN 978 90 8964 232 5)

Raivo Vetik, Jelena Helemäe, Eds.
The Russian Second Generation in Tallinn and Kohtla-Järve: The TIES Study in Estonia
2010 (ISBN 978 90 8964 250 9)

IMISCOE Dissertations

Panos Arion Hatziprokopiou
Globalisation, Migration and Socio-Economic Change in Contemporary Greece: Processes of Social Incorporation of Balkan Immigrants in Thessaloniki
2006 (ISBN 978 90 5356 873 6)

Floris Vermeulen
The Immigrant Organising Process: Turkish Organisations in Amsterdam and Berlin and Surinamese Organisations in Amsterdam, 1960-2000
2006 (ISBN 978 90 5356 875 0)

Anastasia Christou
Narratives of Place, Culture and Identity: Second-Generation Greek-Americans Return 'Home'
2006 (ISBN 978 90 5356 878 1)

Katja Rušinović
Dynamic Entrepreneurship: First and Second-Generation Immigrant Entrepreneurs in Dutch Cities
2006 (ISBN 978 90 5356 972 6)

Ilse van Liempt
Navigating Borders: Inside Perspectives on the Process of Human Smuggling into the Netherlands
2007 (ISBN 978 90 5356 930 6)

Myriam Cherti
Paradoxes of Social Capital: A Multi-Generational Study of Moroccans in London
2008 (ISBN 978 90 5356 032 7)

Marc Helbling
Practising Citizenship and Heterogeneous Nationhood: Naturalisations in Swiss Municipalities
2008 (ISBN 978 90 8964 034 5)

Jérôme Jamin
*L'imaginaire du complot: Discours d'extrême droite en France et
aux Etats-Unis*
2009 (ISBN 978 90 8964 048 2)

Inge Van Nieuwenhuyze
*Getting by in Europe's Urban Labour Markets: Senegambian Migrants'
Strategies for Survival, Documentation and Mobility*
2009 (ISBN 978 90 8964 050 5)

Nayla Moukarbel
*Sri Lankan Housemaids in Lebanon: A Case of 'Symbolic Violence' and
'Every Day Forms of Resistance'*
2009 (ISBN 978 90 8964 051 2)

John Davies
*'My Name Is Not Natasha': How Albanian Women in France Use
Trafficking to Overcome Social Exclusion (1998-2001)*
2009 (ISBN 978 90 5356 707 4)

Dennis Broeders
*Breaking Down Anonymity: Digital Surveillance of Irregular Migrants
in Germany and the Netherlands*
2009 (ISBN 978 90 8964 159 5)

Arjen Leerkes
Illegal Residence and Public Safety in the Netherlands
2009 (ISBN 978 90 8964 049 9)

Jennifer Leigh McGarrigle
*Understanding Processes of Ethnic Concentration and Dispersal:
South Asian Residential Preferences in Glasgow*
2009 (ISBN 978 90 5356 671 8)

João Sardinha
*Immigrant Associations, Integration and Identity: Angolan, Brazilian
and Eastern European Communities in Portugal*
2009 (ISBN 978 90 8964 036 9)

Elaine Bauer
*The Creolisation of London Kinship: Mixed African-Caribbean and White
British Extended Families, 1950-2003*
2010 (ISBN 978 90 8964 235 6)

Nahikari Irastorza
Born Entrepreneurs? Immigrant Self-Employment in Spain
2010 (ISBN 978 90 8964 243 1)

Marta Kindler
A Risky Business? Ukrainian Migrant Women in Warsaw's Domestic Work Sector
2011 (ISBN 978 90 8964 327 8)

IMISCOE Textbooks

Marco Martiniello, Jan Rath, Eds.
Selected Studies in International Migration and Immigrant Incorporation
2010 (ISBN 978 90 8964 160 1)